CLARENDON ARISTOTLE SERIES

General Editor
LINDSAY JUDSON

ARISTOTLE
Metaphysics Book Iota

Translated
with an Introduction and Commentary
by

LAURA M. CASTELLI

CLARENDON PRESS · OXFORD

OXFORD

UNIVERSITY PRESS

Great Clarendon Street, Oxford, OX2 6DP,
United Kingdom

Oxford University Press is a department of the University of Oxford.
It furthers the University's objective of excellence in research, scholarship,
and education by publishing worldwide. Oxford is a registered trade mark of
Oxford University Press in the UK and in certain other countries

Published in the United States of America by Oxford University Press
198 Madison Avenue, New York, NY 10016, United States of America

British Library Cataloguing in Publication Data
Data available

Library of Congress Control Number: 2017957356

ISBN 978–0–19–968298–0 (hbk.)
ISBN 978–0–19–968299–7 (pbk.)

Printed and bound by
CPI Group (UK) Ltd, Croydon, CR0 4YY

PREFACE

This book has been in the writing for quite a few years, during which I have accumulated debts towards several people and institutions. The initial suggestion to direct my attention to Aristotle's *Metaphysics* came from Francesco Del Punta. I remember him with gratitude and affection. As an undergraduate student in Pisa, I worked on Iota under the guidance of Bruno Centrone and Giuseppe Cambiano, whom I thank for their advice over the years. Various parts of the introduction and commentary were presented at seminars and conferences in Pisa, Milano, Oxford, Munich, Paris, Campinas, Santa Monica, and Chicago; I am very grateful to the audiences on those occasions for their questions and objections. In particular, Andreas Anagnostopoulos, Chiara Ferella, and Chris Noble read and commented on a previous version of the introduction. Christian Pfeiffer gave me generous feedback on the general introduction and on the introductions to the single chapters in addition to sharing quite a few hours of conversation about quantities and mathematical entities. Chapters 3 and 4 have profited from the feedback of an anonymous referee. Adam Crager, Lindsay Judson, and Stephen Menn kindly gave me permission to refer to their unpublished work. Unfortunately I have not been able to use Sattler 2017 on Aristotle's theory of measurement since the paper appeared when the book was already at proof stage. Lindsay Judson gave me access to the unpublished notes on I.1–I.4, 1055b11 stemming from a seminar of the London Group organized by G.E.R. Lloyd in 1982–4. I have mostly profited from the discussion of textual variants there included and from Andrew Barker's notes on musical examples in I.1. Barker's notes have been expanded and incorporated in more comprehensive publications by the same author, to which I refer in the notes. Oliver Primavesi gave me access to the data emerging from a new collation of the manuscripts of the *Metaphysics* regarded as independent by Dieter Harlfinger, which was undertaken under his supervision and funded by the G.W. Leibniz-Preis 2007. Oliver Primavesi was also kind enough to discuss with me the main textual issues of Iota, and Christina Prapa gave me advice while preparing the notes on the text.

Alberto Cavarzere helped me to select the bibliography on ancient treatises on meter and rhythm. I am very grateful to Peter Momtchiloff for putting up with a series of delays without making me feel too bad about them. Most of all I would like to thank Lindsay Judson for the patience and competence with which he read and commented on various versions of all chapters. I owe him more than I can express.

The bulk of the commentary took shape during my stay at the Munich School of Ancient Philosophy (MUSAPh) as a Humboldt postdoctoral fellow in 2012–15. The final revisions were added while I was at the same institution as a research fellow sponsored by the Deutsche Forschungsgemeinschaft (DFG). To the A. v. Humboldt Stiftung and the DFG I owe the privilege of being able to work on my research; to my hosts at MUSAPh, Christof Rapp and Oliver Primavesi, and to my other colleagues and friends there I owe the invaluable opportunity to do so in a welcoming and inspiring environment.

Writing this book would have taken even longer without the help and support of my family. I am grateful to my little daughter Francesca for being a very smiley and quite cooperative baby, and to my husband Marcus for his unfading confidence in me and—last but not least—for sharing in all the joys and duties of family life.

L.M.C.

Munich, September 2017

CONTENTS

ABBREVIATIONS

ARISTOTLE

APo	*Posterior Analytics*
APr	*Prior Analytics*
Cat.	*Categories*
DA	*De Anima*
DC	*De Coelo*
DS	*De Sensu*
EE	*Eudemian Ethics*
EN	*Nicomachean Ethics*
GA	*De Generatione Animalium*
GC	*De Generatione et Corruptione*
HA	*Historia Animalium*
Int.	*De Interpretatione*
LBV	*De Longitudine et Brevitate Vitae*
MA	*De Motu*
Met.	*Metaphysics**
Meteor.	*Meteorologica*
PA	*De Partibus Animalium*
Phys.	*Physics*
Poet.	*Poetics*
Pol.	*Politics*
Probl.	*Problemata*
Rhet.	*Rhetoric*
SE	*Sophistici Elenchi*
Top.	*Topics*

*Books of the *Metaphysics*:
A=I; α=II; B=III; Γ=IV; Δ=V; E=VI; Z=VII; H=VIII; Θ=IX; I=X;
K=XI; Λ=XII; M=XIII; N=XIV.

INTRODUCTION

The tenth book of Aristotle's *Metaphysics* (Iota according to the Greek numeration) is divided into ten chapters. Of these, the first two deal with the ways in which things can be said to be one and, more generally, with the relation between being one and being something that is. The remaining eight chapters are devoted to contrariety and various issues connected with it. In particular, I.3, 4, 7, and 8 spell out different aspects of contrariety and its role in the articulation of being into genera and species, while I.5, 6, 9, and 10 address issues concerning specific pairs of opposite notions with reference to the general theory developed in the other chapters.

This is pretty much all that is clear and uncontroversial about Iota. Arthur Madigan concisely captures the widespread uneasiness of interpreters confronted with this puzzling bunch of chapters: 'If *Metaphysics* Iota is the answer, what was the question?' (Madigan 2007, p. 108). I do not have a conclusive answer to this question, but I shall argue that there is at least a family of questions for which Iota provides some answers. In speaking of a family of questions I intend to emphasize at the start that, although different sections of the book address different concerns, Iota displays a relatively unified line of enquiry. There are, however, some objective difficulties in making sense of this book, both with respect to the rest of the *Metaphysics* and, more generally, as a piece of Aristotelian philosophy. Such difficulties might be the reason why Iota has not received much attention in both recent and ancient Aristotelian scholarship (a survey of modern interpreters' views about Iota's composition and chronology can be found in Centrone 2005, pp. 37–49; for a survey and some discussion of late ancient and medieval authors see Castelli 2011; for some new evidence about Alexander of Aphrodisias's views about Iota, see Di Giovanni and Primavesi 2016, pp. 46–7). While I do not hope to give a comprehensive account of (let alone settle) all the problems surrounding this complex text, I should like to approach two main overarching issues which might not emerge as such from the discussion of the more specific problems linked to the individual chapters. The two broad issues are the place of Iota within Aristotle's *Metaphysics* and the place of Iota within Aristotle's metaphysics.

With respect to the latter point, much work has been done on Aristotle's approach to unity and being in I.1–2 and I refer to the commentary for a more detailed discussion of those two chapters and bibliographical references. In the second part of the Introduction I shall rather focus on the more general philosophical relevance of the discussion of contrariety in I.3–10, which, I shall argue, are interesting in their own right and as a piece of Aristotelian metaphysics.

I. THE PLACE OF IOTA WITHIN THE *METAPHYSICS*

I.1 IOTA AND BETA

We have fairly good evidence that the *Metaphysics* as we read it today is the result of a long editorial history. Awareness of this fact casts some doubts on the possibility of individuating the exact place and function of the different parts of this work as parts of a unified original plan. Nonetheless, different sections in the *Metaphysics* do hint at a unified project, and these hints help in making sense of Iota's place within the *Metaphysics*.

One common strategy for interpreters dealing with the structure and unity of the *Metaphysics* is that of tracking the correspondences between other parts of this work and the preliminary difficulties raised in book Beta. Beta provides a preliminary discussion of a series of aporiai, i.e. conceptual knots which have to come loose in order to proceed in the enquiry. The enquiry at stake is an investigation into the first principles and causes. Knowledge of the first principles and causes, according to *Met.* A.1, has to be identified with *sophia*, 'wisdom'. Most interpreters have therefore taken the aporiai in Beta as setting the agenda for a unified project against which the various parts of the *Metaphysics* can be tested. If we apply this strategy to Iota, two main points can be made.

First, I.2, 1053b10–11 explicitly refers to the difficulties in Beta and, more precisely, to the aporia concerning the status of one and being (*Met.* B.1, 996a4–9; B.4, 1001a4–b25): are one and being substances or are they nothing more than general predicate-terms? As we shall see, though, we do not really need Iota to solve this difficulty. As Aristotle himself recalls (I.2, 1053b17–18), the difficulty has already been solved in the discussion of substance (presumably the reference is to Z.13–16). In this sense, I.2 might well be linked to the discussion of one aporia in Beta, but not because I.2 solves that aporia (for further comments on the link between the aporia and I.2 see the commentary on I.2). Furthermore, the connection between Beta and I.2 is clearly relevant only to I.2: the scope and function of all other chapters in Iota with respect to the alleged plan of the *Metaphysics* is not particularly enlightened by the link between I.2 and the aporiai (for a different opinion see Menn (in progress), Iγ2a: From B # 11 to Iota 1–2). Therefore this link does not lead us very far if we are trying to make sense of Iota as a whole within the *Metaphysics*.

However, we can turn to a second and more promising hint. For a large part of Iota, despite the lack of any explicit mention of the aporiai, seems to respond to the difficulties raised in B.1, 995b20–27. In these lines, Aristotle asks whose task it is to enquire into a series of very general notions such as sameness, otherness, similarity, dissimilarity, contrariety, etc., which are usually dealt with by 'the dialecticians'. The task at issue does not only include the enquiry into what each of these 'things' is, but also the enquiry into some of their distinctive properties (e.g. whether only one thing is contrary to another). Aristotle drops the discussion of this difficulty in the rest of Beta, but he goes back to it in Γ.2, 1004a31–b26 and 1005a13–18, where he assigns the task of the discussion to the philosopher. In doing this, Aristotle sketches the guiding lines of a rather articulated project, whose basic features might be worth recalling in order to test Iota's credentials for being the place where such a project is actually carried out.

I.2 THE PROJECT IN Γ.2, IOTA, AND DELTA

Γ.1 opens with a statement: 'there is a certain science which investigates being inasmuch as it is being and things belonging to it in its own right' (1003a21–22). In Γ.2 Aristotle mentions at least two different views about how and why all notions mentioned in B.1 belong to the domain of investigation of the science of being. The first view (1003b22–1004b26) is that these general notions are general properties of things that are and that they form a relatively well-structured conceptual framework. The second view (1004b27–1005a13) is that contraries are principles of being and contraries can be 'reduced' or 'led back' (see below) to the opposition of unity and plurality, which can be regarded as principles of the contraries and, therefore, as ultimate principles of being. The possibility of providing a unified account of the principles of being grounds the possibility of giving a unified account of being.

These two views are not only different (as long as being a property of something is not the same as being a principle of it), but, to some extent, in tension with each other in that they suggest opposite relations of priority between being on one side and unity and the other general notions on the other side. According to the first view, unity and the series of contraries mentioned with it are general features of being whose belonging to being presumably has to be explained by the science of being qua being. According to the second view, unity and contraries are principles of being and can, therefore, be brought in in order to account for at least some features of being. In this part of the introduction I shall mainly focus on the first view, while I shall return to the second one and to the issue of the apparent contrast between them below (see, in particular, section II of the Introduction).

Before taking a closer look at either of them, however, some preliminary difficulties should be mentioned. These difficulties are involved in both views, insofar as both views provide an account of why the science of 'being' (*to on*) should also be the science of 'the one' (*to hen*) and the other general notions mentioned in B.1–2 (from now on I shall use expressions like 'the one' or 'the many', 'the equal', 'the similar', etc. as calques or loan translations to indicate the objects of the enquiry outlined in B.1–2 and Γ.2).

One difficulty is that *to on* (and, correspondingly, *to hen*, see below) can be taken to indicate some general property or the object which has that property, i.e. what is (or beings or things that are) and what is one (or things that are one) (for a detailed account of the ambiguities involved in the use of the equivalent Greek expressions, see introductory notes to I.1). The first difficulty therefore consists in understanding whether an enquiry into being and, correspondingly, an enquiry into the one are mainly enquiries into some specific objects or into some general properties (as we shall see, the two options are not mutually exclusive). Some further problems emerge as soon as we try to spell out those general properties. Difficulties start with grammar and go deeper. 'Being' translates the singular neuter participle of the verb *einai* ('to be'), whereas 'one' translates the singular neuter numeral adjective *hen*. If we are to construe 'being' and 'one' as parallel in the expressions 'the science of being' and 'the science of the one', then we might wonder whether 'one' should be understood in the sense of 'being one' (in this way both expressions would be verbal expressions), or whether 'being' should be construed as adjectival. The reason why this is relevant is that the sense(s) in which 'being' should be understood crucially depends on how we interpret the relation between the use of the participle as a substantive to indicate the object of a certain enquiry (the science of *being*) and the verbal uses of *einai*. For occurrences of finite forms of *einai* and, in particular, the third singular person of the present indicative *esti*, depending on the context, can be translated in different and non equivalent ways. *esti* can be used absolutely in contexts where it can be naturally translated with 'exists' or 'is true', or it can be used as a copula and be translated with 'is' in sentences such as 'Socrates is wise' (for a full survey of the uses of *einai* in Greek see Kahn 2003). However, there is an issue as to whether and to what extent the distinction between the existential, the veridical, and the copulative use of 'is' was perceived as such by Greek speakers in general and by Greek philosophers in particular. As a consequence of this, one may wonder whether the distinction is supposed to play any role in spelling out what an enquiry into being is. For instance, if one thinks that the distinction is relevant, depending on whether 'being' is taken as a nominalization of the existential use, one might think that an enquiry into being is an enquiry into existence (I am not suggesting that this is the case). If, on the other hand, one thinks that 'being' rather relates to the copulative use, one will come up with a corresponding account of what an enquiry into being looks like. For example, given that the copulative use of 'is' requires the addition of a predicate (such as in 'Socrates is a man', 'Socrates is wise'), one might think that an enquiry into being is rather an enquiry into what things are. Important studies on the use of the verb 'be' in Greek (see Kahn 2003) and, in particular, in Plato and Aristotle (Brown 1986 and 1994) have shown, however, that what we regard as a neat distinction does not map on to a neat distinction acknowledged by Greek philosophers. The complexity of being, as it were, in a way impacts on our understanding of the enquiry into the one as long as Aristotle seems to think that *hen* ('one') and *on* ('being') behave similarly in significant respects (for a more specific analysis of the similarities see, in particular, notes to I.2, 1053b16–24 and 1054a9–19). For example, one might wonder whether an enquiry into the one is an enquiry into an absolute feature of things (as existence may be), or an enquiry into the ways in which things can be said to be *one something* (in analogy with the copulative use of *esti*), or an enquiry into what things fit together with each other and what things do not (in analogy with the veridical use of *esti*: cf. *Met.* Θ.10, 1051b11–13). In what follows I will not return to these general difficulties in a systematic way, but I shall sketch the beginning of some responses to them in the course of the commentary.

Bearing these general remarks in mind, we can now take a closer look at the view that the one and the contraries are general features of being. Aristotle goes to great lengths to explain how being can be the object of a unified science and how such a science can be extended to include a series of very general properties of things that are without loss of unity. As for the unity of being, Aristotle notoriously argues (*Met.* Γ.2, 1003a33–b19) that, although things that are are in different ways ('being is said in many ways'), this does not prevent the existence of a science of being as long as 'being' is not a merely equivocal term. In particular, it is possible to have a unified science of being if all ways in which things are something that is can be ordered with reference to one basic way of being something that is. Aristotle thinks that this can be done in the same way in which we can order with reference to one (*pros hen*) the various ways of being healthy. Some things are said to be healthy in that they produce health, some in that they preserve health, some in that they are signs of health, etc. Although things are said to be healthy in all these different ways, all ways of being healthy can be referred back to and explained in terms of one single core notion: bodily health. The unification of the healthy grants the possibility of a unified science of it: medicine is the science of health and disease, of the healthy and of the unhealthy. Similarly for being and the science of being: although there are different ways in which things that are are, i.e. as self-subsisting objects (substances), qualities, quantities, etc., it is still possible to investigate being as a unified subject of enquiry as long as all ways of being can be referred back to and somehow explained in terms of one core way of being: that of substances.

This picture involves a number of problems I will not linger over. What is important for our purposes is that, having explained how it is possible to conceive of a unified science of being qua being, Aristotle moves on to show how such a science can extend its domain without loss of unity. The progressive extension comes to include a series of very general notions such as unity, plurality, sameness, otherness, etc. Extension is based on distinctive views about the relations of dependence obtaining between the various notions at stake. I shall emphasize five points.

1) All things that are can be said to be one and being. It follows that what can be said of the things that are one can be said of things that are, and vice versa. Aristotle expresses this relation by saying that one and being are 'the same and one nature' (Γ.2, 1003b22–23), even if this does not imply that explaining what being is (i.e. presumably, what it is for something to be) is the same as explaining what being one is (i.e. presumably, what it is for something to be one) (1003b24–25). As we shall see in I.2, it is difficult to get a firm grasp on what exactly this claim amounts to. In particular, it is not completely clear whether Aristotle regards 'one' and 'being' as two names for the same object(s) or whether he takes the one to indicate a property of being (as I am inclined to believe). Be this as it may, let me anticipate that the relation between one and being does not seem to be a merely extensional one. In particular, Aristotle believes that, if it is always the case that something that has a property P also has a property Q and vice versa (i.e. if all and only things that are P and Q), then this cannot be an incidental fact, a mere coincidence, but there must be an explanation for it. How much of this explanation can be found in Iota and how much, on the other hand, Iota relies on this assumption without spelling it out, is one problem we have to keep in mind. However, this problematic relation between one and being is the basic tool Aristotle employs to argue in Γ.2 that the science of being has to enquire into the one as well.

2) The one has an opposite, plurality (*plēthos*). According to Aristotle, one and the same science deals with the opposites (Γ.2, 1004a9–10). It follows that the science which deals with the one has to deal with plurality as well. Therefore, since (based on 1) the

science that deals with the one is the same as the science of being, the science of being will deal with plurality as well.

3) In addition to unity and plurality, there is a series of further general notions such as sameness, similarity, equality, and their opposites which are (in a way to be spelled out) linked to unity and plurality. Aristotle expresses this thought by saying (1004a17–22) that the same, the similar, the equal, etc. can be 'led back' or 'reduced' to the one, and their opposites (i.e. the other, the dissimilar, the unequal) can be reduced to the opposite of the one, i.e. plurality. All other notions which are said 'either on the basis of these or on the basis of plurality and the one' will also belong to the domain of enquiry of the same science—which, as in 1) and 2), will be the science of being. On the procedure of 'reducing' the contraries to one and plurality, see section II.2.

4) Things can be said to be one, the same, other, similar, dissimilar, etc. in many ways. However, the ways in which things are said to be one, the same, etc. can be ordered 'with reference to one' (*pros hen*). In this respect, all these notions are structurally similar to being (*on*), which can be the object of a unified science precisely because, despite being said in many ways, all ways in which things are can be ordered *pros hen*. Two problems arise with respect to these *pros hen* structures. With reference to being, Aristotle spells out its *pros hen* structure by saying that all things that are are by being something of substance—e.g. by being qualities of substances, changes of substances, etc. Within this picture, substance is that with reference to which all things that are are said to be. With respect to the other notions introduced in Γ.2, however, Aristotle confines himself to saying (1004a28–31) that, once we have individuated the primary way of being one (or of being the same, equal, etc.), all things which are said to be one will be said to be one 'some in virtue of having that, some other in virtue of producing that, some others in other similar ways'. We shall see some applications of this idea in the course of Iota. However, Γ.2 does not specify what the focus of these other *pros hen* structures is. In particular, nowhere is it said that the focus with reference to which all things are said to be one or the same or similar is substance (as is the case for being). In fact, it is not at all obvious that the clusters of ways in which things are said to be one, the same, similar, etc. display exactly the same structure as the cluster of ways in which things are said to be.

If, therefore, *pros hen* structures are a relatively familiar tool, Aristotle's move in 4) leaves at least two questions open. First, it is not clear what occupies the position of that with reference to which things are said to be one, the same, similar, etc. Second, it is not clear whether and how these *pros hen* structures are mutually related. The only indication in Γ.2 is that there is some relation of dependence between the fact that things which can be 'reduced' to the one are said in many ways and the fact that the one is said in many ways (1004a22–23: 'So that, since the one is said in many ways, also these things will be said in many ways (. . .)').

5) The group of notions belonging together with unity and plurality seem to build a subject of enquiry in its own right: one should not only investigate what each of them is, but also what their properties (or per se accidents) are.

In order to assess whether Iota is or can be the place where Aristotle carries out the project outlined in Γ.2, we have to keep these general guidelines in mind, for within the *Metaphysics* there is at least one other candidate for being the place where Aristotle carries out that enquiry: book Delta. The nature, structure, and origin of Delta are controversial, but the idea that the function of this book is precisely that of responding to the plan outlined in Γ.2 has an authoritative history going back to Alexander of Aphrodisias (Alex., *in met.*, Hayduck 344.2–345.20; for recent endorsements of this view see Halper 2009, pp. 463–9; Bodéüs-Stevens 2014; Menn (in progress), Iγ1b: The Aims of *Metaphysics* Δ). Broadly speaking, Delta can be described as a sort of select philosophical lexicon, in which Aristotle spells out the different ways in which relevant expressions are used. Delta includes all terms mentioned in Γ.2 and several more (including the ways in which things are said to be principle, cause, element, nature, necessary, etc.). The fact that Delta includes more than is actually mentioned in Γ.2 does not rule Delta out as a plausible candidate for being the place where Γ.2's project is carried out. On the contrary: Γ.2 itself alludes to the fact that the list of notions explicitly mentioned is not exhaustive (1005a16–18) and, from this point of view, Delta might even have a better claim than Iota. However, it is debatable whether the case can be adjudicated on the basis of coverage only. For, as we have seen, Aristotle seems to have a rather complex structure in mind when he justifies the progressive extension of the science of being, and this systematic and theoretical framework should be taken into account in establishing whether Iota or Delta (or anything else) fits the bill.

In this respect, at least some sections of Iota appear to be more systematic than Delta (for a more detailed analysis of the correspondences between Iota, Delta, and Γ.2 see notes, and, more generally, for a detailed account of the place of Delta in the *Metaphysics* see Menn (in progress), Iγ1b: The Aims of *Metaphysics* Δ). If this is correct, then Iota might turn out to be a better candidate than Delta *de facto.* However, there are at least some chapters in Delta (Δ.9, 1018a4–11; 10, 1018a35–38; 15, 1021a8–14) explicitly expressing views close to 4) above. Interestingly enough all these passages appear in chapters dealing with the notions mentioned in Γ.2. This might suggest that, independently from further extensions, Aristotle had a relatively well-defined plan as to how this group of notions should be dealt with, taking into account relevant structural similarities and relations of logical dependence.

I.3 IOTA AND THE DIFFERENT CONCEPTIONS OF ARISTOTLE'S ENQUIRY IN THE *METAPHYSICS*

Being one, being the same as or other than something, being contrary to something are all properties ranging over the whole domain of being, without being confined within one specific kind of things. Horses, colours, and numbers can each be said to be one, the same as, or different from, each other, etc.; but horses, colours, and numbers belong to different genera (respectively: substance, quality, and quantity) and this marks a difference between these properties and those ranging over a determinate kind of thing (for instance, being able to be literate is a property of human beings; having sense perception is a property of animals; being odd or even is a property of numbers, and so on). In this respect Iota is interesting because, in dealing with these notions, it is, together with Gamma and Delta, the part of the *Metaphysics* where the enquiry into being qua being takes the shape of an enquiry into general properties of all things that are (cf. Burnyeat 2001, pp. 134–40). A particular version of this reading of Iota is endorsed in Halper 2007 and Halper 2009, p. 18. According to Halper, Delta (rather than Iota) picks out the program of Γ.2, but Iota as a whole carries out an enquiry into unity in the same way in which the central books carry out the enquiry into being. The outcome of such an enquiry would be fully spelled out in I.2: in each genus there is a primary species (the one for that genus) working as a principle of knowledge for the other species of the genus. Since Halper's interpretation is crucially based on a specific reading of I.2 as the key to understand Iota as a whole, I shall defer discussion of his views to the notes to I.2.

The interpretation of Aristotle's metaphysics as an enquiry into the general properties of things that are is in partial contrast with other interpretations, all of which can receive support from the text. Although these are not incompatible with each other, they differ in the focus they ascribe to the philosophical enterprise outlined in the *Metaphysics*. In what follows, I shall sketch some alternative pictures of the *Metaphysics* as a whole and comment briefly on the place that Iota would occupy within each of them.

To start with, even if we accept the idea that the *Metaphysics* is meant to give an account of some general features of being, at crucial places Aristotle suggests that such an enquiry does not only or does not necessarily take the form of an enquiry into the features of things that are in general. Rather, it should focus on the most fundamental kind of being with reference to which all other beings are. In Γ.2, 1003b5–19, all beings are said to be by being something of substance and this feature is precisely what allows for a unified approach to being. Even more explicitly, in Z.1 (see in particular 1028b2–7) and Λ.1, 1069a18–26 Aristotle stresses that the traditional enquiry into being and its principles should be understood as an enquiry into substance and its principles.

The focus on substance in its turn can be taken more or less loosely. Aristotle makes room for three kinds of substance: movable perishable substance (things coming to be and passing away in the sublunary world), movable imperishable substance (celestial bodies), and unmovable substance (unmoved movers). The issue is whether, even if the science of being is understood as the science of substance and its principles, one should think of the science of being as an enquiry into substance in general (i.e. as an enquiry encompassing all three kinds of substance) or whether the enquiry into movable substance (constituting the bulk of Aristotle's analysis of substance that we have) should be rather taken as a preliminary step towards the real object of enquiry, i.e. unmovable substance (for a thorough discussion of the matter with reference to the structure of book Lambda see Judson (in progress)).

The first option seems to require that substance is a univocal notion or that at least it can be ascribed some kind of *pros hen* unity. The viability of this option has been radically questioned (Berti 1975) on the basis of two pieces of evidence coming from I.2 and I.10 respectively. I refer to the commentary for some discussion of the matter. The second option is explicitly presented as a viable one in E.1, 1026a19, where Aristotle characterizes first philosophy as a specific kind of theoretical philosophy having a specific kind of being, i.e. unmovable separate substance, as its object. In this sense, first philosophy would be 'theological' (*theologikē*) philosophy, as contrasted with mathematical and natural philosophy. The reason why this kind of science could nonetheless be regarded as a science of being qua being is that it would be primary, i.e. about what is primary within being. If one follows this line of thought, then the core of the *Metaphysics* is to be found in Λ.6–10, which provide Aristotle's accounts of the unmoved mover(s).

Whether we take Aristotle's enterprise to be a general enquiry into substance or a specific enquiry into one kind of substance, what is quite striking about Iota is that the primacy of substance is quite far from being a crucial concern in this book. This idea is as good as absent in I.3–10. I.1–2 are more complex in this respect and I refer to the commentary for further details, but let me anticipate one point. In I.1 Aristotle distinguishes the different ways in which things can be said to be one in their own right, and in I.2 he spells out how the one for each kind of being should be understood. There is a long and honourable tradition of interpretation trying to bring this discussion to bear on the unity of the unmoved mover as the primary and fundamental way of being one and, more generally, on the more familiar enquiry on substance and its principles (for a review of the literature and some discussion see Castelli 2010, pp. 182–92). However, it seems to me that such attempts are at least partially misleading in that Aristotle's focus in these chapters is quite different. Although the primary ways in which things can be said to be one are the primary ways in which substances are one, I.1–2 emphasize that quantity is the category we should look at in order to grasp what it means to be one in the primary and basic sense. Furthermore, I.3–10 show, if anything, that contrariety is a basic structure of qualitative determinations of objects (by saying this I do not mean that contrariety is restricted to the category of quality, but that the analysis of contrariety Aristotle starts with primarily applies to contrary qualities; I shall return to this point: see xxxiii–xxxv). How the quantitative and the qualitative focus of unity and contrariety respectively is supposed to relate to the 'substantial' focus of being is a deep and complex issue which deserves more attention than it has received so far.

We have seen how Iota relates to Aristotle's enquiry in the *Metaphysics* if we take the latter as an enquiry into being qua being in general, into substance, and into a specific kind of substance respectively. There is one further characterization of Aristotle's enterprise in the *Metaphysics* which, while not necessarily incompatible with any of the aforementioned views, can be taken to carry partly different implications as to the scope of metaphysical investigation. According to the characterization of wisdom (*sophia*) we find in book Alpha, the goal of the enquiry is that of leading to knowledge of the first causes and principles (I shall call this option 'archeological', from *archē*, 'principle'). I take it that there are at least two rather different ways to understand Iota's contribution to the enquiry into the principles.

One way is to regard the analysis in Iota as relevant, but mainly for destructive purposes. In particular, Iota would show what is wrong with various Academic attempts to individuate the first principles of all things. Such attempts are known to us mainly through Aristotle's reports in *Met.* Mu and Nu, which are undoubtedly close to Iota in several respects. For instance, in I.1 and 2 Aristotle shows how there is no such thing as a separate principle which is the One; in I.5 he shows how the equal, the great, and the small and, in I.6, how the one and the many do not stand to each other in the right kind of opposition in order to be regarded as contrary principles. I refer to the commentary for further details.

This approach to Iota has been particularly developed by Stephen Menn (in progress, Iγ2: Iota and the attributes of being). On Menn's reading, Iota's main contribution to the enquiry into the principles is indirect in that the outcome of Aristotle's criticism in Iota will only become explicit in Nu (see introduction to I.5 for more details). This reading certainly rests on an important feature of Iota: all notions discussed in this book figure prominently in Aristotle's discussion of Academic doctrines of the principles. However, this reading does not do full justice to the 'constructive' side of the book (nor does Menn deny that there is more to Iota than its function within the archeological reading of the *Metaphysics*). For in Iota Aristotle hardly confines himself to saying what the one or specific kinds of contraries, which are regarded as principles by other philosophers, are *not*: rather, he spells out what he seems to take as the right way to think about them. Furthermore, although it is undoubtedly true that the table of contents, so to speak, in Iota largely overlaps with fundamental topics in Academic metaphysics, only in two points Aristotle claims explicitly that what he says is of some consequence for the refutation of Academic doctrines in I.2, 1053b11–13, where Plato figures among the supporters of the view that the one is substance; and in I.10, 1059a10–14, where the analysis of the opposition of perishable and imperishable shows that there cannot be Forms as they are conceived by 'some', i.e. as they are conceived by Plato and his followers. However, at several other places in the course of Iota Aristotle alludes to the implications of his analysis for other philosophers' doctrines (see p. 139). This is, of course, hardly a crucial point, but the general impression is that Aristotle's polemical or non-polemical target in Iota is broader. This being said, some work has to be done in order to assess the extent and value of the constructive side of Aristotle's discussion in Iota (see section II and pp. 137–9, 177–9, 254–5).

If the destructive reading might be excessive in one way, the opposite view that Iota, far from being in opposition to Academic doctrines, actually gives Aristotle's primordial version of his own doctrine of the principles seems to go too far in the opposite direction. This reading is endorsed by Leo Elders in his commentary on Iota (Elders 1961, in particular pp. 12–24). Elders's commentary is heavily based on often unjustified assumptions about Aristotle's philosophical development, which led Elders, among other things, to excise all parts of the text which might constitute a problem for this general view. The disadvantages of such an approach are, I think, evident. But Elders is right in detecting some peculiarities in Iota's text such as the reference to categorial distinctions which do not (or, at least, do not in any obvious way) match the distinctions Aristotle draws elsewhere (see e.g. I.6, 1056b34–1057a1; I.7, 1057a37–b4; cf. Elders 1961, pp. 25–36, 149, 156). Furthermore, even if Elders is perhaps too optimistic in taking these as unequivocal signs of Aristotle's contribution to Academic metaphysics, it is true that some sections of Iota have a characteristic Pythagorean-esque flavour (see, in particular, pp. 88, 118–19). However, some main pieces of analysis in Iota do retain general interest and relevance for Aristotle's philosophy independently of the more eccentric aspects which can be observed at different points in this fascinating book. I shall now provide some support for this claim.

II. IOTA, CONTRARIES, AND CONTRARIETY

Both in the *Physics* and in the *Metaphysics* Aristotle repeatedly ascribes to his predecessors the claim that contraries are principles. We can distinguish two aspects in Aristotle's reconstruction of other philosophers' doctrines: first, he identifies pairs of polar principles which can be labelled *enantia* (which I systematically translate with 'contraries'; for some discussion of the problems involved in the translation of this term see Judson (forthcoming)); secondly, he explains what kind of causal function each item in the pair is supposed to perform. As for the first point, both Aristotle and his predecessors are quite liberal in accommodating things of different ontological types in the class of *enantia*: qualities (hot and cold), stuff characterized by those qualities (the hot thing and the cold thing, fire and water), forces or powers carrying out opposite activities (Love as a principle of unification and Strife as a principle of division), etc. As for the second point, the ascription of causal functions to such items has to be understood in light of Aristotle's distinction of the four causes (formal, material, final, and efficient). Aristotle regards his distinction of the four types of cause as an all-or-nothing matter: no type of cause can be adequately accounted for unless all four of them are distinguished. Since none of Aristotle's predecessors has adequately drawn Aristotle's fourfold distinction, their causes and, in particular, their ultimate causes (i.e. their principles) are doomed to play hybrid causal roles. This situation is reflected by the possibility Aristotle envisages of describing other philosophers' causes as anticipating different causal roles at different places (for a particularly clear discussion of this feature of Aristotle's discussion of the views of his predecessors, see Betegh 2012).

With respect to this overall picture, Aristotle retains the claim that the contraries are principles by doing three things: he specifies what kind of relation contrariety is; he specifies what kind of things primary contraries are; on the basis of the first two moves, he is in a position to give a more precise formulation of the question whether the contraries are principles by taking it as a question about primary contraries and by qualifying the causal role they can play with reference to his fourfold distinction of types of cause. While Iota might not tell us much about the third move, I think it tells us much more than any other text about the first two in a way that differs from Aristotle's other main account of the role of the contraries as principles in *Physics* I. In particular, I take it that *Physics* I delivers some information about the first two moves, but its main concern is the third move and the identification of the right kind of principles of change and, more generally, of changeable substances (see Λ.1–5). Note that even if we admit that the question whether and in what sense the contraries are principles is what really animates Aristotle's interest in the contraries in the first place, the importance of the first two moves can hardly be overestimated. For it is only by getting clear on what kind of items contraries are that the issue whether there is any basic sense in which contraries are principles can be properly addressed. This is not to say, however, that Aristotle's general account of contrariety in Iota is independent from his account of change: in fact, on various occasions (I.4, 1055a6–10; 1055b11–17; I.7, 1057a21–33; 1057b23–25) Aristotle resorts to the analysis of change to get a grasp on the kind of items (contraries and intermediates respectively) he is talking about. But what Aristotle does in Iota is, in my view, logically prior in that he explicitly sets out certain formal constraints for any account of the role of contraries as principles. In what follows I shall sketch the main features of the general account of contrariety in Iota and spell out a few overarching issues involved in Aristotle's understanding of the claim that contraries are principles.

From a very general point of view, the structure of the enquiry into the contraries does not significantly differ from the structure of the enquiry into other general notions such as being and substance. Aristotle starts by acknowledging the 'population' of contraries, i.e. of things (of various types) that are more or less uncontroversially regarded as contraries. He analyses the basic features of those uncontroversial cases in order to get to an account of what it is for two items to be contraries. On the basis of the general account, he can then revise the population of contraries, by showing, for instance, that some items are not contraries (cf. I.5 and 6) and that some items are contraries only in a derivative sense (see p. xxxi and p. 124). In the better known case of the enquiry into substance, the interplay between the enquiry into the 'nature' of substance and the enquiry into the 'population' of substance leads Aristotle to address the question of the identification of primary substance(s). Similarly, in the case of contraries Aristotle approaches issues of priority and primacy among contraries. However, Aristotle's approach to such issues in the case of the contraries might strike the reader as particularly complex and, to some extent, peculiar. In what follows I shall address and try to make sense of some of its peculiarities.

II.1 THE GENERAL ACCOUNT OF CONTRARIETY IN IOTA

The analysis of contrariety is introduced in I.3, 1054b31–32. In the immediately preceding lines (b22–31) Aristotle has drawn a distinction between (mere) otherness and difference: otherness is a more generic relation than difference in that difference requires that 'what is different is different from something with respect to something, so that there must be something which is the same with respect to which they are different', whereas otherness does not require any such constraints. Aristotle's formulations of this point are ambiguous (see commentary pp. 115–17, 199–201). The general problem is that Aristotle oscillates between saying that, if x and y are different, then they differ from each other in the same respect (which means: either in genus or in species), and saying that, if x and y are different, then x and y are in some respect the same. For any two things that are, they are either the same as each other or other than each other; but it is not the case that any two things that are are either the same as or different from each other. It is not very clear what it is exactly that qualifies objects as different from each other rather than as merely other. Aristotle's basic idea seems to be that difference requires some sort of homogeneity: if x and y can be said to be different from each other, they must be comparable and therefore, in some sense to be qualified, they must be the same sort of thing. It is clear that homogeneity links to the idea that, if x and y are different, then x and y are in some respect the same. It is less clear how it links to the idea that, if x and y are different, then they differ from each other in the same respect. I shall suggest in what follows that homogeneity links to the latter idea as well in that things that differ from each other must be (in some sense to be specified) comparable.

Difficulties in understanding the requirement of homogeneity for difference immediately impact on contrariety. For in I.4, 1055a3 ff., Aristotle explains that contrariety is a sort of difference: contrariety is the greatest difference—presumably: the greatest difference between objects which are, in some sense, homogeneous. In the course of Iota Aristotle considers three main cases: contraries that differ in species; contraries that differ in genus and contrary genera; contrary differences (for a brief account of the conceptual framework of species, genera, and differences see introductory notes to I.7). The requirement of homogeneity poses partially different challenges for each case.

As for contraries which differ in species, there is a very straightforward sense in which these are homogenous: they are or belong to contrary species of one and the same genus. But things are more problematic in two other cases. First, there is an issue concerning things that are contraries in genus: it is not completely clear whether Aristotle intends to stick with the idea (*Cat.* 11, 14a23–25; *Met.* Γ.2, 1004b33–1005a2; I.10) that there can be contrary genera, and, if so, it is not clear how we should understand the relevant 'genera'. If the genera at stake simply are the result of intermediate divisions of a higher genus which are not lowest species, the same understanding of homogeneity holding for contrary species applies. But it is far from clear that contrariety in genus relies or, at least, is exhausted by genera which happen to be species of a higher genus.

If, on the other hand, 'genera' has to be taken in the sense of highest genus, then the contrary genera to which things that are contrary in genus belong cannot be homogeneous in the sense of belonging to one and the same genus. Furthermore, it is not at all clear what such highest genera would have to do with the more familiar highest genera of Aristotle's ontology, i.e. the categories: categories do not stand to each other in any relation of contrariety. In fact, when Aristotle alludes to contrary genera he does not seem to have 'his' highest genera in mind: in *Cat.* 11, 14a23–25, good (*agathon*) and bad (*kakon*) are contraries which do not belong in a genus, but are themselves genera of other things; in *Met.* I.10 what is perishable (*phtharton*) and what is imperishable (*aphtharton*) are contraries that differ in genus; in *Met.* Γ.2, 1004b33–1005a2, all contraries fall under unity and plurality 'as if they were their genera'. None of these pairs picks out Aristotelian highest genera ('one' and 'good' and, presumably, their opposites are not even univocal predicates). This situation might suggest that, when Aristotle speaks of contrary *genē* or of contraries that differ in *genos*, he is not referring to what he would regard as (highest) genera. It is hard to tell whether the view that good and bad or one and plurality are contrary genera should be rejected as a whole because it rests on a wrong conception of what genera are supposed to be or because it fails to see that good, bad, one, and plurality are not good candidates for being genera or because of both (for some comments on the opposition of perishable and imperishable see notes on I.10). Be this as it may, references to things that differ in *genos* and to contrary *genē* usually appear in conjunction with things that differ in *eidos* and contrary *eidē*, which in turn suggests at least a semi-technical use of the pair *eidos* ('species')/*genos* ('genus'). (For further comments on the use of this vocabulary in Iota see the commentary, pp. 170–2, 198–9.) The view that even in semi-technical locutions such as 'other in genus' (*hetera tōi genei*) the word 'genus' may or may not be used in a technical sense is supported by *Met.* Δ.28, 1024b9–16, where in the course of a few lines the predicate 'other in genus' is applied to form and matter or to things falling under different categories: 'And those things are said to be other in genus (*hetera tōi genei*) whose primary substrate (*hypokeimenon*) is other and which do not resolve (*mē analuetai*) the one into the other nor both into the same thing—in this way form and matter are other in genus (*to eidos kai hē hulē heteron tōi genei*)—, and those things which are said in a different form of predication of being (*kath' heteron schēma katēgorias tou ontos*) (e.g. some of the things that are indicate what is, others a certain quality, and others as it was distinguished earlier): for these, too, do not resolve into each other nor into something one'. This passage suggests that some sort of primitive and unbridgeable ontological difference is what is really at stake in otherness in *genos*. As in Δ.28, in Iota Aristotle characterizes things that differ in genus as things which do not have any 'way' or access (*hodos*) to each other and which do not have any matter (*hulē*) in common (pp. 119–23). This might (but, as we shall see in a moment, need not) be taken as a denial of the homogeneity requirement.

Even if we leave aside the intricacies of contrary genera, Aristotle is clearly willing to say that there are contrary differences which are not in the genus of which they are differences (e.g. sight-piercing and sight-contracting are contrary differences of the genus colour; they are not in the genus colour; see I.7 and the corresponding notes). Of course, nothing prevents differences from being species of some other genus (are sight-piercing and sight-contracting species of some genus of quality?), but nowhere (at least nowhere in Iota) do we find this idea spelled out.

Given the difficulties involved in taking the relevant homogeneity in the sense of belonging to a common genus, we can try to find a better solution elsewhere. In particular, Aristotle seems to be keen on the idea that contraries share the same 'matter' (*hulē*). While there certainly are texts suggesting that the matter in question is, in some sense, the genus of which the contraries are species (*Met.* I.8, 1058a23–24; *GC* I.7, 324b4–9; cf. *Met.* Z.12, 1038a5–8; H.6, 1045a14–25), there are also texts suggesting that the matter that accounts for the homogeneity of the contraries is, rather, the kind of substrate in which the contraries inhere (*Met.* I.4, 1055a29–30; cf. I.3, 1054b27–31; *Cat.* 11, 14a15–20; *GC* I.7, 323b29–324a9 and 324a15–24, where the homogeneity of the contraries is eventually spelled out in terms of the same matter or the same substrate). Emphasizing the homogeneity of the contraries in terms of the kind of substrate in which they inhere does not imply that Aristotle is not aware of the difference between saying that contraries have the same kind of substrate and saying that contraries belong to the same genus: he neatly distinguishes these two claims in at least three places (*Met.* Δ.10, 1018a27–29; I.4, 1055a27–30; *Cat.* 11, 14a15–25). The suggestion is rather that, when it comes to accounting for relevant features of contraries, homogeneity in terms of kind of substrate is clearly something Aristotle has in mind even when (as in *GC* I.7) he expresses himself in terms of sameness in genus. Similarly, when he spells out otherness in genus he refers to the absence of a common substrate or a common matter. How specific the kind of substrate over which the contraries range is supposed to be depends on the level of generality of the contraries: the pair of contraries the same/other range over 'all things that are said to be one and being' (1054b18–22). This feature is what distinguishes the pair of contraries the same/other from the pair of contradictories the same/not the same. Generally speaking, contraries, unlike contradictories, keep within the domain of being. The general picture is that contraries can be more or less general properties and that each pair of contraries is anchored to a correspondingly more or less general subject. Perhaps we can make sense of contrary genera by saying that they are opposite properties determining a full partition of the domain of being—and this restriction to beings is, as in the case of the same/other, what distinguishes contrary genera such as good and bad or perishable and imperishable from contradictories. However, they are not anchored to any more specific kind of substrate which would be a suitable substrate for change and, in this sense, they lack a common matter. Within this picture, contrary genera and things that differ in genus are 'unjoinable' but are not completely incomparable.

Having defined contrariety as the greatest difference, which is, as any difference, tied to some kind in a way to be specified for the individual cases, Aristotle takes a further step in I.4, 1055a33–38, where he identifies primary contrariety with possession (*hexis*) and complete privation (*teleia sterēsis*). Aristotle adds that other contraries are said to be contraries either because they have or because they produce or because they are acquisitions or losses of possession and complete privation. This way of describing the relation between primary contraries and other contraries is reminiscent of the way in which in Γ.2 Aristotle describes the relation of primary being, i.e. substance, and other beings (cf. *Met.* Z.1, 1028a10–20; Θ.1, 1045b26–32). One important aspect of this account of primary contrariety is that the opposition of possession and complete privation provides a second-order description of pairs of qualitative features of objects without isolating any specific pair of contraries as primary. A similar idea can be found in *Met.* Λ.4, 1070b10–21 and Λ.5, 1071a32–33, where form and privation are mentioned among the principles of being that are one by analogy: there is no one single property which performs the role of form and no corresponding privation for all beings, but for any being that comes to be it is possible to identify factors performing analogous explanatory roles.

I take it that one of the reasons why the opposition of possession and complete privation provides an attractive analysis of contrariety is that, in addition to allowing for a unified explanation of several features of the contraries (see pp. xxxv–xxxvi), possession and privation are not only definitionally tied to each other but they also display their ontological dependence on a substrate, and on a substrate of a certain kind. This is made clear in the case of privation by its repeated characterization with reference to a determinate substrate (*Cat.* 10, 12a26–13a36; *Met.* Γ.2, 1004a15–16; I.4, 1055b8). As for possession, not only does possession in its sense of (good or bad) disposition require reference to the subject of the disposition (*Met.* Δ.20, 1022b10–11), but possession in the sense of 'a certain actuality of the thing that possesses and of that which is possessed' (*Met.* Δ.20, 1022b4–5) paradigmatically displays the inextricability of a substrate and of what determines it.

With this account of contrariety and, in particular, of primary contrariety, the issue whether primary contraries can be principles can only be tackled by taking all these formal constraints about the nature and mutual relations of the primary contraries into account. Among the constraints there will be the inevitable reference to a third item, i.e. the kind of substrate that can be formally determined by the pair of primary contraries which, in their turn, cannot be without the kind of substrate of which they are *hexis* and the corresponding complete privation.

These structural features of primary contraries account for two standard pieces of criticism Aristotle often uses against other philosophers' understanding of the claim that contraries are principles: first, contraries are not substances (and therefore cannot be principles of substances); second, contraries do not act on each other, but on a common substrate. Aristotle sometimes expresses the first point by saying that contraries are by being something else. This means that primary contraries only exist as contrary properties of a substrate (*Phys.* I.6, 189a27–32; cf. *Phys.* I.4, 188a5–9; *Met.* Λ.2, 1069b7–9; Λ.4, 1070b10–21; N.1, 1087a36–b4): if C_1 and C_2 are a pair of contraries, C_1 and

C_2 cannot exist as floating properties without a subject nor can anything simply be C_1 or C_2 without being anything else. For example, white and black cannot exist as floating properties nor can there be anything which is just white or just black without being anything else; in particular, if x is white or black, x will also be a surface (and in its turn, a surface can only exist as a limit of a body and so forth).

There are crucial problems in understanding the relation between the contraries and their substrate. In particular, there is a two-sided issue as to how the existential inextricability of contraries and substrate as outlined above links to essential and definitional inextricability. Can the contraries be defined without reference to the kind of substrate they inhere in? And is it ever the case that contraries figure in the definition of a subject they qualify? By introducing the general account of primary contraries in terms of possession and privation of a form of a substrate Aristotle presumably intends to stretch this account in order to cover two rather different cases: the relation obtaining between contrary properties and their subject (e.g. white, black, and surface) and the relation obtaining between form, privation, and substrate in substances (e.g. soul, privation of soul and body). But differences here are as important as similarities. First, while one could argue that the definition of contrary properties must include reference to the kind of subject they are properties of (e.g. the definition of white and black must eventually include reference to surfaces), the extent to which the definition of a substantial form must include reference to its substrate is controversial. Secondly, while substantial forms determine the identity of their substrate, it is less clear whether contrary properties do or do not determine the identity of the subject in which they inhere. There are two main options. One option is to take the claim that contraries must have a substrate to mean, quite simply, that contraries (as any other properties) have to be anchored to some individual subject. If this is all that claim amounts to, then the question of whether any contrary properties can also fix the identity of the subject they are properties of is left open. Alternatively, one can assume that, in order to speak of a substrate for the contraries, such a substrate must be identifiable independently of its being affected or qualified by either of the contraries at stake. The latter stronger view would imply that all contraries can only be incidental (i.e. non essential) features of things.

The reason why the distinction between these two approaches is important becomes clear in connection with Aristotle's claim that contraries are, in some sense, principles of being, despite his objection against his predecessor that contraries are not substances. Are these two claims compatible? Aristotle thinks that beings are primitively divided into ten types of things, which cannot be reduced to each other. The fundamental distinction is the one between substances and things such as qualities, quantities, relatives, etc. Substances enjoy a form of ontological priority in that all other things are by being something of substances; without substances, nothing else would be. Simplifying, the ontological priority of substances is based on two main ideas. In the first place, substances 'support' all other beings by being the ultimate substrates in which other beings are. Secondly, substances are determinate individual objects, which exist (to some extent) and are what they are independently of each other and independently of the particular properties that happen to belong to them; typically a substance is something that can survive the loss or replacement of some of its properties. Importantly, what is not a substance cannot be a principle of substances. Accordingly, if there are any more basic ontological factors accounting for the fact that substances are substrates and determinate beings, those factors will have to be acknowledged the status of substance, too, as long as they are responsible for the distinctive features of substances.

If we go for the first weaker reading, contraries would fail to be substances in the sense that they are not ultimate subjects of predication; rather, they are always predicated of something else. But nothing would be said about the possibility that they be essential or formal features of substances, i.e. nothing would be said about the possibility that contraries are forms (and, therefore, substances) of different substances. According to the second, stronger reading, instead, contraries could not be substance in the sense of being forms (or parts of the forms) of substances either, because they would never express the nature (or the essence) of the subject they qualify. Rather, that subject will always be already characterized by its own nature independently of its being characterized by either of the contraries. It follows that, if contraries fail to be substance both as substrates and as formal determinations of substances, they simply will not do as principles of being. We shall see below that the lack of a neat distinction between these two approaches accounts for further issues in Aristotle's account of contrariety such as the problematic onto-logical status of differences (see section II.2 and pp. 173–7) and the oscillation between contraries as properties of being and contraries as principles of being (see pp. xiii–xiv, xliii–xliv).

To conclude this section, I should like to return to the claim introduced above (p. xxxii) that Aristotle relies on his general account of contrariety in order to explain other features of con-traries and of the causal interaction between them. This is inter-esting from a methodological point of view in a rather precise sense. As we saw (see points 1–5) on pp. xvii–xix), in *Met.* B.1, 995b20–27, Aristotle introduces an aporia about the enquiry into some general notions, one of which is contrariety, and he suggests that one should not only enquire into what each of these is, but also into their per se accidents (e.g. whether one thing is contrary to one only). Γ.2, 1004a31–b10 states that such an enquiry should be carried out by the science of being qua being. Interestingly enough, the account of contrariety in I.4 does provide a unified explanation of several features of contraries which can be regarded as their per se accidents.

I have already mentioned how in *GC* I.7, 323b29–324a9, the formal account of contrariety provided in Iota is used to ground the possibility of causal interaction between the contraries. Even if the way in which the analysis of contrariety and primary contraries is sketched in Iota precedes, at least conceptually, the ascription of more or less determinate causal roles, it is tempting to think that in other passages such as *GC* I.7, 323b29 ff. and *Phys.* I.5, 188a31–34, where the nature of contraries as principles is at stake, Aristotle spells out different aspects of this unified picture in accounting for the fact that neither acting and being acted upon nor coming to be can take place between randomly chosen items—in particular, those items cannot be completely different nor can they be exactly the same. It is by understanding the structure of the relation between primary contraries and their substrate that one can come up with an appropriate appreciation of the constraints on sameness and otherness which are required for explaining causal interaction and change. Furthermore, in I.4,

1055a19–23 the account of contrariety as greatest and, therefore, complete difference provides the ground to decide on the issue whether only one thing is contrary to another. In Γ.6, 1011b15–22 and K.6, 1063b15–24, the incompatibility of the contraries with each other and with their intermediates is explained with reference to the account of contraries in terms of privation given in I.4, 1055a33 ff., and to the account of intermediates as joint privation of the corresponding contraries in I.7, 1056a22–b2 (cf. I.5, 1056a22–b2). In I.4, 1055b3–29 (in particular: b7–11 and b23–26) the distinction between contraries which have intermediates and contraries which do not have intermediates is accounted for by appealing to the fact that there are different forms of privation, in terms of which primary contrariety is defined. Finally, the identification of primary contrariety with the opposition of possession and complete privation gives a model for understanding Aristotle's description of differences in terms of more and less (or excess or defect) (*Met.* I.7, 1057b19–25; the model is applied in *De sensu* and in the biological writings in that the more and the less account for differences between parts of different species of animals; see Lennox 1980).

II.2 PRIMARY CONTRARIES AND REDUCTION(S)

We have seen that, when in Γ.2 Aristotle argues for the claim that the enquiry into unity and the other general notions should be the object of the science of being qua being, he is not very clear on the role that such notions play in the economy of being. He suggests at least two different ideas: on the one hand, the existence of pairs of opposite properties is a general feature of being. On the other hand, Aristotle's predecessors are unanimous on the intuition that the ultimate principles of being display a certain form of polarity which might be adequately captured by the opposition of contrariety if properly understood. As we shall see, these two approaches may turn out to be less far apart from each other than it might look at first sight. However, whether we look at the enquiry into the contraries as primarily an enquiry into (some) principles of being or if we look at it as primarily an enquiry into general properties of being, the task of individuating primary contraries is linked to the project of a unified science of being qua being.

In order to see why this is the case, it might be worth recalling that in setting up the issues concerning the nature and structure of the science of being in Beta and Gamma, Aristotle is concerned with the individuation of three basic constitutive elements of the science of being in agreement with some of his tenets on the structure of scientific knowledge in the *Posterior Analytics*. Each science is about a subject genus and it shows why some determinate per se attributes of such a subject belong to it by resorting to some principles. The extent to which the science of being qua being is structurally analogous to particular sciences is a notoriously difficult issue. However, all I intend to emphasize here is that all three aspects involved in the determination of the science of being (i.e. subject genus, per se attributes, and principles) raise problems of unity for Aristotle.

While the issue of the unity of the subject genus of the science of being and, at least in part, the issue of the unity of the principles of being have received attention in the literature, I would like to stress that there are passages suggesting that the unity of per se attributes of being is an issue in its own right. For instance, B.2, 997a18–19 clearly states that the reason why a unified science of all kinds of substance is problematic is that 'there would be one demonstrative science of all attributes' and *this* is taken as a problematic outcome. If one sees this as a problem, one has reasons to come up with some sort of unification of the per se attributes of being which might be at least partially different from the unification of being understood as a subject genus. More generally, there are passages suggesting that some project of unification of the basic qualitative/formal determinations of objects might be complementary to and distinct from a project of unification of beings as a subject genus. In K.3, 1061a10–15, 1061b4–5, b11–17 we explicitly find two distinct lines of enquiry: on the one hand, being has to be unified in order to be an appropriate subject genus; on the other hand, the differences and contrarieties of being have to be unified and reduced to some primary ones. But even if one does not trust Kappa as a genuine Aristotelian source, a similar distinction is at least alluded to in *Met.* A.4, 985b4–13, where Aristotle describes the views of the atomists, who assume atoms and void as matter and substrate of beings, while taking the rare and the dense as 'principles of the affections' of beings and making the differences causes of other things. The relevance of a unified approach to the

xxxvii

differences of being understood as basic formal determinations of being as matter is taken over by Aristotle himself in *Met.* H.2, in particular at 1042b9–15, 31–35. The idea that basic contrary differences should be understood as principles of other beings is spelled out and developed in I.7 (see, in particular, 1057b19–25). As we shall see, there are problems in understanding what Aristotle is after in I.7 as well as in the other passages I mentioned, but at the very least we can look at these passages as expressing a relatively unified family of concerns and not as isolated episodes of idiosyncratic metaphysical thinking.

In the course of Iota references to the identification of primary contraries can be found in three different contexts: in I.3, I.4, and I.7. While all three discussions are problematic in several respects, I.4 introduces problems which might sound familiar to the reader of the *Metaphysics* from other texts, whereas I.3 and I.7 pose more specific issues. I shall briefly present these texts in the order which I take to be from the least puzzling to the most puzzling: I.4, I.7, and I.3.

We have seen above what Aristotle might find attractive in describing primary contraries as properties of a subject displaying an opposition of possession and complete privation (I.4, 1055a33–38). One important aspect of this account of primary contrariety is that possession and complete privation provide a second-order description of pairs of qualitative features of objects without isolating any specific pair of contrary properties as primary.

I.7 addresses issues of priority from a rather different point of view. In this chapter Aristotle approaches the issue of the nature of intermediate beings. The general picture Aristotle sketches is the following: determinations of being come in ranges and, for each range, there is a pair of basic opposite determinations enjoying logical and ontological priority over all other determinations of the corresponding range. Such basic opposite determinations come in pairs, and they are called primary contraries (1057b18, b32) and principles (1057b23) of the other determinations. The chapter does not address the issue whether there is a pair of primary contraries for all determinations of being or whether the provided account should be understood in the distributive sense that, for any range of determinations, there is one pair of primary contraries. I think the second distributive reading is more likely, but I do not think the first all-inclusive reading can be excluded, especially if one compares I.7 with I.3, on which see below. I refer to the commentary for further details and discussion of the constitutive account of the relation between primary contraries, derivative contraries, and intermediates. In these preliminary notes I shall emphasize only two points: I.7 is perfectly compatible with and perhaps even complementary to I.4, to which it adds an account of how contrariety determines basic structures of reality such as the articulation of being into genera and species. Furthermore, I.7 is perfectly general. In their generality, I.4 and I.7 can be read as two possibly complementary pieces of general metaphysics providing rather systematic insights on contrariety as a feature of being.

A less perspicuous project is undertaken in I.3 and referred to in I.4, where Aristotle uses two peculiar expressions to describe the relation of other contraries to one and plurality. First, he says (I.3, 1054a29–32) that the same, the similar, and the equal are 'of the one' (*tou henos*, in the genitive), whereas the other, the dissimilar, and the unequal are 'of the plurality' (*tou plēthous*, also in the genitive). Secondly, he says that the other contraries can be 'reduced' or 'led back' (I.4, 1055b29: *anagetai*; cf. Γ.2, 1003b36–1004a2; K.3, 1061a10–15) to one and plurality. For a fuller account of the procedure applied in this chapter Aristotle refers to a 'division' of the contraries (I.3, 1054a30).

There is some debate about the number and nature of Aristotle's lost writings on the contraries and on the opposites, but at least the basic outline of the project has been made convincingly clear (Guariglia 1978; see also Berti 1973; Rossitto 2000). Aristotle's work on the contraries was probably an attempt to order the contraries into two columns, in a way analogous in structure to the Pythagorean tables of contraries (see e.g. *Met.* A.5, 986a22 ff.). From Γ.2 we can gather some additional details: one column (*sustochia*) of the contraries is privation (1004b27); all contraries can be 'led back' or 'reduced' (*anagetai*) to being and non-being or to one and plurality, e.g. rest belongs (or falls under) the one and change belongs (or falls under) plurality (1004b27–29); all other contraries (and, a fortiori, all other contraries that are assumed as principles) can be 'led back' or 'reduced' to one and plurality, under which they fall as if the latter were their genera (1004b33–1005a2; cf. I.4, 1055b27–29). In this way, one and plurality can be regarded as the principles of the contraries (1005a2–13).

This picture is problematic for several reasons, but I intend to focus only on two intertwined issues: can we say anything about the vertical relation obtaining between items within the same column? And is this ordering of the contraries meant to provide any clue about the structure of reality?

As for the first question, something more precise on the relation between the one, the same, and the similar can be gathered from the analysis in I.3. I refer to the commentary for further details, but the general impression is that sameness, equality, and similarity are at least logically dependent on unity in the sense that unity is mentioned in the definition of each of them. Further information on the nature and purpose of such a 'reduction' can be gathered by looking at *GC* II.2 and *Meteor.* IV.1, 378b10 ff., where Aristotle presents the reduction of properties of a certain kind of subject to a few basic pairs of properties which are then regarded as principles of the properties and of the subject at issue. I shall confine myself to a brief survey of *GC* II.2, but similar considerations apply to *Meteor.* IV.

In *GC* II.2 Aristotle 'reduces' (cf. 330a25: *anagontai*) all tactile contraries to the two basic pairs of warm–cold and wet–dry. The conceptual framework and the technical vocabulary there deployed are similar to those described above with reference to the reduction of the contraries to the one and plurality. In short, Aristotle is enquiring into the principles (*archas*) of sensible body; he explains that in this case 'sensible' should be understood in the sense of 'tangible'. Therefore, the contrarieties which determine the differences of the sensible body can only be restricted to those that are perceptible with the sense of touch. These tactile contrarieties apply to body as their common substrate and give place to the basic distinction of the species of the simple bodies. Aristotle explains that the contraries that make for the differences between the simple bodies must be such as to account for the mutual relations of acting and being acted upon obtaining between the simple bodies themselves.

Aristotle makes a list (329b18–20) of tactile contraries: warm and cold, dry and wet, heavy and light, hard and soft, glutinous and friable, rough and smooth, coarse and fine. Of these, heavy and light cannot be the primary differences of the simple bodies because they do not account for the mutual interaction of the elements (329b20–24). Warm and cold have an active capacity, whereas dry and wet have the passive capacity of being acted upon. The other contraries (fine and thick, glutinous and friable, hard and soft, etc.) are made 'out of these' or 'from these' (329b34). Aristotle explains this in the following terms.

The basic four contraries are so defined:

Warm = what brings together homogeneous things;
Cold = what contracts (or brings together) both things of the same kind and of different kinds;
Wet = that whose shape is determined by its container and not by its own determination;
Dry = that whose shape is determined by its own determination and not by its container.

The other pairs of contraries are accounted for in terms of the definitions of basic contraries given above. For example, what is 'fit for filling up' is 'of', i.e. belongs together with or falls under the wet (*tou hugrou*, in the genitive); the fine is fit for filling up; therefore the fine belongs to the wet; accordingly, the coarse belongs to the dry. Furthermore, there are different kinds of dry and different kinds of wet; each kind of dry has a corresponding contrary kind of wet; they belong together with or fall under the primary dry and the primary wet (330a15).

In *GC* II.2 Aristotle suggests that it is possible to give a unified account of the properties of a certain subject by identifying some basic properties of it and showing how all other properties are modifications or further specifications of the basic ones. The basic properties can then be labelled 'principles' of derivative properties as well as of the objects they determine. A similar strategy is described in *Met.* Γ.2 and I.3—where, presumably, the subject determined by the opposite properties which can be reduced to one and plurality is being qua being.

If we now compare this reconstruction of the reduction of the contraries with the analysis we find in I.4, we can see that while the primary contrariety (i.e. the opposition of possession and complete privation) in I.4 provides a second-order description of the relation between any two contraries belonging to the same pair, primary contraries in Γ.2 and I.3 (i.e. one and plurality) are, so to speak, first-order contraries, whose relation to each other can be described in terms of the primary contrariety of I.4 (plurality is the complete privation of unity). If we take seriously the parallel with *GC* II.2 (as I am inclined to do), the reduction to unity and plurality suggests that, for any pair of contraries, one of them is a way of being one and the other is a way of being many (in the same way in which being glutinous is a way of being wet and being friable is a way of being dry). How can we make sense of the relation between these two pieces of analysis? And what kind of insight does either of them provide into being?

There are two opposite and equally radical ways to play down the difficulties emerging from the co-existence of these two approaches, neither of which is, in my view, fully satisfactory. One could endorse the view that the reduction in Γ.2/I.3 is really nothing more than what we find in I.4: in some texts Aristotle speaks of unity and plurality, being and non-being, whereas in others he rather speaks in terms of possession of a form and corresponding privation; but what he is after is really the same kind of analysis. The other view would be that we do have to do with two distinct and incompatible projects: in Γ.2/I.3 Aristotle is still after a project analogous to that of his predecessors, i.e. that of identifying some basic contrary properties somehow determining all further properties of being. In I.4, on the other hand, Aristotle proceeds towards a different (possibly more mature) approach to the contraries as principles of being: there is no pair of basic properties determining all beings, but it is possible to give a unified description of the formal determination of subjects through contrary properties. Such a description would not pick out any pair of contrary properties in particular, but would account for what it is for two items to be contrary to each other.

While I do not think there are conclusive arguments against these two approaches, I would rather look at the results in I.3 and I.4 as two distinct but intertwined aspects of one and the same unification project. If we look at more familiar pieces of Aristotle's ontology, we can see that the enquiry into what it is to be a primary P and the identification of the objects which happen to be primary Ps are but two sides of the same general issue: what is P? For instance, in the case of substance the enquiry into what it is to be a primary substance is also supposed to contribute to the identification of objects that are primary substances; similarly for being and, as we shall see in I.1, for the one. When it comes to the identification of the objects that are primary Ps Aristotle tends to restrict the number of tokens that are primary Ps by individuating some P which stands to all other P in some relations of onto-logical priority. In the case of substance, we end up with a first substance (the unmoved mover); in the case of unity, we end up with the one (i.e. the numerical unit) which is the principle of numbers. Similarly, we can look at the reduction in Γ.2 and I.3 (as well as in GC II.2 and Meteor. IV) as an attempt at individuating, among the objects which are primary contraries in the sense of I.4, some pair of contraries enjoying some form of ontological priority over other contraries.

The outcomes of this strategy in the case of contraries might look less appealing than in other cases, and it is certainly possible that at some point Aristotle just gave up the reduction of contraries to unity and plurality, possibly in favour of more local reductions such as those we find in GC II.2 and Meteor. IV. Interestingly enough, in Met. Λ.4, 1070b10–21, where Aristotle spells out the different ways in which one could say that the principles of all things are the same, he mentions the sense in which hot and cold, wet and dry are principles of sensible bodies in addition to the general sense in which form and privation can be said to be prin-ciples of all things. This again suggests that the two approaches are regarded as complementary.

Despite difficulties, a relatively unified picture emerges which makes Aristotle's enterprise on the contraries a philosophically interesting one. Let us assume (as Aristotle does) that we can distinguish two basic ways of being: things are either by being a substrate of properties or by being a property of a substrate. It seems to be a general feature of properties that they come in pairs of opposites of a certain type (i.e. as possession and privation) or in derivative forms of it (e.g. in ranges bounded by pairs of opposites). This general view is articulated into two basic intu-itions emerging at different points in Aristotle's writings. First, each pair of contraries is homogeneous or anchored to a genus (this anchorage can take different forms depending on the pair of contraries one considers). Second, for each kind of being there is one pair (or a small number) of basic opposite features that characterize objects belonging to that kind. We have seen how the first idea links to the identification of possession of a determin-ation/privation of that determination/subject of the possession as structurally inextricable. The second idea is behind a series of more or less local 'reductions' of properties of a certain kind of subject to a small number of basic contraries. I contend that both ideas play for Aristotle a fundamental role in determining the formal constraints for an appropriate description of being.

If an adequate analysis of being has to include a general account of the basic structures of determination of being understood as the subject of those determinations, one might wonder whether it makes a big difference to say that what we are looking for are the principles of the attributes of being rather than, more simply, principles of being. This is all the more true if, as I suggested, there are genuine difficulties in accounting for the ontological nature of differences between objects, i.e. the properties which determine objects and distinguish them from each other. Aristotle's oscillation between treating differences simply as affections of an independently identifiable subject and taking them as formal determinations affecting the identity of the substrate which they determine is a notorious problem. The same oscillation, however, might help us to understand why the enquiry into some general features of being eventually also becomes an enquiry into (some) principles of being.

NOTE ON THE TRANSLATION

The translation is based on Ross's critical edition of the Greek text (Ross 1924, II).

* indicates passages where I depart from Ross's text (see Notes on the Text).

< > indicate possibly controversial supplements in the translation which are discussed in the commentary.

Paragraphs in the translation correspond to sections of the commentary.

TRANSLATION

CHAPTER 1

That the one is said in many ways has been said before, in the **1052a15** works which distinguish in how many ways things are said. Given that it is said in many ways, there are four principal ways of being one for the things that are primary and said to be one in their own right and not incidentally.

For what is continuous, either without qualification or, most of all, by nature and not by contact nor in virtue of bonds, is said to 20 be one; and, of these things, those are more one and prior, whose motion is more indivisible, i.e. simple in a higher degree.

Furthermore, what is a whole and has some shape and form is such in an even higher degree, and most of all if something is such by nature and not by force—like those things that are a whole in virtue of glue or nails or bonds—but has in itself the cause of its being continuous. And something is such in virtue of the fact that 25 its motion is one and indivisible in place and time; so that it is evident that, if something has by nature the primary principle of the primary motion, as circular motion is—I say—with respect to local motion, this is the primary magnitude which is one.

Some things, then, are one in this way, i.e. inasmuch as they are continuous or a whole. Other things are one if their account is one, and things of this kind are those of which the thought is one; 30 and things of this kind are those of which the thought is indivisible, and a thought is indivisible which is of what is indivisible in form or in number: and the particular is indivisible in number, while what is indivisible with respect to what can be known and knowledge is indivisible in form, so that the cause of the one for substances would turn out to be a primary one.

The one, then, is said in these many ways: the continuous by nature and the whole, and the particular and the universal; and all 35 these things are one because, in the former cases, their motion, in the latter cases, their thought or their account is indivisible. One **1052b** ought to understand also that saying what sort of things are said to be one and what it is to be one and what its account is should not be taken as the same. For the one is said in these many ways,

I

and each of those things to which one or other of these ways
5   belongs is one; but being one sometimes will be being in one or
other of these ways, but sometimes it will be being something else
which is rather close to the name—while those are rather close to
its power. This is the same as in the case of element and cause, if
one had to speak by defining them with reference to things and by
giving the definition of the name. For in a way fire is an element
10 (and perhaps also the infinite and something else of this kind is
<an element> in its own right), but in a way it is not: for being fire
and being an element are not the same. Rather, fire is an element
as a certain thing and nature, whereas the name signifies that this
feature belongs to it, namely that something is made out of it as a
primary constituent.

15   This is the case also with reference to cause and one and all
such things. For this reason, too, being one is being indivisible,
which is precisely being a this and being inseparable* either in
place or in form or in thought, or also with respect to* what it is to
be a determinate* whole, and most of all by being the primary
measure* of each genus and, in the strictest sense, of quantity: for
from this case it has been extended to the other things.

20   For measure is that through which quantity is known; and
quantity as quantity is known either through the one or through
number; but every number is known through the one, so that every
quantity as quantity is known through the one; and the primary
thing through which it* is known, this very thing is one. For this
reason the one is a principle of number as number.

And from this case in the other cases, too, the primary thing
25 through which each of them is known is said to be a measure, and
the measure of each is one, in length, in width, in depth, in weight,
in speed (for weight and speed are common in the contraries: for
each of them is double, namely 'weight' indicates either anything
that has downwards inclination in whatever quantity or what has
an excess in downwards inclination, and 'speed' indicates either
30 anything that has motion in whatever quantity or what has an
excess of motion: for what is slow has some speed and what is
lighter has some weight).

In all these cases, then, something one and indivisible is a
measure and a principle, since also in the case of lines people
use the foot as if it were atomic. For in each case people look for
the measure as something one and indivisible: and this is what is

simple either in quality or in quantity. And when it seems that it is 35
impossible to remove or to add anything to it, then this measure is
precise. For this reason the measure of number is the most
precise: for they posit the unit as indivisible in all respects. In **1053a**
the other cases they imitate such a condition: for when something
is added or removed from the stade or the talent and, in general,
from what is bigger, it escapes notice more than when the same is
done to something smaller. So that everyone establishes as measure
of liquids and of solids and of weights and of magnitudes the 5
primary thing to which it is not possible to add or remove anything with respect to perception. And they think they know the
quantity when they know it in terms of this measure. And more-
over, they think they know motion, too, through the simple and
fastest motion (for this takes the shortest time); for this reason in 10
astronomy a one of this kind is a principle and a measure (for they
set down the motion of the universe as uniform and as the fastest
and judge the other motions with reference to it); and in music a
semitone is a principle and measure because it is the smallest
<interval>, and in the case of vocal sound a vocal element is a
principle and a measure. And all these things are something one
in this way, not as if the one were something common but as it has
been said.

And the measure is not always one in number, but sometimes 15
there are more than one: e.g. the semitones are two—not with
respect to hearing but in their ratios—and the vocal sounds we
use to measure are more than one, and the diagonal and the side
are measured by two measures, too, as well as all magnitudes.

In this way, then, the one is a measure of all things, in that we
know the things from which substance is by dividing on the basis
of quantity or on the basis of form. And it is for this reason that 20
the one is indivisible, because what is primary in each case is
indivisible.

But not everything is indivisible in the same way, for instance
the foot and the unit: for the latter is indivisible in all respects,
while the other is meant* to fall under the things that are indivisible relative to perception, as has already been said; for certainly
every continuous thing is divisible.

The measure always belongs to the same kind as the things it is
a measure of: for the measure of magnitudes is a magnitude, and, 25
in particular, of length it is a length, of width it is a width, of

3

vocal sound it is a vocal sound, of weight it is a weight, of units it is a unit. For this latter case must be understood in this way, and not in the sense that the measure of numbers is a number: and yet one ought to say so, if the cases were similar. But actually, if one claimed this, one would not think of this case in a similar way, but rather as if one thought that the measure of units is
30 units, and not a unit: for in truth number is a plurality of units.

And we say that knowledge as well as perception is a measure of things for the same reason, namely because we come to know something through them, although, rather than measure, they are measured. But what happens to us is the same as if someone else was measuring us and we knew how tall we were in virtue of the
35 fact that the cubit-rule applies to this much of us. And Protagoras says that the human being is the measure of all things, as if talking
1053b of the human being who knows or who perceives: and <he says that> these <would be the measure of all things> the one because he has perception and the other because he has knowledge, which we say to be measures of their objects. And, without saying anything extraordinary, they appear to say something remarkable.

It is evident then that, for those who define* in accordance with the name, to be one is most of all a certain measure and, in
5 the strictest sense, of quantity, and then of quality; and, in one case, that which is indivisible in quantity, in the other case that which is indivisible in quality will be of this sort. And it is precisely for this reason that the one is indivisible either without qualification or as one.

CHAPTER 2

And we must investigate how it is with respect to substance and
10 nature, as we did in presenting the difficulties, when we approached the issue of what the one is and how we ought to think of it: whether we should think of it assuming that some sort of substance is the one itself, as first the Pythagoreans and then Plato maintained; or whether it is rather the case that some nature of some sort underlies it and it should be spoken of more intelligibly and rather as the philosophers of nature did—for one of
15 them says that the one is love, another says that it is air and another that it is the infinite.

If in truth it is not possible that any of the universals be substance, just as we said in the discourses about substance and being, nor is it possible that this very thing be substance as something one over and above the many, for it is common— unless it is only something predicated—it is clear that the one cannot be substance either: for one and being are predicated most 20 universally of all things. So that neither are genera determinate natures and substances separate from other things nor can the one be a genus for precisely the same reasons that neither being nor substance can.

Furthermore, it is necessary that things be similar in all cases: and one and being are said in the same number of ways. So that, if it 25 is true that in qualities the one is something and some nature, and similarly in quantities too, it is clear that we must investigate what the one is in general, as also what being is, assuming that it is not enough to say that this very same thing is its nature.

The one in colours, at any rate, is a colour, e.g. the white, and accordingly the others appear to come to be from this and the 30 black, and the black is privation of white, as darkness, too, is privation of light; so that if things that are were colours, things that are would be a certain number, but of what? It is clear that they would be a certain number of colours, and that the one would be a one of a certain kind, e.g. the white.

Similarly, if things that are were tunes, they would be a num- 35 ber, but a number of semitones; but their substance would not be number; and the one would be something whose substance would not be the one, but a semitone. And similarly, in the case of **1054a** articulate sounds, too, things that are would be a number of vocal elements, and the one would be a sounding vocal element. And if beings were rectilinear figures, they would be a number of figures, and the one would be the triangle.

The same account applies to the other genera too, so that, given 5 that there are numbers and there is something one in affections, qualities, quantities and motion, if it is true that in all things the number is of things of a certain kind and the one is a one of a certain kind, and yet this is not its* substance, then it is necessary that in the case of substances, too, things be in the same way: for things are similar in all cases.

It is therefore evident, on the one hand, that the one in each genus is a certain nature and that this very same thing, i.e. the 10

5

one, is not the nature of anything, but as in colours the one itself must be investigated as one colour, so in substance, too, the one itself has to be investigated as one substance.

On the other hand, that the one in some sense signifies the same as being, is clear in virtue of the fact that it follows the categories in the same number of ways and that it is in none of them (e.g. it is
15 neither in the category of the what-it-is nor in the category of of-what-quality, but it behaves in the same way as being), and in virtue of the fact that 'one human being' does not add anything else in predication to 'human being' (as being, too, is nothing over and above being a certain something or of a certain quality or of a certain quantity), and in virtue of the fact that being one is being for each thing.

CHAPTER 3

20 The one and the many are opposed in many ways, in one of which the one and the plurality are opposed as indivisible and divisible. For what is divided or divisible is said to be a certain plurality, whereas what is indivisible or not divided is said to be one.

Since, then, the oppositions are said in four ways, and, of these, one of the two is said according to privation, they would be
25 contrary—and they would not be opposed as contradiction nor as things which are said as relatives.

The one is called after and is revealed by its contrary—the indivisible by the divisible—because plurality, i.e. the divisible is more perceptible than the indivisible, so that plurality is prior in account to the indivisible in virtue of perception.
30 As we outlined also in the *Division of the contraries*, the same, similar and equal belong with the one, while the other, dissimilar and unequal belong with plurality.

Given that the same is said in many ways, in one way, that which* we sometimes call 'it itself' is said according number; in another way, when what is called the same is one in account and
35 in number, as you are one with yourself both in form and in matter. Furthermore, we call things the same when the account
1054b of the primary substance is one: for instance, the equal straight lines are the same, and so also quadrangular figures that are equal

and have equal angles, even if they are more than one. But in these things equality is unity.

We call things similar when, even if they are not the same without qualification and are not undifferentiated with respect to the composite substance, they are nevertheless the same with 5 respect to the form, as the bigger quadrangular figure is similar to the smaller one, and as the unequal straight lines: for these are similar, but they are not the same without qualification. And in another way we call things similar if they have the same form and are neither more nor less in those respects in which the more and the less occur. In another way, when the affection is the same and one in form (e.g. the white), in higher or lower degree, people 10 say that things are similar because their form is one; in another way when things have more features that are the same than features that are different, either without qualification or with respect to evident features, e.g. tin is similar to silver or fire is similar to gold* in that it is flame-coloured and golden.

So that it is clear that the other and the dissimilar are also said in many ways. And the other and the same are said in opposition 15 to each other; therefore each thing in relation to each thing is either the same or other; in another way, we call things other when the matter and the account are not both one; therefore, you are other than your neighbour; in the third way we call things other as in the case of mathematical objects.

For this reason, then, each thing of those that are said to be one and being is said to be either other or the same in relation to each thing: for the other is not the contradiction of the same, and 20 therefore the other is not said of things that are not (whilst not-the-same is said of things that are not as well), but is said of all things that are. For all things that are and that are one are naturally such as to be either one or not one.

The other and the same, then, are opposed in this way; but difference and otherness are distinct. For what is other and the thing it is other than are not necessarily other in a certain respect: indeed, anything that is a being is either other than or the 25 same as anything that is a being. On the other hand, what is different is different from something with respect to something, so that there must be something which is the same with respect to which they are different. And this, which is the same, is the genus or the species. For anything which is different differs either in

7

genus or in species: in genus those things of which there is no common matter and no coming to be into each other—as is the case with things whose figure of predication is other—and differ-
30 ent in species, on the other hand, those things whose genus is the same (what is called 'genus' is that with respect to which both different things are said to be the same according to substance).

The contraries are different and contrariety is a certain difference. The fact that we are right in supposing this is made clear from induction: for it appears that all these things too are different, which are not only other than each other, but are such
35 that some of them are other with respect to the genus, and some
1055a belong to the same column of predication, so that they are in the same genus and are the same in genus. It is distinguished in other places which things are the same and which are other in genus.

CHAPTER 4

Since differing things can differ from each other more and less, there is also a certain difference which is the biggest, and I call
5 this contrariety. That contrariety is the biggest difference is clear from induction. For things differing in genus do not have any access to each other; rather they are quite apart from each other and are unjoinable. On the other hand, for things differing in species the processes of coming to be are from the contraries regarded as the extremes, and the distance between the extremes is the biggest, so that the distance between the contraries is also the biggest.
10 But the biggest in each genus is complete. Biggest is that which cannot be exceeded, and complete is that beyond which it is not possible to take anything; for the complete difference has an end (as other things are also said to be complete in virtue of having an end) and there is nothing beyond the end. For the end is an extreme in
15 each thing and embraces it; therefore there is nothing beyond the end nor does the complete lack anything.

That contrariety is complete difference is clear from these things. And given that the contraries are said in many ways, the way in which completeness belongs to them will follow the way in which being contraries belongs to them.

Given these things, it is evident that there cannot be more than one contrary to one thing (for neither there could be something 20 more extreme than the extreme nor could the extremes of one single distance be more than two); and in general, if contrariety is a difference and difference is between two things, then the complete difference is also between two.

Necessarily then the other definitions of the contraries are also true. For the complete difference differs the most (for it is not possible to take anything further beyond things which differ in 25 genus and things which differ in species: for it has been shown that there is no difference in relation to things which are beyond the genus and, of things which are in the genus, this is the biggest); and things which differ the most in the same genus are contraries (for the complete difference is the biggest difference between them); and things which differ the most in the same receptive thing are contraries (for the same matter is matter for the con- 30 traries); and things which differ the most and fall under the same capacity are contraries (for the science which is one is concerned with one single genus). In these things the complete difference is the biggest.

The primary contrariety is possession and privation—not any privation (for privation is said in many ways), but whichever privation is complete. The other contraries will be said on the 35 basis of these, some in virtue of having them, some in virtue of producing or of having the capacity to produce them, some in virtue of being acquisitions and losses of these or of other contraries.

If then contradiction, privation, contrariety and relatives are **1055b** opposed, and of these contradiction is primary and there is no intermediate for contradiction, whereas there can be for the contraries, it is clear that contradiction and contraries are not the same. But privation is a certain contradiction; for either what cannot possess the corresponding property at all, or what would be naturally apt to possess it but does not possess it, is 5 deprived, either completely or in a certain determinate way (and we say this, too, in many ways, as we have explained in other places); so that privation is a certain contradiction or a determinate incapacity or an incapacity considered together with what is receptive of it. And for this reason there is no intermediate for contradiction, but there are intermediates for some cases of

10 privation: for everything is either equal or not equal, while not everything is either equal or unequal—or, if at all, only in what is receptive of the equal.

If, then, processes of coming to be for the matter are from the contraries, and things come to be either from the form, i.e. from the possession of the form, or from some privation of form and shape, it is clear that every contrariety is a privation, while

15 perhaps not every privation is a contrariety (the reason for this is that the thing which is deprived can be deprived in many different ways): for the extremes from which changes take place are contraries.

This is evident also from induction. For every contrariety includes the privation of one* of the two contraries, but not in the same way in all cases. For inequality is the privation of

20 equality, dissimilarity of similarity, and vice of virtue, but they differ as has been said: for in some cases <the privation of the contrary obtains> if the subject is just deprived, in other cases if it is deprived at a certain time or in a certain part—e.g. at a certain age or in the principal part—or in all respects. For this reason for some contraries there are intermediates, and there can be a human being who is neither good nor bad; but for others there are not any, but the thing is necessarily either odd or even.

25 Furthermore, some contraries have a determinate subject, some others do not.

So that it is evident that one of the two contraries is always said on the basis of privation. And it would be enough even if this were true in the case of the primary contraries and of the genera of the contraries, e.g. the one and the many: for the other contraries are reduced to these.

CHAPTER 5

30 Since one thing is contrary to one thing, one could be puzzled as to how the one and the many are opposed and as to how the equal is opposed to the great and to the small.

For* we say 'whether ... or ...' always within an opposition, e.g. 'whether white or black' and 'whether white or not white' (we do not say 'whether human being or white', unless this is

35 understood on the basis of a hypothesis and while enquiring into

whether, e.g., it is Cleon or Socrates who came—yet this is not necessary in any genus. But this derives from there too: for only the opposites cannot be at the same time, and this fact is relied upon also in the question whether this or that came. For, if both could be at the same time, the question would be ridiculous; and if **1056a** the two could be at the same time, they would fall into an opposition in this way also, whether one or many: e.g. whether they both came or only one of them did). So, if the enquiry into whether something or something else is the case is always concerned with the opposites, and we ask whether <something is> greater or smaller or equal, what is the opposition in which the 5 equal stands to these?

For, it cannot be contrary to only one of them nor to both: for why should it be contrary to the greater rather than to the smaller?

Furthermore, the equal is contrary to the unequal, so that it will be contrary to more than one thing.

But if the unequal indicates the same as the two of them taken together, <the equal> would be opposite to both of them (and the difficulty runs in aid of those who say that the unequal is a dyad); 10 but then it turns out that one single thing is contrary to two, which is precisely what is impossible.

Furthermore, the equal appears to be intermediate between the great and the small, but neither there seem to be an intermediate* contrariety nor is this possible on the basis of the definition: for it would not be complete if it were intermediate between some things; rather, it is always contrariety that has something intermediate within itself.

The only options left, then, are that they are opposed as neg- 15 ation or as privation. Certainly it cannot be <the negation or the privation> of only one of them (for why should it be of the great rather than of the small?); therefore it is a privative negation of both, and for this reason 'whether . . . or . . . ' is referred to both and not to only one of them (e.g. we do not ask whether something is greater or equal, or whether it is equal or smaller), but there are always three terms. But it is not a privation of necessity: 20 for not everything which is neither greater nor smaller is equal; rather, this is the case only with things in which these are of a nature to be. The equal, then, is what is neither great nor small, but which is by nature such as to be great or small; and it is opposed to both as a privative negation, and this is why it is also intermediate.

25   What is neither good nor bad is opposed to both, too, but it has no name: for each of them is said in many ways and what receives them is not one thing only; rather what is neither white nor black. This, too, is not said to be one single thing, but the things of which this negation is privatively said are determined in a certain way: for what is neither white nor black is necessarily either grey or

30   yellow or something else of this sort.

Consequently, those do not assess the matter correctly who consider that all things are said similarly, in such a way that what is neither shoe nor hand will be intermediate between shoe and hand, if it is also true that what is neither good nor bad is intermediate between the good and the bad, as if there were going to be some intermediate between any two things. But there is no

35   necessity that this turn out to be the case. For there is a joint negation of the opposites for those things for which there is some intermediate and which are by nature such as to have some

1056b   distance between them. But no difference obtains between those things: for the things that are jointly negated are in different genera, so that the subject is not one.

CHAPTER 6

Similarly one could be puzzled about the one and the many. For, if the many are opposed to the one without qualification, some impossible consequences follow.

5   For the one will be what is few or few, since the many are also opposed to the few.

Furthermore, two will be many, if it is true that the double is said to be a multiple on the basis of two; hence the one will be few. For relative to what will two be many if not relative to one and what is few? For nothing is less.

10   Furthermore, if, as long and short are in length, so much and few are in plurality, and if what is much is also many and the many are much (unless perhaps there is some difference in the case of continuous fluids), what is few will be some plurality. So that the one will be some plurality, if it is also few; but this is necessarily so, if two is many.

But perhaps, in some sense, the many are also said to be much, 15 but in a different way. For instance, water is said to be much, but not many, whereas <many> is said with reference to those things that are divisible—in one way, if there is a plurality which has excess, either without qualification or relative to something else (and in the same way what is few, too, is a plurality which has a deficiency), and in another way, as number, which is also opposed to the one only.

For, in this sense we say one or many, as if one were to say one 20 and 'ones' or white and 'whites', and the things which are measured and what is measurable* in relation to the measure. And multiples are said to be <many> in this way, too: for each number is many because it is several 'ones' and because each is measured by the one, and as what is opposed to the one and not to the few.

In this sense, then, two are also many, and not in the sense that 25 they are a plurality which has an excess either relative to something or without qualification, but primarily. On the other hand, two are few without qualification: for two is the primary plurality which has a deficiency. (This is why Anaxagoras did not leave things in a correct state saying that all things were together, infinite in plurality and smallness, while he should have said 'in 30 fewness' instead of 'in smallness'; for they are not infinite.) For the few is not on account of the one, as some people say, but on account of two.

In fact, the one is opposed to the many* as measure to measurable; and these are opposed as those relatives which are not relative in their own right. We have distinguished in other writ- 35 ings that relatives are said in two ways, some as contraries, some as knowledge is relative to what is knowable, because something else is said relative to it.

Nothing prevents the one from being less than something, e.g. **1057a** less than two: for it does not follow that, if it is less, it is also few.

Plurality is like a genus of number: for number is plurality measured by one, and in a way one and number are opposed to each other, not as contraries but as we have said that some of the 5 relatives are. They are opposed in that one is measure and the other is measurable, and for this reason not everything which is one is number, as in the case of something which is indivisible.

Although knowledge is said to be relative to what is knowable in a similar way, this case is accounted for differently. For one

would think that knowledge is measure, while the knowable is the
10 measurable; but it turns out that all knowledge is knowable, but
not all that is knowable is knowledge, because in a certain way
knowledge is measured by what is knowable.

Plurality is neither contrary to the few (rather, what is much is
opposed to what is few as a plurality which exceeds is contrary to
a plurality which is exceeded) nor to the one in every way: rather,
15 in one way, as has been said, because it is divisible while <the one>
is indivisible, and in another way as a relative, as knowledge to
knowable, if <plurality> is number and the one is measure.

CHAPTER 7

Since it is possible that there is something intermediate between
the contraries and, in some cases there is, it is necessary that
intermediates be from the contraries.
20   For all intermediates are in the same genus as those things
between which they are intermediate. For we say that those things
are intermediate, into which what changes necessarily changes
into before changing into the opposite (for instance, if something
moves from the lowest note to the highest note through the
smallest <interval>, one will reach the intermediate notes before
<coming to the highest>; and in the case of colours, if something
25 <moves> from white to black, one will reach red and grey before
coming to black; and similarly in the other cases, too). But there is
no changing from one genus to another genus except incidentally,
as, e.g., from colour to figure. Therefore, it is necessary that the
intermediates be in the same genus as each other and as the things
between which they are intermediate.
30   But all intermediates are between opposites of some sort: for
it is only from these that things can change in their own right
(for this reason it is impossible that there be intermediates of
things which are not opposite: for, in that case, there would be a
change which was not from the opposites). Of the opposites,
there is no intermediate in a contradiction (for a contradiction
35 is this, namely an opposition such that one part or the other is
present in anything whatsoever and which does not have anything intermediate), while, of the remaining opposites, some are
relatives, some are opposed as possession and privation, and

some are contraries. And, of relatives, those that are not contraries do not have any intermediate: the reason for this is that they are not in the same genus. For what would be intermediate between knowledge and knowable? But <there is an intermediate> **1057b** between great and small.

If the intermediates are in the same genus, as has been shown, and are intermediate between contraries, it is necessary that they be composed out of these contraries. For either there will be a genus of them or there will be none.

And if there is to be a genus in such a way as to be something 5 prior to the contraries, the differences which produce* the contrary species (i.e. the species of a genus) will be prior and contrary: for the species are from the genus and the differences (e.g. if white and black are contraries, and the first is piercing colour whilst the latter is contracting colour, these differences, i.e. piercing and 10 contracting, are prior; so that these are contrary to each other and prior).

But things which differ in a contrary way are contraries to a higher degree; and the remaining <contraries> and the intermediates will be from the genus and the differences (for instance, those colours which are intermediate between white and black, these must be said to be from the genus—and the colour is the genus— 15 and from some differences; but these will not be the primary contraries: otherwise each <intermediate colour> will be either white or black; therefore <the differences out of which intermedi­ate species are> are other differences; and therefore these will be intermediate between the primary contraries, and the primary differences are piercing and contracting).

Hence we have to enquire, with respect to these primary contraries which are not in <a> genus, what their intermediates are 20 from (for it is necessary that things in the same genus be either composed of things that are incomposite with respect to the genus or themselves incomposite). The contraries, then, are not composite from each other, so that they are principles; as for the intermediates, either all of them or none of them is composite.

And it is from the contraries that something comes to be; hence change will be into this before being into them: for it will be less of 25 one contrary and more of the other. And this, too, will therefore be intermediate between the contraries. Therefore all other intermediates will be composite as well: for that which is a composite

of more of one thing and less of another thing is somehow
from those things of which it is said to be more of one and less
of the other.

And since there are no other things of the same kind prior to
30 the contraries, all intermediates would be from the contraries, so
that also all things lower down, both contraries and intermediates, will be from the primary contraries.

It is clear, then, that the intermediates are all in the same genus
and that they are intermediate between contraries and that they
are all composed from the contraries.

CHAPTER 8

35 What is other in species is something other than something, and
this must belong to both of them: for instance, if it is an animal
other in species <than something else>, they are both animals.

Therefore it is necessary that things that are other in species be in
the same genus. For I call 'genus' such a thing, i.e. the one and same
1058a thing which both are said to be and which has a difference not
incidentally, be it as matter or in another way. For not only must
what is common belong <to both of them> (for instance, they are
both animals), but this very thing—the animal—must also be other
for each of them: for instance, in one case it is <a> horse and in the
other case it is <a> human being. For this reason they are this
5 common thing, other in species than each other. So they will be in
their own right the one <an> animal of this sort, the other <an>
animal of this other sort—e.g. the one will be <a> horse, the other
will be <a> human being.

Therefore, it is necessary that the difference be this otherness
of the genus. For I call 'difference of the genus' an otherness
which makes this same genus other.

This, then, will be contrariety, and this is clear also from
10 induction. For all <genera> are divided by the opposites, and it
has already been shown that the contraries are in the same genus.
For contrariety was complete difference, and every difference in
species is from something with respect to something, so that the
latter is the same and is the genus in both cases (for this reason
also all the contraries which differ in species and not in genus are
in the same column of predication, are other than each other in

the highest degree—for the difference is complete—and do not 15
come to be at the same time as each other). Therefore the difference is contrariety.

Therefore being for things which are other in species is this, i.e.
having a contrariety while being in the same genus and being atomic,
and those things are the same in species which, being atomic, have
no contrariety. For contrarieties come to be in the division and in the 20
intermediate steps before coming to the atomic things.

Hence it is evident that with respect to the so-called genus none
of the species of the genus is the same or other in species (with a
reason: for matter is shown by negation and the genus is matter of
what it is said to be the genus of—I do not mean the genus in the
sense of that of the Heraclides, but I mean the genus as that which
is in nature), nor <is any of the species of the genus the same or
other in species> with respect to things which are not in the same 25
genus; rather, they differ in genus from these and in species from
the things which are in the same genus. For it is necessary that the
difference of things that differ in species is a contrariety; and this
belongs only to things that are in the same genus.

CHAPTER 9

One might also wonder why a woman is not different in species
from a man, given that female and male are contraries and that 30
the difference at stake is a contrariety, and why a female animal
and a male animal are not other in species; and yet this is a
difference of animal in its own right, and male and female belong
to it not as paleness and darkness do, but insofar as it is animal.
This difficulty is almost the same as the one concerning why one
contrariety makes things other in species, whereas another does 35
not: e.g. the footed and the winged do, whereas paleness and
darkness do not.

Is it perhaps because some are affections proper to the genus,
while others are less so? And since one thing is account and one is 1058b
matter, the contrarieties that are in the account make a difference
in species, whereas those that are in the compound taken with the
matter do not.

For this reason neither paleness nor darkness make a difference
of human being, nor is there a difference in species of the pale

17

human being in relation to the dark human being, not even if
5 one assigned one name <to each of them>. For the human being
<is considered> as matter, and matter does not make a differ-
ence: human beings are not species of human being because of
this, and yet the flesh and bones out of which this human being
and this human being are made are other. Rather, the compound
is other, but not other in species, because there is no contrariety in
10 the account. And this is the last atomic thing; and Callias is the
account with the matter; and in truth the pale human being is
because Callias is pale—therefore, the human being is pale incidentally. Nor are a brazen circle and a wooden circle other in
species; nor do a brazen triangle and a wooden circle differ in
species because of their matter, but because there is a contrariety
in their account.
15 But is it true that matter does not make things other in species
by being in some way other, or is there a sense in which it does?
For, why is this horse other in species from this human being? In
truth their accounts are with matter. Is it rather because there is a
contrariety in their account? For there is a difference between the
pale human being and the dark horse, and it is a difference in
20 species, but not insofar as the one is pale and the other is dark,
since, even if they were both pale, they would be other in species
all the same.
Male and female are proper affections of the animal, not on
account of substance, though, but in the matter and the body; for
this reason the same seed becomes female or male by being
affected in a certain way. What it is to be other in species, then,
25 and why some things differ in species whereas some others do not,
has been said.

CHAPTER 10

Since contraries are other in species and the perishable and the
imperishable are contraries (for a determinate incapacity is privation), it is necessary that the perishable and the imperishable be
other in genus.
Now, then, we have spoken with reference to universal names as
30 such, so that one might think that it is not necessarily the case that
anything which is imperishable and anything which is perishable be

18

other in species, just as it is not necessarily the case that anything which is pale and anything which is dark be other in species (for it is possible that the same thing be pale and dark, and this is possible at the same time if it is a universal, e.g. human being would be pale and dark; and if it is a particular, this is possible too, for the same human being could be pale and dark, if not at the same time; and yet the pale is contrary to the dark). 35

But, of the contraries, some belong to some things incidentally, for instance those we just mentioned and many others, whereas for some others this is impossible, and the perishable **1059a** and the imperishable belong to the latter: for nothing is perishable incidentally, because what is incidental can fail to belong, while the perishable is among the things that belong of necessity to the things they belong to. Otherwise, one and the same thing will be perishable and imperishable, if it is possible for the 5 perishable to fail to belong to it. Therefore, it is necessary that the perishable be the substance or belong in the substance of each perishable thing. And the same account applies to the imperishable as well: for they both are among the things that belong of necessity. Therefore, <the perishable and the imperishable> have an opposition in the respect in which and according to the primary thing on account of which one thing is perishable and the other is imperishable, so that it is necessary that they be other in genus. 10

It is evident, then, that there cannot be forms such as some people say: for there will be one perishable human being and an imperishable one. And yet the forms are said to be the same in species as the particulars and not homonymous; but things that are other in genus differ more than things that are other in species.

COMMENTARY

CHAPTER 1

Aristotle deals with unity in a number of places. Apart from
I.1–2, *Met.* Δ.6 provides the most extensive survey of the ways
in which things are said to be one, including ways of being
one which do not appear in I.1 (see pp. 24–5). Other texts focus
upon issues of unity for some specific kind of thing: for instance,
Met. H.3 sets up the issue of the unity of definitions, numbers,
and composite substances, which is taken over in H.6; *Pol.* II.1–2
deals with the unity of the *polis* and *Poet.* 23, 1459a18–24 with the
unity and sameness of tragedies and narrative epic poems. Other
texts touch upon unity in the context of criticism directed against
other philosophers' views: e.g. *Phys.* I.2–3 deal with unity within
the discussion of Eleatic monism; *Met.* M.7, 1080b37–M.8,
1083a17 discusses whether numerical units should be conceived
of as all combinable and undifferentiated in connection with
Aristotle's criticism of the Academic doctrine of ideal numbers; *Met.* N.1, 1087b33–1088a14 and N.4, 1091b15–26 refer
to Aristotle's views about the one in the context of his criticism
of Academic views making of the One a principle of being. The
list could be longer and further references can be found in the
notes.

A number of interesting philosophical questions emerges from
these passages: what is it for something to be one? Is unity one
and the same property for all things that are? Or are there
different ways in which things are one? Is there any object
whose being just consists in being one? And is unity a primitive
and unexplainable feature of things, or can it be grounded and
explained by bringing in some cause of unity? If there is some
cause of unity, is it one and the same for all things that are one or
is there a plurality of causes of unity? What sort(s) of thing are
causes of unity? Furthermore, what is the relation, if any, between
regarding an object as something unified and counting it as one,
and, correspondingly, between distinguishing the parts of a unified object, regarding it as many and ascribing it a number? What
sort of things are mathematical units? Is there any relation

between mathematical units and unified non-mathematical objects such as human beings, colours, sounds, etc.? Although not all of these questions are considered in I.1–2, these two chapters can be read as the starting points (with some qualifications) of a systematic enquiry into such problems and this is what sets them apart from other passages dealing with more specific issues of unity. Broadly speaking, I.1 mainly focuses on the question of what it is for something to be one, whereas I.2 focuses on whether there is any object whose being consists in being one—or, as Aristotle puts it: whether the one is a substance (or whether there is a substance whose nature consists exactly in being one).

There are a few general difficulties making the interpretation of each of I.1 and I.2 and of their mutual relation particularly challenging. I shall briefly spell out what these are before moving on to a closer reading of the text. One general difficulty is that Aristotle does not disentangle what we would regard as rather different questions.

a) What does 'one' mean?
b) What does 'the one' refer to?
c) What is it for something to be one?
d) What is the one? (Or: what is the essence of the one? What is it for something to be the one?)
e) What objects/what sorts of object can be said to be one?
f) What object/what sort of object is the one?

All these questions receive at least partial answers in the course of I.1–2. But, although in the course of I.1 Aristotle draws some distinctions (1052b1–20), questions a)–f) are never neatly distinguished. Rather, they can all be regarded as aspects of one complex issue: what is the one?

The difficulties in disentangling a)–f) are partly due to some specific features of the Greek language. One source of difficulty is that the linguistic formulation Aristotle resorts to in order to indicate the object of the enquiry, *to hen*, i.e. the neuter singular article *to* ('the') with the neuter numeral adjective *hen* ('one'), is ambiguous in two ways. In the first place, it can either indicate an object, i.e. the thing that is one, or a general property, i.e. oneness or being one. This is a general feature of Greek and on other occasions Aristotle draws attention to it (see, for instance,

Phys. I.3, 186a28–31; *Met.* Z.6, 1031b22–28): 'the white', *to leukon* (morphologically similar to *to hen*, i.e. constructed from the neuter singular article *to* followed by the singular neuter adjective *leukon*) is ambiguous as it can indicate the white thing or the colour white. The fact that Aristotle does not draw a sharp distinction between the two options in Iota requires some caution on the part of the reader. Issues relating to the characterization of the property of being one (questions a), c), d) above) and issues relating to the characterization of object(s) that can be said to be one or the one (questions b), e), and f)) are tightly intertwined. In the second place, ancient Greek has no quotational devices such as inverted commas, but the singular neuter article *to* can (but does not have to) be used to quote the expression that follows. Accordingly, there is no way to draw any systematic distinction between texts concerning the one and texts concerning the expression 'one' (unless the context makes it unmistakably clear that the discussion is about an object rather than about a linguistic expression—which is hardly ever the case). This makes a sharp distinction between questions a)/b) and c)/d) very difficult to draw. Similar considerations apply to all abstract notions discussed in the course of Iota such as the same, the other, the similar, the dissimilar, the equal, the unequal, the great, the small, etc.

Despite the lack of a neat distinction, I shall suggest in the course of the commentary that two threads of the enquiry into the one can be disentangled by spelling out the answers to c) and d) respectively: being one amounts to being indivisible, in some respect or other; being the one amounts to being the measure of a certain domain of objects. I am not suggesting that Aristotle would express the distinction in this way. Note, in particular, that Aristotle, unlike Frege (1884, §§ 29–54), does not distinguish between 'one' as the name of an individual object (number one) and 'unit' as a predicate which can be said of a plurality of objects. This can be seen quite clearly in I.6, 1056b23–24 (cf. I.1, 1053a27–30), where numbers are described as pluralities of 'ones', i.e. of units. The distinction I intend to make is that between the answers to two questions: what it is for things to be one (and I take it that Aristotle's main answer to this question is that it is to be indivisible); and in what sense we can say that the one is a principle (and Aristotle's answer to this is that the only sense in which the one is a principle is that the unit is a principle of number). For Aristotle the one which is a principle of number, i.e. the numerical unit, is not a number (for a number is defined as a plurality of units) and, more generally, is not a unique object. In *Met.* M.8, 1083a24–35 he explicitly criticizes the view of those who assume the one as a unique object alongside mathematical units (which, for Aristotle, are the only objects that can be regarded as unqualifiedly one; about the status of mathematical units, see below). In this sense, Aristotle's enquiry into the one as the principle of number is nothing more than the enquiry into what it is for something to be a unit. Since, according to some of Aristotle's predecessors numbers and their principles are causes and principles of other beings, Aristotle's understanding of the claim that the unit is a principle of knowledge of number impacts on his views about the existence (or non existence) of a causal relation between the one which is a principle of number and the fact that each thing that is, is—in some sense—one. There is some debate on Aristotle's views about the relation between the one that is a principle of number and the one which is convertible with being (i.e. the one that can be predicated of anything that is) and I shall address the main points of the debate in the course of the commentary.

The numerical unit is one in an unqualified sense (it is indivisible in every respect) and its relation to number provides a sort of paradigm for the analysis of the relation between the unit of measure and the measurable more generally. Speaking of 'the numerical unit' or of 'the one' in numbers should not be taken to imply that we are talking about one unique token: units are indefinitely many indiscernible objects exclusively characterized by the essential feature of being indivisible (cf. *Met.* M.7, 1081a5–6, 10–11, 19–20; see, however, notes to I.3, 1054b1–3 about the sense in which indiscernible mathematical entities can be said to be one and the same; about being one as the essence of the unit cf. *Met.* B.4, 1001a26–27). Numerical units (and, more generally, mathematical objects) for Aristotle do not exist as separate objects: units are what we think of when we consider objects exclusively insofar as they are indivisible (M.3, 1077b22–30; 1078a21–30). Units can be added to each other in order to obtain numbers (M.7, 1081b12–17, 28–30, 34–37; 1082b4–9; M.8, 1083a1; for a very clear account of Aristotle's views about numbers and units also relying on evidence from Iota see Annas 1976, pp. 26–41).

All things that can be said to be one are indivisible in some respect or other. All things that can be said to be the one in their respective domain work as a unit of measure (in a sense to be specified) in their domain. I.1 and I.2 do not push the idea of the extension of the conceptual framework of units and numbers for kinds other than numbers equally far. While I.1 considers not particularly controversial examples of measurable quantities, I.2 presents a series of examples suggesting that the one in a kind K is some specific sort of K which is also a constitutive principle of the other Ks. Other Ks can therefore be regarded as numbers precisely in the sense that they are complex objects made out of K-units. I refer to the commentary for further details and some assessment of this view.

As I mentioned, I.1 addresses the issue of what it is for something to be one. The chapter can be divided into four main sections. 1052a15–b1 presents four basic general ways in which things are one in their own right; 1052b1–24 unpacks the idea that, in some cases, being one consists in being the unit of measurement for a certain kind of objects; 1052b24–1053b3 spells out various features of measures; 1053b4–8 sums up the main results of the discussion starting at 1052b1.

1052a15–19:   1052a15–16 presumably refers to *Met.* Δ.6, where Aristotle distinguishes the ways in which things are said to be one incidentally and the ways in which things are said to be one in their own right (for a survey and some discussion of the ways in which things are said to be one see Demos 1946, Castelli 2008, and Castelli 2010, pp. 67–83). I.1 focuses on the four principal ways (*sunkephalaioumenoi tropoi*) of being one for 'the things that are primary and said to be one in their own right and not incidentally'. This restriction requires some comments.

In Δ.6 Aristotle does not provide a general account of the distinction between being one incidentally and being one in one's own right. However, the distinction can be illustrated in the following way. Broadly speaking, a subject S is P in its own right if S is P (or P belongs to S) on account of what S is or on account of what P is. S is incidentally P if this is not the case (for this distinction between properties belonging to a subject in its own right and properties belonging to a subject incidentally see *APo* I.4, 73a34–b5). Things are incidentally one if being one does not belong to them on account of what they are nor on account of what being one is. In particular, things that are incidentally one are not genuinely unified objects, but compounds of a plurality of items which are not characterized by a unified essence. All examples of incidental compounds in Δ.6 are examples of compounds whose unity rests on the unity of some more basic ontological component and on more basic ontological facts about how the compound is made. The white and the musical are one incidentally in the sense that they form a unity only if they happen to inhere in one and the same subject, e.g. Socrates. The wise and Socrates are one incidentally in that they are one if and only if Socrates happens to be wise and Socrates is an individual substance that is one in its own right. A similar analysis applies to the claims that the wise Socrates is incidentally one or that the white musical thing is incidentally one. Corresponding descriptions of incidental compounds can be found in *Met.* Δ.7, 1017a8–22, and Δ.9,1017b27–1018a4, on incidental being and incidental sameness respectively. The ontology of incidental compounds is puzzling and several studies have been devoted to it; for some discussion see Matthews 1982; Lewis 1982; Kirwan 1993, pp. 210–14; Shields 1999, pp. 155–75; Mariani 2000; Cohen 2008 and 2013.

I.1 focuses on the ways in which things can be said to be one in their own right (a17–19). In this sense, I.1 covers only a part of the distinctions provided in Δ.6. Furthermore, there is no uncontroversial correspondence between the distinctions drawn in the two chapters with respect to the ways in which things are said to be one in their own right.

At a18–19 Sylburg and, following him, Jaeger correct *prōtōn* (plural genitive: 'of the primary things') into *prōtōs* (adverb: 'primarily'). The correction is not implausible (cf. *Met.* Δ.6, 1016b8), but does not seem necessary (cf. 1052a33). In Jaeger's text, both 'primarily' and 'in their own right' qualify the way in which things are said to be one. This understanding would yield the translation: 'the principal ways of being one for things that are said to be one primarily and in their own right'. The formulation with the genitive kept in Ross's text leaves room for two interpretations yielding two different translations: (1) 'the principal ways of being one for the things that are primary and said to be one in their own right'; (2) 'the principal ways of being one for the primary things <that are said to be one and that are> said to be one in their own right'.

Jaeger's emendation does not make much of a difference if we opt for (2), but it makes some difference with respect to (1). For (1) suggests that there is some relation between things that are primary in being and things that are one in their own right (Berti 2005, pp. 66–7), whereas (2) neither excludes nor strongly suggests this possibility. In *Met.* Δ.6, 1016b6–11 Aristotle distinguishes between the ways of being one of things that are said to be one in virtue of producing, having, being affected by, or standing in relation to something else that is one and things that are said to be one because their substance is one in one of the principal ways, i.e. on account of continuity or of the form of the matter or of their account. Things whose substance is one in these basic ways are substances. I.1 does not introduce any explicit distinction between things that are one in their own right and things that are one by being something of them. However the way in which the four principal ways of being one are described from the beginning of the chapter down to 1052b1 suggests that, in drawing the distinction, Aristotle is thinking of different ways of being one for substances (whereas I do not think that reference to substances is equally relevant at 1052b1 ff.; see notes on 1052b1–14 for further comments on this point). For this reason translation (1) (for which I opt) seems appropriate. Halper 2009, pp. 130–1, suggests that I.1's emphasis on ways of being one for substances is due to I.1's reliance on Z.13–16; it is not clear to me how much of Zeta is presupposed in Iota, but see Burnyeat 2001, pp. 134–40, for some comments on the relation between Zeta and Iota. Further references to priority and to some sort of ranking can be found at 1052a20–21, a22, a23, a27, a33–34, b18, 1052b18, b23, b25, 1053b4–6.

1052a19–21:   The basic meaning of the Greek verb *sunechō*, from which the adjective *suneches*, 'continuous', derives, is 'to hold together'. Some things are one by being continuous. The way in which a continuous object is 'held together' can be further specified: things are continuous either **(a)** without qualification or

(b) by nature, i.e. not by mere contact or because they are kept together by an extrinsic bond, but because they are naturally assimilated parts of an object. Furthermore, of things that are one by nature, **(b*)** those whose motion is more indivisible, i.e. simpler, are more one than and prior to those whose motion is divisible, i.e. less simple.

As for (a), 'without qualification' can introduce a restriction or a generalization. If it introduces a restriction, then the restriction might be specified by (b) or might point to some specific kind of continuous objects such as geometrical entities. Geometrical entities such as lines, planes, and volumes, are defined as continuous quantities extended in one, two, or three dimensions respectively (*Met.* Δ.13, 1020a10–12; cf. Δ.6, 1016b26–29). These objects can be said to be continuous without qualification in the sense that their being consists in being continuous quantities. Alternatively, one can take 'without qualification' as a restriction spelled out by (b). According to this interpretation, objects that are continuous without qualification are continuous by nature in such a way that their motion is simple (see below for further comments on this option).

If, on the other hand, 'without qualification' introduces a generalization, then Aristotle's point could be that any objects displaying a certain ontological structure (broadly speaking: extended non-scattered objects) can be said to be continuous, quite irrespective of the causes or structures that keep their parts together. According to this interpretation, artefacts and bundles can be said to be one by being continuous, although they are continuous in a lesser degree than objects that are naturally assimilated and are characterized by simple motion.

It is not clear whether (b) is meant to exclude artificial objects from the domain of continuous objects or whether the specification 'not by contact nor in virtue of bonds' simply spells out 'by nature', without necessarily implying that only objects that are continuous by nature can be regarded as continuous. I think the second option is more likely, especially if one compares this passage with 1052a22–28 on wholes, where natural wholes are distinguished from artificial wholes: the latter can still be regarded as wholes. Examples of artificial continuous objects would be bundles of parts of artificial wholes as well as, more generally, bundles of objects held together by means of glue, nails, bonds, etc. For a thorough discussion of the mereotopology of bodies in Aristotle see Pfeiffer (forthcoming).

(b*) introduces motion as a criterion for ascribing continuity to objects and for ranking degrees of continuity: the simpler the motion, the more one and continuous the object. 'Simple' has to be taken as explanatory of 'indivisible', since every change, being continuous, is potentially divisible into segments of change, so to speak, which are in turn further divisible. In this sense there is no change that is, strictly speaking, indivisible. At a21 I translate the comparative form *mállon haplē* as 'simple to a higher degree' (instead of just 'simpler'). I take it that the use of this comparative form (instead of the usual *haploustera*: 'simpler') is meant to emphasize difference in degree (cf. Kühner 1890, I.1, §157 sect. 1, pp. 571–2 on the uses of the comparative form with *mállon* in the sense of 'rather' or in the sense of 'in a higher degree'; cf. 1052b6 *mállon engus*—instead of *enguteron*—which I translate as 'rather close').

The use of simplicity of motion as a criterion to ascribe continuity to objects raises two questions: first, what is simplicity of motion? Second, what relation obtains between features of motion and features of the moving object? In *Phys.* V.1, 224a34–b1, Aristotle analyses the factors responsible for the features of motion. These are the mover (*to kinoun*), the object that is in motion (*to kinoumenon*), the time in which (*en hōi*) motion occurs, the starting point (*ex hou*) and the ending point (*eis ho*) of motion. In *Phys.* V.4 he then resorts to these criteria to spell out the different ways in which motion can be said to be one. As for the mover, the only mention of a principle of motion we find in I.1 is at 1052a27: see notes to 1052a22–28. As for the other criteria, simplicity of motion is not exhausted by motion's temporal continuity (*Phys.* V.3, 226b27–34; V.4, 228a25–b10; 229a1), i.e. by the fact that motion occurs without temporal breaks. Simple motion must comply with a number of further conditions: the rate of change must be uniform; its beginning and end points and its intermediate stages must be on the same qualitative spectrum. For instance, a motion from A to B which is the result of the conjunction of different motions in different directions is not uniform (and, according to Aristotle, it is not even strictly speaking temporally continuous as the moving object needs to stop at the end of one segment of motion to change direction: see

Phys. VIII.9, 261b28 ff.). Similarly, the conjunction of different kinds of change (e.g. a change in place from A to B and a change in colour from white to red) is not a simple motion. These or similar considerations are likely to provide the background for the account of continuity in terms of simplicity of motion in I.1.

The most puzzling aspect of the relation between the analysis in *Phys.* V and I.1 is that in *Phys.* V the unity of the object that moves is a factor determining the unity of motion, whereas in I.1 it looks as if Aristotle intends to resort to the unity or simplicity of motion as a criterion to ascribe a certain kind of unity to the object that moves. I shall discuss some of the issues which this raises in the notes to 1052a34–b1. In order to understand Aristotle's point here, it is enough to stress that he seems to assume a basic correspondence between the ontological simplicity of the objects of change and the simplicity of their respective motions. This aspect is particularly explicit in *DC* I.2, 268b14–269a2, 269a8–9. Aristotle claims that there are only three kinds of simple motion: rectilinear from the centre of the universe to the extremity of the universe (i.e. upwards); rectilinear from the extremity of the universe to the centre of the universe (i.e. downwards); circular. To each simple motion there corresponds a simple body (a natural element). None of the simple motions can be analysed into more basic components and, in this sense, each of them is simple and indivisible. On the basis of these considerations, masses of natural elements would be good candidates for being the kinds of objects which are one by being continuous (but see p. 30 for the problems involved in identifying natural elements as the continuous bodies which Aristotle has in mind).

However, natural elements are not the only bodies which Aristotle describes as continuous. In *DC* III.8, 306b22–29, IV.6, 313b6, 17, 19, Aristotle refers to homeomerous bodies in general as 'continuous bodies' (*suneche sōmata*). Homeomerous bodies are bodies whose ontological simplicity consists in that their parts have exactly the same ontological features as the whole: *GC* I.1, 314a19–20; *DC* I.7, 275b32–276a1, 276a15; *Met.* Δ.3, 1014a26–31.

Again, homeomerous parts do not conclude the list of candidates for being continuous objects. Passages such as *Met.* Δ.6, 1016a9–12, *MA* 1, 698a18–21 and 8, 702b10–12 suggest that anhomeomerous parts of animals (i.e. parts characterized, unlike tissues, by a distinctive shape and structure, such as legs and arms) can be said to be continuous as well. In particular, the motion of some parts of animals endowed with locomotion cannot be divided into distinct motions of distinct parts, whereas the motion of parts with articulations can be divided into the motions of the parts joined by the articulation. For instance, the whole arm can be moved, but its parts can also be moved relatively independently (e.g. one can move her forearm without moving the arm from the shoulder to the elbow, or one can move her hand without moving the forearm). In this sense the motion of parts which do not present articulations is indivisible; and in this sense the forearm is more continuous than the whole arm. Following this train of thought, anhomeomerous parts of living beings can be ascribed different degrees of continuity, depending on the complexity of their internal structure and, more specifically, on the presence of joints. Note also that in *Met.* Δ.6, 1016a12–17 the remarks on the continuity of geometrical objects such as the straight line and the bent line are clearly a follow up on the remarks about the continuity of parts of natural beings without or with articulations respectively. This is a nice example of how mathematical entities are 'abstracted' from natural beings and how there is no tension between ascribing continuity to geometrical entities and to natural beings. The respect in which the latter are continuous is exactly the respect in which they are considered, by making abstraction of all other sensible properties, when they become the object of mathematical thought—otherwise said: the objects of geometrical thought are natural beings regarded only insofar as they are continuous and have some limits.

This list of kinds of object (simple natural bodies, homeomerous parts such as flesh and bones, anhomeomerous parts without or with articulations) that can be said to be continuous on account of some features of their motion is interesting in that it suggests a scale of continuity as the basic form of unity of natural bodies which are not wholes. As we shall see, at 1052a22–28 Aristotle keeps following this train of thought and describes wholeness as a higher form of unity which is characteristic of other natural bodies.

A continuous object is something that moves as a compact chunk, not incidentally. 'Compactness' has to do with the relation between the parts of an object, with the way in which its parts 'hold together'. Lumps of matter and parts of wholes, however, despite being compact chunks, are not genuinely unified objects. In fact, *Met.* Z.16, 1040b8–10 suggests that simple bodies and material parts of substances are nothing more than heaps when they are not parts of something one—and a heap (*sōros*) is something paradigmatically lacking unity. This perhaps explains why wholes are one in a higher degree (see 1052a22–28): wholes do not only display the topo–mereological structure of continuous objects, but are characterized by a determinate form which determines how their parts are supposed to hold together. In particular, natural wholes are characterized by an internal cause of their continuity and this gives them a particularly strong claim to being one.

On this score, note that in *Met.* Δ.6, 1016a17–24, Aristotle distinguishes continuity from the perceptual homogeneity of matter of objects like fluids. Presumably, elemental masses and, more generally, homeomerous masses enjoy this form of unity, which is described as a lack of differentiation of the form (*eidos*) of a substrate to perception. Note that no reference to motion is contained in this account. I.1 does not include any explicit reference to this kind of unity, even if it cannot be excluded that it falls under the partition considered at 1052a29–34 (cf. *Met.* Δ.6, 1016b8–11).

1052a22–28: Things that, in addition to being continuous, have a determinate shape or form, are wholes. They are also said to be 'such', i.e. one, in an even higher degree (cf. *Met.* Δ.6, 1016b11–17) than merely continuous objects. As in the case of continuous objects, natural wholes, i.e. wholes that have in themselves the cause of their own continuity (a23–25), have a stronger claim to wholeness and unity than artificial wholes. Continuity has been accounted for in terms of indivisibility and simplicity of motion. Beings that have in themselves the cause of their own continuity are, therefore, beings that have in themselves the cause of the simplicity of their own motion. These are natural wholes. However, this account does not seem to exclude objects having an external (possibly artificial) cause of their continuity from the domain of wholes—even if such objects will be one in a lesser degree than natural wholes. On contact (*aphē*) and unity cf. *Met.* H.6, 1045a8–12; on glue, nails, bonds, etc. as differences in the arrangement of material parts of composite substances cf. *Met.* H.2, 1042a15–20. For *phusis* ('nature') as an internal principle of motion see *Phys.* II.1, 192b20–23 (cf. *Met.* Δ.4, 1014b18–26, about *phusis* as an internal principle of change, and *sumphusis* as the natural continuity of parts of natural beings that 'grow together', *sumphuetai*, as naturally assimilated parts of a whole). For the soul as a cause of continuity which 'holds together' the body cf. *DA* I.5, 411b6–14; II.4, 416a6–9; *Met.* M.2, 1077a20–24.

Paradigmatic wholes display a motion which is indivisible 'in place and time'. Indivisibility in time can either indicate that the whole moves all at the same time or that the whole moves continuously, without temporal breaks. Both features are characteristic of the continuous rotation of the sphere. As for indivisibility in place, Aristotle usually expresses in this way the characteristic feature of a motion which does not involve any displacement of the whole object that moves. This is, again, a distinctive feature of the rotation of the sphere. In this way Aristotle identifies the object that is a whole in the highest degree by displaying the appropriate kind of motion with the outermost heavenly sphere (cf. *Phys.* VIII.9, 265a13–27; cf. *Met.* I.1, 1053a8–12). Note that Aristotle does not refer here to an external unmoved mover.

On the priority of locomotion over other kinds of change see *Phys.* VIII.7, 260a20–261a26; on the priority of circular motion over other kinds of locomotion see *Phys.* VIII.7, 261a27 ff.; *DC* I.2, 269a18–30. The reason why the object naturally characterized by the internal principle of primary motion can be identified as the primary magnitude that is one could be the following. 1052b19–28 introduces indivisibility or simplicity of motion as a criterion to ascribe unity to objects that are characterized by motion. Any movable object is a body, i.e. a magnitude (or continuous quantity) finitely extended in three dimensions. If the degree of unity and the rank of an object corresponds to the degree of simplicity and rank of its motion (cf. p. 29), the object characterized by the primary motion, which is indivisible in time and place will be the primary magnitude that is one (*DC* I.1, 268a1–10; I.2, 269a18–b2). The fact that Aristotle identifies a primary *magnitude* that is one (as opposed to, say, a primary sensible imperishable substance that is one) may suggest that Aristotle is interested in establishing some ranking in the domain of quantities based on the features of the natural objects from which those quantities are abstracted.

As mentioned above (see in particular notes on 1052a15–19), the correspondence between degrees of unity and priority in being is problematic. However, if we try to map the degrees of unity alluded to at 1052a19–28 on kinds of beings, we can track a relatively neat correspondence between degrees of unity and kinds of movable substances. Whole substances are more one than simply continuous substances (assuming that the continuous parts of substances can be regarded as substances in some sense: cf. *Met.* Δ.8, 1017b10–13; Z.2, 1028b8–13). Among whole substances, those characterized by the simplest motion, i.e. the heavenly spheres, are more one than those characterized by more complex motions (presumably: natural substances and, perhaps, artefacts in the sublunary world).

For an account of the relation of parts and whole in Aristotle see Koslicki 2008, pp. 122–64.

1052a29–34: A new criterion for the ascription of unity to objects is introduced. Things are said to be one if their account (*logos*) is one, i.e. if they are grasped by an indivisible thought (*noēsis*). The new criterion, while compatible with the criterion of indivisibility of motion (e.g. one and the same substance can be one as a whole and one in account), also applies to objects that are not in motion.

As in the previous section, Aristotle starts by giving a criterion which is progressively specified and ends by identifying the objects that turn out to be primarily one with respect to the criterion at issue. If the criterion is simplicity of motion, what is primarily one is the body which has the internal principle of its continuous and homogeneous motion; if the criterion is indivisibility in account, what is primarily one is the cause (or the causes) of unity for substances. The reference to the cause of unity of substance is presumably to the form or the essence of substances (Halper 2007, p. 175, takes this more specifically as a reference to the human soul). Simplifying, the essence of x is for Aristotle an intrinsic ontological principle of x which determines the kind of object x is and x's unity (see *Met.* Z.17, 1041b11–33, on the necessity of introducing something responsible for the unity of the material parts of a compound; see also *Met.* H.6, in particular 1045a30–35 and 1045b14–23 on the idea that there is no further cause of unity of matter and form understood as what something is in potentiality and what something is in actuality, unless one wants to mention the role of the efficient cause in bringing something that is only in potentiality into actuality). It is hard to tell how much of Aristotle's theory of substance is presupposed by this remark. At different places (see, for instance, *Met.* Γ.2, 1003b32–33; H.6, 1045b3–7, but see below about H.6) Aristotle suggests that the essence of (at least some) things is primitively one and primitively something that is. However, depending on how much of Aristotle's theory of substance one is willing to bring in, the point at 1052a29–34 can have more or less rich implications.

To start with, in spelling out the new criterion, Aristotle touches upon several levels of unity: indivisibility of account, indivisibility of thought, and indivisibility of the objects of thought. As for the unity or indivisibility of the account, Aristotle distinguishes between the syntactic unity and the semantic unity of a *logos* (*Int.* 5, 17a8–17; *APo* II.10, 93b35–37; *Met.* H.6, 1045a12–14). The former consists in being a unified syntactical structure, the latter consists in signifying something which is in itself one. Semantic unity is accorded priority over syntactic unity, in particular as far as the account in question is the 'account of the essence' (*logos tēs ousias*) or 'definition' (*horismos*). The definition of x is a complex linguistic formula that spells out what x is. The problem of the unity of the definition arises from the idea that the parts of a definition pick out real ontological components of the defined thing (see, e.g., *Met.* Z.11, 1037a18–20; Z.12 1037b11 ff.; H.6, 1045a7 ff.). Why should it be the case that the result of the composition of such components is not a mere aggregate, some sort of incidental compound (cf. notes on 1052a15–19), rather than a unified object? How is it possible to reconcile the ontological analysis required by and reflected in the formulation of a definition with the unity of the defined object? For instance, let us assume that the definition of (the species) human being is 'biped rational animal'. If each of 'biped', 'rational', and 'animal' picks out a genuine ontological component of human being, how is the composition of biped + rational + animal supposed to pick out something unitary (i.e. what it is to be a human being) rather than an aggregate of relatively independent features? Why should there be any difference between the compound biped–rational–animal and the compound white–human being? Issues relating to the unity of definition are complex and have attracted a great deal of attention in the literature: for some discussion see the articles collected in Scaltsas, Charles, and Gill 1994; in particular, on the solution provided in H.6 see Halper 1984; Harte 1996; Koslicki 2006; Gill 2010; Keeling 2012.

Despite difficulties, one basic point is clear: the unity of the definition ultimately depends on the unity of what is defined. This core assumption about the semantic unity of definitions is relevant to I.1. For an account can always be divided into its material parts (cf. *Met.* H.3, 1043b34–36), but it can be said to be one and indivisible as long as the object it refers to is one and indivisible. This implies that, if the objects of definition admit of degrees of unity, definitional accounts, too, will correspondingly admit of degrees of unity. While the formulation in I.1 ascribing priority to the causes of unity of substance as what is primarily one in account suggests that there will be other things whose account will be one in some degree, Iota does not expand on this suggestion and it is difficult to establish how far one should go in unfolding it. In the first part of the chapter the criterion of unity in motion points at some ranking in degrees of unity of material substances, but not much can be found in I.1 on other kinds of substance and other kinds of beings such as incidental compounds. Other texts point out that degrees of unity can be envisaged at different levels. Substances can be more or less complex: composite substances such as natural living beings, made of matter and form, are less simple than simple substances such as the unmoved movers, which do not include any matter. In the case of simple immaterial substances there is no difference between the substance itself and its essence, which is also the cause of its unity (cf. *Met.* Z.6, 1032a4–6; Z.11, 1037a33–b4; Λ.8, 1074a33–37). In the case of material substances, the composite substance is ontologically richer than its essence (*Met.* H.3, 1043a29–b4; H.6, 1045a36–b7; cf. *DC* I.9, 277b30–278a23; see also *Met.* Z.11, 1037b4–7, reading *oude* at b5 with the manuscripts: material substances are neither unqualifiedly the same as their essence nor are they only incidentally the same, unlike incidental compounds which are only incidentally the same as their essence).

Furthermore, *Met.* Z.4–5 (see, in particular, the formulation in Z.4, 1030b7–12) make room for the idea that items belonging to other categories as well as incidental compounds are definable. The accounts of such items will be less simple—and, in this sense, less one and indivisible—than the accounts of the essence of substances. This is because accounts of non-substances signify objects that are ontologically more complex than substances. This applies in different ways to incidental compounds and items belonging to categories other than substances. The definition of incidental compounds will necessarily refer to a plurality of items which do not make a genuine ontological unit (e.g. the white and Socrates are distinct beings belonging to two different categories). The definition of items from non-substantial categories, although categorially simple, will presumably include some reference to the category of substance (i.e. to the fact that the defined object is by inhering in substances).

The simplicity of the account of the essence and its indivisibility into accounts spelling out relatively independent parts of the essence of the defined object is perhaps what Aristotle has in mind in *Met.* Δ.6, 1016a32–35: 'Furthermore, those things are said to be one whose account of the essence is indivisible with respect to another account showing the thing (for each account is, in itself, divisible)'. However, the formulation is not particularly clear and it cannot be excluded that the passage is about the way in which a *plurality* of objects sharing the same definition can be said to be one in account (see the examples at 1016a35–b1: 'For in this way the thing that grows and shrinks is one, too, because the account is one, as in the case of plane figures the account of the form is one'). In I.1 Aristotle distinguishes between the unity in account of universals and individuals, where the unity in account of universals can be understood as the unity in account of all those objects that share the same account.

Before referring to the ontological features of the objects whose account is one, Aristotle spells out the unity of the account in terms of indivisibility of thought. For thought as intermediate between language and extramental objects cf. *Int.* 1, 16a3–13. The indivisibility of the thought through which we grasp an object of thought is dependent on the indivisibility of the latter. A discussion of how we think of indivisible objects can be found in *DA* III.6, and some of the issues emerging from *DA* III.6 are relevant to the discussion in I.1 (for some discussion see Berti 1978). In particular, *DA* III.6 makes it clear that indivisibility of thought in the relevant sense cannot be understood in merely temporal terms. We have the capacity to put together several contents of thought (*noēmata*) and think of the result of this composition as something one (*DA* III.6, 430a27–b6). This operation of composition is responsible for mistakes and falsehood if the contents we put together are thoughts of objects which are not together in reality. By thinking of the composite object that is the result of this synthetic operation, we think at once of some complex contents which do not correspond to any unified object in reality. A similar analysis of composite mental contents is given in *DS* 7, 447b24–26, where Aristotle explains how we perceive individuals: the composite object which is numerically one (e.g. Socrates) is not itself the object of a unified perception. Rather, it is acknowledged as a unified object in virtue of the simultaneous perception of the different qualia which are the objects of the single sense perceptions (cf. *DA* III.1, 425a31–b4). The different components of such a complex object can in turn be discerned by some specific activity of the soul (*DA* III.2, 426b8–427a14).

Furthermore, Aristotle introduces a distinction between things that are actually undivided but potentially divisible and things that are both actually undivided and potentially indivisible (i.e. things that do not have the potentiality to be divided and that, therefore, cannot possibly be divided). Things that are actually undivided but potentially divisible can be grasped through an indivisible act of thought and in an indivisible time. For instance, we can think of a line through an indivisible act of thought in an indivisible time even if the line is in itself always divisible. However, we can also think of the parts of the line one after another and, in this sense, the thought of each part can be divided from the thought of other parts (*DA* III.6, 430b7–14). By way of contrast, objects that are potentially indivisible (e.g. points, units, and for Aristotle presumably: simple substances) cannot be divided into parts that can be thought of separately from each other.

These considerations show that temporal at-once-ness of thought is compatible with different degrees of unity in the objects of thought. A different characterization of indivisibility in thought can be indirectly found in *DA* III.6, 430a26–27, where the thought of something indivisible is said to be a thought about something which cannot be false. This characterization, too, is difficult to spell out since indivisibility of thought does not necessarily imply the impossibility of any conceptual analysis. Presumably, Aristotle would concede that the thought of a point or the thought of the unmoved mover is indivisible in some relevant sense; however, this does not seem to imply that no conceptual analysis can be carried out on the notion of a point or of the unmoved mover (and *Met.* Λ.6–7 and 9 can be taken as indirect confirmation of this). Rather, it looks like indivisibility of thought, like indivisibility of account, ultimately rests on some basic ontological facts of unity: if the object of thought is one in some relevant sense, then the thought and the corresponding account will be indivisible in the relevant sense. That unity in thought (as well as unity in account) allows for degrees is confirmed by *Met.* Δ.6, 1016b1–6: 'And in general, those things such that the thought of their essence is indivisible and <such that they> cannot be separated in time nor in place nor in account, such things are most of all one, and, of these, those that are substances. For, in general, those things which do not have a division, inasmuch as they do not have any division, are said to be one in this respect; for example, if something does not have a division inasmuch as it is man, then it is called "one" man, if as animal, "one" animal, if as magnitude, "one" magnitude.' Cf. *Met.* N.1, 1087b33–1088a14.

We are then left with a basic ontological question: what objects can be regarded as ontologically simple? And what is ontological simplicity exactly? To neither of these questions does Aristotle give a full answer—at least, he certainly does not give such an answer in Iota. Among things that are one in account he distinguishes between what is indivisible in *eidos* ('form' or 'species'; see pp. 170–1, 198–9) and what is indivisible in number. Under the former rubric Aristotle understands what is indivisible for knowledge. I take this to mean: indivisible for scientific knowledge. Aristotle thinks that scientific knowledge is knowledge of why general properties belong to certain kinds of subject on the basis of some general principles such as definitions and general axioms (e.g. the principle of contradiction). Definitions can only be general accounts which are in principle applicable to a plurality of individuals (see *Met.* Z.15, 1040a9–14, a33–b2). For example, we can only define what it is to be a human being in general, but we cannot define what it is to be Socrates in particular. In this sense, the definition of the human being is supposed to grasp the what-it-is of human beings, i.e. the ontological factor common to all human beings which makes them precisely what they are, i.e. human beings. Universals can be more or less general (e.g. animal is more general than human being), but scientific knowledge cannot reach beyond the boundary of the most specific universals (this, of course, does not imply that we cannot have any knowledge whatsoever of particulars, but the forms of knowledge we have of particulars, such as sense perception or experience, are different from scientific knowledge; see *Met.* A.1, 981a7–12, a15–24, b10–11; *DA* II.5, 417b22–23). Furthermore, Aristotle distinguishes explicitly between the knowledge we can have of an object and the knowledge we can have of what that object is: the latter is always a matter of thought and intellection, even if the object is a perceptible object (*DA* III.4, 429a11). In this sense, the definitional account of something x, expressing what x is, always rests on the thought grasping what x is, independently of whether the object at stake is a sensible object or an intelligible one. The universal account applies to each of the single individuals falling under the universal grasped by the universal account and, in this sense, it is true that each individual is also one in account (cf. *Met.* Δ.6, 1016b31–1017a3: numerical unity implies unity in species but not the other way round). The definition of an object remains a general account, in principle applicable to a plurality of particulars, even if, as a matter of fact, there happens to be only one single particular object falling under it. Aristotle acknowledges a number of universals that are instantiated by one single individual: e.g. heavenly bodies (*Met.* Z.15, 1040a28–b2), the first unmoved mover, and the universe (*Met.* Λ.8, 1074a31–38; *DC* I.8, 276a18 ff.; I.9, 277b27.ff.) are unique specimens of their species.

Ross (1924, II p. 281, *ad* a17; p. 282, *ad* a35) suggests that the contrast between the two kinds of unity falling under unity in account corresponds to the contrast between lowest species and genera. I find this reading hard to reconcile with the claim that the particular is one in number. Be this as it may, Ross is right in stressing that the inclusion of universals under what is one in account does not distinguish between what is one object of thought by having or being a certain ontologically unified nature, and what is one object of thought by being logically unanalysable. Perhaps examples of the latter kind could be the categories: these are immediately and primitively something one and something that is and no account in terms of simpler items can be given of them (cf. *Met.* H.6, 1045a36–b7, although it is not clear whether the whole passage is about the categories as 1045b1–2 suggests).

1052a34–b1:   The summary of the four principal ways of being one emphasizes the common element running through all of them: things are said to be one as long as they are indivisible in some respect. In some cases (continuous objects and wholes) things are said to be one based on the fact that their motion is simple. In other cases (particulars and universals) things are said to be one based on the fact that their thought or account is indivisible.

In order to appreciate the philosophical relevance of the distinction of the two basic criteria (indivisibility of motion/indivisibility of account), some parallels between I.1 and some passages from *DA* might be useful, even if no explicit cross-reference can be found in the text. I have mentioned above that the role of the criteria of unity of motion and unity of account should be investigated: as long as the unity of motion and of account are dependent on the unity of the objects whose motion or account they are, it might be better to think of indivisibility in motion and indivisibility in account not as grounds for unity, but as the ways in which unity appears to us. Indivisibility of motion and indivisibility of account can be taken as basic phenomena intimately linked to the nature of the objects characterized by those features, but they are not, in themselves, what determines the unity of their underlying objects. Rather, they reflect some more basic ontological facts about those objects and we can resort to them in order to explore further ontological features of those objects. The idea is the following: the ontological structure of an object (and, ultimately, what the object is) determines the kind and degree of unity of its motion or of its account and, in this sense, the structure of the object is causally prior to the unity of its motion and account. However, the unity of motion and account enjoy some priority 'with respect to us' in that they are starting points we have access to in order to undertake the enquiry into the unity of their underlying objects (note that at other places such as *Met.* Z.5 Aristotle is inclined to rely on considerations about the accounts of things in order to infer some features of those things).

This idea gains in credibility if we consider that the basic bipartition between ways of being one, with respect to motion and with respect to account or thought, corresponds to the bipartition of the domain of objects we can know into objects of perception and objects of thought. With respect to objects of perception, Aristotle mentions motion, shape, number, and unity (*DA* III.1, 425a14 ff.) among the common sensibles, i.e. the features of the external world we get acquainted with through more than one sensory channel. For instance, we can perceive motion through sight, touch, and hearing, whereas we can perceive colours only through sight, sounds only through hearing, and so on. Number is perceived as a privation of continuity (*DA* III.1, 425a19–21), which in I.1 is defined in terms of motion. It seems possible that Aristotle thinks of the basic acquaintance with a whole in terms of the perception of a continuous object with a determinate shape (also a common sensible). What we perceive is simple motion and shape. The way in which we perceive them is causally determined by some features of the extra-mental objects characterized by them. Similarly for objects of thought. As for the latter, Aristotle further emphasizes our capacity to distinguish between a certain object and what it is for something to be that kind of object (*DA* III.4, 429a11). As we saw, the account of what it is for something to be a certain kind of object is a universal account; depending on what the object at issue is, such an account can be simple (e.g. the definition of the unmoved mover) or make reference to a plurality of different beings (e.g. the definition of the white Socrates). Since, according to Aristotle, our cognitive faculties are naturally apt to grasp extra-mental ontological structures, the fact that we perceive something as continuous or that we think of it as something simple reflects some fundamental ontological facts (in our case: facts about unity) about the objects of perception and of thought.

In *DA* III.1, 425a20 Aristotle mentions a further way to get acquainted with unity and number, through an exercise of discernment of similarities and differences in our perception. Number and unity can also be conveyed by the special sensibles, since each sense perceives one kind of object. I take it that this means that each sense perceives one homogeneous field within the domain of perceptible objects which we can distinguish from the field of perception of any other sense. This seems to be some hybrid form of unity with respect to perception and with respect to thought or account. *Met.* Δ.6, 1016a17–24 and *DA* III.6, 430b7–20 might count as further passages where this kind of unity is considered. I.1 does not mention this way of being one.

One might wonder why, with respect to objects of perception, Aristotle focuses on motion rather than, say, on shape in order to describe the unity of continuous things. I have no conclusive answer, but one consideration might be relevant to the point. At different places (*PA* I.1, 640b30–35; 642a24–30; *Met.* A.4, 985b10–20; cf. H.2, 1042b12–36) Aristotle criticizes Democritus's use of differences in shape as somewhat too superficial and extrinsic forerunners of his notion form. Perhaps the preference accorded to motion rather than shape in I.1 can be explained by resorting to similar considerations: the way in which something moves and is active might tell us more about its unity than its shape. After all, one could argue that, from the point of view of shape, artefacts do not radically differ from natural beings in that they, too, exhibit a unified structure. However, artefacts lack an internal principle of motion: their parts do not naturally grow as assimilated parts of a whole, but must be put together by force, by resorting to glue, nails, bonds.

1052b1–20: The passage introduces some general considerations on the nature of *pollachōs legomena* ('things said in many ways'). How far this analysis applies to cases other than those mentioned in the text ('one', 'cause', 'element') deserves further investigation.

The text can be divided into three main sections. In the first section (b1–9) Aristotle introduces a distinction by means of three questions whose mutual relations must be analysed: **(i)** What kind(s) of things are one? **(ii)** What is it to be one? **(iii)** What is the account of the one? Compared to the issues distinguished on p. 21, it might look like Aristotle is working on the distinction between question e) (corresponding to (i)) and question d) (corresponding to (ii) and (iii)). However, the discussion actually bears on all of a)–f). The second section (b9–14) illustrates the distinction with reference to an example: saying what things are elements (e.g. fire) is not the same as saying what being an element is. Finally, the third section (b14–20) spells out what it is to be one in the primary sense. Since the second section is crucial to make sense of the first one, I shall deal with them together.

1052b1–14: Two main problems arise: first, how exactly we understand the relation between (i) and (ii), and second, how we understand the relation between (i) and the distinction of the different ways of being one in the first part of the chapter. Aristotle starts by drawing a contrast between (i) and (ii)/(iii). In particular, (iii) seems to spell out the way in which (ii) should be understood. One could take this to imply that (i) is just a different question from (ii). One might (but need not) go even further and say that (i) has been accounted for in the first part of the chapter, where Aristotle has spelled out what kinds of thing can be said to be one, while from now on the discussion will bear on (ii) and (iii). This reading of the relations between (i)–(iii) and of the corresponding structure of the chapter is quite natural and is more or less implicitly endorsed by most interpreters.

However, a more nuanced and complex option can be sketched out by taking a closer look at the development of the chapter. As the analysis of the example (b9–14) shows, Aristotle seems to think that (i) (or something very similar to it) could be understood as a way to spell out (ii): we can answer the question: 'What is an element?' by saying: 'Fire'. While this answer is not fully satisfactory, it is not completely off the mark either. Accordingly, we can take the passage as making a point about the different ways in which (i) and (iii) can contribute to an enquiry about (ii). Furthermore, and even if we want to keep (i) as opposed to (ii)–(iii), we can still question the idea that what we find in the first part of the chapter is an account of (i) with no particular relevance for (ii). In fact, b5–6 make quite clear that the ways of being one distinguished in the first part of the chapter have something to do with (ii): for at b5–6 Aristotle draws a contrast between being one in some of the ways (i.e. as continuous, as a whole, etc.) specified above and being one in the sense of being something else 'which is rather close to the name'.

Leaving aside for a moment the exact meaning of b6–7 and the contrast between name and power, it is important to distinguish the general ways (*tropoi*) of being one per se in the first part of the chapter from the things to which each of these ways belongs (1052b4–6). Things (or, presumably, primary things) are mainly said to be one because some or other of these ways of being one belongs to them. Similarly, at b12–14, being an element, i.e. a constituent, belongs to objects which are said to be an element precisely by being constituents of something else. I take it that all different ways of being one (i.e. both those introduced in the first part of the chapter and the one Aristotle will talk about shortly) correspond to being an element in the example, while all things which are said to be one in virtue of the fact that some or other of these ways of being one belongs to them correspond to the determinate things and natures (e.g. fire, the infinite, etc.) which are said to be an element in virtue of having this property.

This reading of the relation between (i)–(iii) can be illustrated with reference to 1052b9–14. In this section Aristotle explains how we can 'talk about element and cause' in two ways: with reference to things or by giving a definition of the name. The formulation at b7–8 suggests that what is accounted for is the general notion at issue, i.e. 'element' or 'cause'. In spelling out what an element or a cause is, we can either define the notion at stake with reference to things or we can give an account of what the word indicates, i.e. of the general features the name picks out in those things that are said to be elements. In the first case, we give an account of the notion at issue (e.g. 'element') by giving an example of something that typically or uncontroversially falls under it (e.g. fire). In the second case, we provide a general account (we spell out the property we intend to ascribe to things when we say that they are elements, i.e. the property of being a constituent of other things—and this is what being an element amounts to).

Before going back to b6–7, two further points deserve some attention. First, in the parenthesis at 1052b10–11 Aristotle refers to things that are elements in their own right. Perhaps the point of this qualification is that Aristotle intends to restrict the attention to beings which can only exist as constituents of other beings: one cannot spell out what the property of being an element is by giving examples of elements, not even if the examples are of beings which are necessarily elements. The view that fire is one of the elements is relatively common (it is supported, among others, by Empedocles) and can be ascribed to Aristotle himself. The view that the infinite is an element (i.e. a constitutive principle) of things existing in its own right is ascribed to the Pythagoreans and to Plato (*Phys.* III.4, 203a4–16), whereas the view that the infinite exists as a property of some material constituent characterized by its own nature is ascribed to Anaxagoras and Democritus (*Phys.* III.4, 203a16–b2).

Secondly, the idea of spelling out what it is to be an element or a cause in terms of some determinate thing and nature is reminiscent of Aristotle's characterization of the approach to the one of the philosophers of nature (*Met.* B.4, 1001a12–19; see notes to I.2, 1053b14–16) as well as to other notions such as the infinite (*Phys.* III.4, 203a16 ff.). The philosophers of nature say that the one is Love or fire, or that the infinite is water or air or something intermediate between them. For Aristotle this approach captures some truth, but is still too simplistic and, to a certain extent, misleading: for in this way no general account is given of what it is to be an element (or of what it is to be a cause, infinite, one, etc.). At the same time, Aristotle's specification of the other option in terms of an account of what it is to be one shows how wrong is the approach of those who go too far in the opposite direction. Some philosophers such as the Platonists and the Pythagoreans (*Met.* B.4, 1001a5–6, a9–10; *Met.* A.5, 986a13–28; cf. *Met.* Z.11, 1036b12 ff.) assume that what it is to be one is the same for all things, that there is one single cause of unity for all things that are one, and that the single cause of unity is also what is one in the highest degree: the One (see introduction to I.2). Against this approach Aristotle shows that there is no single account of what it is to be one for things—let alone one object which is the cause of unity for all things that are one. Rather, in some cases being one is being a continuous object or being a whole, in other cases being one is something else. Note that in the case of 'element' there seems to be a unified account of what it is to be an element, which corresponds to the general trait common to all ways in which things are said to be an element in *Met.* Δ.3, 1014b14–15. On the common trait between the different accounts of what it is to be one see p. 51.

We can now return to b6–7 and the distinction between being one in the sense of being 'something else which is rather close to the name' and being one by being something 'rather close to the power'. The odd phrase 'to the power' translates *tēi dunamei* at b7; *dunamei* without the article (*tēi*) could have the standard sense of 'potentially', but the presence of the article seems to rule out the standard translation for the expression without the article. Different interpretations have been given of the distinction Aristotle is trying to draw. Ross takes 'the power' to be the power of the name, in the sense of the force or application of the word and refers to Lys. 10.7; Plat., *Crat.*, 394b3. He takes the point of the passage to be a semantic distinction corresponding to extension and intension, or denotation and connotation (Ross 1924, II p. 282; similarly Stokes 1971, p. 12). The problem with this semantic distinction is that it does not seem to apply without qualification to what Aristotle is doing: as we have seen, the first four ways of being one (as continuous, wholes, etc.) do not immediately pick out the objects that are one; rather, they are general descriptions under which those objects fall. This is perhaps what Halper 2009 has in mind when he speaks of 'non-categorial essences' (pp. 69–71) falling between a name and the things referred to by that name (in our case: between the term 'one' and things that happen to be one in one way or other). I am not sure whether by 'non-categorial essences' Halper means something like the nominal definitions in *APo* II.10, 93b29–32, where Aristotle speaks of accounts spelling out what a word means without providing a full account of what it is for things falling under that term to be the kind of thing they are (for some discussion about the relation between the different kinds of account in *APo* II.10 see Bolton 1976; Demoss–Deveroux 1988; Charles 2000). Morrison (1993a, p. 151) elucidates the clause 'rather close to the power' with reference to the phrase *kata to onoma* ('in accordance with the name') at 1053b4. He reads the latter in analogy with *Phys.* II.6, 197b29 and *Probl.* X.40, 895a19, where the phrase refers to the etymological meaning of an expression, and takes the distinction at b6–7 accordingly, as a distinction between the etymological meaning of an expression (in our case: 'one' in the sense of 'measure') and its current meanings (as continuous, wholes, etc.). Furthermore, he suggests that the meaning of 'one' as the unit of measurement would be phenomenologically more basic. It is not clear to me in what sense being a unit of measurement would be the phenomenologically basic feature of things that are one nor in what sense this would be closer to the etymology of the word 'one' (or, rather, *hen*; note that the words spelled out *kata to onoma* in *Phys.* II.6, 197b29 and *Probl.* X.40, 895a19 are composite words: *automaton*, 'chance', which Aristotle spells out in terms of *auto*, 'it', 'the thing itself', and *matēn*, 'in vain', 'at random', 'without reason'; similarly *ischnofōnia*, 'stammering', i.e. a 'hindering' or 'keeping in check' of the voice. It is hard to see how a similar analysis could be applied to *hen*). On Morrison 1993a see also Pakaluk 1993. Centrone (2005, p. 50) sees in the essence of the one (understood as indivisibility) a common and general meaning associated to the word 'one', under which other ways of being one can be brought. It seems to me that Centrone's proposal gets closer than others to the point Aristotle is trying to make. However, whether the account of what it is to be one is being indivisible or being a unit is controversial (see below). If the account on the basis of the name is that being one is being a unit or a measure, then it does not seem true that this is a common and general account associated to the word 'one' of which the other accounts of ways of being one are different specifications.

1052b14–20: The passage expands on the claim made at 1052b5–7 that in some cases being one amounts to being one in one of the four ways in which things are said to be one, whereas in some other cases being one amounts to something 'rather close to the name'. How this is done is controversial since the Greek at 1052b16–18 is extremely problematic. The α-text and, more generally, the manuscript tradition differs significantly from Ross's text (see Notes on the Text). For facility of reference I provide a translation of both texts here. Ross's text yields the translation: '[. . .] being one is being indivisible, which is precisely being a this and being *in itself separable* (*idiai chōristōi*) either in place or in form or in thought, and also being a whole and *indivisible* (*adiairetōi*), but most of all *it is being the primary measure* of each genus and, in the strictest sense, of quantity [. . .]'. The α-text yields the translation: '[. . .] being one is being indivisible, which is precisely being a this and being *inseparable* (*achōristōi*) either in place or in form or in thought, or also *with respect to* what it is to be a *determinate* (*diōrismenōi*) whole, and most of all *by being the primary measure* (*tōi metron einai prōton*) of each genus and, in the strictest sense, of quantity [. . .]'. At b17 the α-reading 'inseparable' was regarded as suspicious by Bonitz (1849, p. 417) based on the consideration that Aristotle usually uses the language of lack of separation to indicate conceptual or ontological inseparability rather than indivisibility in place or form or thought. However, 'inseparable' is much less puzzling when compared to Δ.6, 1016b2–3, where the language of separation is used to make the same point. At b17–18 'determinate' seems in any case preferable to 'indivisible' in that Aristotle is spelling out how being indivisible should be understood: being a whole, i.e. something with a determinate shape and form, is a way of being one and indivisible (cf. 1052a22–29). In Ross's text 'being a whole and indivisible' is an alternative account of what it is to be one: 'being one is being indivisible [...] or also being a whole and indivisible'. In the α-text 'with respect to what it is to be a determinate whole' specifies a further respect (in addition to place, form, and thought) in which being one is being something 'inseparable'. The point would be that, in some cases, being one amounts to being a 'this', i.e. a determinate something, which, despite being a composite entity, is a unified, non-scattered object whose unity is determined by its essence, i.e. by what it is to be a whole of a certain kind.

At b18 in Ross's text (*to metrōi einai prōtōi*), Aristotle adds a further account of what being one is, in addition to 'being indivisible' and 'being a whole and indivisible': being one is most of all 'being the primary measure' of a genus and, in particular, of quantity. However, the manuscript tradition is basically unanimous in transmitting *metron einai prōton* and splits in the transmission of the article (see Notes on the Text *ad loc.*). The β-text as it stands (*to metron einai prōton*) makes little sense and some correction along the lines of Ross's text would be required. However, the α-text was presumably *tōi metron einai prōton*, which makes sense, even if the point in this case would be quite different from the point in Ross's text: being a primary measure would not be an alternative account of being one. Rather, being one sometimes is being a 'this' and something inseparable 'by being a primary measure'. I take this to mean that in some cases objects are regarded as one and indivisible simply insofar as they are regarded as units of measure for a certain domain. Crager (in progress), who follows the α-text, takes this as a blow against the view that the one which is a principle of number is the same as the one which is convertible with being (cf. *Met.* Γ.2, 1003b22–33; Z.4, 1030b10–12; I.2, 1053b20 ff.; K.3, 1061a15 ff.; see notes on I.2, 1053b20 ff.; the debate about whether the one which is a principle of number is the same as the one which is convertible with being starts with Avicenna, who argues in favour of their identification, and Averrois, who criticizes Avicenna: see Menn 2011; Menn (in progress), Iγ2a: From Δ6 to Iota 1: the one as indivisible and as measure, defends the view that being one is being a measure; Menn's view rests, among other things, on his analysis of I.1 as addressing the issue of how the one is a principle). Like Crager, I believe (even if for different reasons: my account in what follows is a refined version of Castelli 2010, Ch. 6, when, among other things, I was not aware of the α-text) that there is a distinction between the one which is convertible with being (or, as it is sometimes labelled in the debate, the transcendental one) and the one which is a principle of number. However, it does not seem to me that the α-text makes the opposite view considerably weaker (nor, for that matter, that Ross's text makes it much stronger). Even if one opts for the α-text here (as I am inclined to do) there are other passages where Aristotle spells out what it is to be one by saying that it is being a measure or being a principle of number (see 1053b4–6; *Met.* Δ.6, 1016b17–21, where, however, there are textual issues; Λ.7, 1072a33). Furthermore, on several occasions Aristotle seems quite keen on the idea that anything that is can be regarded as indivisible and counted as one, and this seems to me enough to say that each thing that is is one precisely in the sense that it counts or can count as a unit (cf. *Met.* Δ.6, 1016b3–6; M.7, 1082b16–19; M.3, 1078a21–26; N.1, 1087b33–1088a14). It does not seem to me that 1052b15–19 in the α-reading need say anything against or in support of this view. The α-reading may suggest that in those cases (such as continuous magnitudes) where there is no indivisible unit strictly speaking, it is by establishing something as a measure that we come to regard it as one and indivisible (cf. 1053a20–24).

No matter what text we follow, what is crucial for the debate is what is at stake in being the primary measure of a genus and, in particular, of quantity. I take it that the claim that the transcendental one and the numerical one are the same consists in saying that there is nothing more to being a unit of measure of a genus than being counted as one in the genus. One could, however, argue that there is more to being a measure than to be counted as one. At some places (e.g. M.8, 1084b13–32 and see below) Aristotle distinguishes between being indivisible and being a principle of number. To start with, Aristotle emphasizes that a unit of measure is necessarily relative to a measurable in such a way that the unit belongs to the same kind as the measurable and, once the measure is identified, what is measured turns out to be a plurality of units of measure. This suggests that numbers are regarded as groups of homogeneous objects and that finding the unit of measure amounts to identifying the kind of object a plurality is a plurality of. Crager (in progress) explores this picture and proposes a distinction between the one, which is regarded as a repeatable type, and the monads, which are the tokens of that type and which constitute a plurality or a number. Crager's emphasis on the distinction between type and token is important and achieves a good deal of conceptual clarity, even if it may not be a distinction Aristotle has present to his mind in this context (cf. pp. 106–7 about taking all equal mathematical entities as one, which would allow for the use of the singular without introducing types). But there is an issue as to how robust the requirement that there be a type under which all units of a number fall is supposed to be. In particular, it is not clear whether Aristotle intends to introduce any restriction on the types with reference to which one can speak of units and numbers. If the requirement can be just taken in the sense that the units qua units must be comparable and combinable (cf. *Met.* M.7, 1080b37 ff.), it would seem that 'object' would be enough of a type (I take it that Aristotle would be ready to say that one quality and, say, one elephant equals two; cf. perhaps M.7, 1082b16–19). I.2, however, clearly pushes the idea that the measure in each kind is a certain nature which works as a principle of knowledge as well as an ontological principle of other members of the kind, which are regarded as pluralities of corresponding units (for the details of this view see notes to I.2). It is in any case clear that neither in the less committal type-reading of the one as a principle of number nor in the more committal account of I.2 the principle of number is the same as the one which is convertible with being in that not every being is a principle of number in the relevant sense (on one account because the principle of number can only be a type, on the other account because the principle of number can only be the kind of thing that is an ontological constituent of other members of the corresponding kind).

Independently of the stand one eventually takes in the debate about the relation between transcendental and numerical one, it is important to spell out how being indivisible and being a measure interplay in the course of I.1 and how the different parts of the account at 1052b14–20 relate to each other and to what precedes. Aristotle has just illustrated that, in giving an account of general notions such as 'cause' or 'element', one can focus on the things which happen to be causes or elements, or one can give an account of the 'name' by spelling out the feature belonging to the objects that we call 'cause' or 'element' (b13) on account of which we apply that name to them. I take it that the whole of b16–19 unpacks the account of the 'name' of the one in that it gives a general account of the feature(s) belonging to the objects that we call 'one'.

We have seen that indivisibility is a common trait of the four ways of being one distinguished in the first part of the chapter. In each of them indivisibility is qualified and b16–18 provides a general account of the possible qualifications which may enter specific ways of being one. As for b18–19, according to the α-text Aristotle would add to the general account of the 'name' that being (or being set down as) the primary unit of measure of a genus provides the basic ground (b18: *malista*, 'most of all') for something's being regarded as indivisible (note that, on this reading, 'being a this' and being 'inseparable' apply to numerical units as well; cf. again, *Met.* Δ.13, 1020a7–8, where 'a this' indicates the result of a division in quantity). According to Ross's text, Aristotle would be adding a somewhat more specific account of what it is to be one and indivisible by saying that being one and indivisible consists most of all in being the primary measure of a genus and, strictly speaking (b19: *kuriōtata*), of quantity.

I take it that in the next section (1052b20–24) Aristotle moves from giving a general account of what it is to be one to identifying the kind of object (the numerical unit) which paradigmatically responds to that account by being indivisible in all respects and by being the primary measure of quantity in that it is the primary measure of number. The one which is the principle of number is defined as what is indivisible without qualification (the one is what is indivisible in quantity without position; *Met.* Δ.6, 1016b24–25; cf. *APo* I.2, 72a21–23). Furthermore, the only function of the numerical unit is that of being a unit of measurement with respect to the domain of objects to which it belongs (see p. 53 ff. and I.6 for further details).

If this is right, Aristotle strategy in I.1 down to 1052b24 resembles quite closely his strategy in the enquiry into substance. In the enquiry into substance, Aristotle starts by giving a survey of kinds of objects that are generally acknowledged to be substances such as bodies, living beings, etc. (*Met.* Δ.8, 1017b10–14; Z.2, 1028b8–27). He then considers the general features of such objects on the basis of which they are regarded as substances (Z.3, 1028b33–36, setting the agenda for the discussion in Z.3, Z.4–11, and Z.13–16). One could take this part of the enquiry as an attempt to answering a general question: what is it for something to be (a) substance? (cf. question c) on p. 21). The answer to this question will at the same time yield an answer to a question concerning what the primary substance(s) is (or are; cf. Introduction, xxvi–xxvii). In the enquiry into unity, one can start with a survey of things or kinds of things that are generally acknowledged as one. In this case, the first result of this survey might appear discouraging: in some way or other, anything that is is also one (*Met.* Γ.2, 1003b22–33; Z.4, 1030b10–12; I.2, 1053b20 ff.; K.3, 1061a15 ff.). However, it is possible to identify a few principal ways of being one (and this is where I.1 starts): these are the ways in which continuous things, wholes, at least certain universals, particulars are said to be one. By working on these ways of being one, it turns out that being one in all these cases is being indivisible in some respect or other. That indivisibility is what matters is confirmed by the fact that, if something is regarded as a primary measure, i.e. as something basic and unanalysable, in its kind, then that object is identified as the one in its kind just in virtue of the role it plays within its kind, i.e. just because it is (or is set down as) basic and indivisible in that kind. Objects that are primary measures in their kinds are objects standing to other objects in their domain as the numerical unit, which is essentially what is indivisible in all respects, stands to numbers. The identification of these ways of being one leads to the identification of the kind of objects that are primarily one (or primary 'ones'): the outer sphere of the cosmos is a primary one by being a paradigmatic whole; the form or essence of substances is a primary one by being the cause of unity of substances and what is primarily one in account; the numerical unit is the paradigmatic one in that it is the simplest and most precise measure, i.e. the measure of numbers. If this is the structure of Aristotle's approach to unity, then the attempt at neatly disentangling unity as indivisibility and unity as measure might turn out to be artificial, at least to a certain extent.

Numerical units are not self-subsisting objects in Aristotle's ontology, but they can be regarded as if they were self-subsisting objects as long as the assumption of their separate existence is not used in proofs about their properties. Stressing that the enquiry into the one somehow ends up in the category of quantity could be one way to show that a certain approach to being and its principles is inadequate: the ultimate focus of the enquiry into being radically diverges from that of the enquiry into unity. The enquiry into primary being ends up in the category of substance, while the enquiry into the primary one ends up in the category of quantity (see notes on 1053a18–21 on the basic categorial partition of indivisibility into quantity and quality and pp. 89–90 in I.2 for further comments on this point). The opposite view, that the enquiry into being coincides with the enquiry into the one, has been supported, with different emphasis, by Couloubaritsis 1983, 1990, and 1992; Morrison 1993a; see also Gloy 1985. It seems to me that the only way in which the enquiry into the one can come to coincide with the enquiry into being is by being corrected in light of Aristotle's views about the ontological priority of self-subsisting beings, i.e. substances. But those views are part of Aristotle's approach to being rather than to unity (for a more elaborate account of this view see Castelli 2010, pp. 206–11; in the same direction also Berti 2005, p. 74).

1052b20–24: These and the following lines spell out two intertwined ideas: first, the one is the primary measure of quantity (cf. 1052b18–19); second, the relation between measure and measured obtaining between the numerical unit and numbers extends from the domain of numbers to other kinds of beings. Both ideas and several related points are discussed in more detail in I.2 and I.6 (see notes on those chapters).

As for the first point, a measure is that in virtue of which quantity is known. Aristotle's train of thought can be paraphrased as follows. Knowing a quantity is knowing how much something is. We know how much something is when we can ascribe a number to it. We can ascribe a number to something once we have established what parts of it we count as one. The basic idea on the relation between the one and number is that a number is a plurality of units (a plurality of 'ones').

1052b24–31:   Aristotle illustrates the extension of the notion of measure beyond the domain of numbers. The extension takes two steps: from numbers to other quantities (1052b24: *enteuthen*, 'from this case', i.e. from the case of numbers) and from quantity to other kinds of being (1052b19: *enteuthen*, 'from this case', i.e. from the case of quantity). I.2 provides more details about the second step. The core idea is that, by analogy with the case of numbers and quantities, 'measure' comes to indicate the primary thing in virtue of which each domain of objects is known; the measure in each domain is the one with respect to its domain. In our passage in I.1 all examples (length, surface, weight, speed) belong to the domain of quantities and this suggests that, at this stage, Aristotle is still mainly interested in spelling out the first and less problematic step of the extension.

The parenthesis at 1052b27–31 introduces a clarification about the last two members in the series of kinds of quantity, i.e. weight and speed. In this context both notions are used to indicate the genus of weight and the genus of speed, rather than the weight of heavy things or the speed of fast things respectively.

1052b31–1053a14:   The section spells out two features on the basis of which something is singled out as a measure and, in this sense, as a principle within a given domain of objects. Plat., *Resp.* VII 524d–526c certainly belongs in the backdrop for Aristotle's discussion. The choice and analysis of the examples is almost exclusively confined to cases of quantifiable objects (such as length, weight, speed) that can be measured in a straightforward sense. As we shall see, I.2 will consider more controversial cases (but see the case of musical intervals and vocal elements at 1053a12–13). The two features of a suitable measure are simplicity and precision. Simplicity with respect to quantity or quality is introduced at 1052b34–35 in order to spell out indivisibility. Whether the gloss on indivisibility in terms of simplicity is really helpful depends on whether one thinks that simplicity picks out a more basic ontological feature (cf. *Met.* Λ.7, 1072a32–33) which is reflected by the impossibility or difficulty to divide the object at issue in quantity or quality. Cf. notes to 1053a18–21.

Precision is often mentioned as a feature of sciences depending at the same time on the conceptual simplicity of their object (see, e.g., *Met.* M.3, 1078a9–14) and on the accuracy of their methods of enquiry (e.g. *Met.* α.3 995a8–16). The accuracy a science achieves in dealing with its object depends on the simplicity of its objects: the simpler the objects, the more accurate the science. So for instance, arithmetic is more precise than geometry because the objects of geometry are more complex than the objects of arithmetic. The claim that the objects of geometry are more complex than the objects of arithmetic is to be understood in the relatively straightforward sense that objects of geometry are ontologically richer than objects of arithmetic, starting from their principles: the numerical unit is what is indivisible in all respects and does not have a position whereas the point is what is indivisible in all respects *and* has a position.

In I.1, precision is a desirable feature of the measure. The idea is that a unit of measure is precise if and only if all token units are recognizably equal. In the case of numerical units, all units are undifferentiated, both in quantity and in quality: a numerical unit cannot be divided in quantity (by definition) and it cannot be divided in quality because, being a merely quantitative object, it has no qualities (cf. *Met.* M.7, 1082b1 ff.; M.8, 1083a11). Nothing can be added or subtracted to it because addition would result in something that is divisible either in quantity or in quality, and nothing can be subtracted to it since, being indivisible, one cannot subtract a part of it without subtracting the whole unit, which would result in the elimination of the unit.

In the case of measures for liquids, weights, etc., it can happen that token units differ from each other, where slight differences may escape notice. People try to avoid this problem by choosing measures that seem to be responsive to the test for precision with respect to perception, whatever such a test may turn out to be. In the case of musical intervals Aristotle speaks of a minimal audible interval (cf. I.1, 1053a14–18; see also notes on I.2, 1053b34–1054a1 and I.7, 1057a22–24); as for other magnitudes cf. 1053a21–24 and corresponding notes. On the fastest motion as a unit of measurement for astronomy cf. *DC* II.4, 287a23–30.

Having shown that there is no common account of what it is for something to be one, at a13–14 Aristotle takes a further step and stresses that, even if we focus on the notion of measure, we cannot single out one single measure of everything that is. Rather, a measure is always relative to the nature of the measurable. A few lines later (1053a18–21) Aristotle spells out the kernel of truth in the complementary claim that the one is a measure for all things.

1053a14–18:   The existence of more than one unit of measurement even in one and the same kind radically undermines the idea of finding one single item which is the one and the measure for all things. Of course the existence of more than one unit of measure for one kind should be understood with reference to types of units (it is obvious that there is a plurality of tokens).

In Greek musical theory *diesis* does not univocally designate one interval, but a number of intervals small enough to deserve this name (among which quarter-tones and a third of a tone). For this reason it is difficult to provide an uncontroversial translation. I translate 'semitone' because it seems likely (Barker 1989, p. 73 n. 17) that Aristotle is thinking of the two unequal 'semitones' (e.g. 17:16 and 18:17) into which the tone (9:8) can be divided (note, by the way, that those semitones can be in turn divided into smaller *dieseis*). The translation 'semitone' should not be taken to imply that a *diesis* is half a tone as in the equal temperament, in which the interval between two adjacent pitches is constant and is the smallest interval in this system of tuning.

The distinction between two methods for establishing a system of measurement for musical intervals, one based on acoustic perception and the other based on ratios, refers to two relatively well known schools of thought about harmonic studies: one school supported an empiricist approach to the analysis and measurement of the relations between pitches, whereas the other favoured a mathematical approach (cf. Plat., *Resp.* 530c–531c; for an extensive analysis of the two approaches see Barker 2007; in particular, for an account of the two approaches as different approaches to issues of measurement, see Barker 2007, pp. 19–30). For the empiricists, the problem of finding a unit of measurement is the problem of identifying the smallest interval between two pitches which is perceptible to human ear. Furthermore the empiricist approach to differences of pitches as gaps between pitches suggests a conceptualization of pitches as points on a line, which can be more or less close to each other (Barker 2007, pp. 23–5 and chs 2–3). This conceptualization of differences between pitches might have some intuitive appeal in that it might be taken as a relatively straightforward representation of how different pitches 'appear' to our acoustic perception (I say 'it might' because it is not obvious that this was the standard way to describe differences in pitches for the Greeks: see Barker 2007, pp. 21–2, about the use of pairs of opposites such as 'sharp' and 'heavy' or 'tense' and 'slack', instead of our 'high' and 'low', to indicate relative differences between pitches). The opposite approach, presumably of Pythagorean origin, regards intervals not as 'distances' between points on a line, but as ratios—perhaps originally as ratios between the lengths of the strings or of the pipes that are used to produce the sounds, and later, in a more refined theory, between the speeds of the movements of the bodies that are the sources of sound or through which sound propagates (Barker 2007, pp. 25–9).

One difference between these two approaches seems particularly relevant in the context of I.1 (and I.2, 1053b34–1054a1). While the empiricist approach leads to a sort of system of direct measurement in which 'larger' intervals are measured by smaller ones, there is no obvious way in which the analysis of intervals in terms of ratios can be used to obtain a similar result. This is so because there is no clear correspondence between the 'size' of the interval and the 'size' of the corresponding ratio. More generally, it does not seem to be the case that in the mathematical approach larger intervals were meant to be 'measured' by smaller ones in any straightforward sense. Furthermore, the approach in terms of ratios would show that there are even more than two different *dieseis*. These would not measure larger intervals rather than be the result of the analysis of relatively small intervals. If this is correct, it is not clear in what sense the two intervals distinguished in ratios would work as measures of other intervals in the first place. If so, Aristotle's remark might be misleading (so Barker 1989, *cit.*).

As for the distinction between the two different semitones, some interpreters think that the distinction is that drawn by Philolaus between *leimma* and *apotomē* (Bonitz 1849, p. 418; Menn (in progress *ad loc.*); others (Ross 1924, II p. 283; Centrone 2005, pp. 46–7) take it as the distinction drawn by Aristoxenus, Aristotle's pupil, between different kinds of *diesis* for different kinds of tetrachord (in particular Ross refers to the distinction between the enharmonic diesis, i.e. a quarter-tone, and the chromatic diesis, i.e. a third of a tone). Centrone (2005, pp. 46–7) uses this reference to make a hypothesis on the date of Iota's composition after the foundation of the Lyceum (335 BC), when Aristotle and Aristoxenus's relationship would have grown stronger. Elders (1961, p. 75) deletes 1053a14–18 as a later interpolation in order to avoid ascribing Iota to a relatively mature phase of Aristotle's philosophical career based on the assessment of Aristoxenus's influence. However, if the considerations above about the plurality of *dieseis* in ratios (which would be in any case more than two) and the possibly misleading nature of Aristotle's remark are correct, the attempt at identifying with certainty a specific pair of *dieseis* may well be hopeless. For further comments on semitones see notes to I.2, 1053b34–1054a1 and I.7, 1057a22–24.

As for the measures of vocal sound, *stoicheion* is usually translated with 'letter', but since Aristotle is interested in distinguishing phonetic components I shall translate as 'vocal element' (note that in other contexts 'element' is the standard translation for *stoicheion*). See *Poet.* 20, 1456b22–34 for Aristotle's classification of *stoicheia*: these are said to differ in several respects (among which length and brevity) and reference is given to the works dealing with metre (*en tois metrikois*) for a fuller account. In the passage in I.1 it is not clear what Aristotle has in mind when he refers to the plurality of vocal sounds 'with which we measure'. I.2, 1054a2 refers to the vocal element which is 'sounding' (possibly: vowels, but see notes *ad loc.*) and says no more about the plurality of such units of measurement. Perhaps we can form an idea of the measurement Aristotle is thinking of by looking at ancient treatises on metre. In particular, in some treatises metre is regarded not only as a tool for measuring feet arranged according to a certain pattern, but more generally as a tool for measuring the quantity of syllables based on the vocal elements they are composed of (Mathiesen 1985, pp. 163–4, 167). The basic idea is that 'the combination of [. . .] letters produces syllables, which are measured (or, metered) by their vowels and by certain combinations of semivowels and mutes' (Mathiesen 1985, p. 164). Interestingly enough, Aristides Quintilianus, *De musica* 1.21, establishes a correspondence between the length of the syllables and the size of musical intervals by ascribing a determinate length to the consonants (and not only to the vowels) which constitute a syllable:

'It has been demonstrated that the magnitudes of the elements are equal in number to the intervals of the tone, for the smallest of these is a fourth part of the largest—as the diesis is of the tone, and the intermediate is half of the larger and double the smaller. A short syllable is half of a long and a simple consonant is half of a short; it is evident that from the juxtaposing of either a double consonant or one vowel, a short becomes a long' (quoted in Mathiesen 1985, p. 164). Dionysius of Halicarnassus, *De compositione verborum*, ch. 15, gives some examples of how to measure syllables based on the vocal elements out of which they are made (for translation and commentary see Roberts 1910). For a survey of Greek metre, see Hephaestion, *Manual on metre* (Van Ophuijsen 1987).

On the two units of measurement for the side and the diagonal of the square cf. Plat., *Theaet.* 147d–148b. The reason why one might think that we need different units of measurement for the side and the diagonal of the square is that they are incommensurable, i.e. there is no segment by which both are measured (whereas the squares built on the side and the square built on the diagonal do have a common unit of measurement; Cattanei (1996, pp. 52–3) seems to take the square-unit as the second kind of unit for the side and the diagonal).

1053a18–21: Aristotle spells out in what sense one could say that the one is a measure of all things. The passage looks like an attempt at making sense of an *endoxon* about the one (cf. 1053a31–b3; see also Plat., *Pol.* 283c11–d2, on the importance of the art of measurement for ontological investigations; note the reference there to an enquiry 'into the precise itself': *peri auto to akribes*).

We can distinguish a general idea from more specific and problematic tenets about the relation between the one and all things. The general idea is that knowledge and the acquisition of knowledge can be thought of as an exercise in discernment and analysis. This very general idea can be found in Aristotle's description of philosophy as an enquiry into the principles and 'elements', i.e. basic constituents, of being (see *Met.* A.3, 983b6–11; Λ.1, 1069a26; Λ.4, 1070a33–b35; *Phys.* I.1, 184a10–23), which Aristotle inherits from his predecessors. If one thinks of advancement in knowledge in these terms, namely as a sort of ongoing process of discernment or 'division', then one can also regard what remains as unanalysable and indivisible at the end of this process as an inner principle of things, through which they can be known. On this idea cf. I.2, pp. 78–80. Aristotle insists in both I.1 and I.2 that there is no single ultimate one for everything that is and emphasizes that analysis and division proceed along two main trajectories: quantity and quality (on the relevance of this distinction see notes to 1053b4–8). By following these two trajectories we can find out the quantitatively and qualitatively simple constituents of things and, in this sense, we can find out what things are by identifying their basic constituents.

Alongside this general idea on the nature of knowledge and of the principles of knowledge, in I.2 Aristotle seems to endorse the more specific and problematic view that for each kind of objects there are some members of that kind out of which other members of the kind are constituted. For example, he suggests that colours are constituted out of the basic colour-unit (the white) in combination with its opposite (the black). The basic members of the kind are then regarded as the one(s) and the measure(s) of the kind by being epistemic *and* ontological principles of the other members of the kind. It is hard to tell how far Aristotle intends to push this account of the relation between measure and measured in each kind.

Aristotle's reference to the things out of which 'substance' is made and to the process of division of 'substance' at a19–20 can be interpreted in two ways, depending on whether we take 'substance' (*ousia*) to refer to items belonging in the category of substance or, more generally, to being and what things are. The second reading squares better with the generality of the initial claim that the one is a measure of everything, once this claim is understood in the distributive sense. Accordingly, the point could be paraphrased: '[. . .] because we know the things out of which things are by dividing either on the basis of quantity or on the basis of form [. . .]'. However, Aristotle's formulation is ambiguous enough not to exclude the first reading. For more comments on the division of substances into their 'units' see notes to I.2, pp. 85–8.

The interpretation of this passage impacts on the more general issue of the relation between the enquiry into the one in I.1–2 and the enquiry into substance and being (cf. Introduction, part I).

If the passage is about substances, then Aristotle is building a bridge between the enquiry into unity and measure and the enquiry into substance and its principles. If the passage is, more generally, about what things are, then we have a link between the enquiry into unity and measure and the enquiry into being and its principles. As we have seen (pp. xxi–xxiii), the two approaches to first philosophy as an enquiry into substance and its principles or as an enquiry into being and its principles respectively are not incompatible, but carry slightly different implications.

At 1053a20 the two possible trajectories of division are 'either according to quantity or according to *eidos*'. The context, in which substance (*ousia*) is mentioned twice, might support a restricted interpretation of *eidos* in the sense of substantial form. However, it is not obvious that the distinction at stake is anything more specific than the distinction of indivisibility in quantity and indivisibility in 'quality' at 1052b35 and 1053b7, especially if 'substance' does not refer to what falls under the category of substance but, more generally, to what things are. In this sense, indivisibility in quality should be taken broadly speaking as indivisibility with respect to any non-quantitative aspect (and not just, strictly speaking, as indivisibility with respect to some feature falling within the category of quality). What is primary (I take this to mean: in the way in which elements are primary) in a genus is what is indivisible in that genus, and the one is identified with what is primary in this sense.

1053a21–24: Not all units of measurement are indivisible in the same way. Aristotle illustrates the point through examples drawn from different kinds of quantity. The numerical unit which is used to measure numbers is defined as what is indivisible in every respect, but the units that are used to measure the different kinds of continuous quantities are not indivisible in every respect since they are the same kind of object as the things they measure, i.e. continuous quantities (see 1053a24–30). However, they are assumed as indivisible. These units are chosen as indivisible with respect to sense perception (cf. 1053a5–7). Perhaps indivisibility with respect to sense perception is regarded by Aristotle as a sort of indivisibility with respect to quality: in *DA* III.6, 430b7–20 (keeping b14–15 where they are in the manuscripts) the apprehension in thought of the continuous line is described as the apprehension of some sort of qualitative or formal unit, which can, in principle, be divided in quantity.

1053a24–30: The unit of measurement must be of the same kind as the objects it measures: magnitudes (i.e. continuous quantities) are measured by magnitudes of the same kind (lengths by lengths, surfaces by surfaces, articulate sounds by articulate sounds, weights by weights, etc.). However, in spelling out the relation between measure and measured in the case of numbers it is not correct to say that numbers are measured by numbers. Rather, one should say that units are measured by a unit ('for' at a27 explains the last case in the list, *monadōn monas*). This is so because a number is a plurality of units and pluralities of units are ultimately measured by a unit, not by further pluralities of units. Accordingly, 'if one claimed this', i.e. that the measure of numbers is a number, she would not be thinking of the case of numbers and their measure as similar to the others, despite appearances.

1053a31–b3: Aristotle unpacks the kernel of truth of claims such as 'knowledge is the measure of things', 'sense perception is measure', 'the human being is the measure of all things' (the last one being Protagoras's famous motto). All these formulations can be ultimately led back to the idea that a measure is something in virtue of which we come to know something else. Aristotle applies this explanation to the first two claims directly: knowledge and sense perception are something in virtue of which we know something else. The same explanation is indirectly applied to Protagoras's motto. Aristotle specifies that the human being figuring in the motto has to be understood as the subject endowed with knowledge or sense perception. As the subject of knowledge or of perception, the human being is said to be the measure of things precisely in virtue of knowledge or sense perception, i.e. in virtue of the faculties through which he acquires knowledge. On the basis of this analysis, Aristotle underlines that Protagoras's formulation sounds deep and peculiar without saying much more than the more sober formulations about knowledge and sense perception.

Even the more sober formulations, though, should not be taken at face value. The point of Aristotle's remarks here is not fully clear. At 1053a32 *epei* seems concessive rather than causal (for the concessive use of *epei*, see Bonitz, *Index*, *s.v.*; cf. I.10, pp. 241–2 for an occurrence of *epeidē* which has been taken by some interpreters as concessive: 'although'). Aristotle specifies that, even if it is true that knowledge and sense perception are that through which we come to know things (and, in this sense, one could say that they are measures), they are 'measured' rather than measure. This specification suggests that all these claims rest on equivocation. When we say that a measure is that in virtue of which we know things, that in virtue of which we acquire knowledge is itself a piece of knowledge, some object we assume as known. But when we say that science or perception is that in virtue of which we acquire knowledge, that in virtue of which we acquire knowledge is not itself a piece of knowledge, but an epistemic disposition which, when activated, allows us to get to know things. It is not clear whether Aristotle wants to keep these two aspects radically distinct and claim that 'measure' is used equivocally in sentences like 'the one is the measure of numbers' and 'science is the measure of things' or whether he wants to leave room for a derivative and not fully equivocal use of measure with reference to epistemic dispositions.

There are some further problems in spelling out the claim that science and sense perception are measured by things. Such problems are partly due to the difficulties in disentangling the notion of measure as a principle of knowledge and the notion of measure as a principle of being. Knowledge and perception are ontologically determined by their objects and we can only know what knowledge and perception are by understanding what their objects are (cf. *DA* II.4, 415a14–22). Aristotle's claim that we come to know how tall we are (i.e. that we have a certain property) by the application on us of the cubit might be a rather convoluted way of stressing the priority of the objects of knowledge and perception by emphasizing that such objects play an active role in determining that and what we know or perceive. In I.6, 1057a10–11 Aristotle returns to similar considerations after a fuller analysis of the relation between measure and measurable. In that context, too, there will be an issue as to whether a measure is only supposed to be a principle of knowledge or also a principle of being; cf. notes on I.2 p. 79. More generally, the problem is whether there are any reasons to believe that Aristotle would subscribe to the claim that x is a measure of y only if x is the cause of y's being or coming to be in a sense to be specified. If these considerations are relevant to Aristotle's claim in I.1 that knowledge is measured rather than measure, then his point could be that it is the objects of knowledge that determine knowledge rather than the other way out.

1053b4–8: Aristotle summarizes the basic results of the chapter: if we want to define what being one amounts to 'in accordance with the name', then being one is being the one in a certain domain, i.e. being a measure. In the strictest sense, being one is being the measure of numbers and of quantity, whereas in a derivative sense being one is being the measure of some quality. Being the measure of a kind X is a prerogative of what is indivisible in X; therefore, what is indivisible in quantity is a measure of quantity, what is indivisible in quality is a measure of quality. Given this characterization of the one, the one is always what is indivisible, either without qualification (which is the case of the numerical unit) or 'as one', i.e. with respect to a metric system or, more generally, with respect to a certain kind of measurable objects.

Aristotle's insistence on the priority of quantity in the characterization of the one is significant: while in the distinction of the ways of being the basic categorial partition is between substance and non-substantial categories, in the distinction of the ways of being one the basic partition is between quantitative and (broadly speaking) qualitative determinations.

CHAPTER 2

In I.1 Aristotle has explained what kinds of thing can be said to be one in their own right, what features of things make them recognizable as something one, and, more generally, what it is for something to be one. One clear upshot of I.1 is that there is no simple answer to the question what it is for something to be one: being one is being indivisible, but things can be regarded as indivisible in different respects; in some cases, it is just postulated that a certain magnitude is a unit of measurement and is therefore regarded as indivisible with respect to a certain system. However, one could say that there is something whose being consists precisely in being indivisible in all respects: the numerical unit.

The numerical unit is the unit of measurement of number. Things standing to their kind in the same relation as the numerical unit stands to number can be said to be the one, i.e. the measure, in their kind. We have seen (p. 23) that for Aristotle numerical units (and objects of mathematical sciences in general) do not constitute a separate domain of being: rather, a unit is just any object considered precisely and only with respect to its indivisibility. However, such claims cannot be extrapolated from I.1. I.1 as such is silent as to the kind of thing that a numerical unit is and does not fully spell out the features of the relation between measure and measured which are supposed to be instantiated in other kinds. Are numerical units self-subsisting beings? If not, how are they supposed to be thought of? More generally, what kind(s) of object can be regarded as measures of their respective kind? I.2 provides some partial answers to these questions by setting them within a broader framework: is there any self-subsistent being whose essence just consists in being one? Otherwise put: is there a substance whose being just consists in being one?

In addressing the latter question, Aristotle explicitly returns to one of the difficulties raised in book Beta (*Met.* B.1, 996a4–9; 4, 1001a4–b25; about the eleventh aporia see Bell 2000; Cavini 2009). The first part of I.2 (1053b9–16) is devoted to a summary of the two main theoretical options outlined there. In I.2 Aristotle does not take over all the points raised in the expanded formulation of the difficulty in B.4, but focuses on the denial of the twin Pythagorean/Platonic claims that one and number are substances, and that one and number are the substances of other beings (see, in particular, *Met.* A.5, 987a15–26 for the Pythagoreans and *Met.* A.6, 987b18–25 for Plato; cf. *Met.* A.8, 990a18–32). There are some structural correspondences between the difficulties raised by the denial of the Pythagorean/Platonic claim that the one is a substance in B.4, 1001a19–29, and the three main parts in which the bulk of I.2 can be divided. In B.4 Aristotle argues that (i) if one and being are not substances, no other universal will be (a) substance (1001a19–24); that (ii) if the one is not (a) substance, number(s) will not be substance(s) either (1001a24–27); that (iii) if there is anything that is one and being in itself, one and being will have to be its substance (1001a27–29). I.2 can be divided into three parts: (i) 1053b16–24, about the view that universals are not

65

substances; (ii) 1053b24–1054a13, about the claim that neither the one nor numbers are the substance of anything; (iii) 1054a13–19, on the sense in which 'one' and 'being' in a way signify the same. I shall return to the nature and limits of the correspondences between B.4 and I.2 at the end of the commentary on this chapter, but let me anticipate that I take I.2 to revolve around the three main difficulties raised in B.4.

I have mentioned that in addressing the aporia on the nature of the one in I.2 Aristotle focuses on a pair of Pythagorean/Platonic claims: the claim that the one (and, correspondingly, number) is substance and the claim that the one (and, correspondingly, number) is the substance or true nature of other beings (for the correspondences between theses concerning numbers and theses concerning the one cf. *Met.* M.6, 1080b4–9). The relation between these two claims is not obvious and deserves some attention. As for the Pythagoreans, Aristotle outlines an argument which may hint at how they might be interrelated. The argument seems to rest on two distinctively Pythagorean assumptions: first, numbers enjoy ontological and causal priority over other things that are; secondly, there are correspondences between sensible beings and their properties on the one hand and numbers and their properties on the other hand (for both assumptions see *Met.* A.5, 985b26–986a6). Once these two assumptions are in place, the argument unfolds as follows: if there is a set of objects sharing a property P and a number n to which P primarily belongs, P will be said to be the substance of n and being P will be regarded as the same as being n. Accordingly, for any object x that is P, n will be regarded as x's substance. Aristotle illustrates this reasoning with an example in which P is being double and n is two: being double is a property of many things, but it belongs primarily to number two. From this the Pythagoreans infer (according to Aristotle) that being double is the same as being two and that two is the essence of all things that are double. In this way number two turns out to be not only a substance but also the substance of other things (*Met.* A.5, 987a22–27; cf. 987a13–19). A similar argument can be used to claim that the one is the substance of all things that are one. Although Aristotle regards this way of thinking as too simplistic, he praises this approach as a first rudimentary attempt at thinking in terms formal causes (*Met.* A.5, 987a22–28; cf. Z.11, 1036b7–20).

Alongside this way of thinking of one and number as formal causes of things, Aristotle uncovers the application of a different conceptual framework in the Pythagorean approach, according to which units and numbers are constitutive elements, and, in this sense, the material cause, of things. For instance, in *Met.* A.5, 986a15–17 numbers are assumed as principles both as matter and as affections of other beings; in *Met.* B.3, 998b9–11 some people, claiming that one, being, the great and the small are elements (i.e. constitutive principles), actually use them as genera (i.e. as universal formal features of things), but nothing can be a principle in both ways. Finally, in *Met.* M.8, 1084b4–32 the two ways of thinking of the one as a material constitutive element and as a formal principle are led back to two different ways of carrying out the enquiry into the one. By treating the one in a mathematical way, people have come to regard it as a unit and as a constitutive element or matter of numbers; by looking at the one from the perspective of the enquiry into the universals, the one turns out to be something that is predicated of something else and a sort of formal determination.

Given that the positions Aristotle criticizes do not distinguish these two types of enquiry, it is not particularly surprising that the arguments in I.2 target different aspects of this rather complex picture without explicitly flagging any switch of focus. This consideration is important to account for some peculiarities of I.2, which moves back and forth between the reasons why the one and number cannot be substance or the substance of other beings and the sense in which the one can be regarded as a sort of constitutive principle of other beings in the same kind.

1053b9–16: The enquiry concerning how things are 'with respect to substance and nature' unfolds with reference to the corresponding aporia in book Beta (see pp. 65–6). The problem is that of establishing whether the nature of the thing which is called 'the one' consists simply in being one or whether 'the one' is a name for an object characterized by a different nature, which does not consist in being one. There are two main options. On the one hand, the Pythagorean/Platonic claim is that there is some substance, i.e. some determinate self-subsisting being, whose being amounts to being one; this can be said to be the one itself. On the other hand, what the philosophers of nature call 'the one' is always some determinate being, with its own specific nature (e.g. being love or air or infinite). In B.4 Aristotle adds some information on why some beings within the different philosophical systems of the philosophers of nature come to be singled out as 'the one': in Empedocles's philosophy, Love is the primary cause of unity (*Met.* B.4, 1001a14–15); those who admit a unified principle out of which everything else is and comes to be (cf. *Met.* A.3, 984a27–b1; A.8, 988b22–23; Λ.2, 1069b20–23; *Phys.* I.4, 187a12–23) regard that unique and homogeneous principle as the one, e.g. air for Anaximenes (*Met.* A.3, 984a5), the infinite (*apeiron*) for Anaximander (*Phys.* I.4, 187a20–22; *Met.* Λ.2, 1069b22).

Although the intuitions behind the Pythagorean/Platonic position and the naturalistic position differ considerably (cf. I.1, p. 45), they share the basic tenet that whatever is picked out as the one is a principle of things that are, i.e. something which enjoys some form of ontological and explanatory priority with respect to all other beings (cf. *Met.* B.4, 1001a18–19). As has already emerged from I.1 and as I.2 will further emphasize, Aristotle intends to drop the assumption of a unified principle of unity for all things. Furthermore, although I.1 makes it clear that both positions attract criticism, Aristotle appears to be more sympathetic to the approach of the philosophers of nature than to that of the other party. This becomes evident in I.2, where he almost exclusively engages with the position he intends to deny more strongly, i.e. the Pythagorean/Platonic view that the one and numbers are substances and substances of beings.

See Notes on the Text about 1053b14.

1053b16–24:   In this section Aristotle relies on already established results to argue **(a)** that the one is not a substance (1053b20) and **(b)** that the one is not a genus (1053b22–23).

The argument in support of (a) can be reconstructed in two ways, depending on what one takes 'this very thing' at b18 to refer to: it can either refer to the universal (b16) or to being (b17). It seems to me that the second option makes better sense and makes the argumentative step at b19 (from the case of being to the case of the one) smoother (see below). It has the disadvantage that, in this case, 'being' would be picked out from the back reference to the topic (if not the title) of some other works at b16–17, which I translate: 'just as we said in the discourses about substance and being'. The Greek text is compatible with a different translation: 'just as we said about being, too, in the discourses about substance'. The latter translation yields the right sense (see below) but seems unlikely on syntactical grounds: the two nouns, 'substance' and 'being', are introduced by means of two syntactically identical phrases (*peri* followed by the genitive, 'about' or 'concerning' the object expressed in the genitive) joined by the copulative conjunction 'and' ('about substance and about being'). Either way, there might be a further difficulty at b18, where I translate Ross's text: 'nor can this very thing [. . .]'. Jaeger points out that the negative conjunction *oude* ('nor') cannot be the continuation of the hypothetical starting at b16, presumably because the correct coordinate negation would be *mēde* ('nor'). In order to obviate to this grammatical difficulty, Jaeger follows Bywater and inserts the conjunction *hoti* ('that') before *oude*. In this way the negative clause introduced by *oude* would be part of an objective subordinate spelling out the relevant contents of the discourses about substance and being. This would yield the translation: 'just as we said in the discourses about substance and being that it is not possible that this very thing (*scil.* being) be substance as something one, etc.'. Although Jaeger is right in pointing out the syntactic irregularity, it is not clear whether and how one should intervene in the text. Besides, the overall point of the argument does not change.

Be this as it may, if we take 'this very thing' to be being, the argument in support of (a) rests on three assumptions: (1) that it is not possible that any universal be a substance, (2) that being is something universal, and (3) that one and being behave similarly, in that they are both the most universal predicates of all. From (1) and (2) one can show that being is not a substance, which, in conjunction with (3), delivers the wanted conclusion that the one is not a substance. If, on the other hand, we take 'this very thing' to refer to any universal, then the argument would mainly rest on (1). One disadvantage of the latter reading is that the similarity between one and being stressed in the remark at b20–21 ('for one and being are predicated most universally of all things') would not explain anything that has been said before and its argumentative function would be less transparent.

As for (1), the general claim that universals are not substances is mainly argued for in *Met.* Z.13. Z.13 takes over one thread of the enquiry into substance introduced in Z.3, 1028b33–36, where Aristotle distinguishes four possibilities as to what kind of thing can be substance: essence, universal, genus, and substratum. Z.13, 1038b1–8 sets off to show that none of the things said universally can be substance. This result is then explicitly applied to universals such as one and being in Z.16, 1040b16–27. The back reference to the discourses about substance and being is presumably to these chapters.

Aristotle's arguments in support of the view that universals are not substances are complicated and often puzzling, but the general strategy is to show that universals fail to meet more or less uncontroversial criteria for being (a) substance (on such criteria see *Met.* Z.3, 1028b36–37 and 1029a27–28). In particular, substances are supposed to be subjects of predication, rather than predicates. But universals, being general properties, only exist in that they are features of (and, in this sense, predicated of) particulars (cf. *Met.* Z.13, 1038b15–16). Furthermore, being a substance is being a certain determinate thing (a 'this something'), whereas universals rather seem to indicate general quality-like features of things (cf. *Met.* Z.13, 1038b34–1039a2). Such common features cannot exist, according to Aristotle, independently of the particular subjects to which they belong—or, as Aristotle puts it, they cannot be 'separated' from their particular subjects. But separability and some form of ontological independence and priority is a basic feature of substances (cf. *Met.* Z.16, 1040b26–30). Aristotle infers that being, like any other universal, is not a separate unified entity over and above things that are (1053b18–19).

It is difficult to make full sense of the clause at 1053b19–20. Aristotle distinguishes between univocal general terms and non-univocal ones. A predicate is univocal if the property which it ascribes to the different subjects of which it is predicated always has the same definition. For instance, 'red' is a general term and what it is to be red is the same for all red things. All terms for genera ('animal', 'plant', 'colour', etc.) are of this kind. By way of contrast, 'healthy' is a general term, but what it is to be healthy differs for different subjects: for instance, a healthy diet is a diet which helps to preserve or to reestablish health, whereas a healthy complexion is a complexion which can be taken as a sign of good health. Similarly in other cases. This shows that there are differ-ent, even if not completely unrelated, senses of what it is for something to be healthy. These two cases contrast with merely equivocal general terms (e.g. 'bank'), which are used to indicate completely unrelated things. In the latter case, the use of one and the same term to signify completely unrelated things is just a matter of chance and does not point at any more basic fact about those things. 'Being', according to Aristotle, belongs to the second group. Any item which is said to be a being has being predicated of it either because it is a substance or because it is a quality or a quantity or a disposition or, more generally, a property of a substance; however, there is no general unified property picked out by the general term 'being'. This feature of being is spelled out in *Met.* Γ.2, 1003a33–b19, and extends to all predicates ranging, like being, over the whole domain of things that are; in particular, it applies to the predicate 'one'. What we say exactly when we say of something x that it is one or that it is (or that it is a being) depends on what x is, and there is no unique account of what it is to be one or what it is to be a being. In *Met.* Δ.6, 1016b6–11 Aristotle's formulation of the relation between the different ways in which different kinds of thing are one is clearly reminiscent of the corresponding point about being in Γ.2, 1003a33–b19 (cf. Introduction, pp. xvi–xx). No similar formula-tion can be found in I.1 (or I.2), but this might be due to the fact that in I.1 Aristotle intends to restrict the focus to the four principal ways in which things are said to be one and, as we saw, there are reasons to think that those four principal ways are primarily ways of being one for substances.

The distinction between univocal and non-univocal terms might be a point Aristotle has in mind at 1053b18–20. The most literal translation of these lines is the following: 'If in truth it is not possible that any of the universals be a substance [. . .], nor is it possible that this very thing be a substance as something one over and above the many, for it is common, *unless only something predicated* (*all' ē katēgorēma monon*)'. This translation reflects the problematic syntactical structure of the Greek and provides the most natural reading of the (usually) concessive expression *all' ē* as 'unless'. It is not clear what the phrase 'unless only something predicated' is supposed to qualify. If this is a conces-sive clause, the idea that being is only a predicate is supposed to introduce an exception to something that has been said before, but it is not clear to what. The reading suggested by the punctuation adopted by modern editors, putting 'for it is common' into brackets, is that being cannot be a substance as something one over and above the many, unless it is only something predicated. But this does not make much sense, given that Aristotle seems to treat the view that something is a substance and the view that something is just something predicated as opposite. A different option is to take b18–20 as saying that the only way in which one could say that being is something one over and above the many is by saying that being is one general predicate-word (i.e. to which no single general property corresponds), and not a substance. On the idea that the ascription of one predicate to a plurality of different subjects may occasion the thought that the universal predicate is something separate, over and above the many particulars of which it is predicated, cf. *Met.* B.3, 999a19–21. Note that, independently of whether one wants to unpack the remark at b19–20 in this way, the non-univocal nature of one and being is referred to at 1053b22–28. Perhaps we should take the problematic clause at b19–20 as a sort of gloss to the remark that being is something common based on the considerations about the non-univocal nature of being. The sentence could then be paraphrased as follows: 'we have said that being cannot be a separate substance since it is common—if it is something common at all and not rather a general term to which no common property corresponds'. The translation I give reflects this interpretation of the text. For a similar point cf. *Met.* Γ.2, 1005a8–11.

The argument for (b) comes at 1053b21–24, where Aristotle draws two conclusions: first, (b21–22) genera are not determinate natures and substances separate from other things; secondly, (b22–24) the one cannot be a genus (= (b) above).

The first conclusion can be regarded as a consequence of the claim that no universal can be a substance, together with the uncontroversial assumption that genera are universals. Genera are universals that are univocal and are predicated in the essence of their subjects (cf. *Met.* Δ.28, 1024b4–6; *Top.* I.5, 102a31–36). In *Met.* Z we do not find any specific arguments in support of the claim that genera are not substances, but this seems to follow from Aristotle's arguments about universals, despite the introduction of genera as a distinct candidate for the role of substance in *Met.* Z.3, 1028b35 (cf. *Met.* H.1, 1042a21–22).

As for claim (b), that the one is not a genus, Aristotle has at least two arguments in store: one argument is based on the universal extension of the predicate 'one', the other on its homonymy. Neither of them is explicitly mentioned in I.2. Both arguments raise some issues in their application to the case of substance, which is mentioned alongside being in the text.

The argument based on the universal extension of one and being is given in *Met.* B.3, 998b22–28 (cf. *Top.* VI.6, 144a28–b3; for some ontological reasons not to take one and being as genera, cf. *Met.* H.6, 1045b2–6). The genus cannot be predicated of its differentiae (on the relation between genus and differentiae see introduction to I.7, pp. 173–7). But one and being can be predicated of everything. If they were genera, their differences should not be one or beings; but this is impossible, given that everything is one and a being (for some discussion of the logic of the argument see Loux 1973; Lowe 1977; Wein 1983; Berti 2003). This argument specifically concerns predicates ranging over all beings and it is difficult to see whether and how it is also meant to apply to substance understood as the category of substance, given that, by definition, no category ranges over all beings. Certainly one can find philosophical texts in which *ousia* ('substance') is used as a synonymous of *on* ('being'), but it is not obvious that Aristotle would avail himself of this usage next to *to on* (cf. *Met.* Z.1, 1028b2–7). A different option consists in taking *ousia* in the sense of 'what-it-is' (*ti esti*) (cf. the formulation at 1054a15 and a18). One could ask what something is with respect to any being and, in this sense, one could come up with the (wrong) idea that there is something that all beings are. This is clearly not Aristotle's view: in fact, one way to explain the origin of the distinction of the categories is to ask one single question—what is it?—of things. Aristotle's view is that there are ten distinct and irreducible types of answer to that question, i.e. ten distinct and irreducible kinds of things. On this as a possible explanation of the origin of the categories and on an alternative to it see Ackrill 1963, pp. 78–9.

The argument based on homonymy might apply to substance in a more straightforward way, provided that one identifies what are the different ways of being a substance which make of substance a universal that is not a genus. On more than one occasion (see, for instance, *Met.* Δ.8, 1017b10 ff. and Z.3, 1028b33–34) Aristotle suggests that substance is said in many ways and he is certainly willing to make room for differentiation (different kinds of thing are said to be substance: cf. *Met.* Z.2, 1028b8 ff.), revision (some of the things such as parts of living beings, which are commonly regarded as substances, are substances only in potentiality: cf. Z.16, 1040b5–16), and a plurality of complementary criteria for substantiality (being an ultimate subject of predication, being something determinate and separable: cf. *Met.* Z.3, 1028b36–37 and 1029a27–28). However, it is at least not obvious that these specifications are meant to introduce some radical ambiguity threatening the status of genus of the category of substance.

The view that substance is not a genus is explored in Berti 1975. Berti takes the passage in I.2 in conjunction with the argument in I.10 to show that the different kinds of substance (imperishable and perishable) cannot be unified under one genus. As for I.10 see the corresponding notes. With respect to the claim in I.2, Berti 2005 suggests that the passage at issue is ambiguous and can be taken in either of two senses: 'nor can the one be a genus for precisely the same reasons why neither being nor substance can' or 'nor can the one be a genus for the same reasons why being cannot, nor can it be substance'. The latter reading would eliminate the problem of explaining in what sense substance is not a genus. However, I am not sure the latter reading is an option (I suppose that to get that sense out of the text we should have *oute* at b24, coordinate with b22, and we should have *ousian* without the article). If we were to speculate, we could also think that *oude ten ousian* is a mistake (possibly deriving from the joined mention of being and substance at 1053b17–18); but the manuscript tradition seems to be unanimous here. In any case, the sense in which (b) could follow from what precedes is not obvious. If the reference to substance were eliminated, the claim that one and being are the most universal predicates which are said of all things could provide the reason why neither one nor being can be regarded as genera.

One further issue is how claim (b), that the one is not a genus, relates to claim (a), that the one, being a universal, cannot be a separate substance. I can only see two (perhaps compatible) options. The first option is that (b) blocks a possible countermove against (a), in that (a) would still leave room for the possibility that the one, while not being a separate substance, is nonetheless the substance of other beings. In *Top.* IV.2, 122b12–17 the genus of x is described as the predicate belonging in the definition of x which most of all expresses the substance of x, while the differences add qualitative determinations. The idea would then be that, even if the one is not a separate substance, it could still be the case that the one is a genus of things and that it therefore expresses what such things are. If the one were the genus of something x, being x would consist in being one in such and such a way or in being a one of such and such a sort (in the same way in which, if animal is the genus of human being, being a human being consists in being an animal of such and such a sort). Note that Aristotle himself seems to admit the possibility that the forms of composite substances, while not enjoying independent existence separated from the compounds, are substances by being the substance of the compound. b22–24 could be meant to prevent such a move: not only one and being are not substances, but they cannot even figure in the definition of substances (or of whatever other beings) as genera. In addition, Aristotle provides an explicit argument (b24: 'Furthermore') establishing precisely the further point that being one is not the substance of anything (see 1054a10–11: '[. . .] this very same thing, i.e. the one, is not the nature of anything'). One consequence of this is that, in enquiring into what the one is, we cannot lead the enquiry thinking that being one is the nature and essence of the thing which is in each case said to be the one: the one in each case is a determinate kind of being, whose essence does not consist in being one.

The second option is that the one's failure to be a genus would prevent the application of the procedure of *ekthesis* ('exposure' or 'setting out' of a particular instance) to the one. In geometrical proofs *ekthesis* is the step in which a particular instance of some geometrical object is produced. For example, if the geometer intends to show something about triangles, she can start the proof by drawing an arbitrary triangle ABC which she will use to unfold the proof. Aristotle resorts to this term in his logical writings (see Einarson 1936, pp. 161–2) and in discussing the arguments used in support of the introduction of a Form as one particular alongside the many particulars participating in it (cf. *Met.* A.9, 992b10; Z.6, 1031b21; M.9, 1086b10; N.3, 1090a17; see comments by Ross 1924, II pp. 208–9). In his commentary to *Met.* A.9, 992b9 ff. Alexander (Hayduck, 124. 9 ff.) provides a reconstruction of such arguments. Those who propose such arguments start by 'setting out' particular human beings and establish that there is a similarity among them insofar as they are all human beings. Once this has been established, they 'lead back' all human being to the one and the same thing that they have in common and call such a thing 'the human being itself' (*autoanthrōpos*). They do the same by 'setting out' particular dogs or particular horses and so on. Following the same procedure they 'set out' particulars falling under more and more general universals (particular animals, particular substances, etc.), until they set out particulars which are similar only in that they are all something that is. This similarity is explained, as in all other cases, by the participation of all things that are in one and the same thing, i.e. being itself. Alexander's reconstruction of the argument suggests (see e.g. 124. 16–17; 125. 6–9) that what is 'set out' are the particulars, whereas in *Met.* M.9 and N.3 what is 'set out' is the universal form. Be this as it may, this discrepancy does not affect the gist of the argument in I.2. The idea that the procedure can be applied only with respect to genera or univocal universals (e.g. 'human being', 'animal', etc.) and that the one fails to be one of them and, therefore, is not the kind of universal to which a separate substance corresponds is suggested in *Met.* A.9, 992b9–13. The passage is extremely concise, but it seems to suggest that the procedure of *ekthesis* cannot be applied to general predicates which are not genera; and non-univocal predicates such as 'one' or 'being' are not genera (cf. Alex., Hayduck, 126. 25–37). If this is the gist of the argument, then it is clear how (b) relates to (a): (b) can be used to block the Platonic procedure leading to the introduction of Forms as separate substances and, therefore, to block the introduction of the one as a separate substance.

1053b24–1054a9: The text can be divided into three sections: the first (1053b24–28) gives the outline of an argument leading to a conclusion about the way in which the enquiry into the one should be approached; the second (1053b28–1054a4) illustrates through examples taken from different domains of beings in what way the one and number should be understood in each case; the third (1054a4–9) generalizes the procedure displayed in the analysis of the examples and extends it to the domain of substances. 1054a9–13 syntactically belong together with the last lines of the chapter (1054a13–19), but sum up the achievements of 1053b24–1054a9.

1053b24–28:   This section sketches an argument in support of the general claim that, in enquiring into what the one is, we should not assume that being one is the nature and essence of the thing which is picked out as the one. This is established on the basis of two further claims: **(c)** something similar holds in all cases (1053b24; 1054a9); **(d)** the one is said in as many ways as being. (d) hints at what the relevant cases for the generalization in (c) are: like being, the one ranges over all categories (see below). Although Aristotle uses examples of different categories, his argument does not seem to require categorical difference. For different genera within a category seem to be enough to establish the point: if one manages to show that, in some kind, the one is something with a determinate nature which belongs to that kind, in virtue of (c) it will be possible to conclude that this must be the case in all genera. Examples of the relevant cases will be given and discussed at 1053b28–1054a4. The analysis of such cases will then be applied to the case of substances and this step will be legitimated by appealing to (c): as in all other cases, if there is a substance which plays the role of the one within the category of substance, its essence will not consist in being one (1054a8–9; 12–13). More generally, being one will not be the essence of any substance.

(c) is a very general claim and it is not immediately clear what the relevant cases for the application of this principle of similarity are. As already mentioned, its proximity to (d) with reference to the number of ways in which one and being are said, the recurrence of 'similarly' (*homoiōs*) in introducing different genera of being (1053b26, 34, 54a1) and the explicit extension of the same reasoning 'to other genera' (1054a4–5) suggests that the relevant cases are given by domains of objects of a certain kind, with respect to which it is possible to identify a unit of measurement (the corresponding one). The identification of such a unit will allow us to establish the number of objects in that domain (in a sense to be specified). I.2 resorts to examples of domains of being clearly described in terms of a common essential trait (colours, sounds, affections, etc.). This is in line with Aristotle's general tenet that measure and measured have to belong to the same kind.

Furthermore, the use of such examples might suggest that the domains of objects with respect to which the one can be determined are natural kinds. Whether this is the case or not can only be established once the analysis of the examples has clarified how and in what sense the model of units and numbers can be applied to other cases. I shall return to this point in the analysis of the examples.

As for (d), although there are passages suggesting that for any way in which being is said (incidental; per se according to the categories, per se according to potentiality and actuality, and per se according to truth; see *Met.* Δ.7) there is a corresponding sense of being one (see notes on 1054a14–16), the only relevant distinction in the following argument is that according to the categories and, more generally, to kinds of being. Note that neither in Δ.6 nor in I.1 the ways in which the one is said correspond to the ways in which being is said according to the categories in any straightforward sense (but see pp. 88–9 about the similarities between ways of being and ways of being one).

1053b28–1054a4: Aristotle illustrates through a series of examples how one and number are to be identified in different domains. From the recurrent references to one and number (1053b33, b35, 36, 1054a2, 3, 6) it is quite clear that the aspects of similarity between the different cases have to do with the identification and nature of measure and measured in the different cases. Since a measure is relative to what is measured by it, the question 'what is the one' for a given domain cannot be answered in general without taking into account the kind of thing for which the one will be a unit of measurement (correspondingly, what is measured in a given domain is, in some sense to be specified, a plurality of units of that domain). This general point has already been emphasized in I.1: the measure always belongs to the same genus as the measured. Accordingly, the measure for colours will be some sort of colour (the white: 1053b29), for musical intervals some sort of musical interval (the *diesis*, i.e. the smallest musical interval: 1053b36–1054a1), for articulate sounds some sort of articulate sound (presumably: some phonetic element which counts as the simplest articulate sound: 1054a2), and for rectilinear figures some sort of rectilinear figure (the triangle, i.e. the simplest rectilinear figure: 1054a4).

Aristotle's analysis of the examples swings between two quite different models of analysis. The first and relatively natural model consists in claiming that one counts Ks by taking a K as a unit. For example, in order to count colours we have to establish what counts as one colour; in order to count lengths we have to establish what counts as one length; in order to count articulate sounds we have to establish what counts as one articulate sound. This analysis need not be restricted to natural kinds: K can be any countable noun. Aristotle seems to be aware of this (cf. *Met.* M.7, 1082b16–19), even though he voices some reservations on the choice of the appropriate sortal (*Met.* N.1, 1087b33–1088a14). Note that on this reading of what it takes to be a unit of measure, any being can be regarded as a unit and being one in the sense of being a unit of measure will be co-extensive with being something that is, provided that an adequate sortal is given.

However, this model is far from being exhaustive of what Aristotle seems to be doing in I.2. For the analysis of the examples in I.2 suggests that he is not merely interested in the basic idea that, in order to count objects of kind K, we have to fix a unit of measurement by determining what counts as one K. Rather (and this is the second model) Aristotle brings in a series of assumptions concerning what it is for something to be a measure for something else. In particular, the measure of a kind K turns out to be some basic sort of K (the one for K) such that the ascription of a number to other items belonging to K has something to do with the ontological analysis of those items into K-units. The basic idea is that for each kind K there is some K which works as a constitutive principle of the other Ks and into which other Ks can be analysed, whereas the one in K is not analysable into further constituents which in turn belong to K. By being the basic constituent of Ks, K-units turn out to be both ontological principles and principles of knowledge of K. This account of the relation between the one in K and other items in K is modelled after the relation obtaining between the unit and numbers: the unit is the measure of number and units are the basic ontological constituent of numbers. If this is the model Aristotle intends to apply, then the constraints on the domains that are suitable for such an analysis are stronger. The attempt at finding an element which is a constitutive principle of the others in a collection of random objects is simply misguided. This suggests that in order to apply the second model of analysis some restriction to natural kinds would be necessary.

Halper 2007 labels I.2's approach to the relation between one privileged species of a genus which is a principle for the other species of the same genus 'paradigmatism' and discusses some examples from Aristotle's political and biological writings showing structural resemblances with the analysis in I.2. The problems with the idea that some species is a principle of other species of the same genus will become apparent in the analysis of the examples below and at 1054a4–9. More generally, the application of the second model is far from being straightforward in at least two ways: first, it is not clear how the relevant unit of measurement is chosen in the different cases; secondly, it is not obvious that there is a clear structural analogy in the relation obtaining between the measure and the measured in the different examples Aristotle considers. In order to see why this is so, we can turn to the examples. I shall start from what I take to be the least puzzling one and then tackle the most controversial ones.

I.1 has already introduced the idea that *quantities* of kind K can only be measured by a unit which is some K: lengths are measured by some length, weights by some weight, and so on. The application of this idea to the case of musical intervals (1053b34–1054a1) is relatively straightforward as long as one adopts the empiricist approach (see notes to I.1, 1053a14–18). If one adopts a 'linear' conception of pitches as points along a line, one can think of larger musical intervals as measured by some musical interval which is assumed as the smallest. In particular, according to the empiricist approach, the smallest musical interval is the smallest interval perceptible to human ear. Being the one for musical intervals does not simply consist in being one: the one in musical intervals is something of a specific sort, i.e. a certain musical interval. If, on the other hand, one adopts the mathematical approach interpreting musical intervals not as gaps between pitches but as ratios, it is not obvious whether and how the idea of measuring larger intervals through smaller and indivisible ones could be implemented. The only option I can envisage is that of taking *dieseis* as small intervals into which other small enough intervals can be analysed, but this would be a significantly restricted and deflated reading of the relation between measure and measured: restricted only to the analysis of those intervals that are small enough to be divided into *dieseis*, and deflated in that the measures would be nothing more than (unequal) parts. Note, however, that, despite its difficulties, the mathematical (rather than the empirical) approach to musical intervals and the corresponding analysis of concords provides the model for the application of numbers (in a sense to be specified) to qualitative domains such as colours, flavours, and odours (see below and notes on I.7, pp. 182–4).

Following the empirical approach to musical intervals, both the idea that a certain quantity of kind K measures other quantities of kind K and the idea that units of measurement are constitutive of other quantities of the same kind make some sense. By using the semitone as a unit of measure, we can measure other musical intervals: we can say by how many semitones each interval is constituted and ascribe it a number. Note that 1053b35 makes it plain that, if beings were musical intervals, which would be constituted by semitones, beings could also be said to be a number: a number of semitones. This is important because it points out a rather specific sense in which Aristotle is talking of the number of a certain domain of being: the point is not so much that of counting the members of that domain of being, but that of assigning them a number corresponding to the number of units that constitute them. Accordingly, in the course of the analysis of the examples, the issue Aristotle raises concerning the number of Ks (where K is the kind of being at stake in each example: colour, musical interval, vocal sound, etc.) is not the issue of how many Ks there are, but, rather, that of identifying each K with a certain number of K-units. But number as such (i.e. the number considered in abstraction from the semitones it is a number of) does not express what each interval is: in other words, number as such is not the substance of any musical interval.

What makes the case of musical intervals interpreted in this way (as the case of lengths, weights, and quantities in general) relevantly similar to the case of number is that there is an intuitive sense in which more complex or greater items of a kind can be divided into simpler or smaller items of the same kind, which can be regarded as constituents of the former. As we move through the other examples, though, analogies with the paradigmatic case of units and numbers become harder to draw. Let us consider the example of rectilinear figures (1054a3–4). If we apply to this case the idea outlined above, then in order to ascribe a number to rectilinear figures we have to choose the simplest and indivisible rectilinear figure in terms of which the others can be analysed. Such a figure is the triangle. Note that in this case it is plain that Aristotle cannot be explaining how we can count geometrical figures by establishing what counts as one geometrical figure. Furthermore, the case of geometrical figures is unlike the case of musical intervals in that the point does not seem to be that there is some minimal geometrical figure of given area which works as a unit of measurement for areas of other rectilinear figures, whereas a semitone was a musical interval of given extension. The idea that there are atomic triangles which are the basic constituents of more complex geometrical figures (and, eventually, of everything that has an extension) can be found in Plat., *Tim.* 53b–55c. Aristotle criticizes this view in *GC* I.2, 316a12 and *DC* III.1, 298b33–300a19. In his notes on *GC* I.2, Rashed (2005, pp. 101–2) stresses Plato's failure to distinguish between material atomic constituents and items that are irresoluble into conceptually simpler parts. If Aristotle sees the difference (as his criticism of Plato's views suggests), perhaps his point in I.2 could be that there is no simpler rectilinear figure than the triangle and that for each rectilinear figure there will be a smallest number of triangles it can be analysed into. If so, there will not be one triangle of a given area or of a given kind that measures all figures, but for each figure there will be a smallest number of triangles which is its number (I owe this last point to Lindsay Judson). Note that the fact that there are three kinds of triangle (equilateral, isosceles, and scalene) does not affect the claim that there is one figure, i.e. the triangle, which measures all other figures: Aristotle accepts the claim that the three kinds of triangle are the same kind of figure, i.e. triangles (*Met.* Δ.6, 1016a29–32).

The case of articulate sounds is puzzling in several respects. Again, the point of the example seems to be that of identifying some phonetic element in terms of which articulate sounds can be analysed (for similar ideas cf. Plat., *Phlb* 17b3 ff.; *Leg.* 701a1; *Crat.* 424c; *Soph.* 253a4). The example distinguishes between two levels of analysis: articulate sounds (whatever they are: see below) can be regarded as numbers of vocal elements; furthermore, the one for vocal elements is a vocal element which is 'sounding', *phonēen. phonēen* is commonly used in the sense of 'vowel'.

However, it is hard to make sense of how the vowel (or a vowel) would be a unit of measurement of articulate sounds: for even if one takes articulate sounds as compounds of vocal elements (possibly: as syllables and words), it is not clear why vowels alone would be the unit of measurement of articulate sounds. One possibility is that *phonēen* is here not used in the sense of vowel, but in the more general sense of 'sounding' (cf. I.1, 1053a17, on the 'vocal sounds (*phōnai*) we use to measure', and corresponding notes). If so, the point at 1054a2 would simply be that the unit of measurement in vocal elements is the minimal unit that has a sound. The remark then falls under the general claim that the one within the domain of articulate sounds is not simply one, but is some sound (cf. I.1, 1053a13–14). In the case of articulate sounds there is no single unit of measurement, given that vocal elements (presumably: simple vocal sounds) are more than one (cf. I.1, 1053a13–17 and notes).

As for the case of colours, I translate *leukon* with 'white' and *melan* with 'black'. This translation is not uncontroversial in that it is well known that colour words in Greek indicate different degrees of saturation as well as different hues; the reader should keep this in mind all along. Accordingly, one could translate 'light' or 'pale' and 'dark' instead of 'white' and 'black'. I opt for 'white' and 'black' in this context since this avoids ambiguity at 1053b30–32, where both the colours *leukon* and *melan* and light (*phōs*) and darkness (*skotos*) are mentioned together. More generally, I translate 'white' and 'black' whenever Aristotle speaks about species of the genus colour, whereas I use 'pale' and 'dark' in contexts where this translation is not ambiguous and makes better sense of the text (e.g. in I.9–I.10, where one and the same human being can turn from pale to dark). For further comments on the analysis of colours see notes to I.7, pp. 183–4, 194–6.

Aristotle does not only single out one specific colour (white) as the one within the domain of colours, but he also comments on the constitutive role that it plays, together with its privation (black) in the ontological constitution of other colours. Furthermore, the claim that, if beings were colours, they would be a certain number and, in particular, they would be a number of colours, is presented as following from the claims concerning the white as the one and as a constituent of colours. Explicit reference to the role of the one and its privation in the constitution of other objects of the domain is dropped in the analysis of the other examples, and it is hard to tell whether Aristotle means to extend it to other cases. However, I.7 expands on the idea that, if there are two contraries within a genus and there are intermediates between them, then the intermediates are made out of their corresponding contraries (e.g. intermediate colours are made out of white and black).

Aristotle's claim that different hues are ratios of black and white has roots in Parmenides's and Empedocles's philosophy and can count on some empirical basis (Kalderon 2015, pp. 92–108). But even assuming that the general account of colours in terms of ratios of black and white (or dark and light) makes sense, there are two general problems linked to Aristotle's application of this general idea. One problem derives from taking one of the elements in the composition of colours as the privation of the other. A privation is the absence of a certain property in a certain kind of subject (cf. pp. xxxi–xxxii, 129–30). How can the absence of a certain feature in a certain subject contribute to a composition? The second problem is how to explain the quantification of colours that the application of the conceptual framework of unit and numbers seems to import.

Indirect answers to both question can be found in *DS* (see notes to I.7, pp. 194–6). In I.2 the modality of interaction between white and black is left completely unspecified and this has some consequences for the interpretation of the example in I.2. For, as has been noted (Kalderon 2015, pp. 120–4), in *GC* I.10, 327b10–22 Aristotle claims that qualities are not the appropriate subjects for mixture: mixture can only take place between substances. Simplifying, Aristotle's basic idea is that what gets mixed are the bodies which are constituted by fiery stuff in different amounts. The more fiery stuff they contain in proportion to other materials, the brighter they are; the less fiery stuff they contain, the darker they are. According to this account, what is quantified is the bodies entering a mixture. Privation enters the picture only as a feature of those bodies. It is hard to tell whether the same account is at work in I.2—if not, I have no idea how the example is supposed to be spelled out if it is taken seriously. At any rate, the example in I.2 does not seem to refer to features of coloured things in order to explain the point about the relation between colours and their measure—whatever that point is supposed to be.

1054a4–9: For each genus, what counts as the one for that genus belongs to the genus and, as such, it has a determinate nature which does not consist in being simply one. Similarly, when we say that beings belonging to a determinate genus are a certain number we should not think that such things are nothing but numbers, but that they are a number of units of a certain kind, units which are in their turn determinate beings. At 1054a8–9 Aristotle suggests that a similar analysis can be applied to the case of substance, but the point is not spelled out. Menn ((in progress), Iγ2a: Consequences: against the one as an *archē*) takes the point of the remark to be that the analysis spelled out in the former part of the chapter will apply to substance 'only if (at least some relevant kind of) substance are numbers', as many of Aristotle's Pythagorean/Academic opponents think. However, Aristotle's main point is that, even if there were such substances, one and numbers in substances would not be an absolute one or pure numbers: as in the other cases, the one will be some kind of substance and the number will be a number of substances of a certain kind. Menn's account suggests that the extension to the case of substance is not necessarily accommodated within Aristotle's account of substance. It is not clear to me whether the account in I.2 is supposed to find any resonance in Aristotle's theory of substance (see below), but I think Menn is right about the main point of the passage. The emphasis on substance in the conclusion of the argument can be explained by taking into account the general goal of the chapter, i.e. that of denying that the one is a substance or that there is a substance whose being consists simply in being one and nothing else. The former examples have shown that unity and number do not express the essence of anything. In particular, they do not express the essence of any substance. It follows that there is no substance whose nature simply consists in being one. This is the direct negation of the Pythagorean/Platonic claim that there is a substance which is the one and whose being consists in being one and nothing else. Cf. Met. Λ.7, 1072a31–34.

A rather different view is outlined in Halper 2007. According to Halper, I.2 sketches a general view which, while not pursued in the *Metaphysics* (Halper 2007, p. 103: 'For the *Metaphysics*, book I is the path not traveled [. . .]'), may help us understand certain features of other parts of Aristotle's philosophy, such as his biology and political theory (*ibid.* pp. 102–3). According to this general view, which Halper labels 'paradigmatism', there is a species in each genus which is independently intelligible and allows us to know the other species in the genus in that 'features of imperfect species are intelligible in reference to the one species that serves as the qualitative unity of the genus' (*ibid.* p. 82). For example, in Aristotle's biological works the human being 'is the standard against which Aristotle measures other substances' (*ibid.* p. 80). While Halper takes the idea that in each genus there is a species which somehow works as a principle of intelligibility of the other species in the genus, we have seen in the analysis of the examples that the way in which the model of unit and number is spelled out in the single cases suggests more than this. In his comments to Halper's article, Madigan (2007) stresses precisely the difficulty to make sense of the exact way in which the relation between the one in a genus and the other members of the genus is supposed to be understood.

Perhaps the analysis of I.2 is not really supposed to be applied to the case of substance in any detail. But nothing in I.2 rules this out explicitly. For the sake of the argument, we can explore some ideas emerging from the analysis of the other cases. The basic idea is that the identification of the one for a kind and the ascription of a number to other beings of that kind has something to do with the individuation of some member-type of the kind which can be regarded as the simplest member-type of the kind and whose tokens can be regarded as constituents of the other members of the kind. Furthermore, the ontological complexity of the other members of the kind compared to the one can be expressed by saying that they are some number of corresponding units. The precise way in which this general framework is specified varies with the examples. Although no neat distinction is drawn, I.2 makes room for two different models of analysis of complex objects into simpler ones. According to one model, the complex entity (the number) can be straightforwardly analysed into the units that constitute it. This kind of analysis can be described (in Aristotelian terms) as a sort of partition of number into its material parts. This approach links to the Pythagorean understanding of units as constituent parts of objects (cf. introductory notes to I.2, p. 67) and to the understanding of number as a plurality of units (cf. I.1, 1053a27–30; I.6, 1056b20–24; N.1, 1088a5 ff.). According to another model, the complex entity can be analysed into two basic ontological components standing to each other in some relation of opposition. In the example of colours, black or dark, which is the privation of the one in colours (i.e. white or light), operates with the one to bring about other beings in the genus. This model differs from the former one in two important respects: it introduces two opposite components and it introduces the idea that measuring has to do with establishing the correct proportion between the different components. These two aspects (opposite components and ratios) can occur independently from each other. For it is possible to analyse things with reference to opposite principles without saying that those opposite principles are both constituents of complex objects in different ratios (cf. *Met.* A.5, 986a16–21, 987a15–26; 6, 987b18–25 and Plat., *Phlb.* 16c5 ff.). The idea that numbers come to be as the result of the interaction of two opposite principles is both a Pythagorean and a Platonic idea (*Met.* A.5, 986a17–21; M.8, 1085b4–12).

Both approaches are entangled in difficulties in their own right and with reference to the case of substances. According to the first model, we should find one or more kinds of substance (the one for substances) which should turn out to be constituents (i.e. material parts) of other substances. We can distinguish two ideas in this approach. One idea is that composite substances can be analysed into simpler components which are substances in their turn. The second idea is that the material components out of which composite substances are made are substances in the same way in which composite substances are. Aristotle endorses the view that no non-substance can be a principle of substances (cf. N.1, 1088b2–4). Accordingly, if there are constituents of substances which are their principles, they must be substances too. To this extent, Aristotle's 'official' views about substance are not in contrast with the first idea. However, Aristotle also insists that the material parts of substances do not enjoy the same ontological status as the substances they are parts of: a human being is a substance in actuality, whereas its material parts (her limbs or the elements that make her limbs) are substances only potentially (Z.16, 1040b5–10). Equivalently, he states that the parts in which a substance can be divided cannot be in actuality (Z.13, 1039a3–14). In this sense, if one thinks of numbers as collections of discrete units, for Aristotle it is clear that this model might be misleading in suggesting that substances too, like numbers, are made out of relatively independent units (although there are passages suggesting that the account of numbers as mere collections of units is in important respects too simplistic for Aristotle precisely in that it does not account for the unity of each number: see H.3, 1044a2–5; H.6, 1045a7 ff.; cf. Z.13, 1039a11–14).

Given that substances are not numbers by being collections of discrete units, one could try out the second model. According to this second model, at least material substances could be regarded as numbers of elements in that each substance is made of the four elements in certain ratios. Interestingly enough, Aristotle seems to think that ratios (*logoi*) between numbers, unlike simple numbers, can be regarded as formal causes of things (cf. A.9, 991b13–21; N.5, 1092b8–23). The endorsement of this view on ratios can perhaps be taken as Aristotle's way to revise and rescue the Pythagorean intuition that numbers are the substance and cause of other things (for a move similar in spirit cf. H.3, 1043b32–1044a11, where both the correct intuitions behind the identification of definition and number and the reasons why it is wrong are accounted for). Note, however, that if it is essential to the second model that the components entering the ratio be one the privation of the other, the model cannot apply to substances. Privation for substances (unlike privations of some qualities such as black or blindness, which may look as robust properties) is not a property, but a conceptual construct introduced to account for processes of coming to be and passing away.

Note, finally, that although the basic goal of the examples in Iota is that of showing that unity and number are not the substance or nature of things, the Pythagorean flavour of Aristotle's approach in I.2 is retained in other parts of the corpus (see I.7 and Sorabji 1972 about the Pythagorean ontology of colours).

1054a9–19: The syntactical structure of the period makes it clear that these final lines belong together (1054a9: *hoti men* 'It is therefore evident, on the one hand, that [. . .]'; 1054a13: *hoti de* 'On the other hand, that [. . .] is clear'). 1054a9–13 summarizes the main results of the section starting at 1053b24, while 1054a13–19 gives new arguments in support of some form of identification of one and being. It is not clear whether this is just meant to provide evidence for the moves based on the parallelism between one and being in the preceding argument (cf. 1053b16–21, 21–24; 25, 27–28) or it is supposed to lead to a new point. I shall first go through the arguments and then say something on what the point of this whole final section might be, also with references to the other two places (Γ.2, 1003b22–33 and K.3, 1061a17–18) where similar arguments are used. More generally on the relation between one and being see Berti 1979; Couloubaritsis 1983; Halper 1985; Jeannot 1986; Makin 1988.

The claim for which Aristotle provides some support here is that 'one' and 'being' in some sense 'signify the same' or 'indicate the same'. In order to make sense of this claim we have to take a look at what it is exactly that the arguments show.

First argument (**1054a14–16**): That one and being somehow indicate the same can be gathered by the fact that they behave in a similar way with respect to the categories: they both **(f)** follow the categories in the same number of ways and **(g)** are not in any category in particular. (f) is probably meant to express the fact that all items in all categories are each one and being. *Parako-louthein*, literally indicating local following (cf. e.g. *HA* VI.12, 566b22), is also used to indicate relations of logical consequence or ontological connection (cf. *Cat.* 7, 8a33; *APo* II.17, 99a17; *Top.*, IV.5, 125b28–31; cf. *Top.* II.4, 111b17–23; II.5, 112a16–23; II.8, 113b15–114a6; II.9, 114b13–15; IV.5, 125b20–27). A property that follows or accompanies a subject can be referred to as *akolouthon* (e.g. *Top.* II.5, 112a16–23) or *parakolouthon* (e.g. *Top.* IV.5, 125b28). One and being 'follow' or 'accompany' any object belonging to any category—otherwise said: for any item belonging to any category, that item is one and being. Furthermore, unity, like being, can be incidental or per se (*Met.* Δ.6, 1015b16–17), or in actuality and in potentiality (*DA* II.1, 412b8–9). What is incidentally is incidentally one, what is per se is per se one (in particular, incidental beings, e.g. the courageous Socrates, are incidentally one and vice versa); what is in actuality is one in actuality and what is in potentiality is one in potentiality. One possibility is that it is with respect to these different ways that the one is said to follow the categories 'in as many ways' (for a similar interplay of distinctions cf. the way in which the determinations of prior and posterior, incidental and per se, actual and potential interact with the four-fold division of causes in *Met.* Δ.2, 1013b28 ff.). Alternatively, 'in as many ways' can be taken as a somewhat redundant reference to the plurality of the categories. Commentators tend to endorse the latter option without really distinguishing between the two, but the first option seems to be a viable one, too.

It is more difficult to establish what the point of (g) exactly is. There is some sense in which being has a categorial focus in the category of substance and unity has a categorial focus in the category of quantity. Accordingly I take the point in (g) to be that there is no category in which one and being can be exclusively found, even if it is possible to distinguish between primary and non-primary beings and ones. More particularly, I take (g) to provide the second part of an argument whose aim is that of showing that one and being are predicated of all and only the same things and that one and being do not have anything predicated of them: one and being are in no category in the sense that no predicate belonging to any category can be predicated of them. If this is correct, the two parts of the argument correspond to the two prescriptions of the *topos* (a general standard argumentative strategy) on sameness (*Top.* VII.1, 152a31–36 or 152b25–29) according to which, in order to assess whether A and B are the same, we have to check whether they are predicated of the same things and the same things are predicated of them. More explicitly, in order to check whether A and B are the same, we should check how they behave with respect to the categories, for if they are not both 'in one genus of predication' (*ei mē en heni genei katēgorias*), then they are not the same (*Top.* VII.1, 152a38–b2). As we shall see in a moment, the second argument, too, is built on a *topos* of sameness.

Partially similar arguments can be found in *Met.* Γ.2, 1003b22–24, where one and being are said to 'follow each other as principle and cause do', without being 'revealed by the same account', and in K.3, 1061a17–18: even if one and being are not the same, they convert in the sense that whatever is one is being and vice versa. These two arguments differ from the argument in I.2 in that they do not make any reference to the division into genera and in that, if my interpretation of the function of (f) and (g) is correct, they only account for the sameness of one and being in terms of the things of which one and being are predicated (corresponding to (f) in I.2). The explicit reference in Γ.2 and K.3 to the fact that one and being are not exactly the same even if they are extensionally equivalent is captured in I.2 by the cautionary 'in some sense' (*pōs*) at 1054a13. On the idea that anything that is one is something that is and vice versa cf. Plat., *Tht.* 188e5–189b3, *Soph.* 237d6–238e3. For some discussion of the arguments for the convertibility of one and being see Halper 1985.

Second argument (**1054a16–18**): The predication of unity or of being of a subject does not result in the ascription of a new property to the subject. If we say of something that it is one man (or that it is one and a man) or that it is a man that is (or that it is and that it is a man) we do not say anything more than when we say that it is a man. The point here is that 'one' and 'being' behave in the same way with respect to predication and, in particular, that if added to another predicate they do not add anything to the content of that predicate; the composite predicate made out of 'one' or 'being' and another predicate is equivalent to the other predicate. In this respect 'one' and 'being' are different from any categorial predicate: for, even if within one line of predication, genera do not add anything to their species, e.g. saying of something that it is an animal human being is not more than saying that it is a human being, there is no categorical predicate which behaves in this way with respect to every other predicate to which it might be added. If we add 'animal' to the predicate 'white' and we say of something that it is a white animal, we are saying something more than what we say when we say of it that it is white (or that it is an animal). With 'one' and 'being' this is never the case (on this feature of 'one' and 'being' see Breton 1981). The idea seems to be that since one and being follow any predicate in any category they are already implicitly predicated of any subject with any other predicate, and this is why their addition to or subtraction from a compound predicate does not make any difference. A similar argument can be found in Γ.2, 1003b26–32. For the opposite view, that ascribing unity to something might amount to some form of addition cf. Plat., *Soph.* 238a5–c6. Note that the argument is only about the predication of one and being in addition to another predicate and does not necessarily say much on the predication of one and being in isolation.

Like the first argument, this argument, too, is construed according to a *topos* of sameness (*Top.* VII.1, 152b10–16). If we want to check whether A and B are the same, we can check how they behave when they are added to or subtracted from the same C: if the result of the addition or of the subtraction is different, then A and B are not the same; if the result is the same, this can be used as an argument in support of the claim that A and B are the same.

Third argument (**1054a18–19**): The text is very compressed and probably corrupted. The manuscripts have 'and being one being each thing'. Editors have intervened in different ways. Christ adds *tōi* at a18 before 'being one' (*to heni einai*) and Ross adds *einai* after *tōi*. In this way we would have here a third argument introduced by *tōi einai* ('in virtue of the fact that being one is being for each thing'). The construction would be the same as the construction introducing the other two arguments, with the infinitive preceded by the neuter article in the dative.

Jaeger opts for a different solution: he rejects Christ's and Ross's additions, but he changes the article preceding 'being each thing' (*to*) into the genitive case (*tou*), which he reads as depending from 'does not add anything else in predication' at a16. The translation of Jaeger's text would be: '[...] in virtue of the fact that 'one human being' does not add anything else in predication to 'human being' [...] and that being one <does not add anything in predication> to being each thing'. On this reconstruction, the last lines would not give a third argument but spell out the ontological grounds of the second: the addition of 'one' to 'human being' does not contribute anything to the constitution of a complex predicate because, for each thing of which 'human being' is predicated, being one is nothing other than being a human being. I am not sure whether 'being one' (*to heni einai*) and 'being each thing' (*to hekastōi einai*) could be appropriate subject and complement for the predicate 'not to add anything else in predication' (*mē proskatēgoreisthai heteron ti*—the genitive would depend from *heteron*, 'other than'). The construction with being (*einai*) and the dative ('for the one'/'for each thing') is one of Aristotle's characteristic constructions for indicating the essence of the thing picked out by the noun in the dative. Whatever he is saying about being one and being each thing this does not seem to be a point about how adding predicates and forming compound predicates works—which I take to be the point of the preceding argument in a rather technical sense. Accordingly, I take Christ's and Ross's emendations to give a text suggesting a likelier argument. The point of the remark would then be: what it is for something to be one is nothing other than what it is for that thing to be the kind of thing it is. A similar argument can be found in Γ.2, 1003b32–33, where the point seems to be that the essence of each thing is one and being non-incidentally. Even if the two arguments are not phrased in the same way, I take them to be aimed at one and the same target: each thing is one not in virtue of participating in some distinct substance and cause of unity, but just by being what it is. There is no separate cause of unity—as there is no separate cause of being—for all things that are one. On things being one by being affected by the one, cf. Plat., *Soph.* 244e2–245b10.

As we have seen, similar arguments to those deployed in this section of I.2 are used in *Met.* Γ.2. This similarity should not obliterate some important and problematic differences between the two chapters. In Γ.2 (and, similarly, in K.3) the arguments are used to show that, in some fundamental way, one and being are the same and that therefore the series of notions that can be led back to the one (cf. Introduction, section II.2) must fall within the scope of the science of being qua being. Within this context, the focus of the overall discussion is not so much the enquiry into the nature of the one, but the possibility of extending the domain of the science of being to the enquiry into some notions linked to the one. I.2 is quite different. The chapter is introduced explicitly as a discussion of the nature of the one, and nothing suggests that the discussion is supposed to yield further meta-theoretical results. This is important for two reasons: first, from the point of view of the relation between Γ.2 and I.2, the results achieved in I.2 seem to be presupposed by Γ.2 rather than the other way round. This does not necessarily imply that I.2 was written before Γ.2, but it does imply that at least some of the arguments included in I.2 had already been formulated when Γ.2 was written. Second, if Aristotle's views on one and being have to be criticized, I.2 is the place at which criticism should be primarily addressed.

There remains a problem about the function of 1054a13–19 within the economy of I.2. As already mentioned, there are two—not mutually exclusive—options. The first is that 1054a13–19 is meant to provide support for the claim at 1053b25, that the one is said in the same number of ways as being, in the same way in which 1053b28–54a9 provides support for the claim at 53b25–28 that, if the one in qualities is one determinate nature, the same must holds in quantities and other domains of being. These are the two claims on which the general statement about the correct approach to the enquiry into the one (1053b27–28; 1054a11–12) rests.

The second option is that the last lines rule out the possibility that there be something more to the enquiry into the one than there is to the enquiry into the one with respect to each domain of being. Among the implications of this view we would have that, once we have explained what each thing is, there is nothing left to explain as to why that thing is also one. If the one is nothing over and above being and if being one amounts to being a determinate being, then once we have explained what it is that makes something the determinate being it is we have also explained what it is that makes it one. This option is perhaps supported by Γ.2, 1003b31–32, where the point is made that the one is nothing beyond (or, over and above) (*para*) being.

To conclude, let me briefly return to the relation between I.2 and the eleventh aporia in Beta. In B.1 and B.4 the aporia is introduced as a general one, concerning the status of the most universal predicates, i.e. one and being. As we have seen, I.2 relies on the fact that that general problem has already been solved, at least as far as being is concerned. One basic assumption throughout the chapter is that there is some fundamental analogy in the behaviour of one and being with respect to all things that are and the general aporia on the status of the one is solved by applying to it considerations which seem to be taken as established and uncontroversial as far as being goes. This procedure might tell us something on the place Aristotle ascribes to the enquiry into the one: although in the aporia in B.4 one and being are introduced as on the same level, the enquiry into being takes priority not only in terms of length within the *Metaphysics* as we read it, but also and perhaps more importantly in as much as it provides the basic conceptual tools to solve the corresponding difficulty on the one.

Nonetheless, I.2 does provide Aristotle's reply to some aspects of the difficulties unfolded in B (cf. pp. 65–6). In particular, in I.2 Aristotle may be interested in accounting for the difficulties allegedly arising from the denial of the Pythagorean/Platonic position. (i) In B.4 1001a19–24 one of the consequences of the denial of the substantiality of one and being was the denial of the criterion of universality as a criterion for being a substance. In I.2 (as elsewhere) Aristotle fully embraces the assumption that universals cannot be substances and in this way indirectly replies that the first consequence of the denial of the Pythagorean/Platonic thesis is not a problem. More specifically, the identification of one and being as principles on the basis of the assumption that the highest genera are principles of all things (B.3, 998b14–999a23) is rejected on the basis of the argument that one and being cannot be genera in the first place (1053b16–24). (ii) The second difficulty raised in B.4, 1001a24–27 is that, if the one is not a separate substance, then number will fail to be separate too, given that number is composed of units (or 'ones'). I.2, 1053b24–1054a9 does not insist on separation, but it indirectly shows that there are no separate numbers and that numbers are not the substance of anything by showing that there are no things that are numbers without being anything else. (iii) Finally, the last section of I.2, 1054a9–19 could be taken as a response to the last difficulty raised in B.4, 1001a27–29: if there is anything which is itself one and being, one and being must be its substance (I shall leave aside the compressed and problematic argument in support of this claim). I.2 argues that, on the contrary, one and being are predicated of each and every thing in such a way that not only they do not express the essence or substance of anything, but they do not even add any content to any other predicate. This does not imply that things are not one or being: on the contrary, anything that is is one and being precisely by being the kind of thing it is.

CHAPTER 3

After the first two chapters entirely devoted to the analysis of the one, I.3 opens with an account of one of the ways in which one and many are opposed to each other. In the course of Iota, two kinds of oppositions are envisaged: being one understood as being indivisible is opposed as a contrary to being many understood as being divisible; the one understood as measure is opposed as a relative to the many understood as what is measured. I.3 sketches the opposition of one and many as contraries and gives a first explanation of the sense in which one of them is the privation of the other (the opposition of one and many as measure and measured will be dealt with in I.6). I.3 then considers the ways in which some one-related notions (the same and the similar) are said. The chapter is structured after the assumption that a parallel distinction must be drawn for the ways in which the corresponding opposite notions (i.e. the other and the dissimilar) are said. Having considered the ways in which the other is said and the way in which the opposition of the same and the other is applied to things, Aristotle turns to the distinction between the other and the different. Finally, he introduces the notion of contrariety as a particular kind difference. A fuller account of contrariety will be given in I.4, which will provide the starting point for the ensuing discussion of particular cases of opposites which are usually (and wrongly, as Aristotle will argue) regarded as contraries (I.5, 6), of contrary-related notions such as intermediates (I.7), and of contrariety with respect to the articulation of species and genera (I.8–10).

There is a general question as to the philosophical point of the distinctions drawn in I.3. Menn ((in progress), Iγ2b) takes the discussion in I.3 ff. to focus on the criticism of Academic conceptions of the principle opposite to the one (see introductory notes to I.5). On this interpretation, I.3 would be confined to distinctions that are useful to prepare Aristotle's criticism in later chapters. It is not very clear to me how exactly the discussion of sameness and similarity are relevant to what follows, but other texts suggest that the enquiry into similarities and dissimilarities is relevant to the analysis of things into genera and species and, more generally, for the enquiry into definitions: see, for instance, *Top.* I.16–17 and the remarks in *Top.* I.18, 108a38–b6 and 108b7–9, 19–31.

1054a20–23: One and many are opposed to each other in more than one way, depending on whether the one is taken as indivisible or as measure. In these lines Aristotle considers the opposition of one and many understood as the opposition of indivisible (or undivided) and divisible (or divided). He will consider the opposition of one and many understood as the opposition of measure and measurable (or measured) in I.6, 1056b20 ff. As for the correspondence between the different ways in which opposite terms are said cf. *Top.* I.15, 106a9–b4.

1054a22:   *plēthos ti*, 'a certain plurality'. The Greek word corresponding to 'plurality' is difficult to translate because in some contexts (*Met.* Δ.13, 1020a10–11; cf. I.6, 1057a2–4) it does not indicate discrete plurality, but what can be made into discrete plurality once a principle of division and determination is introduced (whereas the English 'plurality' seems at least to allude to a discrete multiplicity of items). In fact the Greek *plēthos* can indicate both what is actually divided (a discrete multiplicity) and what is just potentially divisible without being an actual discrete multiplicity. It is probably in this more comprehensive sense of the word that the *plēthos* is regarded as a principle of multiplicity opposed to the one (regarded in its turn as a principle of unity and determination) in some version of the Academic doctrine of the principles (cf. *Met.* N.1 1087b27; on the relevance of this and other formulations of the doctrine of Principles for Aristotle's Iota see introduction to I.5, pp. 137–9, and notes to I.6, 1057a2–7; see also Plat., *Parm.* 158d4, 164b5 and, in particular, 164c6 ff. for an account of what is completely deprived of unity and which can only turn into a plurality through participating in the one).

1054a23–26:   At a24 I take *toutōn* ('of these') to refer to the divisible and the indivisible (a22–23) and not to the oppositions (a23–24). See Notes on the Text for an alternative text.
    The gist of the argument can be made clear with reference to I.4, 1055a33 ff., where Aristotle argues in support of the claim that primary contrariety is an opposition of possession of a form and complete privation of the same. Based on I.4, the argument in I.3 can be reconstructed in the following way: **(1)** there are four kinds of opposition (1054a23–24), i.e. possession and privation, contrariety, contradiction, and the opposition of relatives. **(2)** Contrariety is the opposition of two items, one of which is said on account of the possession of a form, whereas the other is said on account of the privation of that same form (this premise is not explicit in the passage, but will be explained in I.4; see in particular I.4, 1055a33–35 about complete privation). **(3)** In the opposition of one and many understood as the opposition of

97

indivisible and divisible respectively, the one is thought of as the privation of the many because the indivisible is the privation of the divisible (see 1054a26–29). **(4)** Based on (2) and (3), one and many (understood as indivisible and divisible) are opposed as contraries and not as contradictories or as relatives. In order to derive (4), (2) and (3) must be qualified in such a way that (2) expresses a necessary and sufficient condition for contrariety and that one and many in (3) satisfy this condition. In I.4 Aristotle says that, although privation is said in many ways, A and B are contrary if and only if A is the complete privation of B (or B of A). According to this qualification, (3) should say that the indivisible is the complete privation of the divisible.

1054a26–29: Aristotle spells out the claim at 1054a24 that one term of the pair indivisible/divisible is said according to privation. In particular, he says that we 'call' and 'reveal' the indivisible through reference to the divisible. This is because what is divisible is 'more perceptible' than what is indivisible. The idea would be that we start with a sort of direct acquaintance with what is divisible (i.e. any extended object) and coin the word and the corresponding notion of the divisible. We get a grasp on what it is to be indivisible by denying the property to which we have access through sense perception: to be indivisible is to be non-divisible. I take this to be the sense of priority in account (*tōi logōi proteron*) that Aristotle ascribes to the divisible over the indivisible.

Aristotle's considerations about indivisible and divisible are at least partly based on the morphology of the Greek words, which is also reflected in the corresponding English words: *adiaireton* ('in-divisible') is construed with the privative *alpha* (*a-*) and the adjective *diaireton* ('divisible'). In this sense the word for one of the contraries (*adiaireton*) is coined from the word signifying its contrary (*diaireton*).

In this passage Aristotle seems to endorse the view that the divisible has definitional priority over the indivisible and that, therefore, the many has definitional priority over the one. This view may be in contrast with a traditional set of considerations concerning the opposition of one and many, according to which the many is characterized as what is deprived of unity (cf. Plat., *Parm.* 158d4; 164b5 and in particular c6 ff.), whereas unity is regarded as formal determination and, as such, as ontologically prior to multiplicity. If the ontological priority of the one implies the definitional priority of the one over the many, then our passage seems to be at least superficially in contrast with this opposite view. Menn ((in progress), Iγ2a: From Δ6 to Iota 1: the one as indivisible and as measure) takes this as an explicit blow at the Academic assumption of the One as a principle: if to be one is to be indivisible, it turns out that to be one amounts to being a privation; if to be one is understood as to be a measure, then to be one amounts to being a relative; either way, the one cannot be a principle of being. However, Aristotle himself seems to adopt the traditional view that plurality is the privation of unity (rather than the other way round) in the account of the way in which other contraries can be led back to the primary opposition of possession and complete privation (1055a33–b26), which is paradigmatically exemplified by the one and the many as the primary contraries (cf. 1055b26–29) (cf. notes to I.4, 1055a33 ff. and Introduction, section II.1). For in I.4, 1055b17–22 it is quite clear that the notions belonging together with the many (cf. 1054a29–32), such as the unequal, the dissimilar, vice, etc., are regarded as privations of the corresponding opposites belonging together with the one. And it seems likely that the ways in which the pairs of particular contraries behave is somehow modelled after the way in which the primary opposition of one and many works. Note, however, that in I.5, 1056a22–24 the equal is defined as the privative negation of the great and the small, which, jointly, are the unequal. This move is similar to saying that the indivisible is the privation of the divisible in that the opposite falling under the one (i.e. the equal) turns out to be the privation of the other. This raises the more general issue of how to identify the privation in a pair of contraries. The Pythagorean model of *sustoichiai* suggests that one contrary's belonging to one column rather than to the other carries some implications as to its 'value', as it were: the contraries falling under the one or the limit have a positive metaphysical and axiological connotation, whereas those falling under the many or the unlimited have a negative metaphysical and axiological connotation. Although there are contexts in which a negative connotation is associated to privation, Iota's stand on this point is not clear.

Perhaps conflicting claims about the priority in knowledge of the one or of the many can be accommodated by saying that what is divisible is prior in knowledge for us (to sense perception), whereas indivisibility is prior in knowledge in its own right. Aristotle often resorts to this distinction in order to sort out apparently contrasting claims of priority in knowledge of different items (e.g. *APo.* I.1–2; *Phys.* I.1; cf. also *Met.* Δ.11, 1018b30–34). For instance, we are directly acquainted with the world of sensible phenomena in our pre-scientific everyday experience, while we might ignore their causes. Nonetheless the philosopher or the scientist, starting with the sensible phenomena, will be able to find out their causes—in fact according to Aristotle philosophical or scientific knowledge is knowledge of the causes and principles of determinate sets of data. By the end of this process of discovery, the causes and the principles will appear to the scientist as clearer and intrinsically more intelligible than the phenomena they are meant to explain. In this picture the phenomena we start with are the first thing we know and, in this sense, are prior for us; on the other hand, the principles and causes are prior in their own right and can be known through scientific investigation. Following this train of thought, one could claim that divisibility is a feature of everything we perceive as long as objects of perception are extended objects and every extension is in principle divisible. We do not perceive indivisible objects, but we can form the concept of indivisibility by denying divisibility.

1054a29–32:   Aristotle introduces three further pairs of opposites (the same and other, similar and dissimilar, equal and unequal) and refers to one of his lost writings, the *Division of the Contraries* (cf. *Met.* Γ.2, 1004a2). In the *Division* he may have shown that, for each pair of contraries, the positive term (i.e. the same, similar, and equal) belongs with the one (literally: 'is of the one' or 'belongs to the one'), whereas the respective opposite belongs with plurality (see Introduction, pp. xxxix–xlvii). On the definitional dependence of sameness, similarity, and equality on unity cf. also *Met.* Δ.15, 1021a9–14.

1054a30:   *diegrapsamen*: literally 'we marked out by lines', 'we drafted', or 'we drew out a list'. For other occurrences of the same verb see *APr* I.30, 46a8, *Rhet.* II.1, 1378a27. This may suggest that the *Division of the Contraries* was or included tables of contraries.

1054a32–b3: Aristotle provides an extremely compressed distinction of three ways in which things can be said to be the same (for other accounts cf. *Met.* Δ.9, 1017b27–1018a11, *Top.* I.7, *SE* 24, 179a26–b7, *Phys.* III.3, 202b14–16; for some discussion see White 1971; Miller 1973; Barnes 1977; Pelletier 1991; Crivelli 2002; Mignucci 2002; Mariani 2005). Despite the shortness of the passage, the conceptual apparatus here deployed is quite rich. Accordingly, the need to bring in materials from other texts in order to make sense of the distinction is pressing, but this makes the reading of the passage inevitably controversial. The difficulties concern both the interpretation of the single cases of sameness and their mutual relations. I shall first present the distinction as it appears in the text and then say something on the concepts used to express it. I shall then analyse each way of being the same in the light of these considerations.

In the first place Aristotle distinguishes three ways in which 'the same' is said.

The Same$_1$: with respect to number.

The Same$_2$: if things are one both in account and in number; Aristotle spells out these two parameters (unity in account and unity in number) in terms of unity of form and unity of matter respectively.

The Same$_3$: if the definition (i.e. 'the account of the primary substance') is one.

First, note that Aristotle appeals to different forms of unity (unity in account, unity in number, unity of form, unity of matter, unity of definition) to spell out The Same$_2$ and The Same$_3$. There are reasons to think that some reference to unity is included also in The Same$_1$, but I shall defer the discussion of this point until the discussion of the corresponding form of otherness. Secondly, the forms of unity to which Aristotle refers in order to explain the different cases of sameness do not coincide in any straightforward way with the ways in which the one is said as distinguished in I.1. Unity in account (in The Same$_2$) and unity in definition (in The Same$_3$) can be linked to unity in thought in I.1 (see notes to 1052a29–34), whereas unity of matter is more problematic (see notes pp. 103–4). In The Same$_2$, 'form' translates *eidos*, which can also be translated as 'species' (see introductory notes to I.7 and I.8).

A definition (*horismos*) is a particular kind of formula or account (*logos*), i.e. the account which specifies the essence of what is defined. When Aristotle says that something is one in account or that A and B are one and/or the same in account, he usually means to refer to the unity of the account of their essence, i.e. to the unity of their definition. Accordingly I shall refer to unity in account and unity in definition interchangeably.

There are two main contexts in which unity in account or in definition can appear, depending on whether it is presented as a feature of one or of more subjects at a time. What it is for *one* object to be one in account can be illustrated by looking at cases in which Aristotle denies unity in account. For instance, the item resulting from the composition of a substance—say: a human being—and a qualitative determination—say: white—is not one in account. If we want to spell out what the white human being is, we have to make reference to two more basic and irreducible components (a human being is a substance, white is a quality). A human being, on the other hand, is one in account because it is not the result of the composition of different items belonging to different kinds (for some discussion of what it is for a definition to be one see notes to I.1, pp. 34–6). *Several* subjects can be said to be one in account if they share the same definition. In this polyadic sense, unity in account is the same as sameness in account.

Both monadic and polyadic unity in account can be best understood with reference to Aristotle's tenets about the ontology of substances and, in particular, of natural substances. This does not mean that unity in account cannot apply to simple substances, but only that the distinction between monadic and polyadic unity in account and the contraposition of unity in account to unity in number can be most easily grasped by looking at natural substances such as human beings, horses, and the like. Natural substances are usually such that there are many individuals which have significant properties in common and, by having these properties, belong to the same species, while they differ from each other in other respects (there are exceptions to this picture in that there are species represented by a single individual: see notes to I.1, p. 39). The ontology of natural substances and the similarities and differences between members of the same species can be explained by introducing the distinction between a material substratum (roughly speaking: the stuff of which the composite substance is made) and a form, responsible for the unity of the composite individual and for its specific identity, i.e. for determining the kind of being it is and, therefore, the species it belongs to. In this sense both monadic and polyadic unity in account are determined by the unity of form of the items which are one in account. For instance, Socrates is (monadically) one in account because his substantial form, which is what makes of him a human being, is one; the very same form is responsible for Socrates's belonging to the species of human beings. Socrates and Plato are (dyadically) one in account because they are both human beings and their belonging to the species of human beings is determined by the fact that both Socrates's form and Plato's form make them human beings (whether Socrates and Plato share one form or have two identical individual forms is a controversial issue which I shall not address).

Given this general picture, one can start to see why the unity of matter invoked in The Same$_2$ is problematic: if the form of x determines and unifies x's matter, it is difficult to see in what sense matter could be one independently from formal determination in such a way as to justify Aristotle's appeal to unity in form and to unity in matter in order to spell out unity in account and unity in number respectively. Although there are passages where Aristotle seems to appeal to unity of matter in a rather problematic way, the difficulty is perhaps not so grave in our passage. For in the example for The Same$_2$ Aristotle probably just wants to convey the relatively intuitive idea that the matter of A and B is one if A and B are made of the same chunk of stuff.

However, the connection established in The Same$_2$ between unity in number and unity of matter remains puzzling in at least two respects. There is a more specific and a more general problem. The more specific problem is: does this connection imply that The Same$_1$ should also be accounted for in terms of unity of matter? The more general problem is: Does this connection imply that numerical unity in general should be defined in terms of unity of matter? As for the second problem, see the considerations on numerical unity as the unity of particulars in I.1, pp. 33–40. As for the first problem, see pp. 111–14.

If we leave aside the intricacies of the conceptual framework employed in Aristotle's account of the three ways in which things can be said to be the same and focus on the different states of affairs justifying the application of one or the other description, The Same$_2$ provides the most straightforward case thanks to the example Aristotle uses to illustrate it. Every individual is The Same$_2$ with itself in the sense that it has one form and one matter with itself. In short, The Same$_2$ seems to grasp the notion of self-identity which, in the case of composite substances, is spelled out in terms of unity of form and unity of matter which are the two basic ontological components jointly responsible for the identity and differentiation of composite substances.

The mention of the two criteria of unity of form and unity of matter need not imply that The Same$_2$ is restricted to composite beings and, in particular, to composite substances. Clearly enough, a non-material being and, notably, a non-material substance can be said to be the same as itself even if the criterion of sameness cannot be split into a requirement for form and a requirement for matter strictly speaking. However, it would still make sense to distinguish the two requirements of unity in account and unity in number (i.e. even if in the case of immaterial beings and, in particular, of immaterial substances the explanation of numerical unity cannot be based on unity of matter). And in fact the two requirements of unity in account and unity in number are applied to non-sensible substances: in *Met.* Λ.8, 1074a36–37 Aristotle qualifies the unmoved mover as one in account and in number (*hen ara kai logōi kai arithmōi*). In this context, unity in number simply indicates the kind of unity of the individual in opposition to the kind of unity of the species to which it belongs. On the opposition of numerical unity as the unity of the particular individual and unity in account as the unity of the species see notes to I.1, pp. 36–40.

In the account of The Same$_2$ Aristotle mentions numerical unity and definitional unity. Numerical unity can also be coupled (in a different way) with plurality in account, i.e. it can be the case that something is one in number and many in account. Aristotle reckons a relatively varied range of cases under this rubric and the ontology of such cases is somewhat controversial (see pp. 24–5 for incidental compounds and Castelli 2010, pp. 259–78 for some discussion of the different cases). Such cases could be what Aristotle has in mind here when he considers items which are The Same$_1$, on the basis of number only (i.e. and not also in account). I shall postpone the discussion of this characterization of The Same$_1$ until the discussion of Other$_1$ at 1054b13 ff.

The Same$_3$, is the relation obtaining between items belonging to one and the same species, all responding to the same definition. Sameness in account as such is compatible with a certain range of variety with respect to the features which are not included in the definition of the species at stake. For instance, all human beings are one in account, i.e. they all share the same definition and have the same essential properties. Nevertheless every human being can be distinguished from any other human being on the basis of a potentially infinite number of features which do not appear in her definition. For example, some human beings are male, some are female; they are differently tall or short; some have fair hair, some have dark hair, and so on. This seems to be the case for natural substances in general, even if, for instance, the differences between a particular lily and another may be less evident than those between individual human beings. Furthermore, the very same individual throughout its ontological career has always the same essence (and it belongs always to the same species) even if it comes to realize itself fully only when it flourishes. Given these features of the ontology of natural substances, which offer a paradigmatic case of a plurality of items being one in account, Aristotle's use of examples of mathematical entities such as straight lines of equal length and congruent figures may be puzzling in that they convey the idea of a multiplicity of individuals not necessarily discernible from each other. See below for some discussion of the examples. I shall return to the characterization of The same$_3$ in the discussion of Other$_3$. For some considerations on the mutual relations between the three ways of being the same, see comments on 1054b13–18.

1054b1–3:　Aristotle introduces the case of equal straight lines and the case of congruent quadrangular figures as examples for The Same$_3$. On other occasions, though, Aristotle illustrates the case of sameness in account with reference to items which have one and the same account even if they differ in other respects such as, e.g., size (cf. *Met.* Δ.6, 1016a32–b1). In fact, the requirement of equal size does not seem to be necessary to explain unity in account. In any case Aristotle regards the case of things which are the same in account and different in size or quantity as a case of similarity at 1054b3 (see Similar₁). Therefore it might be the case that with The Same₃ Aristotle wants to focus on particular cases of sameness in account, such that the single items sharing the same account cannot be distinguished from each other in terms of positive quantitative or qualitative features. What we read at 1054b2 makes some difference (see Notes on the Text): the α-text ('things that are equal and quadrangular figures that have equal angles') leaves room for two different cases (i.e. congruent and similar figures), whereas the text printed by Ross ('quadrangular figures that are equal and have equal angles') only makes room for the case of congruent figures.

Depending on whether we take the reference to geometrical entities in the example as essential to The Same₃, we can take The Same₃ to capture indiscernibility (rather than sameness in account more generally, if we take the examples as crucial without insisting on the fact that they are about geometrical entities), equality (if we take the reference to geometrical entities to point at quantities or mathematical entities in general) or congruence (if we do take the reference to geometrical entities as essential to The Same₃).

A further option is that in these lines Aristotle is introducing his considerations on the equal, which appeared together with the same and the similar in the list of notions belonging with the one. This would be supported by 1054b3, where Aristotle says that in these cases 'equality is unity'. With this remark Aristotle might want to stress the definitional link between the equal and the one (cf. *Met.* Δ.9, 1018a7: *hē tautotēs henotēs tis estin*, 'sameness is a sort of unity', in the context of the explanation of correspondences between ways of being the same and ways of being one). Equal and unequal are primarily said of quantities (cf. *Cat.* 6, 6a26–35; *Met.* Δ.15, 1021a12). In the domain of quantities equality (i.e. sameness in quantity) is unity in form. As for numbers, in *Met.* M.7, 1082b1–9 Aristotle discusses the way in which numbers differ from each other; he says that they cannot differ in quality (because they are merely quantitative entities); they only differ from each other in quantity. In the domain of numbers, we can have a plurality of indiscernible items, which are equal (i.e. do not differ in quantity) and do not present any difference in any other respect as they do not have any qualitative determination. One can say of these items that they are the same in account, but in addition to being the same in account they do not differ from each other in any respect. Aristotle specifies that in the case of numbers things that are equal (*isa*) and completely undifferentiated (*holōs adiaphora*) are regarded as the same (*tauta*) (M.7, 1082b7–9). In the case of geometrical entities, one might want to distinguish between two cases in which geometrical entities are the same in form and account: all equilateral triangles (bigger and smaller) are the same kind of triangle, i.e. they are the same in form and in account, but one might want to distinguish the case of incongruent equilateral triangles from the case of congruent ones. Perhaps Aristotle's point is that congruent geometrical figures look 'more' the same than non-congruent ones (in fact, at 1054b3–7 he speaks of non-congruent geometrical figures as similar).

There are some problems with taking these lines to be about the equal: for these would be the only lines devoted to the equal in the chapter and they diverge from the preceding treatment of the same and of the similar both in length and style. Compared to the sections on the ways of being the same and similar, this section does not divide the different ways in which the equal is said, nor is it introduced as a new section about a new notion (rather than as an expansion about The Same$_3$). Furthermore, when Aristotle introduces the account of the notions opposite to those belonging together with the one (1054b13–14), he only mentions the other and the dissimilar, without saying anything about the unequal. None of these considerations is compelling, but all in all it seems unlikely that b1–3 are meant to deal with the equal as such.

1054b3–13:   Aristotle distinguishes four ways in which things are said to be similar (cf. *Met.* Δ.9, 1018a15–18; the correspondences between the two distinctions are far from being evident). The first three, together with the equal geometrical objects mentioned at b1–3, are further cases of items that are the same in form or account, whereas the last one is a more generic and in a way less ontologically committed account of similarity.

1054b3–7:   For the first sense in which things are said to be similar (henceforth: Similar$_1$) Aristotle gives three qualifications. The first qualification is that the items at issue are not the same *haplōs* ('without qualification' or 'simply'). I shall refer to this qualification as non-identity (henceforth: **NI**). Sameness without qualification could be self-identity as in The Same$_2$. However, at 1054b5–7 Aristotle contrasts the case of mathematical entities which are Similar$_1$ by sharing the same form and being of different sizes with the case of equal mathematical entities used to illustrate The Same$_3$. So being Similar$_1$ seems to be contrasted with indiscernibility or congruence (The Same$_3$) rather than with self-identity (The Same$_2$). The example in The Same$_3$ is about items which are numerically many, have the same form and are indiscernible from each other in any respect apart from numerical multiplicity, whereas the example for Similar$_1$ is about items which have the same form and can be discerned on the basis of other properties (Similar$_1$).

The second qualification is that items that are Similar$_1$ are not without differences from each other insofar as they are composite beings. I shall refer to this qualification as difference of the compounds (**DC**). Again, I take this qualification to be meant in contrast to the example of objects which are numerically distinct and indiscernible in any other respect.

The third qualification is that items which are Similar$_1$ are still the same in form: the bigger square and the smaller square are the same in form (they are both squares and respond to the same definition). I shall refer to this qualification as sameness in form (**SF**).

As for the mutual connections of (NI), (DC), and (SF), (NI) seems to voice the distinction between sameness and similarity, which is then further articulated through (DC) and (SF). (NI) says that items which are similar to each other are the same as each other only in some respect and not without qualification. In this sense, similarity is definitionally dependent on sameness, as (SF) makes explicit. At the same time, though, similar items must be at least in principle distinguishable and discernible from each other in virtue of some positive (possibly non-relational) property. (DC) makes explicit that the properties in virtue of which similar items are distinguishable are grounded in their ontology: similar items are composite beings, which share some formal properties (and in this respect are the same) while not sharing others (and in this respect are different). As we shall see, both (SF) and (DC) are preserved and qualified in Similar$_2$ and Similar$_3$. As it will become apparent in the discussion of the following cases, one problem is that it is not clear whether (SF) concerns substantial forms only or a more or less restricted selection of qualitative features more generally. In the latter case, sameness of form would cover all cases of sameness in account with reference not only to the account of substantial forms but also to the account of qualitative features.

1054b7–9:   Similar$_2$: the items at issue must be such that (SF) they have the same form; **(DC$_{2a}$)** they can receive the more and the less (in some respect to be specified); **(DC$_{2b}$)** they do not exhibit actual differences of degree. A and B are Similar$_2$ if they have a property which can be present in different degrees but is present in the same degree in both A and B. There are some difficulties. In the first place, it is not clear whether the property shared by A and B in the same degree is the same as the 'form' (*eidos*) which is mentioned in (SF). If the form in (SF) indicates the substantial form of A and B, then it is difficult to see in what sense such form could be present in degrees (*Cat.* 5, 3b33–4a9 states quite clearly that substance does not receive the more and the less: for instance, one man cannot be more of a man than another man). Similar$_2$, then, could be made clearer by specifying three criteria: **(SF$_2$)** A and B must have the same substantial form (i.e. they must be the same kind of thing); (DC$_{2a}$) apart from their essential features, A and B are characterized by certain properties (say: a certain colour) which can vary over a determinate range of values (the range is pre-determined for the species to which A and B belong); (DC$_{2b}$) with reference to such range of values, A and B happen not to differ. For instance, Plato and Socrates could differ in the shade of their skin, but as a matter of fact they do not and, in this respect, they are Similar$_2$.

One further problem for this sense of similarity is that it is not obvious whether by 'the more and the less' Aristotle means degrees of intensity of a certain qualitative property or might also have variation of size in mind. A property P receives 'the more and the less' if and only if it makes sense to say that something is more P or less P than something else. In the *Categories*, for each category Aristotle asks whether the specific predicates which fall under the category can in principle receive the more and the less. As already mentioned, he excludes this for predicates belonging to the category of substance. He excludes this possibility also for quantitative determinate predicates (*Cat.* 6, 6a19–25). The reason for this is that it does not make any sense to say that A is more three than B, or that A is more two-foot-long than B. This is fair enough, but it would still seem that a statement like 'Plato is taller than Socrates' makes sense and is based on quantitative properties of Plato and Socrates (their height). Aristotle accommodates cases like this by saying that 'taller than' is a relational property and relatives can receive the more and the less (*Cat.* 7, 6b19–27). So it seems that, although determinate quantitative properties do not receive the more and the less, relational properties based on quantitative properties can receive them. Of the other categories, some qualities (*Cat.* 8, 10b26–11a14), acting and being acted upon (*Cat.* 9, 11b1–8) can receive the more and the less. In *PA* IV.12, 692b4–5 dimensional (and therefore quantitative) differences are regarded as differences in terms of the more and the less which determine not only smaller variations among the individuals of the same species, but also—and perhaps more importantly—the differences of the same part (say: the wing) in the different species of animals (for instance, the wing of the albatross is bigger than the wing of the swallow, but both are wings). It might be relevant that in this context the ascription of the more and the less to dimensional variations is connected with the idea that the range of values is not indefinitely extensible, but is fixed for the species (the wings of a swallow can be slightly bigger than those of another swallow, but cannot be as big as those of an albatross) and for the genus (there cannot be an indefinitely small wing nor an indefinitely big one for any species of bird). For some discussion of how ranges of properties between extremes can be accounted for in terms of the more and the less cf. I.7.

1054b9–11:   Similar$_3$: the items at issue are such that **(SF$_3$)** they are one and the same affection (*pathos*) in form, as, for instance, (being) white. **(DC$_3$)** The affection at issue is present in different degrees. There are some difficulties with this account. In the first place it is not completely clear whether Aristotle is talking of the concrete particular objects which are characterized by one and the same affection (say: white objects) or of particular qualities (say: different shades or portions of white). In the second place, it is not clear whether the qualification at b11 that **(SE)** they are said to be similar 'because their *eidos* is the same' is just a repetition of (SF$_3$) or adds a requirement for the objects that share one and the same affection in different degrees. In the latter case, (SF$_3$) would spell out a feature of the shared affection (it must be one and the same in form), whereas (SE) would add a further requirement on the objects that are said to be similar. On the other hand, if (SE) simply repeats (SF$_3$), then unity in *eidos* of the previous cases does not necessarily refer to sameness in substantial form. If the difference between substantial and incidental properties is not relevant, then Similar$_3$ is complementary to Similar$_2$: in Similar$_2$ the items at issue do not present differences in degree, even if they are such that they could; in Similar$_3$, the items at issue can and in fact do present a difference in degree of the same feature (on this point perhaps *Met.* Δ.9, 1018a17–18 offers a parallel).

1054b11–13:   Similar$_4$: the items at issue are such that the features they share are more than those for which they differ (cf. *Met.* Δ.9, 1018a16). The comparison may extend to any feature or be restricted to the most superficial ones (such as colour). For the philosophical relevance of the distinction between different ways of being similar see comments p. 96.

1054b13–22:   Since the same and the similar are said in many different ways, their opposites too, i.e. the other and the dissimilar, will be said in as many corresponding ways. On the application of the general principle that, if A and B are opposites, if A is said in many ways, then B is said in many ways too, cf. *Top.* I.15, 106a9–b4. Aristotle does not go back to the dissimilar, but analyses the ways in which the other is opposed to the same. First (b13–18), he explains the three ways of being other in opposition to the three ways of being the same; secondly (b18–22), he explains why any item which is one and being is either other than or the same as any other item which is one and being.

1054b13–18:   Other$_1$: in the first sense, the other is opposed to the same in such a way that one of them holds of any being with respect to any being. This seems to be a rather unqualified and possibly determinable sense of 'other' and, correspondingly, of 'the same'. One might therefore wonder whether The Same$_1$ should be also intended in a correspondingly broad sense. Perhaps we could compare this unqualified sameness (which can be made more determinate with reference to different parameters) to the unqualified 'belonging' (*huparchein*) of predication in the *Analytics*. By way of analogy, as the unqualified 'belonging' is a generalization over the different modalities of predication of the four predicables in the *Topics*, the generic numerical sameness corresponding to Other$_1$ would amount to the basic extensional coincidence of the two items which are The Same$_1$, quite independently from the precise modality of such a coincidence. In particular, extensional coincidence can turn out to be mere occasional co-reference (incidental sameness in *Met.* Δ.6, 1015b16–34, Δ.9, 1017b27–1018a4, *Top.* I.7, 103a29–39) or co-extensiveness (as in the cases of *proprium*, definition and their subjects and in the case of synonymous terms in *Top.* I.7, 102b9–10, 103a26; and as in the case of the regular coincidence of mutually related beings such as the act of the mover and the act of the moved in *Phys.* III.3, 202a20–b22). In fact, extensional coincidence seems to be the only basic trait common to all cases recognized by Aristotle as cases of (polyadic) numerical unity or sameness. If this is correct, then the reference to numerical unity in The Same$_1$ must be different and more generic than the reference to numerical unity as the unity of matter in The Same$_2$. In particular, I have suggested that The Same$_2$ applies to individuals, whereas The Same$_1$ is not similarly restricted. According to this reading, we could take The Same$_1$ in the sense of a not better qualified extensional coincidence (which can be modally determined for the different cases) of the items which are said to be the same, whereas The Same$_2$ would require the numerical unity of a particular individual. This is neither exegetically nor philosophically impossible, but in order to support any reading of the passage we need to bring in quite a lot of information from other texts. Both uses of numerical unity (i.e. as dyadic property of extensionally coincident items and as monadic property of the particular individual) belong to Aristotle's philosophical vocabulary. Perhaps a clue to a link between the locution *kat'arithmon* which specifies The Same$_1$ and unity can be found in *Met.* Δ.15, 1021a9–14, where Aristotle explains that in some sense the equal, the similar, and the same are said on the basis of number, i.e. on the basis of the one, because they can all be spelled out with reference to some form of unity.

A different interpretation of The Same$_1$ (and, correspondingly, of The Same$_2$–The Same$_3$) is given by Fait 2005, pp. 84–8. Fait departs from Ross's text in that he restores (correctly, in my opinion; cf. Notes on the Text) the Greek text at 1054a33–34, following the reading of E and J. He strengthens the case for the use of *auto* ('it', 'itself') to indicate the opposite of *to allo* ('the other') rather than *to heteron* (also 'the other') in I.3, 1054b14–16, on the basis of *Met.* N.1, 1087b29–30. Both these moves are convincing. However, Fait goes further and takes the restored text for The Same$_1$ to allude to a use of sameness applying to immobile substances, whereas The Same$_2$ would apply to natural substances and The Same$_3$ to mathematical objects. In this way, the distinction of the three uses of the same would match the partition into three kinds of substance in *Met.* E.1. It does not seem to me that the text need carry these implications. I think Fait is right that The Same$_1$ does not correspond to incidental sameness, but (as Fait himself acknowledges) taking it as ranging over immaterial substances conflicts with the very general reading of the opposition of The Same$_1$ and Other$_1$ explicitly given in the account of Other$_1$ at 1054b15–16. As for the possible restrictions of The Same$_2$ and The Same$_3$ to specific domains of object, see pp. 101–7.

Other$_2$: The second sense of 'other' corresponds to The Same$_2$. X and Y are The Same$_2$ if their form is one and their matter is one; X is Other$_2$ than Y if it is not the case that both their form and their matter is one. This characterization of Other$_2$ is very general and covers three different cases: (i) if matter is the same and form is not the same; (ii) if matter is not the same and form is not the same; (iii) if matter is not the same and form is the same. However, the provided example (you are Other$_2$ than your neighbour—in the masculine and therefore indicating a person as the 'you' whom Aristotle addresses) suggests that Aristotle is considering case (iii) as providing the typical case or the preferred reading of Other$_2$. It is not clear how the different varieties of otherness ((i)–(iii)) interplay with the different varieties of sameness. For instance, (i) could be a case of The Same$_1$ and of Other$_2$. In addition, if The Same$_1$ and Other$_1$ must be regarded as generic and determinable sameness and otherness, it would follow that all other cases of sameness imply The Same$_1$ and all other cases of otherness imply Other$_1$.

Other$_3$: Aristotle's remark is very brief. He just says that this sense of 'other' conforms to the mathematical usage of the term. On the one hand, this characterization of Other$_3$ clearly suggests that we should attach some importance to the mathematical examples in The Same₃. On the other hand, the paradigmatic use of 'the same' and 'other' with reference to mathematical objects does not seem to exclude the extensions of such usages to other kinds of being—unless one shares the worries expressed in Plat., *Phaed.* 72e–78b, that perceptible objects such as two logs can only be imperfectly equal (for some comments about Aristotle's take on the problem see notes to I.1, 1052b31–1053a13). Therefore we still have the problem of understanding not only the possibly restricted mathematical sense of the terms, but also their broader application. Depending on the strength that we attach to the requirement of indiscernibility in The Same₃, we can think of two main cases of Other₃: (1) cases like Similar₁–Similar₃, in which the form is the same, but the items sharing the same form are actually discernible in virtue of other features; (2) cases in which the form is not the same. In the latter sense, Other₃ would apply to cases in which items differ in that they have different forms and, therefore, different definitions.

The analysis of the ways in which things can be said to be other than each other has provided some additional elements for the understanding of the ways in which things are said to be the same. To sum up, The Same₁ seems to cover all cases of co-reference. Co-reference for Aristotle is a minimum requirement for sameness, including incidental sameness; co-reference can be strengthened in terms of co-extensiveness in cases of non-incidental sameness. Co-extensiveness in turn covers different cases such as the relation between a subject and its *propria* and between *definiendum* and *definiens*. The Same₂ is self-identity of individuals. The Same₃ can be taken more or less loosely as sameness in account (compatible with the possession of different and distinguishing properties of the items which are the same in account); as indiscernibility; as equality (confined to mathematical objects or quantities); as congruence (confined to geometrical objects).

1054b18–22: I take the *gar* ('for') at b19 to refer back to *dia touto* ('for this reason') at b18. What is explained is the fact that the disjunction of otherness and sameness in the sense of Other₁ holds of all things that are one and being, but not of what is not (presumably: non-existent objects). Aristotle intends to draw a contrast between this opposition between other and the same and

the opposition between contradictory predicates and contradictory propositions (cf. *Cat.* 10, 13a37–b35; *Int.* 7, 17b16–34), whose
disjunction is always true. In particular Aristotle thinks that the
negative contradictory is true either if its subject does not have
the property expressed by the predicate or if its subject does not
exist. For instance, 'Socrates is not the same as Plato' is true either
if Socrates exists and is other than Plato or if Socrates does not
exist; on the other hand 'Socrates is other than Plato' can only be
true if Socrates exists. More generally, in the proposition 'x is either
the same as or other than y' each of x and y must be something that
is and that is one. The reason for this is that otherness and sameness
are not opposed to each other as contradictories and, more particularly, that neither of them is a (syntactically or morphologically) negative predicate. Since both 'the same' and 'other' are
positive predicates, they can only be said of things that are with
reference to things that are.

1054b21–22: 'For all things that are and that are one are
naturally such as to be either one or not one.' Since this sentence
is supposed to explain why all and only things that are can be said
to be the same as or other than any other thing that is, I take 'one'
in 'either one or not one' in the dyadic sense of 'either one or not
one with each other'. If they are one with each other (in some
sense of the term) they are the same, if they are not one with each
other, they are other than each other. For a similar use of unity to
indicate ontological composition of several items in a state of
affairs cf. *Met.* Θ.10, 1051b9–10.

This reference to unity and plurality in the account of the
opposition of other and the same is relevant, despite its brevity.
For, together with the references to different forms of unity in The
Same$_1$–The Same$_3$, it emphasizes that all these general properties
of beings are definitionally dependent on unity and plurality (i.e.
unity's privation).

1054b22–31: Having explained the ways in which the other
and the same are opposed to each other, Aristotle now moves to
the distinction between 'other' and 'different'. I have tried to keep
in the translation the lexical variety of the Greek text by translating *to diapheron* (the participle of the verb *diapherō*, 'to differ') as
'differing thing' or 'thing that differs' and *diaphoros* (the adjective

with the same root) as 'different', but the two expressions do not seem to be used differently.

As has been said, any being is the same as or other than any being. Other$_1$ does not require the specification of any respect in which two things are other than each other. By way of contrast, something is different from something else in some determinate respect; more particularly, two items which are different from each other differ from each other in the same respect. Aristotle's text could be misleading when he says that 'there must be something which is the same with respect to which they are different'. This should not be taken in the sense that things which differ from each other have something in common (although in some sense this is also true: cf. *Met.* Δ.9, 1018a12–13, and see below), but rather in the sense that things which differ from each other are different in the same respect. As we proceed in reading, we see how Aristotle qualifies such respect: things can be different in genus or in species. This qualification of difference implies that different things are always picked out from an ordered and structured series of items displayed by the division into genera and species, and that difference obtains between items lying on the same level of the division (for the conceptual apparatus of the division into genera and species see introduction to I.7, pp. 170–7). Aristotle resorts to this conceptual apparatus to define a technical notion of difference which he will further analyse in I.7–9. Aristotle's account of difference seems to be oriented towards his notion of specific difference (*differentia*) which divides the genus into species. For instance, if we consider the genus of substance, mobile/immobile are the first opposite specific differences which divide the genus into immobile substance (the unmoved movers) and mobile substance. Mobile substance is in turn further divided by the specific differences perishable/imperishable. Perishable substance is then divided into the different genera and species of natural substances (for this division of substance cf. *Met.* Λ.1, 1069a30–b2). It is not clear whether Aristotle is here providing an account of this philosophically loaded notion of the different (i.e. that which differs in virtue of a specific difference) or of the use of *diaphoros* and *diapherōn* in common Greek. At any rate Aristotle's account of the distinction between 'other' and 'different' matches our understanding of difference as something which can have degrees and can be of several kinds (things can be more

or less different from each other and there can be many differences, whereas there do not seem to be degrees or several kinds
of otherness).

Aristotle characterizes as different in genus those items
which have no matter in common and such that there can be
no change from the one to the other. These qualifications of
difference in genus implies that such items cannot be a suitable
pair of extremes for a process of change (on this see also note to
1054b28–29). Different in species are those items which have
the same genus and—we may add—come about through one
and the same division of the genus (see I.7–8). The genus is here
described as 'that with respect to which both different things
are said to be the same according to substance'. This means
that the genus is part of the definition of its species, which are
different from each other. For instance, black and white are
different in species, but have the same genus (colour): white is
defined as sight-piercing colour, while black is defined as sight-
contracting colour. 'Colour' is present in the definitional
account of both. Given that the definitional account is supposed
to express the substance or the essence of what is defined, colour
is what both white and black are said to be with reference to
their substance.

The remarks on the role of the contraries in change make it
clear that Aristotle is thinking of the contraries as opposite properties. In I.4 we shall see that other items can be said to be
contraries in virtue of a certain ontological relation to contrary
properties.

1054b28–29:   Two items that differ in genus cannot work as
the extreme stages of a process of change. Since the contraries
that can work as the extremes of change can be received by the
same matter, Aristotle can express the inadequacy of contrary
genera to be the extremes of change by saying that there is no
common substratum which can receive both of them and that,
therefore, can go through a process of becoming from one
contrary to the other. On the relation between contraries and
a common substratum see Introduction, pp. xxvii–xxxii and
notes to I.8, pp. 210, 216–18; for things that differ in genus see
notes to 1054b31–1055a2, Introduction, pp. xxviii–xxx, I.7,
pp. 193–4, and I.10, pp. 253–4.

1054b31–1055a2: Aristotle introduces the opposition of contrariety as a certain difference (*diaphora tis*). I.4 is devoted to the specification of this account. Depending on how we read b34 (see Notes on the text), in the closing lines Aristotle either gives support for his account of *difference* by way of induction or he gives support for his claim that *contrariety* is a certain difference by showing by induction that, for any pair of contraries, the one appears to differ from the other by being either different in genus or the same in genus and different in species.

At 1054b35–1055a2 one feature of items that differ in species is expressed in three equivalent ways: they are 'in the same series of predication' (*en tēi autēi sustoichiāi tēs katēgorias*), 'in the same genus', 'the same in genus'. Aristotle contextually refers to an account, to be found elsewhere, of what it is for things to be the same or other in genus. The reference is not clear. Among the passages where Aristotle explains sameness in genus we can count *Top.* I.7, 102b13–14; *Met.* Δ.6, 1016a24–32; 1016b33–34; for difference in genus *Met.* Δ.28, 1024b9–16. Δ.10, 1018a38–b8 deals with otherness and sameness in species, but does not consider otherness and sameness in genus. Jaeger's reference to Δ.9, 1018a4 (Jaeger 1912, p. 118) is puzzling in that the passage includes no explicit reference to sameness or difference in genus. Elders (1961, p. 111) takes the reference to be to the *Divisions*. For the equivalence of sameness in genus and being in the same series of predication cf. I.8, 1058a13–14 and corresponding notes.

sustoichia derives from the same root as the verb *sustoicheō*, which means 'to stand in the same line or rank'. The basic meaning of *sustoichia* is 'series' or 'column' of items ordered under or after one main item. In Aristotle logical writings (*APr* II.20, 66b27; *APo* I.15, 79b7) and with reference to the progressive division of general predicates into more specific ones, it indicates the same 'line of predication', namely the series of predicates which stand on the same side in the progressive stages of the division. Aristotle also records a more metaphysically loaded use of the term in connection to Pythagorean philosophy (*Met.* A.5, 986a23; N.6, 1093b12; cf. Λ.7, 1072a32). In this context a *sustoichia* is each of the two parallel columns which result from the ordering of ten basic pairs of contraries under the main opposite headings of the Limit and the Unlimited. The 'positive' member of each pair is listed under the Limit, while all 'negative' members are listed under the Unlimited. Each column is a *sustoichia*. In Pythagorean philosophy the partition was supposed to have metaphysical and axiological value. On the influence of this model on Aristotle see Introduction, section II.2, and notes to 1054a29–32. Note that, after I.2's account of the relation between members of a kind and their unit(s), I.3's arrangement based on the two columns of opposites falling under the one and the many continues with the application and revision of Pythagorean conceptual frameworks. The introduction of difference and contrariety in the last part if I.3 provides a clear link to the discussion in I.4–6.

CHAPTER 4

I.4 proceeds with the account of contrariety introduced at the end of I.3. The chapter opens with a general account of contrariety and gives support for it by induction (1055a3–10). In what follows two general features of contrariety are analysed: first, contrariety is complete or perfect difference (1055a10–16) and completeness follows from any correct account of contrariety (1055a16–19); secondly, contrariety is a dyadic relation (1055a19–23). A list of alternative accounts of contrariety is given in order to show that all accounts turn out to be in agreement with the general account of contrariety and its features given in the first part of the chapter (1055a23–33). Finally, Aristotle shows that every pair of contraries can be regarded as an opposition of possession of a form and complete privation of it (1055a33–b29), and provides three arguments in support of this analysis: an argument based on the analysis of change (1055b11–17), an argument by induction (1055b17–26), and an argument based on the relation obtaining between the genera of contraries (1055b26–29). As for the general philosophical relevance of I.4 see Introduction, part II. More generally on the use of contrariety in Aristotle's philosophy see Anton 1957; on contraries and change see Bogen 1991 and 1992.

1055a3–10: Having said in I.3 that contrariety is a certain difference, in these lines Aristotle qualifies the kind of difference that contrariety is. In particular, he says, given that there are degrees of difference (on degrees of difference and intermediates see I.7), contrariety is defined as the biggest difference (I shall refer to this account of contrariety as Contraries$_1$). That this account of contrariety is correct can be shown by induction on the two cases (distinguished in I.3) of items that differ in genus and items that differ in species.

The argument by induction can be interpreted in two ways. On one reading, the argument establishes that both difference in genus and difference in species can be regarded as cases of contrariety. On the second reading, the argument establishes that difference in genus should be discarded and that in all cases of difference in species contrariety is the biggest difference in species (and is, therefore, intrageneric). The relation between difference in genus and contrariety is one of the main problems of this chapter.

In support of the first reading one may turn to *Met.* Δ.10 1018a30–31, where Aristotle acknowledges that contrariety is the biggest difference 'either without qualification or according to genus or according to species'. A reference to contraries which differ in genus can be found in the same chapter at 1018a25–27 ('those items are said contraries which differ according to the genus (*tōn diapherontōn kata genos*) and cannot be present at the same time in the same subject'). The idea would be that items which are different in genus are so far apart from each other that their ontological distance cannot be bridged: their ontological distance, as it were, is so big that they cannot be joined by any process of change taking them as extremes, although they might look like the kind of opposites which might function as extremes of change. This last qualification is necessary in that there are indefinitely many pairs of items which cannot function as extremes of change without being opposite to each other (e.g. being a cat and being a dog). On this account, things that differ in genus are still 'comparable' in some relevant respect, but are not 'joinable' or 'they have no access to each other' (cf. 1054b28–29 and I.10; on the translation of *asumblēta* at 1055a7 see note to 1055a7).

The very fact that items that differ in genus are so far apart that their distance cannot be bridged would count as the first step of the inductive argument that contrariety is the biggest difference: the difference between two contrary genera is so big that it cannot be bridged. According to this line of interpretation, the fact that two items differing in genus cannot work as extremes of a unitary process of change would not count by itself as evidence against the possibility that such items are opposed as contraries. However, the fact that items differing in genus cannot be the extremes of a process of change is in contrast with the case of things that differ in species, which can be the extremes of change (cf. 1055b11–17). By definition the distance between the extremes of something is 'the biggest'. Therefore, if the contraries are the extremes, the distance of the contraries from each other will be the biggest.

On the second reading, we should take Aristotle's claim that what differs in genus is 'incomparable' in the sense that difference in genus is somehow beyond contrariety. The main idea in support of this interpretation would be that degrees of difference between the contraries can be described in terms of more and less and in terms of closeness to one contrary rather than to the other. Contraries would then be the extremes of ranges of properties that can be compared to each other based on their position within such a range. Items that differ in genus cannot belong to a range—not even as its extremes—because they cannot be compared to each other. Therefore, they are simply excluded from the domain of contraries. The case for this interpretation could be strengthened on the basis of 1055a26–27, where Aristotle seems to say that it has been shown that there is no difference with reference to things which are outside the genus (the passage, however, is perhaps more compatible with the first reading than it might appear at first; see notes below).

The two readings are not clearly distinguished and discussed in the interpretations of this passage (Ross 1924, II does not comment on this point, but his paraphrase on p. 289 seems to support the second reading; similarly, Bonitz 1849, pp. 430–1, says that we should add the implicit premise that two items cannot be contraries unless they admit a process of change from the one to the other). However, contrary genera (and, therefore, some difference in genus that can be regarded as contrariety) are explicitly admitted in other texts (see references in Introduction, pp. xxviii–xxx) and seem to be required to make sense of I.10. Some further distinctions may be useful. We have already pointed out (see Introduction, p. xxvii, and Notes on the Text *ad* 1054b34) that the characterization of what differing items have in common is ambiguous: it swings between the claim that differing items must have something in common in the sense that they must share something, and the claim that differing items differ from each other in the same respect. Furthermore, the requirement that they have something in common is open to further qualifications, making it a more or less loose criterion (see, e.g., *Met.* Δ.9, 1018a12–13: 'Those things are said to be different which are other while being the same something, not only in number, but either in species or in genus or by analogy'). The highest genera (the categories) could be said to differ in genus as in the second claim, but not as in the first. However, the categories are at least formally comparable: they are the same kind of item in that they are all highest genera of being and lie at the same level of generality. Furthermore, 'genus' and 'species' in Aristotle's vocabulary may but need not be used absolutely to indicate absolute levels of generality (see introduction to I.7, pp. 171–3). They can be used relatively. A genus can be further divided into species and a species is the result of the division of a genus; but nothing prevents what is regarded as a genus of certain species from being in turn regarded as the species of a more general predicate, which is correspondingly a genus. Similarly, nothing prevents the species of a genus from being the genus of other species. According to this scheme, only the ten categories, which are not the result of any higher division, are genera without qualification and only the *infimae species*, i.e. the ultimate results of division under which only particulars fall, are species without qualification. Based on this picture, it could be the case that Aristotle thinks of items which differ in genus as belonging to two genera which are in their turn species of one higher genus. Items belonging to two genera which do not in their turn fall under one higher genus are not different at all (they are just 'other'), because they just do not have anything in common—whereas having something in common and being somehow the same is the mark of difference in contrast to otherness. Finally, when Aristotle refers to contrary genera (see Introduction, pp. xxviii–xxx), he tends to refer to opposites that mark a primitive partition of things that are, but are not genera in any of his technical senses.

It follows that we can distinguish four different cases: (a) contrary species, to which there belong contrary items that differ in species; (b) contrary genera that are the result of the division of a higher genus and under which there fall items that differ in genus; (c) items that differ in genus and are not the result of the division of a higher common genus; (d) items which are comparable in some formal respect and mark some basic partition of things that are. The problematic case is (c) in that it is not clear whether there are any contraries belonging to this group or even whether items belonging to this group can be said to be 'different' from each other.

1055a7: *asumblēta*: 'unjoinable' or 'incomparable'. The word is used in *Phys.* IV.9, 217a10, where Aristotle dismisses the hypothesis that the void can move or that something can move through the void by showing that in either case we would have a motion of indefinitely high speed. The speed of such motion could not be compared to the speed of any other motion, and this would go against the principle that there must be a *logos* (ratio) of each motion with respect to any other (of *kinēsis pros kinēsin*). In this sense the speed of the motion of or through the void and the speed of any other motion would be 'incomparable'. For a similar context see *Phys.* VII.4, 248b5 ff. In *PA* IV.2, 677a10–11 Aristotle speaks of quantities of bile that are *asumblēta*. Finally, *Met.* M.6, 1080b9 is about ideal units, which are qualitatively different and, for this reason, cannot be put together to make a number and in this sense are *asumblēta*, i.e. in the sense that they cannot be combined. I have rendered the idea that items belonging to different genera cannot be joined by a unitary process of change in terms of being 'unjoinable', whereas I have rendered the idea that two items are too different to be compared with 'incomparable' (see note on 1055a3–10 on how the two senses of the word could be functional to two different interpretations of the passage). The two properties are not mutually exclusive, but they are different.

There is a problem as to what the notion of 'comparability' requires. It seems clear that terms expressing contrary properties must belong to the same semantic area in some relevant sense. One interesting case to test Aristotle's intuitions on this point is analysed in I.10, discussing the opposition of perishable and imperishable. These are contrary properties marking a primitive partition of being between two domains which cannot be joined by any process of change (in this sense they are 'unjoinable'). However, perishable and imperishable are the kind of opposites which could work as extremes in a process of change in the sense that they are formally similar: they fill in corresponding gaps in the full description of different kinds of objects, so to speak.

1055a8:   *geneseis*: 'processes of coming to be'. This should be understood in a very general sense as to cover all kinds of change and not only change in substance (i.e. generation and corruption strictly speaking).

1055a10–16:   Aristotle has established that contrariety is the biggest difference. He now establishes that, precisely in virtue of this qualification, contrariety is also the complete or perfect (*teleios*) difference. In order to elucidate this point he resorts to a morphological feature of the words he is using: the complete (*teleia*) difference has an end (*telos*), and it is precisely in virtue of having an end that things are said to be complete. It belongs to the very nature of the 'end' (*telos*) to be the extreme or the conclusion of what it is the end of. Hence it is not possible to take anything beyond the end of what is complete and perfect, because what is complete and perfect does not lack anything.

1055a16–19:   Contrariety is complete or perfect difference. Since, the contraries are said in many ways (cf. *Met.* Δ.10, 1018a25–35), Aristotle argues that completeness belongs to the contraries according to any account of contrariety. Note that in Δ.10 Aristotle provides two distinctions. First, he provides different definitions (1018a25–31) of the contraries, which (with the exception of 1018a25–27, quoted above on p. 120) correspond to the accounts given at 1055a23 ff. Second, he distinguishes items which are said to be contraries by answering to the given accounts from items which are contraries only derivatively—by having, being receptive of, being able to produce or to be affected by, being rejections, acquisitions, possessions, or privations of contraries of the first kind (1018a31–35). I shall refer to this distinction as a distinction between primary and derivative contraries. Primary contraries are properties standing to each other in a certain relation of opposition, whereas derivative contraries are more or less ontologically complex items that have a certain relation to basic contraries. For the extension of completeness to all kinds of contraries cf. *Met.* Δ.16, 1022a1–3.

In this section of I.4 Aristotle takes over the first distinction of accounts of contrariety, while he recalls the distinction between basic and derivative contraries at 1055a35–38.

1055a19–23: It is not possible to give a literal translation of the Greek at 1055a22–23 as the text is anacoluthic. The translation I provide gives a grammatically acceptable English sentence which is as close as possible to the Greek text.

In this passage Aristotle argues that any contrary is contrary to one and only one item (in other words, contrariety is a 1–1 relation). This was one of the properties of contrariety whose investigation Aristotle characterized as pertinent to the science of being in *Met.* Γ.2, 1004b3–4 (cf. *Met.* B.1, 995b25–27; *Top.* VIII.3, 158b24–28; see Introduction, pp. xxxv–xxxvi). This property of contrariety is established through three arguments, two based on the specific nature of the contraries as extremes and one on the generic characterization of contrariety as a kind of difference. The text is concise, but the three arguments can be spelled out comparatively clearly. (i) The first argument is that the contraries are the extremes of a certain ontological interval; there cannot be any extreme more extreme than the extreme (1055a20). This is true by definition (i.e. by the definition of extreme). Therefore there cannot be any further extreme than the contraries which are the extremes and, therefore, there cannot be any further contrary. (ii) Second argument: contraries are the extremes of a certain ontological interval; there are no more than two extremes of one single interval (1055a21); therefore, there are no more than two contraries as extremes of a certain ontological interval. (iii) The third argument seems to introduce a more general point (see *holōs* l.22, 'in general'). The generality could be accounted for by the fact that Aristotle here resorts to a general property of difference, which is in a way the genus of contrariety. The argument is: contrariety is (a certain) difference; difference is between two items (i.e. difference is a dyadic relation); therefore complete difference (i.e. contrariety), too, is between two items.

1055a23–33: In this section Aristotle presents three different accounts (1055a27–28; 29–30; 31) of the contraries, which turn out to be correct ('true') given what has been said so far. In particular, all alternative accounts are expressed in terms of 'differing the most' or 'in the highest degree' (*pleiston diapherein*), which is taken as a necessary property of complete difference (i.e. as following from Aristotle's account of Contraries₁). The correspondence of difference in the highest degree and complete difference explains (see *gar* l.24: 'for') why the truth of the alternative accounts follows from Aristotle's previous account.

1055a23–27: Aristotle explains why complete difference is difference in the highest degree by giving an explanation parallel to 1055a6–10. In the latter passage he has shown that contrariety is the biggest (and, therefore, complete: a10–11) difference by considering the cases of difference in genus and difference in species. Similarly, he now starts by saying that there are no different items beyond pairs of items that differ in genus and pairs of items that differ in species (a25–26). The explanation is problematic. Aristotle reminds us that he has shown (i) that there is no difference with respect to items which are beyond or outside the genus and (ii) that of 'these' (I take this to mean: of things within the genus) 'this' (i.e. complete difference) is the biggest difference. As for (i), items which are different in genus belong to two genera and are, therefore, each beyond or outside the genus of the other. So it might sound as Aristotle were saying that there is no difference of things that are different in genus, which looks like a contradiction.

1055a27–29: Contraries₂ (cf. *Met.* Δ.10, 1018a27–28): The first alternative account of the contraries is not particularly problematic. It replaces the notions of biggest difference with that of differing the most (i.e. in the highest degree) within the same genus.

1055a29–30: Contraries₃ (cf. *Met.* Δ.10, 1018a28–29): The second alternative account takes up Aristotle's hint at 1055a9 that contraries are involved in change. The basic idea is that the same substratum can assume either contrary and can change from having one of them to having the other. For instance, the same surface can change from being white to being black. The 'matter' (*hulē*) in the parenthesis corresponds to the 'receiver' (*dektikon*) at a29 and it indicates what persists through change and assumes ('receives') opposite properties. It is not clear whether Aristotle means to cover all four types of change (in quality, in quantity, in place, and in substance). In *Phys.* V.1, 224b35 ff., he says that change in quality, quantity, and place is between the contraries, while change in substance rather requires the shift from negation to affirmation (generation from non-being to being) or from affirm-ation to negation (ceasing to be). The second part of I.4 (1055a33 ff.) opens up the logical space for a unified account of all extremes of change in that they are all opposed as possession and privation. For further details on the role of the contraries in the ontology of change see Introduction, pp. xxv–xxvii and I.7, pp. 177, 180–6.

1055a31–32: Contraries$_4$ (*Met.* Δ.10, 1018a29–30): The third alternative account is that the contraries are 'things which differ the most and fall under the same capacity'. The elucidation in the parenthesis (one science embraces one whole genus) hints at two main ideas which Aristotle expounds elsewhere. First, the unity of a certain domain of knowledge (say: of a science) is determined by the unity of its object (in this case: the subject genus which defines the scope of the science itself). Each science deals with a deter-minate genus of objects and the science of one genus of objects is one (cf. *APo* I.28). Secondly, rational capacities (cf. *Met.* Θ.2, 1046b2: *dunameis meta logou*) are defined as principles of change (cf. 1046a10–11; 1046b2–4). Rational capacities are 'of the con-traries' (1046b5) in the sense that they presuppose rational know-ledge of what both contraries are (e.g. the doctor knows both what health is and what disease is; cf. 1046b16–24) and are able to bring about contrary results (e.g. the good doctor is the one who is able to restore health and who would be able to kill one off most efficiently). Scientific knowledge is a rational capacity. A science deals with one whole genus and, with reference to that genus, it is knowledge of the contrary properties that range over that genus. Based on this account, contraries can be characterized as those items which, falling within the scope of the same capacity, differ in the highest degree.

1055a32–33: The final addition ('in these things the complete difference is the biggest') seems redundant. It is not clear whether the relative pronoun in the dative ('in these things') refers back to the most differing items mentioned in the account of Contraries$_4$ or to all three alternative accounts. In the latter case, the remark would recall the point made at a17–19, that completeness belongs to the contraries together with their being contraries, no matter in which of these ways contraries are defined. Given the correspondence between differing in the highest degree and being a complete difference stated at a24–25, Aristotle adds that in all cases covered by the alternative definitions complete difference is the biggest difference.

1055a33–38: With the statement at 1055a33, that primary contrariety is an opposition of possession and privation, we are introduced to the second part of the chapter.

At 1055a34–35 Aristotle explains in what sense privation contributes to the determination of an opposition of contrariety. Privation is said in many ways (cf. *Met.* Δ.22) and these ways are distinguished on the basis of the specifications that can be added to 'being deprived of' a certain property (at a certain time, under determinate circumstances or in all respects and completely). The privation which provides one side of contrariety is not any privation, but only complete privation (cf. *Phys.* I.7, 191a5–7).

1055a35–38: Having said that primary contrariety is an opposition of possession and privation, Aristotle spells out how other contraries are derivatively said with reference to the form of contrariety. Derivative contraries are contraries in virtue of having or producing primary contraries or in virtue of being acquisitions or losses of primary contraries (cf. p. 124). This way of spelling out derivative contraries with respect to a basic form of contrariety is reminiscent of the project outlined in *Met.* Γ.2 (see pp. xvi–xviii). In order to explain what this 'ordering' of derivative contraries amounts to, we can use Aristotle's example of something which is said *pros hen* ('with reference to one') in *Met.* Γ.2 and adapt the example to the case of the contraries. 'Healthy' is said of many different things whose being healthy is defined with reference to health. The primary contraries, which are opposed as possession and privation, are health and sickness (the notion of complete sickness is in itself problematic, but let us assume for the sake of the argument that the opposition of health and sickness as contraries is clear). The healthy person and the sick person designate a pair of contraries in virtue of having, respectively, health and sickness; getting sick and recovering designate a pair of contraries in virtue of being processes of acquisition of those basic contraries; a medicine and a poison are contraries in virtue of producing, respectively, health and sickness.

1055a38–b11: The relation between contrariety and contradiction is spelled out with reference to the analysis of primary contrariety as a relation of opposition between possession and complete privation of a form. The section opens with a list of the four kinds of opposition acknowledged by Aristotle: contradiction, privation (and possession), contrariety, the opposition of relative terms. Although contradiction and contrariety can also be relations between propositions (*Cat.* 10, 13b13: *tōn kata sumplokēn enantiōn legomenōn*; *Int.* 7, 17b16 ff.), in this context Aristotle is not dealing with opposite propositions, but with non-propositional items (predicates or properties). This can be seen from the examples at b9–11 and from the role he ascribes to contraries in the ontology of change. For some discussion of the different kinds of contradictory pairs with reference to I.4, 1055a38–b9, see Gallagher 2014.

Aristotle does not have an abstract noun to indicate the opposition existing between two relative beings (e.g. the master and the slave), whereas he has abstract nouns for the other three kinds of opposition. The proposed translation ('relatives') reflects this feature of the Greek, which might be of philosophical significance to understand the way in which Aristotle looks at the ontology of relations.

Aristotle shows that contradiction and contrariety are two different relations of opposition by exposing a discrepancy between the two: contradiction admits of no intermediates, while there can be intermediates of contraries. That the opposition of *a* and *not a* admits of no intermediate (i.e. that there is nothing which is neither *a* nor *not a*) is accounted for in *Met.* Γ.4, 1008a2 ff., where Aristotle discusses the principle of excluded middle for contradictories. As for intermediates of contraries, see I.7.

Having established that contradiction and contrariety are not the same, Aristotle goes on to argue that privation is a determinate contradiction. What Aristotle means is presumably that privation involves the negation of a positive term as the negative member of a contradiction does. Compared to the negative member of a pair of contradictory items, privation is the negation of a property in a determinate subject which could be able to receive the property of which it is deprived. For instance, blindness is the privation of sight in something which could have sight, while absence of sight can be ascribed in general to anything that has no sight, no matter whether it could have it or not (for instance, a stone has no sight, but is not blind, while an animal which is blind also has no sight). The account of privation as a determinate negation, qualified with respect to a certain subject and to determinate circumstances, explains why the opposition of possession and privation may admit of intermediates, whereas the opposition of contradictories does not. The point is illustrated through some examples. Everything is either equal or not equal, but not everything is either equal or unequal. This is so because, strictly speaking, only quantities can be equal or unequal; thence not everything can be equal or unequal. This is equivalent to saying that there are things that are neither equal nor unequal. The joint negation of two properties (in this case: one property and its privation as in 'neither equal nor unequal') is a way to pick out intermediates (cf. I.5, 1056a16–b2). However, the possibility to deny at the same time two opposite predicates is compatible with two states of affairs: (e) there are subjects to which the opposites in question simply do not apply and to which the joint negation of them applies (e.g. colours are neither equal nor unequal); (f) there are subjects which are characterized by some positive property which is intermediate between the two opposite properties that are denied (e.g. a red surface is neither black nor white). On these two options cf. notes to 1055b17–26 and I.7, 1057a18–19.

1055b11–17: Aristotle provides an argument for the identification of contrariety with the opposition of complete privation and possession of a form (for some assessment of the advantages and the philosophical motivation for this move, see Introduction, part II). The argument is based on the analysis of change (cf. *Phys.* I.5–8) according to which change is always of a certain substratum which changes from having a certain property to having the contrary property. If changes are from one contrary to the other and if they take place from the possession of a determinate form or from the privation of a determinate form to the opposite state, then every contrariety (which is the relation of opposition between the extremes of change) is an opposition of privation and possession. At 1055a34–35 ff. Aristotle has already specified that contrariety is an opposition of possession and complete privation. However, Aristotle admits cases of change in which the initial and the final stage are not contrary to each other, but are intermediates between two contraries (for instance: an object changing its colour from yellow to red—and not from white to black). In these cases, the opposition between two intermediates which work as the initial and the final stage of a process of change resembles the opposition between the contraries (cf. *Phys.* V.5, 229b14–21). The idea seems to be that, when the extremes of change are intermediates between two contraries, the intermediates can be regarded as contextual or functional contraries (precisely in that they fulfil the function of being extremes of change). This suggests a possible distinction between a structural or constitutive account of contrariety as biggest difference and a functional account of contraries as extremes of processes of change. For some discussion of the relation between the structural and the functional account of contraries and, correspondingly, of intermediates, see notes to I.7, pp. 180–6, 194–6.

At 1055b14–15 Aristotle uses two different words in the formulation of the claim that 'it is clear that every contrariety (*enantiōsis*) is a privation, while perhaps not every privation is a contrariety (*enantiotēs*)'. The two words are taken as equivalent by most commentators, but Gallagher (2014, p. 319) suggests that the two words are used differently. In particular, *enantiōsis* would be used in I.4 to indicate the greatest difference, whereas *enantiotēs* would be used more generally to indicate a relation of functional contrariety obtaining between any two extremes of change (in the sense outlined above; the terminology of 'functional' contraries is mine). Gallagher is right that there is a distinction to be drawn between the two cases, but I cannot find support for his view about the different usage of the two Greek words. For example, at 1055a16 *enantiotēs* is used for complete difference.

1055b17–26: After the argument from the analysis of change, Aristotle sets off to show that in any opposition of contrariety one of the contrary is a privation by means of induction. If we look at pairs of particular contraries, we can see that one of them is always the privation of the other, even if in different ways. Aristotle mentions four examples: inequality/equality; dissimilarity/similarity; vice/virtue; odd/even. Before taking a closer look at the way in which one of the contrary in each of these pairs is the privation of the other, let us consider the qualifications of privations specified in the course of the passage. Aristotle says that something can be deprived of a certain property either without further qualification or in a qualified sense: at a certain time (e.g. at a certain age), or in a certain organ (e.g. in the brain or in the heart), or in all possible respects (1055b21–22). It is with respect to these qualifications that some contraries admit of intermediates, whereas others do not (b23–25). In addition (1055b25–26) some pairs of contraries have a determinate subject, while some do not.

Taking these additions into account, we can spell out Aristotle's examples. Aristotle has already resorted to the equal and the unequal (1055b10–11) to illustrate the difference between a negative contradictory predicate (e.g. not equal) and a privative predicate (unequal). Inequality is the privation of equality in those subjects (quantities) which can be equal; there are subjects that are neither equal nor unequal (cf. *Cat.* 6, 6a26–35). Dissimilarity is the privation of similarity; in this case it is not completely clear whether Aristotle has any specific restriction of subject in mind, as at some places he seems to restrict similarity to qualities strictly speaking (*Cat.* 8, 11a15–19), while at other places he seems to endorse a looser notion of what can be said to be similar or dissimilar (cf. Similar$_4$ in I 3).

As for virtue/vice and odd/even, both pairs appear in the Pythagorean table of *sustoichiai* (cf. 1054b31–1055a2; 1055b26–29; see p. 99 and Introduction, section II.2). Within this scheme, vice should be understood as the privation of virtue. In addition, given that ethical vice and virtue according to Aristotle are dispositions of the soul of the adult human being, acquired through practice and exercise, a human baby cannot be said to be 'vicious' because she is not yet in the age in which she could be virtuous. The joint negation of vice and virtue applies to human babies as in (e) on p. 130; but also with reference to their appropriate subjects, some contraries have intermediates as in (f) on p. 130 (an adult human being can be neither vicious nor virtuous), whereas some do not: for instance, any number is either even or odd. To understand the sense in which even and odd are contraries in which one term is the privation of the other, we probably have to resort again to Pythagorean ideas. In the Pythagorean arrangement of the basic pairs of contraries, the odd belongs in the column of the Limit, whereas the even belongs in the column of the Unlimited (cf. *Met.* A.5, 986a15–26). This presumably rests on the idea that the division of an odd number is 'limited' by the one unit which cannot be split (and which makes the difference between an odd and an even number), whereas the division by two of the even number gives place, as it were, to an unlimited fissure between the two groups of units resulting from the splitting (cf. *Met.* M.8, 1083b29–30). In Aristotle's reinterpretation of this model, this makes of the even the privation of the odd.

1055b18: See Notes on the Text.

1055b22: *en tōi kuriōi*: 'in the principal part'. This can either indicate the principal part of the whole body (the brain or the heart) or the principal of two similar parts (e.g. the right hand is the principal hand).

1055b25–26: I follow Ross and translate 'furthermore (*eti*) some contraries have a determinate subject'. Bonitz (see Bonitz 1849, p. 434) conjectures, on the basis of (ps.) Alexander's commentary (Hayduck, 597.7) 'because (*hoti*) some contraries have a determinate subject'. The reason behind Bonitz's move seems to be that at 1055b8–9 intermediates link to the presence of a determinate subject (note that Bonitz regarded the commentary on Iota ascribed to Alexander as authentic, whereas nowadays interpreters regard as authentic only the books up to Delta). However, b25–26 may be making the additional point that some contraries have some positive intermediates (i.e. intermediates which are determinate properties of the type of subject which could also receive the contraries) whereas others do not. The examples for both cases include reference to a specific subject: the specific subject of vice and virtue is the human being with respect to certain dispositions of her soul, whereas the specific subject of equal and unequal is quantities. The difference between the two cases is that in the first case the same subject which could be vicious or virtuous (a human being) can be neither good nor bad, whereas in the second case the subject that can be equal or unequal (quantities) is not the same as the subject that can be neither.

Alternatively, one could perhaps take the reference to a specific subject as introducing the case in which one given contrary necessarily belongs to a determinate subject (e.g. hot to fire, cold to snow). But Aristotle usually refers to this situation by saying that a determinate contrary belongs to a subject rather than by saying that the contraries have a determinate subject. Cf. *Cat.* 10, 13a1–3.

1055b26–29: Aristotle restates the claim that for all pairs of contraries one term is the privation of the other and sketches one last argument in support of this claim. Although the claim has been argued for by induction on particular cases, it would be enough to show that this structural feature of the opposition between contraries obtains in the case of the primary contraries and the genera of the contraries, i.e. the one and the many, to which all other contraries can be reduced. On the doctrine of the one and the many as primary contraries and as genera of the contraries see Introduction, section II.2 and I.3, p. 99 and notes to 1054b31–1055a2.

CHAPTER 5

I.4 has provided an account of the relation of contrariety and of its main properties. In particular, on the basis of the account of contrariety as complete difference, Aristotle has been able to settle the disputed question (cf. *Top.* VIII.3, 158b24–28, *Met.* B.1, 995b27) whether only one thing is contrary to another (in what follows I shall refer to this property as uniqueness of the contrary). I.5 introduces two cases of opposite items traditionally regarded as cases of *enantia* (which I systematically translate as 'contraries') which fail to comply with the requirement of uniqueness of the contrary. This implies that contrariety cannot be the relation obtaining between the items at issue. Therefore, Aristotle sets out to explain what kind of opposition obtains in each case: what can we say about the relation of opposition between the equal, the great, and the small and of that between the one and the many? The opposition between the equal, the great, and the small is dealt with in I.5, the opposition between the one and the many in I.6.

There are two main difficulties in making sense of these chapters. The first concerns some peculiar features of Aristotle's formulation of the arguments, the second concerns the more general philosophical significance of the discussion. The first difficulty is due to the fact that, as we have already seen (pp. 21–2), in Iota Aristotle often resorts to the neuter adjective preceded by the article to indicate the objects he is talking about (e.g. *to ison*, 'the equal'; *to hen*, 'the one', etc.). This locution can indicate the property (equality or being equal) or the thing that has that property (the equal thing(s)) and this ambiguity is of some importance for the interpretation of these chapters.

To start with, in introducing one of the difficulties in I.5, Aristotle refers to the two terms whose opposition has to be clarified as 'the one' (*to hen*) and 'the many' (*ta polla*). The latter term is a neuter *plural*; the fact that Aristotle uses a plural expression here could by itself suggest that he is talking of the many things rather than of the property of being many. I do not think, however, that the linguistic formulation in terms of 'one' and 'many' rules out taking the argument in I.6 as being about properties at the start. For in I.3, 1054a20–22, Aristotle says that the one and the many (*ta polla*) are opposites in many ways, one of which is the way in which the one and plurality are opposite as indivisible and divisible. In this passage the plural is replaced with a singular neuter noun (*to plēthos*) spelled out as 'the divisible' (*to dihaireton*), which in turn can indicate either the property of being divisible or the thing that is divisible. Accordingly, the use of a neuter plural expression does not in itself exclude the possibility that the argument be about properties rather than things. If I.6 is about properties, however, and the opposition of the one and the many is supposed to be problematic with respect to the requirement of uniqueness (on this point, however, see below), then the problem becomes clear only once we add at least one further assumption: the many is also supposed to be the contrary of the few. The many, then, turns out to have two contraries: the one and the few.

If, on the other hand, we take the many to indicate 'the many things', then the many are many (i.e. more than one) things and this may seem to introduce the problem with the requirement of uniqueness already at the start. This understanding of the one and the many may be supported by an argument Aristotle builds in I.6 against the claim that the one and the many are contraries. In short, the argument is this: a plurality of items can be said to be many to convey the idea that the plurality of items amounts to a great number (on this see notes on I.6, pp. 159–60). In this sense, the many are opposed to the few; but the many are also opposed to the one; if both oppositions are oppositions of contrariety, then the one and the few will be the same. But this is absurd, because the few are a plurality, whereas the one is, by definition, the negation of any plurality. One could argue that the natural reading of the claim that the few are a plurality is that things that are few are more than one.

Note, however, that independently of whether one reads I.6 as about properties or as about things, Aristotle must admit that what is one and what is many (i.e. the many things) can stand in a relation of contrariety: for even if he argues that primary contraries are properties rather than things (see Introduction, p. xxxi and I.4, pp. 124, 128), things that have contrary properties can be regarded as derivative contraries. Presumably the one as what is indivisible or undivided is contrary to the things that are many, provided that the latter are taken collectively as what is divisible or divided. This is not a violation of the requirement of uniqueness in that, if the many are taken collectively as what is divided, they can be regarded as one (logically) unified term entering a relation of contrariety. The requirement of uniqueness would be violated if one took the relation of opposition as obtaining between the one and the many taken distributively: if one considers a relation of opposition in which one term is supposed to be the contrary of each of a plurality of items, then that relation cannot be a relation of contrariety. It is doubtful, however, whether such considerations really play any role in the development of the argument in I.6 (are the many that are opposed to the one as what is measured to the measure taken collectively or ditributively?), despite the announcement of the difficulty about the one and the many in I.5 with reference to the requirement of uniqueness. For some discussion of this point see notes to 1056b3–5.

As for the opposition of the equal, the great, and the small, the detection of the difficulty in connection with the requirement of uniqueness is more straightforward: the equal is opposed to (each of) the great and the small. Whatever the great and the small are, they are two, i.e. more than one. Note that in the course of I.5 Aristotle emphasizes that the contrary of the equal is the unequal; although he never specifies the relation obtaining between the unequal and the great and the small, one could think of the unequal as what results from taking the great and the small collectively (rather than distributively) as the opposite of the equal.

As for the general philosophical interest of I.5–6, it may be useful to distinguish between the motivations which might have prompted the discussion of these chapters and the outcomes of the discussion. As for the motivation, there is little doubt that the Academic debate about the principles of immaterial substances (and, therefore, of all things that are), especially as they are reported in *Met.* N.1–2, draws the main lines of the backdrop for I.5–6. More specifically, according to all versions of the doctrine of the principles, the One as a positive and active principle is opposed to another contrary principle. N.1, 1087b4–33 surveys different views about the principle which is opposed to the One: some (Plato and others: see below) identify it with the unequal (*to anison*), which Plato construes as a dyad of the great and the small (*dyas tou megalou kai tou mikrou*); others (presumably Speusippus) rather identify it with plurality (*to plēthos*). The views of those who take the principle opposed to the One to be the unequal differ in that some prefer to take the dyad as the dyad of the much and few (*to polu kai oligon*) whereas others take it as the dyad of what exceeds and is exceeded (*to huperechon kai huperechomenon*). The idea behind the revised versions of Plato's dyad is that much and few, or exceeding and exceeded, are more general than the great and the small in that the latter primarily apply to a specific kind of being, i.e. extended entities. By being more general, much and few or exceeding and exceeded seem more adequate to pick out some ultimate principle of all things that are. Among those who opt for a non-dyadic principle opposite to the One, two versions of the other (either *to heteron* or *to allo*) figure as alternatives to plurality. Aristotle goes through the difficulties involved in these views, and some of the difficulties are explicitly tackled in I.5–6 (see notes for references).

That N.1–2 are needed to make sense of the discussion in I.1–6 is equally acknowledged by those who see a structural link between Iota and Nu (Menn (in progress); see, in particular, his extensive discussion in Iγ2c: Iota 5–6 and N.1–2: critique of plurality and inequality as *archai*) and by those who take the lack of explicit references in Iota to Nu as a sign of Iota's extrinsic character within the *Metaphysics* (Brandis 1834). Menn ((in progress), Iγ2c), in particular, takes I.5–6 as the most important chapters in Iota for the overall argument of the *Metaphysics* understood as an enquiry into the principles—and this despite the fact that (as Menn acknowledges), in the economy of Iota, I.5–6 are rather appendixes to I.4 (cf. introduction to I.3, p. 96). This fact alone is enough to suggest that there may be more to I.5–6 (as to Iota in general) than a more or less indirect response to Academic views. In this respect, it may be helpful to emphasize some important differences between the account in N.1 and in I.5–6. In N.1, 1088a15–b13 Aristotle explicitly spells out a series of objections to the identification of the second principle as a dyad. He particularly insists on two points. To start with, the dyad is conceived of in terms of pairs of affections and incidental features (great and small, much and little, etc.) of the things it is supposed to be a principle of. Affections and incidental features can only be by being in something else and, therefore, they do not enjoy the right ontological status to be principles (N.1, 1088a15–21, b4–13). Furthermore, all pairs of terms used to spell out the dyad are relatives, and, within Aristotle's ontology, relatives are the farthest away from substances; but it is impossible that non-substances be principles and elements of substances (N.1, 1088a21–b4).

These two points are recurrent themes in Aristotle's criticism of Academic doctrines and, more generally, of other philosophers' accounts. Such objections and the ontological and philosophical commitments behind them are absent from I.5–6. In I.5–6, with the exception of the parenthetical hint at 1056a10–11, Aristotle does not mention the function that the notions at issue may or may not have within a more complex philosophical system. Rather, he seems to be interested in spelling out the formal relation of opposition obtaining between determinate triplets or pairs of terms, quite independently from the role that such terms may play in the construction of specific philosophical views. I.4,

1055a19–23 has shown, in general, that contrariety is a dyadic relation. I.5 and I.6 discuss cases of opposites which are problematic with respect to this feature of contrariety. If there is a consequence to be drawn with respect to the metaphysical doctrines considered in N.1–2, it is that those who claim that the equal and the great and the small, or the one and the many, are contrary principles are wrong because those terms are not contraries to start with (independently of whether they are principles or not). Furthermore, the variety of sources chosen for explicit reference (Platonic doctrines in I.5, 1056a10–11; unknown interlocutors in I.5, 1056a30–34; Anaxagoras in I.6, 1056b28–32; presumably Protagoras in I.6, 1057a7–12; cf. I.1, 1053a35–b3) suggests that Aristotle is interested in applying his analysis to the conceptual clarification of the philosophical debate more generally. The reason why the concepts discussed in I.5–6 are interesting for Aristotle is not just that they are on the agenda of Academic debates. Rather, the reasons why Aristotle is interested in them are the same as those who have led other philosophers to isolate them for philosophical investigation and, in some cases, to turn them into principles of things: being one, many, equal, unequal, great, and small are the kind of properties that range over things that are in that they are quantitatively determined and display quantitative features. The same conceptual framework also finds application within the ontology of quantities and mathematical objects. Before seeing whether mathematical objects are in any sense causally responsible for the presence of those properties in the broader domain of things that are, it is necessary to clarify the logical relations obtaining among those concepts. In this respect, I take the constructive side of the discussion in I.5–6 to be logically prior to the discussion of whether any of the concepts at issue in these chapters are supposed to enter any causal account—pretty much in the same way in which I take the discussion of contrariety in Iota to be logically prior to the discussion of whether contraries can be ascribed any causal role (see Introduction, pp. xxvi, xliii–xliv).

1055b30–32: These lines introduce the two issues tackled in I.6 and I.5 respectively. Aristotle sees some similarities in the source of the two problems and resorts to similar strategies in tackling them (cf. 1056b3: 'similarly'). He starts from the assumption that 'one thing is contrary to one thing only'. Given this feature of contrariety, one could ask in what way the one is opposed to the many and the equal is opposed to the great and the small (which are two different things). As we shall see, similarities mainly concern the source of the difficulties (but see notes on I.6, 1056b3–4) and not the two solutions: the kind of opposition obtaining between the one and the many on the one hand and the kind of opposition obtaining between the equal, the great, and the small on the other hand are different.

Aristotle formulates the two problems by means of two different constructions. He says that one might wonder in what way 'the one and the many are opposed' (both in the nominative case) and in what way 'the equal is opposed to the great and to the small' ('the equal' in the nominative case, 'the great' and 'the small' in the dative case). I do not think that the variation is meant to emphasize any deep philosophical concern. One reason for swapping to the construction with the dative in the second case could be that Aristotle intends to emphasize that the equal stands in a similar relation of opposition to the great and to the small. The construction with the dative suggests that, in order to make sense of the problem as a problem about alleged contraries, the problem must be taken as concerning a relation between two poles (the equal on one side, the great and the small on the other side) and not a sort of triangular relation with three poles.

1055b32–1056a6: For the beginning of the sentence at b32 see Notes on the Text. Aristotle explains (cf. *gar*, 'for', b32) why it makes sense to assume that the triplet equal/great/small is a triplet of opposites whose relation has to be spelled out. That those terms are opposites is made manifest by the fact that the triplet can appear in disjunctive questions, disjunctive questions are supposed to refer to mutually exclusive options, and mutually exclusive options are opposites. As for whether the options are supposed to be exhaustive, see below.

The logical structure of the passage is the following: **(1)** (1055a32, repeated at 1056a3): the enquiry into *whether* something *or* something else is the case is always concerned with opposite alternatives; **(2)** (1056a4–5) we ask whether something is greater or smaller (than something else) or equal (to it). Therefore the problem is **(3)** (1056a5–6): in what kind of opposition does the equal stand to the other two terms?

In the formulation of (2), 'the great' and 'the small' are replaced by 'the greater' and 'the smaller' respectively. This is not a problem in itself because Aristotle thinks of the great and the small as relatives; therefore the comparative formulation just stresses this aspect (there are no such properties as being great and being small without qualification: something can only be great or small with respect to something else).

(1) is further spelled out in the long parenthesis at 1055b34–1056a3. First Aristotle resorts to two examples of disjunctive question 'whether [...] or [...]'. The first example is about a pair of contraries ('whether white or black'), the second one is about a pair of contradictories ('whether white or not white'). These are two cases of opposites for which a disjunctive question can be meaningfully formulated. In the parenthesis Aristotle explains that, in general, disjunctive questions are not asked with reference to non mutually exclusive items. If a disjunctive question is formulated with respect to items which, if taken out of the context, are not mutually exclusive, it is only on the basis of the hypothesis that the two items at issue behave as mutually exclusive within the context of the question (I take this to be the sense of 'this derives from there too', b36–9). For instance, the question whether Cleon or Socrates came, or whether something is a human being or white, can (he seems to think) be appropriately asked only under the assumption that the two alternatives are not compatible. In these cases the disjunctive question does not pick out a pair of items such that there is a domain of objects in which, necessarily, if one is the case, then the other is not the case (the reverse claim, that if one is not the case, then the other is the case, holds unqualifiedly only for contradictory pairs). However, the incompatibility of the alternatives is not determined by what the items at stake are (I take this to be the sense of the remark that it is 'not necessary' in any genus of being). The point in the parenthesis can be reformulated as follows: the sense of a 'whether [...] or [...]' question requires that the items picked out by the expressions replacing the dots be mutually exclusive. Accordingly, things or properties or states of affairs that are mutually exclusive in their own right are naturally suitable candidates for replacing the dots in 'whether [...] or [...]' questions. However, the sense of the question is determined by the sense of the pair of conjunctions 'whether' and 'or': that a 'whether

[...] or [...]' question is about mutually exclusive alternatives is part of the semantic of that pair of conjunctions. This feature of 'whether [...] or [...]' questions is therefore retained independently of whether the expressions replacing the dots pick out items that are 'naturally' mutually exclusive or not. For example, being pale and being courageous are not two mutually exclusive properties. But if I ask: 'Is Socrates pale or courageous?', the question makes sense only under the assumption that, within a certain context, Socrates's being pale and Socrates's being courageous are mutually exclusive states of affairs. The further questions whether the context in which such a question is asked is appropriate in such a way that the question is meaningfully formulated is a matter of pragmatics and not of semantics.

It is not clear whether the reference to a genus at b36 is meant to introduce the idea that genuine opposites are linked to a genus (in a way to be specified) or range over a determinate domain of objects. Aristotle is committed to such claims about the relation between the opposites and a genus with respect to contraries and possession and privation (cf. 1056a30–b2; see Introduction, section II.1; I.3, pp. 115–19; I.7, pp. 181–2, 187–97; I.8, pp. 199–201), but the restriction does not apply to contradictories. As for relatives, see pp. 162–5, 186–7.

In the last lines of the parenthesis (1056a1–3) Aristotle explains that, in asking whether Cleon or Socrates came, we can understand the question in two different ways, both depending on the assumption that, if we deal with a disjunctive question, we have to make sense of it by individuating mutually exclusive options. Either (a) Cleon's coming is not compatible with Socrates's coming and we are asking which one of them came; or (b), if Cleon's coming is compatible with Socrates's coming, we are asking whether both came, or only one of them did. Aristotle suggests that (b) rests on the opposition of one and many: if only one of them came, not both of them (a plurality) came; if both of them (a plurality) came, then not only one of them came. (b) might legitimate the introduction of the difficulty about the one and the many dealt with in I.6, but it is not clear that the passage has this structural function.

Having established that the equal, the great, and the small are opposites by showing that they are naturally suitable to appear as mutually exclusive options in a disjunctive question, the problem remains of explaining what relation of opposition obtains between them.

1056a6–15: Aristotle argues that the opposition of the equal, the great, and the small cannot be an opposition of contrariety. In order to do that, he shows that **(4)** neither can the equal be the contrary of just one of them **(5)** nor can the equal be the contrary of both of them.

1056a6–7: The first argument is in support of (4): there is no reason why the equal should be contrary to the greater rather than to the smaller. The argument relies on the idea that the equal seems to stand in exactly the same relation to the greater as it stands to the smaller, independently of what that relation turns out to be. Accordingly, if someone wanted to claim that the equal is contrary to only one of them, they would need an argument in support of the introduction of the asymmetry in the relations obtaining between the equal and the small and between the equal and the great respectively. Aristotle suggests that such an argument would go against some basic intuitions about these three terms. This implicitly introduces a restriction on the solution to the puzzle: whatever the precise relation of opposition between the equal and the great and the small turns out to be, the solution has to preserve the symmetry of the relations obtaining between the equal and each of the other two terms.

1056a7–8: The second argument introduces the relation of opposition between the equal and the unequal and constructs a difficulty about the interplay between this relation and the relation between the equal, the great, and the small. The equal, Aristotle says, is contrary to the unequal (cf. I.3, 1054a31–32). This is assumed as uncontroversial. It is not fully clear whether the argument is meant to be in support of (4) or (5). If it is in support of (4), then the argument is the following: the equal is contrary to the unequal and the unequal is different from the great and is different from the small (i.e. the unequal is different from each of them taken on its own). Accordingly, if the equal were contrary to one of them, the equal would at the same time have two contraries, i.e. the unequal and the great or the unequal and the small. But this is impossible, given the uniqueness of the contrary. Therefore, given that the unequal is the contrary of the equal, we have to deny that either the great or the small is contrary to the equal, too.

If, on the other hand, the argument is meant to be in support of (5), then presumably it is different from the one immediately following at a8–11. The argument at a8–11 is based on the assumption that the unequal and the-great-and-the-small are the same (on the sense of this claim see below). This assumption is introduced at a8–9 and a7–8 are not governed by that assumption. Reading the argument at a7–8 as in support of (5) requires taking the great and the small as indicating one single thing: for, if they were taken to indicate two things, there would not be any need to introduce the unequal to conclude that the equal turns out to be contrary to more than one thing. Furthermore, it requires that the great and the small are not the same as the unequal since the equal is contrary to the unequal and, if the equal were contrary to the great and the small, it would be contrary to a plurality of different items. Given that the unequal is the contrary of the equal, we have to deny that the great and the small are its contrary too.

There is a question as to how plausible the first requirement is, given the absence at this stage of any explicit indication: for since the very beginning of the chapter Aristotle seems to assume that it is clear that the great and the small are two items (no matter what they are). If this were not the case, the initial formulation of the puzzle would not be understandable—at least not without introducing further assumptions. This difficulty casts some doubts on the reading of the argument in support of (5), whereas the first reading, taking the argument in support of (4), gains plausibility on the basis of the simplicity and straightforwardness of the additional premise that the unequal is neither the same as the great nor the same as the small. Be this as it may, the next two arguments (1056a8–11 and 1056a12–15) are clearly meant to be in support of (5).

1056a8–11: If we identify the unequal with the pair of the great and the small, we could spell out the relation between the equal and the unequal by saying that the equal is at the same time contrary to the great and the small. In this way, one thing (the equal) turns out to be contrary to two (the great and the small).

The identification of the great and the small with the unequal is presented as an Academic doctrine in *Met.* N.1, 1087b10–12. One relatively natural reading of the claim that 'the unequal indicates the same as both taken together' is that the names or name-like expressions 'the unequal' and 'the great and the small' signify the same thing (the argument does not say anything about what this would be), but, unlike 'unequal', the expression 'the great and the small' clearly conveys the idea of a duality. The idea would be that these two linguistic expressions are just two names for the same thing, no matter what that turns out to be at closer inspection. For an account of the nature of the great and the small as what lacks determination of equality cf. Plat., *Phlb.* 24a1–25b3; cf. Arist. *Met.* M.7, 1081a23–25 and M.8, 1083b23–26, about the origin of two units out of the indefinite dyad of great and small through some sort of equalization.

The statement that the difficulty 'runs in aid' of the supporters of such a claim could mean that the identification of the unequal with the dyad of the great and the small gains plausibility due to the difficulty of disentangling the relations between equal and unequal and equal, great, and small. The unequal is taken to be the contrary of the equal; but the equal seems to be opposed to the bigger and the smaller, too. Perhaps the remark in the parenthesis has a mocking tone: the verb *boētheō*, 'to run in aid', is typically used by Plato (e.g. *Phaedr.* 275e) in describing the capacity of the true philosopher to 'run in aid' of his *logos* ('discourse', 'account') which cannot defend itself. The true philosopher is able to defend his *logoi* by supporting them with stronger reasons. In our passage, though, a difficulty seems to run in aid of confused philosophers who are at a loss in defending their claims.

Aristotle's views on the relation between the unequal and the greater and the smaller are not spelled out. Later Peripatetic sources analyse analogous cases to the effect that the unequal is taken as the genus of the greater and of the smaller (cf. Alex., *Eth. Probl.* XI, Bruns 131. 26–34). The equal, being the contrary of the genus, is equally opposed to both species.

1056a12–15: The equal seems to be something intermediate between the great and the small. This feature is incompatible with the claim that the relation between the equal and the great and/or the small is a relation of contrariety, i.e. of complete difference. If x is intermediate between y and z, x cannot stand to y or z in a relation of complete difference, i.e. contrariety. At most, x will stand to y or z in a relation of intermediate difference (and y and z will stand to each other in a relation of greater difference than x and y or x and z respectively). About intermediate relatives cf. I.7, 1057a38–39, where Aristotle rules out the possibility that relatives *that are not contrary* have intermediates: the qualification suggests that relatives that are contrary can have intermediates; cf. *Cat.* 7, 6b15–27.

In I.7 Aristotle will present an account of intermediates based on two ideas: first, intermediates are a sort of mixture of the corresponding contraries; second, intermediates are understood as intermediate steps in a process of change in which the corresponding contraries are the extremes (for the latter idea cf. *Phys.* I.5). The idea of intermediates as mixture can hardly be generalized. Later Peripatetic sources (cf. Alex., *Eth. Probl.* XXVII, Bruns 152.34–157.9) introduce a distinction between intermediate quantities and intermediate qualities: intermediate qualities (e.g. intermediate colours between white and black: see I.2, pp. 83–5; I.7, pp. 183–4) are a mixture of the corresponding contraries, whereas intermediate quantities (for instance: 4 as an intermediate between 2 and 6) are not mixtures of the corresponding extremes. The distinction between cases in which the mixture theory applies and cases in which it does not apply at least testifies to signs of uneasiness within the Peripatetic tradition with the generalization of such a theory.

The second idea, that intermediates are intermediate steps in a process of change, is easier to apply to the equal, with some qualification. We can imagine a process of change starting with A's being smaller than B and ending with A's being bigger than B. It is possible to describe such a situation by saying that in the process of getting bigger than B from being smaller than B, if the change is continuous, at some point A will be equal to B—and being equal to B is, for A, an intermediate step between being smaller than B and being greater than B. It is doubtful, however, whether Aristotle would resort to an account in terms of change to elucidate the claim that the equal is intermediate between the greater and the smaller: for Aristotle does not admit change according to the category of relatives, while the smaller, the equal, and the greater are all relatives. The change in the relation obtaining between A and B is parasitic upon A's or B's change in quantity: A will grow and/or B will shrink and these will be the genuine processes of change going on.

The idea that in I.5 Aristotle makes sense of the relations between the equal, the greater, and the smaller with reference to some process is spelled out by Cattanei 2005, pp. 122–4, in a rather different way. Cattanei analyses I.5 in light of the method of *antanhairesis* or *antaphairesis*, an archaic procedure for measuring geometrical magnitudes by way of repeated and mutual subtraction. The procedure is mentioned in Arist., *Top.* VIII.3, 158b29–35 and commented upon by Alexander in his commentary on the *Topics* (Wallies, 545. 9–19). The procedure was used to establish equations between geometrical magnitudes and, in particular, between segments of lines. Consider a segment AB and another segment, CD, shorter than AB. We start by using the shorter segment CD as a measure for AB by progressively subtracting CD from AB. It can be the case that AB is exactly n times CD: if so, we can say that AB is equal to nCD. But it can also be the case that, by progressively subtracting CD from AB, we end up with a segment AE which is smaller than CD. At this point, we adopt AE as our new measure and repeat the procedure by subtracting AE from CD. If CD is equal to mAE, we stop. If we end up with a segment of CD, CF, which is smaller than AE, we use CF as a measure and start to subtract it from CF and so on. The greatest measure between the two segments is the equal, i.e. what is obtained by progressively eliminating what makes the segments the one greater and the other smaller. On Cattanei's account (2005, p. 124) the greatest common measure between the greater and the smaller segment turns out to be intermediate between the greater and the smaller in that it 'mediates' between the two and allows to achieve a sort of equalization between the two. Note, however, that this understanding of the sense in which the greatest common measure is an intermediate does not square in any obvious way with Aristotle's account of what it is to be an intermediate in I.5. On Cattanei's account the equal turns out to be the segment that bridges and, in this metaphorical sense, eliminates the difference between the great and the small and not what is captured by the joint negation of the great and the small. Reference to *antanhairesis* seems, in any case, relevant to I.6, 1057a2–7.

1056a15–24:   Having established that the equal, the greater, and the smaller are not contraries, Aristotle introduces an argument leading to the final assessment of the relation of opposition obtaining between the three terms. The argument is usually read as a (controversial) argument by exclusion (cf. Ross 1924, II p. 294; Cattanei 2005, p. 121). The main reason why the argument is controversial is that, in general, Aristotle acknowledges four kinds of opposites (contraries, contradictories, possession and privation, relatives); but, having ruled out the possibility that the equal, the great, and the small are contraries, he says that two possibilities are left. Presumably here 'negation' has to be understood in the sense of contradictory negation (see below). Accordingly, the two options which are left are contradiction and privation. Why does Aristotle exclude the possibility that equal, greater and smaller are opposed as relatives? Ross 1924, II p. 294, suggests that the equal as a relative is not opposed to the unequal, but to the equal—the core idea being that the relatives are the objects standing to each other in a certain relation and not the relation that binds them. One possibility is that in our passage Aristotle is only interested in oppositions such that one of the opposite can be regarded as some form of negation of the other(s), as his appeal to disjunctive questions on mutually exclusive options suggests. A similarly dismissive attitude towards the relatives can be found in I.4, 1055b1–11: the relatives are mentioned at the beginning, but the passage is really only about the relations obtaining between the other three kinds of opposites.

One further reason why the argument is puzzling is that Aristotle's solution sounds like the conjunction of the two remaining options, negation (*apophasis*) and privation (*sterēsis*), in that the equal is defined as privative negation (*apophasis steretike*) of the great and the small. I am not sure whether the use of this complex expression is best understood as alluding to a conjunction of the two options left in the solution of the puzzle. It could be taken more simply as a periphrasis that Aristotle uses to indicate privation in agreement with his analysis of privation as a certain type of contradiction in I.4, 1055b3–8 (see notes on 1056a16–24).

The arguments in support of Aristotle's solution that the equal is the privative negation of the great and the small (rather than the contradictory negation of them) are to be found at 1056a16–24. This section can be divided into two parts. 1056a17–20 gives an argument to the effect that the equal must be the negation of *both* the great and the small. As at 1056a5–6, Aristotle insists on the symmetry of the relations obtaining between the equal and the great and the equal and the small respectively. 1056a20–24 supports the claim that the equal is a specific kind of negation, i.e. the joint privative negation (as opposed to the unqualified or contradictory negation) of the greater and the smaller. The characteristic feature of privation as opposed to contradictory negation is that it is linked to a determinate kind of subject (cf. I.4, 1055b4–11): privation is the absence of a certain property in those subjects which could or should have that property. This implies that only those things which could be great or small but happen to be neither great nor small can be said to be equal. Menn emphasizes the polemical force of the result that the equal turns out to be a privation against the Academic assumption that the unequal is a principle (cf. p. 99).

The account of the equal as that which is neither great nor small is given at 1056a23–24. At least two non-equivalent paraphrases of this claim can be given, depending on whether we take the argument as an argument about objects or about properties:

(i) x is equal to y iff x is neither greater nor smaller than y.
(ii) <the property of> being equal to something is the same as, or nothing more than, being neither greater than nor smaller than it.

Similar paraphrases can be formulated for the unequal:

(iii) x is unequal to y iff x is greater than or smaller than y.
(iv) <the property of> being unequal is the same as, or nothing more than, being greater or being smaller.

(ii) and (iv) are more problematic than (i) and (ii) because they express a relation between properties which (i) and (ii) need not imply. In particular, in (ii) being equal is said to be the same as the conjunction of two negative properties (being not bigger/being not smaller), and in (iv) being unequal turns out to be the disjunction of two other properties. One might wonder whether there are any such things as negative or disjunctive properties (for some discussion of negative and disjunctive properties see Meixner 1992).

1056a23–24: The conceptual move from x's being the privative negation of y and z to x's being the intermediate of y and z requires some clarification. Not all contraries admit of intermediates (cf. *Cat.* 10, 12b27–13a15; cf. *Met.* I.4, 1055b23–25; I.7, 1057a18–19). For instance, odd and even are contraries ranging over the domain of numbers and not admitting of intermediates. In these cases, necessarily each subject falling within the domain of the two contraries is characterized by one or the other of them: necessarily each number is either even or odd. Some contraries, though, admit of intermediates and, in these cases, the objects belonging to the domain over which the contraries range do not necessarily have either of them. In a more formal way, if C1 and C2 are contraries, W the domain of objects over which C1 and C2 range, then we can describe the two cases in the following way: there are no intermediates between C1 and C2 iff for any x belonging to W, x is either C1 or C2 and not both C1 and C2. There are intermediates between C1 and C2 iff there exists some x belonging to W such that x is neither C1 nor C2.

In these lines Aristotle introduces the possibility that intermediates be picked out by the joint privative negation of the corresponding contraries. In order to avoid confusion, it is important to bear in mind that Aristotle distinguishes explicitly between contradictory negation and privative negation (cf. I.3, 1054b18–22). This distinction (as well as the opposition of contrariety) is not captured by negation in classical logic, but is crucial to understanding Aristotle's point here and his theory of oppositions in general.

We have seen that the main feature of privation (or, as I shall call it, privative negation) is reference to a determinate subject. The privative negation of a property makes sense only with respect to a subject which could or should be characterized by that property. We can say of many things that they do not see: a wall does not see, a table does not see, a stone does not see, etc. Aristotle wants to distinguish between these cases, in which we simply deny that a property belongs to a subject, without any further qualification, from cases in which we deny that a property belongs to a subject which could be expected to have that property. So, if we say of an adult man that he does not see, we are denying a certain property of a subject which would naturally have that property (and which, for whatever reasons, happens to be deprived of it). In this case it is appropriate to say that the subject (the man) is blind. The negative semantic content of privation is not always reflected in the morphology of the linguistic expressions indicating it. For instance, 'blind' expresses the privation of sight, i.e. the negation or absence of sight in subjects which could or should be able to see, but this negative connotation is not reflected in the morphology of the word (there is no part in the word 'blind' expressing a negation). In other cases, the negative semantic content is reflected at the morphological level: 'unequal' indicates the privation of the equal and is composed of the privative prefix 'un-' followed by the adjective indicating the property that is denied. In some other cases, there are no specific words to express privations and we have to resort to periphrastic expressions composed of the negation 'not' or 'non-' followed by the property we want to deny. In this last case (e.g. if we spell out the meaning of 'blind' in terms of 'not seeing' or 'not sighted'), the linguistic formulation is indistinguishable from the linguistic formulation of a contradictory negation.

We can now extend these considerations to the case of the joint negation of contraries and, in particular, to the case of the equal, the great, and the small. Let's consider the following sentence, expressing a joint negation:

(JN)   x is neither bigger than nor smaller than y.

(JN) is true of all objects that are neither bigger nor smaller than y. Aristotle wants to distinguish two cases. In one case, (JN) is taken as true independently of whether the subjects of which it is true belong or do not belong to the domain of objects over which the two properties of being greater than something/being smaller than something range. For instance, no colour is greater or smaller than another colour, given that colours are not the kind of object that can be said to be equal. In this case, the negation in (JN) simply works as a contradictory negation: the predicate of the proposition is the conjunction of the two negations of two properties (being bigger than y, being smaller than y). This conjunction of negations is not meant to pick out any property. In the other case, (JN) is true of certain subjects which belong to the domain of objects over which the two relations being-bigger-than and being-smaller-than range. In this case, Aristotle says, we have to do with a privative joint negation and the privative joint negation picks out some property ranging over the same domain of objects as the negated properties. If (JN) works as privative joint negation, (JN) is equivalent to the proposition stating that x is equal to y.

At a23–24, Aristotle adds that if the joint negation of two properties is privative, then the joint negation indicates some property that ranges over the same domain of objects and that is intermediate between the two negated properties. Let C1, C2, and W be defined as on p. 150; then what Aristotle is saying is that in the second case, for any object x belonging to W, if x is neither C1 nor C2 then 'being neither C1 nor C2' picks out an intermediate property ranging over W.

Aristotle seems to believe that each pair of contraries C1 and C2 and, if they exist, their intermediates range within a genus or specify a genus (see Introduction, section II.1 and I.7). As we have just seen, privation, too, is defined with reference to a determinate subject genus; this feature makes privative (rather than contradictory) negation apt to capture intermediates. As we shall see in the following chapters, Aristotle is not always clear and consistent in spelling out the relation between the contraries and the genus they are anchored to. In I.5 the genus linked to the equal, the great, and the small is the domain of objects suitable to receive such properties, without any further qualification as to the specific predicative link obtaining between such properties and their subjects (for all we know, the properties Aristotle is talking about could be essential or necessary or incidental to their subjects). But see 1056b1–2.

One last point about a22–24: in these lines Aristotle hints at the reason why one could say that intermediates and their corresponding contraries are opposite to each other (cf. p. 131 on functional contraries). Any intermediate can be expressed as the privation of its corresponding contraries and privation is a form of opposition. Furthermore, if there is more than one intermediate between two contraries, the procedure can be extended: each property in the set made of two contraries and all their intermediates can be expressed as the joint privative negation of all other members of the set. This makes available an important bit of theory for Aristotle's otherwise not fully spelled out view that change takes place between opposites and that intermediates behave as opposites when treated as extremes of a process of change (*Phys.* V.1, 225b3–4; V.5, 229b14–21).

1056a24–b2: In the last part of the chapter Aristotle comments on some further cases of intermediate properties (1056a24–30) and on the restrictions applying to the use of joint negation as a formula to pick out intermediates of the negated terms (a30–b2). The latter part of the passage addresses the views of those who believe that such a strategy can be generalized without any restriction, but it is not clear who the polemical target is. Perhaps the same people would resort to cases such as those mentioned in the parenthesis at 1055b36 ff., where non mutually exclusive items appear in 'whether [...] or [...]' questions. If one thinks that any two expressions can appear in 'whether [...] or [...]' questions as opposites, one might also think that joint negation can be indiscriminately applied to any pair of items to indicate something intermediate between opposites. By the same token, someone endorsing this view might deny the distinction between contradictories and contraries or between contradictory negation and privative negation.

1056a24–30: Aristotle considers other cases of intermediates. The first case is that of what is neither good nor bad, which is opposed to both what is good and what is bad. Aristotle says that in this case the intermediate of the good and the bad has no name. In particular, in this case Aristotle links the lack of an appropriate linguistic expression to the fact that both the good and the bad are said in many ways and there is no one single kind of subject to receive them. This statement links to Aristotle's claim that *agathon* ('good') is not a univocal predicate (or a genus) (*EN* I.vi, 1096a19–b35; *EE* I.7, 1217b25–1218a1): different things are good in different ways and there is no univocal definition of what it is to be good for all things that can be said to be good. It is not obvious, though, why, if there is no determinate kind of object which can be said to be good or bad, this impacts on the lack of a word for what is intermediate between good and bad, given that it does not affect the existence of *agathon* or *kakon* as non-univocal terms. Perhaps Aristotle's point here is different. One possibility is that, given the different kinds of object which can be said to be good or bad, one could think that good and bad have or do not have intermediates or have a different number of intermediates in the different cases. For instance, if we talk about dispositions of the human soul, there are at least two intermediate dispositions between a good (virtuous) disposition such as temperance and a bad (vicious) disposition such as intemperance, namely self-control and lack of self-control (*akrasia*). If, on the other hand, we consider external goods, we might want to distinguish between useful, damaging, and indifferent things. One further possibility is that of taking the point to be that the lack of a determinate subject genus makes it difficult to say, in general, whether 'neither good nor bad' is a privative joint negation (and, therefore, picks out an intermediate with respect to the objects referred to within the context) or a contradictory joint negation, which does not pick out any determinate property of any object.

A clearer example of intermediate properties is given by what is neither white nor black: according to Aristotle, there is a range of colours of which white and black are the extremes and the joint privative negation 'neither black nor white' applies to each colour within this range. I take *mallon* at a27 in the sense of 'rather' and not in the sense of 'more'. I take this to introduce a more perspicuous example of a joint privative negation that picks out intermediates. The point of 'rather' would not be that the joint privative negation picks out an intermediate in the case of colours more than in the case of things that are neither good nor bad (whenever joint negation picks out an intermediate properties, it does it in the same way), but that, in the case of colours, the function of the joint privative negation, as a periphrastic way to pick out intermediates, is clearer and easier to observe.

1056a30–b2: We have seen that in some cases (such as that of the good and the bad) there is no given name to indicate the intermediate property even if there is some intermediate property out there. We can indicate such a property through the joint privative negation of the contraries ('neither good nor bad'). In the last lines of the chapter Aristotle objects to the undue generalization of this procedure: it is not the case that for any two items there is an intermediate picked out by their joint negation. We have seen that privative negation differs from contradictory negation by relating to a specific kind of subject. Accordingly, the joint privative negation of two properties only makes sense and picks out an intermediate property if the negated properties range on a unified domain of objects with respect to which privation indicates the lack of those two properties. Being a shoe and being a hand do not range over an adequately unified domain of object to fall within the scope of joint privative negation. Furthermore, given that the opposites between which there can be intermediates are contrary properties, 'shoe' and 'hand' are general terms picking out, if anything, substance-like objects. This point is not explicit in the text, but the choice of the examples might emphasize the complete lack of understanding of the nature of intermediates and of the terms between which there can be intermediates on the part of Aristotle's presumed interlocutors.

In order to express this point Aristotle uses the same language he used to describe things that differ in genus: things that belong to different genera do not have a common matter (I.3, 1054b28–29); similarly, things which do not fall within the scope of joint privative negation do not have a common subject (I.6, 1056b2). The distance between things belonging to different genera cannot be bridged (I.3, 1054b29; I.4, 1055a6–7; I.7, 1057a26–30; cf. I.7, 1057a37–38). Accordingly there is nothing 'intermediate' and no common 'distance' or 'interval' that can be covered between them. At 1056b1 Aristotle describes this situation by saying that there is no 'difference' (*diaphora*) between the two items that belong to two genera that have no 'intermediate' and no 'subject' in common.

CHAPTER 6

1056b3–5: Aristotle seems to think that the difficulties dealt with in I.5 and I.6 belong together (see pp. 134–7, 139–40). There are both differences and similarities in the argumentative structure of I.5 and I.6. The most evident difference is the following. At the beginning of I.5 Aristotle suggests that the common problem in the two cases is the failure of the equal/the great/the small and the one/the many to comply with the criterion of uniqueness of the contrary (cf. introductory notes on I.5 and notes on 1055b31–1056a6). However, I.6 does not explicitly take over this aspect. Aristotle does not spell out the difficulties involved in the opposition between the one and the many by resorting to the criterion of uniqueness of the contrary and, therefore, by showing that there is some sense in which they cannot be regarded as contraries. Rather, he shows that, if we do not qualify the sense in which the one is opposed to the many, the one turns out to be many.

As for similarities, in I.5 Aristotle introduces the unequal as the uncontroversial contrary of the equal and unpacks the relation obtaining between the unequal, the great and the small on the basis of that uncontroversial assumption. Similarly, in I.6 he introduces the few as the uncontroversial opposite of the many and tries to spell out the relation obtaining between the one and the few.

The claim to be discussed and revised in the course of the chapter is:

(1) The many are opposed to the one without qualification.

I take the scope of 'without qualification' to be the whole sentence 'the many are opposed to the one' rather than one specific part of it. The introduction of the relevant specifications can then concern both the terms involved and the relation obtaining between them. This seems to be the strategy Aristotle follows: at 1056b14–25 he focuses on the ways in which things are said to be many (*polla*) before disentangling the relations obtaining between the many and their opposites. The distinction Aristotle introduces between the many in the sense of exceeding quantity and the many in the sense of measured plurality is a distinction between two different kinds of relatives: an exceeding quantity exceeds something which is exceeded; the measured/measurable is what it is (i.e. measured or measurable) because there is a measure of it (see below).

1056b5–14:   Three difficulties are introduced on the basis of (1) and of the additional claim that

(2) The many are opposed to the few.

(2) is assumed as uncontroversial (cf. in I.5 the assumption that the equal is the contrary of the unequal). The three difficulties are presented at b5–6, 6–9, and 10–14 respectively.

1056b5–6: From (1) and (2) the first absurd consequence follows:

(3) The one will be few.

The exact formulation of (3) at b5 is problematic. Aristotle phrases (3) by saying that the one will be *oligon* (singular for 'few', 'little') or *oliga* (the corresponding plural form). One might be tempted to translate the singular with 'little', but Ross opportunely warns against this move: the distinction between *oligon* and *oliga* does not parallel that between 'little' and 'few' in English in that the Greek does not necessarily allude to the distinction between uncountable and countable objects. Aristotle mentions this distinction later on in the chapter (1056b14–20), but at least at this stage of the discussion the difficulties seem to arise partly because the adopted vocabulary is relatively flexible and leaves room for ambiguity. In particular, the use of the singular *and* the plural in the formulation of (3) could be regarded as a remedy to the syntactical oddity of having a singular subject (the one) with a plural predicate (few), without alluding to deep ontological distinctions. English does not decline adjectives and the problem of lack of agreement in number between subject and predicate simply does not arise. In the translation I have tried to keep the presence of two morphologically related predicates by translating *oligon* as 'what is few' and *oliga* as 'few'. In any case, Aristotle is resorting to a vocabulary that, in the singular, can apply to both countable and uncountable nouns; one could therefore express this feature of the Greek by providing a double translation for the singular (e.g. 'little/what is few'). This issue will become pressing at b11–13. For the formulation of the difficulty and of its solution in terms of the opposition of measure and measured cf. N.1, 1087b27–1088a14.

b6–9: The second difficulty unfolds as follows:

(4) The double is a multiple (*pollaplasion*) on the basis of two.

Therefore,

(5) Two will be many.

(6) The only quantity to be less than two is one; so, two can be many only if compared to one.

Therefore,

(7)   One will be few.

The argument is based on the idea that a multiple is something which is many times that of which it is a multiple. According to this account, any number can be regarded as a multiple of one, being many times one. Two, by being the double of one, is a multiple and, being a multiple, it is many times one. Reference to multiplicity is evident in the morphology of the Greek (where *polla-* in *pollaplasion* has the same root as *polu*, 'much', and *polla,* 'many') as well as of the Latin word (*multiplex*—from which the English 'multiple'—where *multi-* has the same root as *multum*, 'much', and *multa*, 'many').

I take this to be one complex argument, in which (7) is the most paradoxical conclusion and (5) a less paradoxical, but still potentially controversial conclusion. Note the singular (*oligon*) in the formulation of (7) at b8.

b10–14:   Third difficulty:

(8)   Being many (*polu*) and being few (*oligon*) are properties of plurality (*plēthos*) in the same way as being long and being short are properties of length.

(9)   What is *polu* is many (*polla*), the many (*ta polla*) are *polu*.

Therefore,

(10)   What is few (*oligon*) will be some plurality (*plēthos ti*).

From (7) and (10) it follows that

(11)   The one will be some plurality.

I take the pairs *to makron kai brachu* ('the long and short') and *to polu kai oligon* ('the much and few') in (8) to refer to properties and I take it that Aristotle's point here is that *polu* and *oligon* are per se properties of plurality in the same way in which *makron* and *brachu* are per se properties of length (cf. *Met.* M.9, 1085a9–14 and 21–22; N.1, 1088a17–21, 1088b4–7; N.2, 1089b11–14). Whatever can be said to be long or short either is a length or has length and it can be said to be long or short precisely because its length is such. In (8) Aristotle draws an analogy between two kinds of quantity (length is a kind of continuous quantity or magnitude whereas plurality is discrete quantity) and their corresponding pairs of per se properties.

The meaning and role of (9) are not clear (cf. notes on 1056b14–20). One possibility is that it introduces a parenthetical remark about one of the two per se properties of plurality: it does not make any difference if we express it in terms of 'much' or 'many', since the two expressions are interchangeable in most cases (granted that uncountable objects are an exception to this rule). According to this reading, (10) would not derive from (9) and the linguistic formulation ('*and if* what is much is also many [...]') would be misleading. However, the final conclusion (11) would rest on (9) in that two, being many, is also much and it is much with respect to the one, which is few and, by being few, is a plurality.

1056b14–20: Perhaps the point of the claim that the many are also said to be much, but 'in a different way' is the same as in *Met.* Δ.26, 1024a8–10, where Aristotle remarks that, with respect to objects composed of a plurality of items, we can use *pan* (singular for 'all') when we talk of the composite object as a sort of collective unity as well as *panta* (plural for 'all') when we talk distributively of the units composing that object (e.g. 'all these units'; Aristotle's example for the use of *pan*, literally: 'all this number', cannot be translated into English, which rather uses 'whole': 'this whole number'). In the first case we refer to the composite object 'as if referring to one thing' (*hōs eph' heni*), in the second case we refer to it 'as if referring to divided things' (*hōs epi diēirēmenois*).

In order to solve the three difficulties Aristotle clarifies the uses of *polla* ('many'). *polla*, as the English 'many', can indicate mere plurality (in opposition to singularity) or a large number (in opposition to a small number). *polu* ('much') is here used as the opposite of *oligon* ('few', 'little') to indicate a greater amount compared to a smaller amount. *polla* and *polu* are interchangeable if referred to countable objects, whereas only the singular can be used with reference to uncountable objects. In the latter contexts the only appropriate way to indicate that there is a large amount of something is by using *polu* (we can talk of 'much water', but not of 'many water'). Aristotle does not express the distinction at stake in terms of countable and uncountable nouns or objects, but confines himself to giving an example: when we talk about an amount of fluid we do not say that there is 'many' of it.

If we now focus on objects that can be said to be many (b16–20), i.e. countable objects, we can see that they can be said to be many in two different senses: **(a)** in the sense that they are in a great number compared to other pluralities of objects; **(b)** in the sense that they are a plurality rather than one single object. In sense (a), 'many' indicates an 'exceeding plurality' as opposed to an 'exceeded plurality' of objects, which will be said to be few. In sense (b), plurality is opposed to singularity and objects are said to be many iff they are more than one. If the distinction is not drawn, one runs the risk of taking 'many' in (1) and (2) as a univocal term, with the consequences outlined in (3)–(11).

At 1056b18 Aristotle speaks of pluralities that are 'exceeding' without qualification (*haplōs*). Aristotle acknowledges that two is the plurality which is exceeded without qualification (cf. *Met.* M.9, 1085b10), but he does not think that there is a plurality which is exceeding without qualification (numbers are infinite by addition; he thinks, however, that there is a greatest body, i.e. the universe). He must be referring to the views of those who claim that ideal numbers are finite and to the claim that ten (or some other number) marks the completion of number (cf. *Met.* A.5, 986a8; Λ.8, 1073a20–21; M.7, 1082a1–11; M.8, 1084a12; 1084a29–b2; N.1, 1088b8–11—in the latter passage Aristotle addresses explicitly the claim that there be a quantity which is *polu haplōs*, 'much without qualification').

1056b20–25: Given the way in which the two relations (a) and (b) are spelled out, i.e. as relations between exceeding plurality and exceeded plurality and between plural and singular respectively, the relation obtaining between the one and the many is (b). Within this opposition the many are regarded as nothing but a plurality of "ones". This is the relation obtaining between unit and number; since the unit is also the measure of number, Aristotle can say more generally that the relation obtaining between the one and the many is the relation obtaining between measure and measured. At b22–25 Aristotle spells out the idea that the relation between one and number is the same as the relation between x and any multiple of x. What is important in this relation is that the multiple of x (or the number or, more generally, the many opposed to the one) is not simply something greater than x, but is precisely many times x—or: many x's. This implies that x is not simply a part into which the multiple can be divided, but is a part that measures the multiple (for this distinction see *Met.* Δ.25, 1023b12–17). For instance, 3 is a part of 8, since 8 can be divided into 3 and 5, but it is not a part that measures 8; 1, 2 or 4 are all parts of 8 that measure 8 and 8 can be described as a multiple of 1 (8x1), 2 (4x2), or 4 (2x4). For further comments on measure and measurable see I.1, pp. 47–59, I.2, pp. 64–5, 78–88, and 1056b32–1057a7.

By explaining that the sense in which the one is opposed to the many in (1) is (b), Aristotle provides a reply to (3): the opposition between the one and the many is not the same as the opposition between exceeded plurality and exceeding plurality displayed by the few and the many. Accordingly, the fact that the one is opposed to the many does not imply that the one is few and, therefore, a plurality.

1056b25–32: Replies to (5)–(7). The claim that two is many (5) should be understood by taking 'many' as in (b): two is many in the sense that it is a plurality of ones, not in the sense that it is a plurality exceeding another plurality. Accordingly, while it is true that the only quantity to be less than two is one (6) (cf. 1057a1–2), it does not follow from this that the one is few (7). Rather, two is the smallest plurality which can be said to be few. This means that two is few, i.e. an exceeded plurality, with respect to any other plurality. In this sense, two is 'few' without qualification and it can be said to be the primary plurality 'which has a deficiency'. I take the latter two claims as equivalent: being the primary plurality that has a deficiency does not mean that two lacks anything, but that it is exceeded by any other plurality.

I take the last lines of this section to spell out one further consequence of the identification of two as the primary plurality. The general idea behind this claim is that x is said to be P on account of y if y is the primary subject of which P can be predicated and any x that is said to be P is said to be P because it stands in a certain relation to y or because it has some basic feature in common with y. Two is the primary subject of being few. Anything that is said to be few either has the property of being two or it resembles two in some relevant respect—in particular, in being an exceeded plurality with respect to some other plurality.

1056b28–31: Aristotle's criticism against Anaxagoras is (as usual) rather difficult to understand and, on the face of it, it rests on more or less deliberate misunderstandings. Aristotle comments on Anaxagoras's thesis that 'all things were together, infinite in plurality and smallness'. The first point Aristotle makes seems to be that Anaxagoras should have said 'fewness' instead of 'smallness'. Why this is the case is quite mysterious. One possibility is that Aristotle's point is just that smallness is not the opposite of plurality and that Anaxagoras should have put his point differently. However, from what we know about Anaxagoras, it seems that Anaxagoras's point is appropriately expressed by his original formulation in terms of smallness rather than by Aristotle's 'improved' version.

Perhaps what Aristotle wants to give here is not a paraphrase of what Anaxagoras meant to say, but a formulation which would have allowed Anaxagoras to move on to what, according to Aristotle, would have been a better position, possibly allowing him to recognize one of his own mistakes (cf. Bowman (1916)). In *Phys.* I.4, 188a13–21, Aristotle gives a (very controversial) argument against Anaxagoras's tenet that there can be indefinitely big or indefinitely small homeomerous parts. Perhaps the final remark in the parenthesis ('for they are not infinite') in our passage alludes to this kind of argument and the point of Aristotle's consideration would be that, if Anaxagoras had moved on to consider fewness rather than smallness, he would have seen that there is a limit to what is few (there is no indefinite fewness). From this he would have been in a better position to draw some consequences about indefinite smallness and to give up on infinity. If this is what Aristotle is trying to say, the argument is very weak, given that, as Aristotle himself admits, continuous magnitudes are indefinitely divisible and this does not imply that something can be divided into fewer parts than two.

1056b32–1057a1: Having provided a reply to the difficulties presented in the first part of the chapter, Aristotle returns to the relation obtaining between the one and the many understood as measure and measurable. On the paradigmatic function of the relation between unit and number for the characterization of measure and measurable more generally cf. I.1, pp. 47–59.

Aristotle introduces two distinctions within the domain of relatives. First, he says that the opposition of measure and measurable is an opposition of relatives that are not relatives in their own right (b34), implicitly introducing a distinction between things that are relatives in their own right (or per se relatives) and things that are relatives not in their own right (non per se relatives). Furthermore (b35–36) he refers to a twofold partition of the relatives into 'contraries' (*enantia*) and relatives that are such by having something else said relative to them (as, for instance, the knowable is relative to knowledge because knowledge is of it, and not because it is of knowledge). For the sake of brevity and clarity I shall refer to the implicit distinction in b34 in terms of per-se-relatives (henceforth: ps-relatives) *vs.* non-per-se-relatives (henceforth: nps-relatives), and to the one in b35–36 in terms of *enantia*-relatives (e-relatives) *vs.* knowledge-knowable-like-relatives (k-relatives). I shall first consider each of the two distinctions and then turn to how they might relate to each other.

Aristotle distinguishes different kinds of relatives in *Cat.* 7 and *Met.* Δ.15. Both chapters contain useful elements for elucidating the distinctions in I.6. In *Cat.* 7, 6a36–b2, relatives are described as beings that 'are said to be precisely what they are of other things or, in whatever other way, with respect to something else'. At 6a36–b2 this characterization seems to apply to all relatives, without singling out any special group. At 7b15–8a12 we find a distinction between the majority of relatives, which are 'together by nature' (*hama tēi phusei*) in that the one cannot be without the other, and those relatives for which such a condition does not obtain: the object of knowledge (the knowable) can be without there being knowledge of it. The idea behind the distinction seems to be that in some cases of relatives, but not in others, one item of the pair enjoys some sort of ontological (possibly: causal) priority over the other, and this introduces a sort of ontological asymmetry between the items of the pair (cf. *Cat.* 12, 14b10–22 for a sense in which things that follow each other can be the one prior to the other). For the idea that the object of knowledge enjoys some sort of priority over knowledge, see pp. 62–4.

A more explicit distinction between groups of relatives is drawn in *Met.* Δ.15, 1021a26–30, where Aristotle distinguishes relatives that are said on account of number (e.g. double and half) or on account of capacities (e.g. capable of heating and heatable) from relatives which are said as knowledge and knowable or measurable and measure. In this case, too, the distinction seems based on considerations of ontological asymmetry (for the way in which ontological asymmetry is described in Δ.15 as opposed to I.1 and I.6 see the detailed discussion in Menn (in progress), Iγ2a: Knowledge and the thing known, the measure and the thing measured).

It is more difficult to understand what Aristotle has in mind when he mentions the distinction between e-relatives and k-relatives. He refers to another treatment of this distinction, but, to my knowledge, a similar partition is nowhere to be found in Aristotle's extant writings. I.7, 1057a37–38 introduces a distinction between relatives that are contraries and relatives that are not contraries and claims that relatives that are not contraries do not have any intermediate, since they are not in the same genus (see notes *ad loc.*). However it is at least not obvious that Aristotle would distinguish e-relatives and k-relatives by saying that the former, but not the latter, belong to the same genus: in I.1 and I.2 he seems quite keen on emphasizing the commonality of genus of measure and measurable, which in I.6's partition would belong to k-relatives.

Furthermore, *Cat.* 7, 6b15–27 specifies that the category of relatives admits of contrariety; his examples are virtue and vice, knowledge and ignorance. But these contraries are not the corresponding relatives: knowledge is contrary to ignorance, and ignorance is not what knowledge is relative to. So this cannot be what Aristotle has in mind in I.6, because in I.6 he seems to have in mind two different cases concerning things that are relative *to each other*. I take it that in I.6 Aristotle is rather referring to cases in which the pair of relatives is also a pair of contraries as opposed to cases such as those of knowledge and knowable. For instance, the great, i.e. the greater, is greater than something which is smaller and vice versa; similarly for the exceeding and the exceeded (about whether these are contrary relatives see, however, *Cat.* 6, 5b11–6a11). Why the distinction between e-relatives and k-relatives is recalled at this point is not clear. Perhaps it is meant to mark one further difference between the opposition many/few and the opposition many/one, where both oppositions are taken as oppositions of relatives, but of relatives of different kinds: many and few fall under e-relatives; many and one fall under k-relatives.

One further point which is not clear is whether the distinction between e-relatives and k-relatives is supposed to be an exhaustive partition of the domain of relatives in the same way in which the distinction between ps-relatives and nps-relatives is exhaustive. This does not seem to be the case: Aristotle acknowledges as paradigmatic cases of relatives items which do not have a contrary and are ps-relatives such as double and half. Furthermore, the distinction between e-relatives and k-relatives is not internal to ps-relatives (k-relatives are nps-relatives) nor to nps-relatives (there are e-relatives that are ps-relatives).

The possibility cannot be excluded that the notion of *enantion* used to mention e-relatives is not Aristotle's refined notion of contrary as it is developed in I.3–4 or that the partition in terms of e-relatives and k-relatives is not a partition within relatives in Aristotle's technical sense of relative. The main piece of evidence in support of this hypothesis is given by the fact that a partition into contraries (*enantia*) and relatives (*pros ti*) is presented as a Platonic distinction of things that are 'with respect to something else' (*pros heteron*) as opposed to things that are in their own right (*kath'hauta*) (cf. Hermodorus, Isnardi-Parente fr. 5 = Simpl. *In Phys.* 247.30–148.15 Diels). Still, in I.6 Aristotle mentions the distinction without taking any distance from it and in I.7 the distinction between relatives that are contraries and relatives that are not contraries is implicitly resorted to without further additions.

1057a1–2: The fact that the one is not few, and therefore does not stand to the many in the relation of exceeded plurality to exceeding plurality, is not incompatible with the one's being less than something else. Being less than something does not imply being few. Accordingly, it makes sense to say that one is less than two without implying that one is a smaller plurality than two.

1057a2–7: Aristotle has argued that the many are opposed to the one as number is opposed to the unit, i.e. as the measured is opposed to the measure. In I.3, 1054a21–29, one different kind of opposition was analysed: one and *plēthos* ('plurality') are opposed as contraries if they indicate the indivisible and the divisible (or divided) respectively. In I.6, 1056b10–14 Aristotle builds an argument based on the claim that *polu* and *oligon* are per se properties of *plēthos*. For the problems involved in translating *plēthos* as 'plurality', which suggests an actual plurality of items, and, therefore, on the relation between *plēthos* and *polla* ('many') see notes to I.3, p. 97, and Castelli 2005.

This section of I.6 spells out the relation between *plēthos* and number, while a12–17 sums up the relations obtaining between *plēthos* and other terms. The general idea is that *plēthos* is more general than number—or, that number is a specification of *plēthos*. Both points are explicitly stated in the passage: **(i)** *plēthos* is a sort of genus of number; **(ii)** number is *plēthos* measured by the one. (ii) is supposed to provide support for (i) (see *gar*, 'for', at a3) and this might imply that Aristotle regards (ii) as in some sense clearer than (i). In order to get a better grasp on (i) and (ii), we have to figure out what a *plēthos* is that is not measured by the one. Otherwise said: we have to figure out what a *plēthos* is that is not number. In *Met.* Δ.13, 1020a8–9, *plēthos* is defined as **(iii)** 'a certain quantity, if it is countable' (*poson ti ean arithmēton ēi*). The modality included in *arithmēton* (literally: 'numerable', 'that can be numbered', or 'that can be counted') is stressed in other passages, too. We have already seen in I.3, 1054a22, that **(iv)** *plēthos* is what is divided *or* divisible. Similarly in *Met.* Δ.13 1020a10–11, *plēthos* is defined as **(v)** 'what is *potentially* divisible into non continuous <parts>' (*to diaireton dunamei eis mē sunechē*), in opposition to magnitude (*megethos*), which is what is potentially divisible into continuous parts. What is the relation between divisibility in (iv) and (v), numerability or countability in (iii), and being measured by the one in (ii)?

I take it that Aristotle regards being numbered and being measured by the one (and, correspondingly, being numerable and being measurable by the one) as equivalent. If so, then the distinction between being divided and being divisible in (iv) corresponds to the distinction between number (i.e. a *plēthos* which is actually divided or measured by the one—see below on the actual division of number) and a *plēthos* which is numerable or measurable by the one or divisible into non-continuous parts. In order to fully spell out the relation between *plēthos* and number one should spell out what is responsible for turning *plēthos* as something countable into number. Broadly speaking, there seem to be two main options: either one takes the *plēthos*'s turning into number in an ontological sense, to mean that a principle of determination makes the *plēthos* an actual plurality of units (cf. Plat., *Soph.* 238a5, b3; *Parm.* 165e–166c). Or one takes the actualization of the *plēthos* into the plurality of units which is number as a psychological act of discernment (cf. *Phys.* IV.14, 223a16–29 where Aristotle raises the question whether time— which is a sort of number—would be if there were no mind doing the counting). For the method of *antanhairesis* as providing the possible background for understanding the way in which a *plēthos* comes to be measured by being progressively divided, cf. notes to I.5, 1056a12–15.

With respect to the divisibility of a *plēthos* into non-continuous parts, the non-continuity of parts tells us something about the relation between parts rather than about an intrinsic feature of the parts: the point is not that each part is a non-continuous item, but that parts are not continuous to each other (cf. *Phys.* V.3, 226b34–227a15). Furthermore, the numerability of a *plēthos* indicates that it can be divided into parts which measure it; but this does not exclude the possibility that the *plēthos* be divided into parts which do not measure it (for the distinction between parts that measure the whole and parts that do not measure cf. notes to 1056b20–25).

1057a6–7: '[. . .] not everything which is one is number, as in the case of something which is indivisible.' A *plēthos* is, by definition, something divisible into parts; number is a certain kind of *plēthos*. If something is indivisible into parts, it is not a *plēthos* and therefore, a fortiori, cannot be a number. Another way to spell out the same point is by saying that some measures are not in their turn measurable (by other measures). In I.1 and I.2 Aristotle makes room for units of measure which are not absolutely indivisible, but are conventionally assumed as indivisible with respect to a certain system (pp. 61–2). The numerical unit, though, is defined as what is indivisible in all respects and it cannot be measured by anything else. Units of measure of extended quantities are unmeasurable within the system for which they are unit of measurement, but can be measured within a different system.

The function of the remark at a6–7 is not completely clear. One possibility is that in this way Aristotle introduces the first part of the parallelism between measure/measurable and knowledge/knowable, the second part being spelled out at 1057a7–12.

1057a7–12:   At 1056b36–37 Aristotle used knowledge and knowable to introduce the kind of relatives under which measure and measurable fall. Now he explains that, although measure and measurable belong to the same kind of relatives as knowledge and knowable, the correspondences between the two cases are not those suggested by the morphology of their nouns. For one might think that knowledge stands to the knowable as measure stands to the measurable. But this is not the case. Aristotle's remarks (a10–11) are very compressed and there are textual issues. I shall start from the latter.

At a10–11 Ross's text yields the translation: 'but it turns out that all knowledge (*epistēmē*) is knowable (*epistēton*), but not all that is knowable is knowledge'. Based on *Cat.* 7, 7b29 Ross suggests that the first *epistēton* is a scribal error for *epistētou* and that *pros* ('relative to') has dropped out before the second occurrence of 'knowledge' (see Ross 1924, II apparatus and notes on pp. 297–8). According to this reconstruction, the text would read 'but it turns out that all knowledge is of the knowable, but not all knowable is relative to knowledge'. The reconstruction is not supported by the manuscripts (nor does Ross himself actually print it in his edition). We should therefore try to make sense of the text as we have it.

We have two claims:

(c) All knowledge is knowable.
(d) Not all knowable is knowledge.

There are two issues. The first issue concerns the argumentative function of the passage; the second concerns the theoretical basis in support of (c)–(d). As for the first issue, I have already suggested above that the passage goes together with 1057a6–7 in spelling out similarities and dissimilarities between measure/measurable and knowledge/knowable. In the passage above concerning one and number we have only one claim: not everything that is one is also number. The claim we lack is that every number is also one—in some sense to be specified. This is a claim Aristotle is committed to, and there are passages in which he criticizes other philosophers' views for not having given an adequate account of why this is the case (*Met.* H.3, 1044a2–8; 6, 1045a7–b23). If 'one' can be replaced by 'measure' and 'number' by 'measurable', one can see that the relations between knowledge and knowable on the one hand and measure and measurable on the other hand are not those one would expect if one had to rely on the morphological similarities of the expressions naming the two pairs of relatives. Rather, they are inverted: all measurable is measure, but not every measure is measurable. It is not clear whether Aristotle intends to draw any more precise correspondences between the two pairs of relatives. He seems rather interested in showing that in both cases there is some asymmetry in the relations obtaining between the two relatives and that it is by exploring such asymmetry that the deeper structural analogies and disanalogies between the two cases become clear.

As for the theoretical backdrop of (c) and (d), the main problem is how to understand (c). In *DA* III.4, 430a4 ff., Aristotle claims that 'in the case of things without matter that which thinks and that which is thought are the same; for theoretical knowledge (*hē epistēmē hē theōrētikē*) is the same as what is knowable in this way (*to houtōs epistēton*)'. Does *DA* III.4 capture the contents of (c) (as ps. Alex., *In met.*, Hayduck 631.26–29, suggests; cf. Bonitz 1849, pp. 419–20 and 441) or not (as Ross 1924, II p. 297, thinks)? The text is too compressed to rule out either option. Cf. I.1, 1053a31–35.

1057a12–17: Aristotle concludes the chapter with a final survey of all relations of opposition in which plurality or the many figures as one side of the opposition: plurality is not contrary to what is few; rather, much is contrary to few in the sense that exceeding plurality is contrary to exceeded plurality (cf. 1056b10–14). Plurality is not contrary to the one in general, but plurality is contrary to unity only if plurality is taken in the sense of being divisible (or divided) and unity in the sense of being indivisible (or undivided) (cf. I.3, 1054a20–23); if plurality is taken in the sense of number, then plurality is opposed to the one as a relative, i.e. as the measured is opposed to the measure.

From this survey it becomes clear that the two senses in which plurality or the many are opposite to the one correspond exactly to the two basic senses of unity emerging from I.1: if the one is taken in the sense of being indivisible, then the opposite sense of plurality is that of being divisible or divided; if the one is taken in the sense of measure, then the many are what is measured. In I.1 being indivisible and being a unit of measurement are two intertwined but non-equivalent properties; I suggested that being indivisible or being regarded as indivisible is a condition for being a unit of measurement; similarly, in I.6 divisibility is regarded as a condition for being measured. From this point of view, a coherent conceptual framework is displayed by the two chapters. Furthermore, the analysis of the opposition between one and many as introduced in I.3 is clearly in the background. These considerations, together with the explicit ties linking I.5 and I.6 (see the beginning of the discussion in the two chapters) and I.5 and I.4 (see the introduction of the difficulties in I.5 with reference to the analysis of contrariety produced in I.4), produce evidence in favour of a unified reading of I.1–6. The Greek commentary of ps. Alexander (Michael of Ephesus) ends with I.6. We do not know why this is so, but it is not impossible to imagine a shorter version of Iota, including I.1–6. Such a shorter version of Iota, if it ever existed, would have looked as a nice self-contained treatise about the one (I.1–2) and the contraries (I.3–6)—or, more specifically, about the one and what is opposed to the one. In fact, Michael (Hayduck 602. 8–10) encourages the curious readers of Iota to look at Plato's *Parmenides* or *Peri ideōn* in order to find out more about the Platonic views about the One (and, presumably, what is opposed to the One). On the historical relevance of this reading of I.1–6 see Castelli 2011, pp. 201–3.

CHAPTER 7

I.7 and I.8 return to two points already touched upon in the previous chapters: I.7 discusses intermediates (cf. I.4, 1055a3–5, b2, b8–11; I.5, 1056a12–15, a18–b2), and I.8 spells out what it is for things to be other in species or form (cf. I.3, 1054a32–b3 and b14–31; I.4, 1055a8; for 'species' and 'form' as translations of *eidos* see introductory remarks to I.8, pp. 198–9). I.9 will then tackle some difficulties raised by the account in I.8, and I.10 will qualify the opposition of perishable and imperishable as an opposition of things that are contrary in genus. All four chapters take for granted some familiarity with the conceptual framework of genera, differences, and species. Some passages (e.g. I.7, 1057b7 and I.8, 1058a22: *hōs genous*, 'as of the genus', to qualify the relevant use of *eidos*; I.8, 1058a21: the 'so-called' (*kaloumenon*) genus) show that Aristotle resorts to a terminology already in use. One could read I.7–9 as unpacking the ontology behind the use of such terminology. It might therefore be useful to sketch the conceptual framework providing the backdrop for these chapters before engaging with the analysis of the text. More detailed accounts of the issues arising from Aristotle's use of this terminology and more thorough reviews of the evidence can be found in Balme 1962 and 1987a; Deslauriers 1990; Falcon 1996; Granger 1984; Krämer 1968; Lennox 1980 and 2001b, in particular pp. 122–3; Pellegrin, 1986, 1987, and 1991.

The Greek words *genos* and *eidos* can be used in a non-technical or in a technical way. In their non-technical use, they can be translated as 'kind' and 'form' respectively and their meaning can be as generic as that of their English counterparts. The technical use can be found in Aristotle's discussions of various aspects of the practice of defining some general subject (a 'species': *eidos*) in terms of its *genos* ('genus') and its *diaphora* ('difference' or 'specific difference' or 'differentia'—the latter two translations emphasize the technical use of the word). The whole of Aristotle's *Topics* relies on this practice (see, in particular, *Top.* I.5, 102a31–b3 for an account of what a genus is, and *Top.* IV and VI for a survey of standard argumentative strategies to deal with definitions given in terms of genus and differences). This approach to definitions rests on the idea that species can be regarded as the results of the division (*dihairesis*) of higher genera through differences. For example, if one wants to give a definition of (the species) human being, one can do this by providing an account specifying the kind of thing that human beings are (i.e. the genus of human being; say: animal) and those distinctive features of human beings that differentiate them from other members of the same genus (e.g. unlike other animals, human beings are rational). To this conceptual framework there belongs the idea that species are parts of their genus and that the genus is a part (of the definition) of the species (*Met.* Δ.25, 1023b17–19, b22–25).

Aristotle's use of the conceptual framework and of the technical vocabulary of division supports the idea that these belonged to common practice in Plato's Academy. However, although the use of division for definitional purposes is portrayed in Plato's dialogues (see, e.g., *Soph.* 265a–268b; *Pol.* 258d–266b), no evidence of rigid technical use of *genos* and *eidos* can be found there. Indirect sources suggest that at some point interest in classification grew in the Academy. For example, in a well-known fragment, the comedy writer Epicrates depicts the members of Plato's Academy as busy with the classification of pumpkin, and Diogenes Laertius (*Lives of Eminent Philosophers*, VI 40) reports the anecdote that the cynic Diogenes of Sinope would have exhibited a plucked chicken with the words: 'Behold! A man!', thus mocking the Academic definition of man as biped featherless animal. Leaving the anecdotal aspects of these reports aside, the very fact that the application of classification was used to depict the activity of Academic philosophers suggests that interest in this practice was seen as somewhat distinctive of them even outside philosophical circles. It is not unlikely that the use of technical vocabulary developed with the activity of Plato's successors (of whom Aristotle was a distinguished one).

Aristotle resorts to the distinction between species and genus in two ways: as a relative distinction and as an absolute distinction. According to the relative distinction (e.g. *Phys.* V.4, 227b11–14), a genus is what is divided into species, but nothing prevents the genus from being in turn a species of a higher genus nor the species from being in turn a genus of lower species. For example, living being is the genus of animal and a species of substance; animal, in turn, is a species of living being and the genus of human being, horse, dog, etc. According to the absolute distinction, a genus is not the species of any higher genus and a species is not a genus of any lower species. In Aristotle's ontology the ten categories (substance, quality, quantity, etc.) are genera in the absolute sense (they are the highest genera), and the species under which the only relevant ontological differentiation is that of individuals belonging to the species are the lowest or atomic species (e.g. human being, horse, dog, etc. are all lowest species). The absolute distinction could be taken as a first step towards a general classification of things that are, and this is how the list of categories can be understood: all things that are can be grouped under the categories. It is not clear whether Aristotle thought that the application of this practice of definition through genera and differences depends upon the existence of a comprehensive classification of things that are (one of Aristotle's contemporaries, Speusippus, may have entertained such a view). What is clear is that Aristotle spells out the difficulties involved with and proposes improvements upon a too simplistic approach to division both as a definitional and as a classificatory method without introducing a neat distinction between its two possible uses. For example, taking division as a definitional method requires spelling out the ontology of genera and differences backing up the use of such a method (*Met.* Z.12). More generally, Aristotle at some point seems to depart from definitions by division in order to endorse a more complex approach in which a definition is supposed to display the causal structure of the defined thing (*Met.* Z.17; *APo* II.8–10). Taking division as a classificatory method, one has to account for cases of items falling under more than one genus (*Top.* IV.2, 121b24–122a2; IV.5, 126b7–12; *Met.* Δ.6, 1016a24–32; for some discussion see Brunschwig 2007, pp. xxxi ff.). Furthermore, in order to account for the complexity of living beings it seems that a simple application of division, consisting in attaching a single difference to the genus, is not adequate; rather, a cluster of differences should be used (*PA* I.3, 643b9–644a11).

With reference to this picture, I.7–10 raise two questions. One question is whether in these chapters Aristotle consistently resorts to a technical use of *eidos* and *genos* and, if so, whether he resorts to the absolute or to the relative distinction (see, in particular, I.10, notes to 1058b26–29). The other question concerns the ontology underpinning the use of the conceptual framework of genera and species and, in particular, the understanding of the nature of and of the relation obtaining between genera, differences, and species (I.7–9). As for the latter question, one general difficulty is that at different places Aristotle seems to endorse radically different views on the nature and role of differences with respect to genus and species. I provide here a sketchy overview of the three main views advocated in the corpus and I shall use this overview as the conceptual background against which Aristotle's account in I.7–9 should be assessed.

The first account of difference can be found in *Top.* I, IV, and VI. From the very beginning of the treatise, Aristotle shows some uncertainty on the nature of difference in that it is not one of the four kinds of predicate he distinguishes (definition, proprium, genus, and accident), but belongs together with the genus (*Top.* I.4, 101b18–19: *genikē*). What this means exactly is matter for debate. One possibility is that the difference, like the genus, belongs in the definition of its subject without being co-extensive with the subject. At any rate, Aristotle is clear on the claim that the genus is more apt to give the 'what it is' of the subject (I.5, 102a31–36), whereas the difference signifies some sort of quality. Similar claims can be found in Books IV (on the genus) and VI (on the definition), where Aristotle underlines the priority of the genus in the definition and the role of the difference as some sort of quality. For instance, in IV.2, 122b15–17 Aristotle comments on why it is wrong to provide the difference instead of the genus: 'for no difference indicates what <the subject> is but, rather, of what sort of quality it is, as the terrestrial and the biped' (*oudemia gar diaphora sēmainei ti estin alla mallon poion ti, kathaper to pezon kai to dipoun*). Similar remarks can be found in *Top.* IV.5, 126b13 ff.; IV.6, 128a20–29; VI.1, 139a27–31; VI.5, 142b20–29.

In most cases, Aristotle does not specify whether the difference is supposed to indicate some sort of quality of the genus or of the species. Interpreters mostly rely on passages such as IV.2, 122b15–17 to settle the issue as far as the *Topics* goes. In this passage Aristotle explains that the extension of each difference is smaller than the extension of the genus. This description applies to the difference that appears in the definition of the species and suggests that the difference indicates a qualitative determination of the species, whereas the genus indicates what the species is. However, there are passages testifying to the opposite view that the difference indicates some quality of the genus. One of these passages is *Top.* IV.6, 128a20–29. The passage is controversial and interpreters' reluctance to take this passage at face value might be motivated by the assumption that the difference (as it is usually understood) cannot be predicated of the genus (see, for instance, Morrison 1993b p. 16 n. 29). But we can distinguish two ways in which Aristotle speaks of *diaphora*. In one way, the difference is a part of the definition of the species; in this case, it is clear that Aristotle refers to a property which is predicated of the species. In another way, though, Aristotle speaks of difference to indicate the pair or set of differences which differentiates the genus in one division. In this sense, Aristotle can speak of the biggest difference or of the complete difference which divides the genus and which is contrariety (I.3 1054b32; see also I.9, 1058a30–31, a32, where taking difference as the set of differences which differentiate the genus is required by the context). By the same token, one can find passages (e.g. *APr* I.31, 46b3–19, *APo* II.13, 96b35–97a22) where the disjunction of the differences that divide the genus is predicated of the genus (every animal is either mortal or immortal; every mortal animal is either footed or a-footed, etc.).

One important qualification for the view that the difference indicates a certain quality (of the species or of the genus) is that this view does not imply that the difference is a sort of merely incidental feature of whatever it is a quality of. In fact, both in *Top.* VI.6, 145a3–12 and in *Met.* Δ.14, 1020b13–18 Aristotle distinguishes the qualitative determination expressed by the difference, which necessarily belongs to its subject, from the incidental qualities with respect to which the subject can change (*Top.* VI.6 criticizes the attempt to offer a *pathos*, 'affection', as a difference, and *Met.* Δ.14 distinguishes two main senses of *poion*, 'quality', as *diaphora tēs ousias*, 'difference of the substance', and as *pathē tōn kinoumenōn*, 'affections of things subject to change'; about *pathos* as an incidental affection with respect to which a subject can change cf. *Met.* Δ.21, 1022b15–18). This qualification will play some role in the discussion about the relation between contrary differences and genus in I.9.

The second account of difference can be found in *APo* I.4, 73a34–b34, where Aristotle distinguishes different ways in which things are said to be in their own right (or: per se) or to belong in their own right (per se) to something else. Two of these ways are relevant to characterize the status of differences as predicates. Something X belongs per se$_1$ to Y iff X appears in the definition of Y; something X belongs per se$_2$ to Y iff Y appears in the definition of X. All parts of the definition belong per se$_1$ to the defined thing (a34–37). It follows that, in a definition given in terms of genus and differences, the differences will be per se$_1$ of the defined thing. For example, if we define human being as 'rational biped animal', the differences ('rational', 'biped') and the genus ('animal') will be per se₁ of human being. Furthermore, differences turn out to be per se₂ to their genus (a37–b3): odd and even, prime and composite belong per se₂ to number, since number belongs in the definition of odd, even, prime, and composite. Similarly, in *APo* I.10, 76b6–8 odd and even are listed among 'per se affections' (*kath' hauta pathē*) that are demonstrated to belong to the subject genus of arithmetic science (i.e. number). Again, 'colour' must be mentioned in the definition of what it is to be sight-piercing or sight-contracting, or 'animal' must be mentioned in the account of what it is to be footed or winged or male or female.

The last view on difference can be found in *Met.* Z.12 1038a18–21 and H.6. Here the difference is the substance (*ousia*) and the 'definition of the thing' (*horismos tou pragmatos*). On this account, the difference turns out to be what the species actually is. This marks a radical shift from the first account, where the genus, rather than the difference, was supposed to express the what-it-is of the defined thing. This approach follows from the discussion of the relation between the difference and the genus appearing in the definition. In particular, Aristotle stresses how difficult it is to come up with a satisfactory account of the predicative relations obtaining between the genus and the difference appearing in the definition of a species. It cannot be the case that the definition of the difference applies to the genus (i.e. it cannot be the case that the difference is synonymously predicated of the genus) because the extension of the genus is greater than the extension of the difference. But it cannot be the case that the relation between difference and genus is one of merely incidental predication either, because in this case the essential unity of the objects of definition would be lost in favour of the composite structure of an incidental compound (see pp. 34–5). Accordingly Aristotle suggests that the relation between genus and difference resembles the relation between matter and form, potentiality and actuality, in which matter and genus cannot be detached (or separated) as such from their form or difference respectively.

With respect to these three approaches to the relation between differences, genus, and species, I.7–9 are not easy to place. On more than one occasion (see below) Aristotle compares genus and matter, and this points in the direction of the third understanding of the relation between genus and difference. Menn ((in progress), Iγ2b: Iota on contraries, and consequences for the *archai*) takes this to be I.7–8's view and reads the chapters as an attack to the Academic view that genera and differences are principles by showing that the genus is only (analogous to) matter and that differences can only be regarded as principles in a qualified way. I shall return to the issue whether differences may or may not be principles. As for I.7–9's approach to the genus, it seems to me that the situation is less clear than Menn submits. For example, in the course of I.7 Aristotle seems to see some analogy between the subject of change and the properties it assumes through the process of change on the one side and the genus and its set of differences on the other side. This may suggest a more extrinsic relation between genus and differences, in analogy to the relation between a subject that retains its identity through change and the properties it assumes in the process (for more details, see notes to 1057a19–30).

We can now take a closer look at the text. I.7 is entirely devoted to the ontology of *ta metaxu*, 'intermediates'. As in the previous chapters, the underlying philosophical motivation and the scope of the discussion are not immediately apparent. I.7 shares with the rest of Iota its interest in aspects and notions figuring prominently in Aristotle's accounts of Academic doctrines. In the case of I.7, this is true in two ways. First and rather superficially, in *Met.* A.6, 987b14–18 Aristotle ascribes to Plato the doctrine that mathematical entities (*ta mathēmatika*) are intermediate (*metaxu*) between Forms (*ta eidē*) and sensible beings (*ta aisthēta*); they differ (*diapheronta*) from sensible beings by being eternal and immobile, from Forms by being many of the same kind (whereas each Form is unique). From Aristotle's account in I.7 it follows that intermediates are always between contraries and that they belong in the same genus as the contraries between which they are. This implies that intermediates cannot be between different kinds of being and that, therefore, mathematical entities cannot be conceived of as intermediates between two radically different kinds of being (i.e. sensible particulars and Forms). In a way, this result would be further strengthened by I.10, where, if one takes perishable and imperishable to indicate Forms and sensible particulars respectively, the outcome is that these are not the kind of opposites between which intermediates can be found.

However, the Academic doctrine of intermediates does not seem to be a suitable polemical target for I.7 in the first place, for I.7 does not touch upon the arguments which Aristotle or Plato provide in support of the introduction of intermediate mathematical entities (for a review of those arguments see Annas 1975). In particular, those arguments do not rely upon any specific account of the ontological constitution of intermediates out of the opposite ontological domains (sensible particulars and Forms) between which they are. Mathematical entities are 'in-between' in that they share some features of sensible particulars (they are many) and some features of Forms (they are eternal), but for sure this does not imply that mathematical entities are conceived of as a sort of mixture between sensible particulars and Forms. In this respect, Aristotle's account of intermediates between contraries is irrelevant to the ontology of mathematical entities in Academic doctrines and to his own criticism against them.

A second and more promising route towards the motivation behind I.7 is the discussion of the extent to which differences and, in particular, contrary differences can be said to be principles. Menn ((in progress), Iγ2b: Iota on contraries, and consequences for the *archai*) takes this to be the main contribution of the chapter in Aristotle's enquiry into the principles. However, unlike Menn I am not quite sure what I.7's conclusion about the status of differences as principles actually is (see notes on 1057b29–34). Furthermore, the discussion in I.7 is ambiguous in at least one crucial sense: it is not clear whether Aristotle intends to allude to the existence of a basic pair of differences for all beings or whether he intends to endorse the weaker claim that, for any genus, there is some basic pair of contrary differences, which are the ultimate principles of its determination. Both claims are problematic but neither is confined to Iota (see Introduction, part II).

Leaving aside the discussion of the role of differences as principles, I.7 makes a contribution to Aristotle's account of the general structures of being in at least two ways. First, the discussion of the existence and nature of intermediates between contraries can be read as the counterpart of the discussion in Met., Γ.7 about the existence and nature of intermediates between contradictories. In particular, both chapters reveal an interest in the issue of the existence of intermediate beings between different kinds of opposites (cf. pp. 179, 186). From this perspective, it is

quite clear that I.7 picks out a topic for which Aristotle shows
interest elsewhere and not just for polemical purposes. Secondly,
I.7 gives a very general account of the ontology of continuous
ranges of qualitative determinations of a subject. The ontology of
ranges of qualities occupies Aristotle at different places and for
different reasons (see Introduction, pp. xxxvi, xliii–xliv). For
instance, perceptible qualities come in ranges; beings are characterized by ranges of features; anything that changes from A to
B changes continuously from A to B and continuously goes
through intermediate stages at which it is neither A nor B, but
something between A and B. I.7 is the only place in the corpus
where a systematic account of the ontology of ranges is given.

1057a18–19: The chapter opens with two claims: **(1)** it is possible that there is something intermediate between contraries; **(2)**
in some cases, there is something intermediate between contraries. Both claims are anticipated in I.4. As for (1), at 1055a3–4
Aristotle has already introduced the idea that there can be degrees
of difference and has already said (1055b2) that contraries may
admit of intermediates. There is an issue about what (1) exactly
means. I take it to mean that, in the case of contraries (unlike the
case of contradictories), it is always possible to jointly deny both
contraries, and joint negation is a way to express intermediates
(cf. I.5, 1056a12–15, a18–b2). More generally, the joint negation
of the contraries opens up the logical space for a third option
other than either contrary. However, Aristotle does not confine
himself to a claim about a *logical* possibility: (2) claims that in
some cases there are intermediate *beings* between the contraries
and I.7 specifies how such intermediate beings are 'made'.

As for (2), I.4 1055b23–25 has already alluded to a distinction
between contraries that have intermediates and contraries that do
not have intermediates. I.7 does not explain the difference
between these two cases, but explains what intermediates are.
This will introduce some restrictions on the pairs of items which
admit of intermediates (as Aristotle will spell out, only items
bound in a certain way to a genus can have intermediates).

The central claim of the chapter is that **(3)** intermediates are
'from' or 'out of' (*ek*) the contraries between which they are.
Aristotle distinguishes different uses of *ek*, two of which are
relevant in I.7. *ek* can be used to introduce the constituents out

of which something is made (e.g. *Met.* Δ.23, 1023a26–29; Z.8, 1033a25–26; *Phys.* I.7, 190a24–26) or to introduce a starting point from which something comes to be (*Phys.* I.7, 189a32 ff.) which is left behind and does not persist through a process of change (*Phys.* I.7, 190a21–23). In the second use, that 'from which' something comes to be is not a constituent of what comes to be. The development of the discussion in I.7 suggests that Aristotle is interested in taking (3) as an ontological claim about the constitution of intermediates as made out of the contraries between which they obtain (see, in particular, 1057b3 and b34), but the discussion resorts to both uses (the non-constitutive use can be found at 1057a27, 28, 31, and 33; the constitutive use at 1057b3, 7, 14, 15, 20, 21, 22, 23, 28, 34). In the course of the commentary I shall discuss whether this is a problem for the development of the argument (see pp. 194–5).

Although (3) is Aristotle's central claim in I.7, two further results are established in the course of the discussion: **(4)** intermediates belong in the same genus as the terms between which they are (1057a19–30), and **(5)** intermediates are intermediates between contraries (1057a30–b1). All three claims are restated at the end of the chapter (1057b32–34) in the order in which they are argued for ((4), (5), (3)).

1057a19–30: The first 'for' (l. 20: *gar*) makes it clear that proving claim (4) is part of the argument in support of (3). The first account of intermediates in I.7 is cast in terms of change: if an object x changes non-incidentally from C_1 to C_2 and x changes into I_n before changing into C_2, then I_n is intermediate between C_1 and C_2 (1057a21–22). I shall refer to this account as dynamic account of intermediates.

Intermediates are here understood as intermediate steps between the initial and the final stage in a process of change (cf. *Phys.* V.3, 226b23–25). Change takes place in a subject which persists while assuming different properties. Accordingly, the initial and the final stage of a process of change can be respectively described in terms of the subject of change's being characterized by the initial property and the subject of change's being characterized by the final property. This picture is further enriched by two tenets: **(a)** change is always from and between the opposites (cf. *Phys.* V.1, 224b25 ff.); **(b)** there is no change from one genus to another. Although these two tenets are most naturally read as concerning the properties assumed by the subject of change in the course of the process and with respect to which the subject of change is said to change, it is not always clear whether Aristotle regards the opposites defining a process of change as the opposite (initial and final) abstract properties or as the compounds of the subject of change taken together with the corresponding property. This difficulty is due to the fact that Aristotle's examples in the relevant texts are often ambiguous or in contrast on this point. For instance, it is not clear whether the extremes between which a process of alteration in which a certain object changes from white to black are the colour white and the colour black or, rather, the white object and the black object. For some discussion of this point see Charlton 1970, pp. 70–3. Furthermore, one might argue that in the case of generation and corruption there are no opposite properties between which change takes place: there is matter characterized by a form and matter deprived of a form, but there is no such thing as a privation of a substantial form. A similar difficulty will emerge at 1057b11–12 as to whether contrary differences or contrary species have a better claim to be contraries.

One point emphasized by (a) and (b) is that the whole range of properties an object assumes while going through one process of change must lie within the same genus, i.e. they must be the same kind of property. For instance, there is no change from colour to shape, if not incidentally. If we say that an object x changes from being white to being triangular, either there are two processes of change incidentally going on at the same time in the same subject x and we are picking out the initial property of one and the final property of the other, or we are simply picking out the wrong properties to describe the initial or the final stage of the process. For instance, in the first case, at the beginning of the process x was both white and circular; at the end of the process, x is black and triangular. There are two processes going on: x is changing from being white to being black and from being circular to being triangular. But being white and being triangular do not work as the initial and the final stage of one single process of change. In the second case (i.e. if there is only one process of change going on), either x is still white at the end of the process or it was already triangular at the beginning of the process. Either way, describing a process of change as a change from being white to being triangular is misleading in the best case and does not make any sense in the worst case. On the idea that change occurs between determinate pairs of properties cf. *Phys.* I.5, 188a31–b26. On the restrictions concerning the nature of the opposites defining a unitary process of change, see *Phys.* V.4, 227b3–228a3.

The dynamic account of intermediates, in conjunction with the analysis of the examples at 1057a22–26, raises some questions. Given that for Aristotle every process of change is continuous and what is continuous can be infinitely divided, the dynamic account might suggest that, for any two opposites that can work as initial and final stage of a process of change, there are potentially infinitely many intermediates between them. Whether Aristotle is committed to this view or rather endorses a more robust account of intermediates is a controversial issue on different grounds. Why this is so can be seen by looking at the examples. Aristotle describes two movements, one from *hupatē* to *nētē* and one from white to black. *Hupatē* and *nētē* are the lowest and the highest note in a tetrachord. The tetrachord (literally: 'four strings') in the Greek musical system is a series of three intervals which divides the interval of a perfect fourth. It is not completely clear to what kind of movement from the *hupatē* to the *nētē* Aristotle alludes. By the same token, it is not clear what is the subject that 'moves' from the *hupatē* to the *nētē* (is it the player? the sound? the material, e.g. a stopper moving along a vibrating string?). Depending on how we fill in the gaps left open by Aristotle's description, we might come up with (at least) two rather different views about the nature and number of intermediates. There is a textual issue at 1057a23 which might be of some consequence (see Notes on the Text). Aristotle specifies that the movement proceeds 'through the smallest thing' (*tōi oligistōi*, A^b-reading followed by Ross and Jaeger) or 'through the smallest ratio' (*tōi oligistōi logōi*, the α-text; see Notes on the Text about *logōi* as an α-supplement). I take it that the more generic 'through the smallest thing', i.e. presumably, 'through the smallest interval', is preferable from the point of view of the meaning. We saw earlier (cf. I.1 1053a12–13, 15–16; I.2, 1053b34–1054a1) that Aristotle alludes to a distinction between the smallest intervals acknowledged in a harmonic system in terms of numerical ratios and the smallest interval that is perceived by the human ear.

Accordingly, the text may refer either to the idea of moving from the *hupatē* to the *nētē* in the sense of moving from the lowest to the highest pitch in the tetrachord through the smallest interval(s) acknowledged within the musical system or through the smallest interval perceived by the human ear. The α-text supports the reading in terms of numerical ratios, but the use of the singular might be relevant here and point towards the empiricist identification of one unit of measure as the smallest interval audible to human ear. Furthermore, the division of the 'path' from the lowest to the highest note suggests a division into intervals of determinate width and, therefore, a division into a finite number of 'steps' from the initial to the final point, which seems to be characteristic of the empiricist approach. Note that if this is the correct interpretation of the example, then the intermediates between the lowest note and the highest note in the tetrachord are not all the potentially infinite pitches in a glissando from the lowest to the highest note, but only some perceptible pitches along a potential continuum. A similar idea can perhaps be found in *DS* 6, 445b29–446a4 (for an analysis of the passage in *DS* 6 and its relation to Theophrastus's and Aristoxenus's approach to the differences between musical pitches see Barker 2004, in particular pp. 108–11; more generally on the issue of the existence of a continuum of pitches see p. 84). In order to make sense of change in sound as a change between contraries we should perhaps think of it as taking place between the sharp and the heavy or the tense and the slack (see p. 57).

Partly similar considerations apply to the second example about change of colour. In this case the example suggests that there will be at least some clearly discriminable stages (red, grey) between the initial and the final stage. Unlike in the musical example, though, no mention is made of some smallest colour interval (whatever that may turn out to be) into which a continuous change of colour can be divided. Other texts such as *DS* 3, 439b26–440a5, 440b18–20 (cf. *DS* 4, 442a12–29 about flavours), *DS* 6, 445b21–446a20 discuss the issue of the number of species of colours, flavours, and sounds in connection with the issue whether perceptible qualities are indefinitely divisible like the bodies to which they belong. Especially in *DS* 6 Aristotle suggests that, although there are indefinitely many potentially perceptible intermediates in an interval bound by two distinctively perceptible colours or sounds, there is only a finite number of species dividing up a spectrum of perceptible qualities. It is not clear how Aristotle's references to a continuous spectrum divided up in a finite number of species should be understood. There are at least two contrasting options. One option is that the qualitative spectrum which is divided up into a finite number of species can be regarded as only derivatively continuous in that qualitative change supervenes upon some continuous change (this idea is suggested by Sorabji (1976, p. 80), with reference to the ontology of pitches: 'What Aristotle seems to have in mind is that a change to the next discriminable pitch, in the discontinuous series of discriminable pitches, may be produced by the continuous movement of a stopper along a vibrating string'). The alternative view is that there are infinitely many potential discriminations to be made, but only finitely many perceptual discriminations are actually made and this determines the finite number of sensible species (Kalderon 2015, pp. 124–36, in particular p. 129). The dynamic account of intermediate in I.7 seems compatible with either analysis.

The dynamic account also raises a problem as to the intended generality of the account of intermediates in I.7. As the second part of I.7 will make plain, Aristotle is interested in the identification of intermediate differences which are intermediate between contrary differences of a genus. The intermediate differences of a genus are those that yield intermediate species. One may wonder whether and how the dynamic account of intermediates and the identification of intermediate differences and species of a genus are related. The division of a genus through contrary and intermediate differences seems to be presented as a structural feature that applies to all domains of being (but see below), while only four categories (substance, place, quality, and quantity) admit of change.

Furthermore, even if one confines the discussion to the four categories which admit of change, it is not clear whether and how the dynamic identification of intermediates matches the identification of intermediate differences and species. The case of substance is problematic in its own right. In *Phys.* I.7–9 the opposites between which change (including substantial change) takes place are regarded as possession and privation of a form. Given Aristotle's account of the contraries in Iota in terms of possession and complete privation of a form, one might think that also the extremes of generation and corruption qualify as extremes between which dynamic intermediates can be found. However, *Phys.* V.1, 225a34–b5 claims that, of the four kinds of change, only those in quality, quantity, and change take place between contraries (*enantia*). The extremes of the two possible changes in substances, i.e. generation and corruption, are opposed as contradictories (being and not being: *Phys.* V.1, 225a12–20). As we have seen and as Aristotle will stress later in I.7, contradictories do not admit of intermediates. One consequence of this would be that there are no intermediates in a process of generation or corruption.

But even leaving the controversial case of substance aside, there are other processes of change in which intermediate stages do not necessarily pick out any intermediate species. Consider locomotion from place A to place B, where B is at A's right. While the claim that in order to move in a straight line from A to B an object has to go through the intermediate distance between A and B has intuitive appeal, it is not the case that any intermediate stage in this process of change picks out a species of place which is intermediate between A and B. One might also wonder whether there is any sense in which A and B can be said to be contraries—unless contraries are defined functionally as the extremes of a process of change (cf. I.4, p. 131). In the case of place, however, Aristotle is ready to make room for the idea that there are species of place which are opposite to each other (up and down, left and right, front and back; see *Phys.* IV.1, 208b12–13 and Morison 2002, pp. 35–47 for some comments), and suggests that the conceptual framework of contrary places may have played a sort of paradigmatic role for the general account of contraries as 'things which are the farthest apart of those that are in the same genus' (cf. *Cat.* 6, 6a11–18). The case of change in quantity is problematic too. Again, one might wonder whether there is any way to make sense of the claim that processes of growing and shrinking are between contraries other than by saying that there are some determinate quantities that happen to be the extremes between which processes of change take place. The only case in which both the dynamic account and the idea that there are contrary and intermediate differences and species of a genus seems to be that of qualities.

If categorial distinctions have to be brought into the picture, then the value of the dynamic account is restricted. For if it is true that there are intermediates between opposites which cannot figure as extremes of change (e.g. relatives), then the dynamic account is not necessary. And if it is true that intermediates must be actually discerned by perception in order to count as intermediate in some robust sense, then the dynamic account is not sufficient either. The dynamic account and dynamic intermediates, however, are as good as any to argue that intermediates belong in the same genus as the items between which they are. One could therefore argue that Aristotle's reliance on dynamic intermediates is functional to establishing (4), by providing a paradigmatic case in which the restriction on the genus of extremes and intermediates are known on different grounds (i.e. through the analysis of change).

1057a30–b1:   Having argued for (4), Aristotle moves on to (5), i.e. the claim that intermediates can only be intermediates of contraries.

The first steps of the argument rely on the dynamic account of intermediates (see 1057a21–22). Aristotle adds that change can only be between opposites (1057a31–32: in the dynamic account given on p. 180: C1 and C2 must be opposites of some kind). It follows that intermediates are intermediate between opposites (1057a30–31). But opposites can be of four kinds: contradictories, relatives, possession and privation, contraries. In order to argue for (5) Aristotle has to show that the only cases in which there are intermediates are cases in which the opposites stand to each other in a relation of contrariety. He starts (a34–36) by showing that there is no intermediate of a contradictory pair. I take this claim to be about pairs of contradictory properties (rather than about pairs of contradictory statements). The point would be that if we take the property of being-A and the property of not-being-A, any object we consider will either have the property of being-A or the property of not-being-A. On the lack of intermediates between contradictories cf. I.4, 1055b1–2 and, more generally on the excluded middle, Γ.7, 1011b23 ff.

At a37–b1 relatives are considered. Aristotle seems to refer to the same partition of relatives into contrary relatives and non-contrary relatives as in I.6, 1056b35–36 (see notes *ad loc.*). In I.7 the distinction links to the issue whether there is a common genus for the relata. The remark might sound puzzling: relatives, qua relatives, by definition all belong to the same genus, i.e. the category of relatives. But Aristotle's point here is a different one and concerns the nature of the objects that can enter a relation when considered each in its own right, independently of the relation. For example, the objects that can be bigger or smaller are quantities of the same kind; knowledge is a specific condition of the soul and what is knowable is some extra-mental object in the world. In the first case, it is possible to have contrary pairs of relatives which admit of intermediates. For instance, consider the case of x and y such that x is bigger than y, and the opposite case such that x is smaller than y. In order for the relations to obtain and for the two cases to be opposite to each other, x and y must be the same kind of thing (numbers, lengths, surfaces, etc.) in both cases. For a number is neither bigger nor smaller than nor equal to a length. And if x and y were, e.g., lengths in the first case and surfaces in the second case, the second case would not be the opposite of the first case. These two opposites admits of an intermediate, i.e. the case in which x is equal to y. It is difficult to come up with even superficially parallel cases with relatives such as knowledge and knowable.

Aristotle says nothing about the case of possession and privation or about the case of contraries. In order to conclude the argument, Aristotle should show that (i) there are intermediates of contraries, and (ii) if (ii.a) there are intermediates of possession and privation, then (ii.b) possession and (complete) privation stand to each other in a relation of contrariety. It is possible that (i)–(ii.b) are assumed as granted premises. For (i) is simply assumed throughout these chapters; (ii.a) is presented as a relatively uncontroversial claim in I.4, 1055a33–b29, where one of the arguments in support of the thesis that contrariety is an opposition of possession and complete privation rests on the claim that both oppositions admit of intermediates; (ii.b) has already been established in I.4.

1057b2–4: Having argued for (4) and (5), Aristotle returns to his initial claim (3). He introduces two exhaustive and mutually exclusive options: either **(c)** there is a genus of the intermediates and/or of the corresponding contraries (cf. 1057b20: *enantia*), or **(d)** there is none. The discussion of these two options determines the structure of the rest of the chapter. (c) is considered at 1057b4–19; (d) is considered at 1057b19–29; the conclusion of the argument is stated at 1057b29–32. Both the formulation of (c) and (d) and their role in the development of the argument are problematic.

To start with, the very introduction of the alternative between (c) and (d) is puzzling. For Aristotle has already said several times that contraries belong to the same genus and that intermediates belong to the same genus as the terms between which they are intermediates. This can be reasonably taken as at least implying that *there is* a genus of the contraries and of their intermediates. Three points should be taken into account in addressing this issue. First, from the way in which the argument unfolds, it seems that the contrast Aristotle is drawing is that between (c) intermediates and contraries that are *species* of a genus (and, in this sense, are in the same genus) and (d) intermediates and contraries that are *differences* of a given genus (which, in this sense, are not in that genus) (this distinction is clearly drawn in Chiaradonna 2005). Secondly, there seem to be different ways in which the relationship between contraries and a certain genus can be specified. If we talk about contrary species (e.g. white and black), there is a genus to which they both belong (colour). If we talk about contrary differences (e.g. sight-piercing and sight-contracting), there is a genus (colour) they differentiate. This suggests that contraries may be bound to a genus even without being 'in' the genus (for some discussion of this and related points see Introduction, section II.1). Thirdly, at different places Aristotle endorses rather different views about the ontological and logical role of differences with respect to their relation to the genus and to the species (see introduction to I.7, pp. 173–7).

1057b4–11: The first case Aristotle considers is (c): there is a genus of the contraries and of their intermediates. Four tenets are characteristic of this view: **(6)** contraries and intermediates are initially understood as contrary and intermediate species of a genus; **(7)** the genus combined with the differences yields the species; **(8a)** the genus and the differences are prior to the species; **(8b)** the contraries that are contrary differences are prior to the contraries that are contrary species.

(6) Until now, Aristotle has spoken of the intermediates within a dynamic framework in which intermediates were introduced with reference to the ontology of change. In this section contraries

and intermediates are discussed within the conceptual framework of the division of genera and species. About the relation between the two frameworks see pp. 184–6.

(7) The general picture Aristotle has in mind is something along these lines: let's consider the contraries black and white. Of these there is a genus (colour) which, in combination with the contrary differences sight-piercing and sight-contracting, produces the contrary species. As anticipated in the introduction to I.7 (pp. 173–7), at different places Aristotle endorses different views about the nature of the combination of genus and differences. I.7 as such does not lead us very far: at 1057b7 Aristotle confines himself to saying that species are 'out of' genus and differences, without going into further details. I.8 (see, in particular, 1058a1–2 and a23–24) suggests that the genus is (a sort of) matter with respect to its species. The idea that the genus is some sort of matter is a recurrent one, with different emphasis: see, for instance, *Met.* Δ.6, 1016a24–28; Z.12, 1038a5 ff.; H.6, 1045a23–25. Of all these texts, it seems to me that in Z.12 and H.6 the analysis of the relation between genus and difference(s) in terms of matter and form is endorsed with full awareness of its metaphysical consequences. Note that both passages deal with the solution to a specific problem, i.e. the problem of the unity of the definition (for a sketchy account of the problem and some comments see notes to I.1, pp. 33–6). Note also that in Z.12, 1038a5–9 one consequence of the claim that the genus is 'either not at all' distinct from the species 'or it is, but is like matter', is that the definition of the species will be an account made of differences (*ek tōn diaphorōn*)—I take this to mean: of differences only, given that reference to the genus is included in the differences. It is not obvious that this analysis of the relation between genus, species and differences is identical with the account presupposed in I.7, 1057b7, where Aristotle stresses that the species are out of (*ek*) 'the genus *and* the differences'. The passages in I.8 are, I think, not decisive either way (see notes *ad loc.*). I.9 is also problematic in that it refers to differences as 'affections' (1058a37: *pathē*) of the genus, which may suggest that, although the genus is a sort of substrate of its differences (and, in this sense, is like matter), it retains its identity when affected by certain properties (and, in this sense, its behaviour resembles the behaviour of subjects rather than the behaviour of matter). I.9's general take on the relation

between genus and difference, however, seems close to Z–H's approach.

(8a) Depending on how we understand the relation between genus, differences, and species, we may come up with different accounts of the sense in which genus and differences are prior to species. Aristotle himself distinguishes different ways in which things can be said to be prior or posterior to each other (cf. *Cat.* 12; *Met.* Δ.11, Θ.8). In particular, he distinguishes priority in nature or being from priority in knowledge. x is prior in knowledge to y iff we can know x without knowing y, but we cannot know y without knowing x. The basic criterion for priority in nature is that x is prior in nature to y iff x can be without y's being, but y's cannot be without x's being. This criterion strongly suggests that priority in nature has something to do with existential priority. However, in some passages a more refined criterion of priority in being seems to be required and different accounts have been given of the refined criterion. The refined criterion can be construed in terms of ontological dependence broadly speaking (x is prior in being to y iff y's being depends on x's being and not vice versa), which would make room for relations of causal priority (y is causally dependent upon x) as well as for relations of existential dependence (Beere 2009, pp. 293–324). Alternatively, the refined criterion can be construed in terms of definitional priority (x is prior in being to y iff x can be defined without reference to y but not the other way round). The latter account of priority in being in terms of definitional priority may run the risk of flattening priority in being with priority in knowledge, but the reason why definitional priority can be understood as priority in being is that the relation between definitions reflects the relation between the essences of the defined things (for an articulated version of this view see Peramatzis 2011, in particular pp. 254–9). The way in which one construes priority in definition is relevant to I.7 in that it is clear that genus and difference enjoy some sort of priority in definition with respect to the species. The question is whether this is also a form of ontological priority or not (for some further comments on this point, see pp. 193–4, 197–8, 207–8, 224–6).

(8b) Contrary differences (sight-piercing and sight-contracting) are prior to the contrary species (white and black) which they constitute. For some discussion see notes to b11–12.

1057b11–19:   Aristotle assumes that all species are constituted in the same way. If contrary species are constituted out of genus and differences, so will intermediate species. In the case of intermediate species, though, the differences constituting the species cannot be the same as those constituting the contrary species. The reason for this lies in the assumption that a species is univocally determined by the conjunction of the genus with its specific differences. Accordingly, the differences of intermediate species must be distinct from the differences of contrary species. In particular, they will be intermediate between the contrary differences which determine the contrary species. For the ontology of intermediate differences see pp. 192–7.

1057b11–12:   *ta enantiōs diapheronta mallon enantia* 'things which differ in a contrary way are contrary to a higher degree'. This is puzzling. The point might be that contrary differences, being responsible for the ontological constitution of contrary species, are more properly said to be contraries than the species (Bonitz 1849, p. 443); cf. *Met.* α.1, 993b24–26. But the opposite interpretation that, despite some priority of the differences, contrary species (rather than contrary differences) have a stronger claim to be contraries than the differences cannot be excluded (Ross 1924, II p. 300: in particular, Ross comments that *ta enantiōs diapheronta*, 'things which differ in a contrary way', seems to apply more naturally to the species than to the differences). In support of this view, one could perhaps refer to *Met.* Δ.10, 1018a31–35 (cf. notes on I.4, 1055a16–19, a35–38), where some things are said to be contrary in a derivative way by producing other contraries; contrary differences are said to produce (1057b6: *poiēsasai*) the species of the genus. Neither of the two readings is fully satisfactory. Perhaps connected with the present passage see *Met.* Δ.10, 1018b3–4: 'And contraries are other in species than each other, either all of them or those that are said to be contraries primarily'. On the idea that species can be said to be other in species (*eidos*) see I.8.

If one takes the things that 'differ in a contrary way' and 'are contraries to a higher degree' to be the contrary species of a genus (cf. Ross 1924, II p. 300; Centrone 2005, pp. 32–3; Chiaradonna 2005, p. 164), one can raise the question whether Aristotle is making a point about contrary species as compared to contrary differences (as Ross, Centrone, and Chiaradonna suggest, taking *alla mēn ge* in the sense of 'and yet', i.e. contrary differences are prior to contrary species, and yet contraries species are more properly regarded as contraries) or whether he is making a point about contrary species as compared to their intermediates. The latter interpretation seems unlikely, but two considerations could be given in support of the idea that intermediates might be regarded as *enantia* to a lesser degree. First, Aristotle sometimes describes the intermediates that work as extremes of change as (functional) *enantia* (see pp. 130–1). His point here could be that, even if one can in some contexts regard the intermediates as *enantia*, those *entantia* whose difference spans a genuine contrariety are more properly regarded as contraries. Secondly, intermediates take part in the contraries between which they are by being a sort of mixture of the two; in this sense, each intermediate is less of a contrary than either of the 'pure' contraries out of which intermediates are made (cf. 1057b25–26).

1057b19–29: The wording of this passage is quite obscure, but the main point is fairly clear. Having established that intermediate species of a genus are the result of the composition of the genus with intermediate differences, Aristotle now approaches the issue 'from what' or 'out of what' (*ek tinos*) such intermediate differences are.

An answer to this question is required in order to understand the ontology of intermediate species. This seems to be what the comment at 1057b20–22 ('for it is necessary that things in the same genus be either composed of things that are incomposite with respect to the genus or themselves incomposite') suggests. I take it that 'things in the same genus' indicates species, whereas the 'primary contraries which are not in <a> genus' refers to the corresponding differences. The passage leaves it open whether the differences are in their turn species of another genus or not: the distinction between contraries in the genus and not in the genus is relative to the genus of the species of which the differences at issue are specific differences (for some additional remark on this point see below).

It is not clear whether the subject of the comment at b20–22 is the intermediates in the same genus or, more generally, species in the same genus. If the subject of the sentence is intermediate species, Aristotle's point would be the following: either intermediate species are constituted out of something added to the genus to which they belong or they are in their turn incomposite. Note that, if this is the sense of the parenthesis, Aristotle does not contemplate the possibility that intermediate species be constituted out of contrary species. The second option would then be excluded, possibly because it has already been shown that contrary species are constituted out of the genus and contrary differences, and it is assumed that all species are constituted in the same way. If, on the other hand, we take the subject of the remark to be species in a genus more generally, the point would be the following: either we think that species of a genus are obtained from the genus through the genus's interaction with something which does not belong to it, or we think that species are primitive and incomposite. The latter option would then be excluded because it has already been said that this is not the case for contrary species (and, therefore, it is not the case for any species) and/or because this simply goes against the common understanding of the relations between species and genus (cf. 1057b7: the idea that species are out of genus and differences is taken as uncontroversial).

One further question is whether the things that 'are not in the genus' should be simply understood as not being in the genus at issue or whether the possibility of some primitive pair of contraries, which are not the result of the division of any genus, should be entertained (on this point, see also notes to 1057b29–32). In the latter case, the doctrine presented in this passage would belong together with the texts emphasizing the role of determinate pairs of contraries as principles of being (see Introduction, section II.2). In the former case, the point of the passage would simply be that contrary differences are incomposite relative to the species of the genus they are differences of, but nothing would prevent them from being the result of a similar composition within a different genus.

Either way, the main idea is the following. Let us consider the differences of a genus. They are not composed out of the genus, so either they are composed out of something else or they are incomposite. The argument starting at b22 suggests that the only relevant available components are the genus (which has been excluded) and the contrary differences. Contrary differences are not composed out of the genus nor out of each other; this seems to be enough to claim that they are incomposite. Their incomposite status makes them 'principles' (cf. *Phys.* I.5, 188a27–30; I.6, 189a17–20; for a recent discussion of some of the issues mentioned above with reference to *Phys.* I.5 see Judson (forthcoming)). Given the connection between the lack of composition and the status of principles of the contraries on the one hand and the constitutive function of contrary differences for contrary species and intermediates on the other hand, contrary differences turn out to be principles in the sense of being primary constituents (on this sense of 'principle', cf. *Met.* Δ.1, 1013a4–7).

1057b23–29: Aristotle establishes a link between the dynamic account of intermediates (b24–25), their relation to contraries (b25–26), and their nature as composite entities (b27–29). According to the dynamic account of intermediates (p. 180) if a subject x changes from being C_1 to being C_2 and x changes into being I_n before changing into being C_2, then I_n is intermediate between C_1 and C_2. To this account Aristotle now adds a remark about the ontological constitution of an intermediate. The idea is that, for any n, when x changes into I_n, x will be more C_1 than when it will be C_2 and more C_2 than it was when it was C_1. In this sense, for any n, being I_n is a certain composition of C_1 and C_2, although the amount of C_1 and C_2 respectively varies for different intermediate stages. I shall refer to this account of the ontological constitution of intermediates as the constitutive account. Aristotle adds that, if something x is a composite of y and z, then x can be said to be 'out of' (*ek*) y and z (1057b26–28). At 1057b28, 'somehow' (*pōs*) voices some caution, but it is not clear where caution should be applied (whether to the claim that what is y and z in different degrees is a composite made of y and z or to the claim that it is 'out of' y and z).

The constitutive account raises a number of questions. To start with, there is a question as to whether the constitutive account essentially rests on the dynamic account of intermediates. If so, the move from the claim that intermediates are from (*ek*) the contraries in the dynamic account to the claim that intermediates are made out of (*ek*) the contraries in the constitutive account may rest on equivocation. Furthermore, we have seen before that the dynamic account may not apply in all relevant cases, whereas the constitutive account is taken to apply in general either to none or to all intermediates (1057b23). One further question concerns

Aristotle's understanding of the constitution of intermediates out of the contraries. Even if, for simplicity's sake, we focus on qualities (therefore leaving aside the more complicated cases of quantities, places, etc.), and even if we grant for the sake of the argument that a continuous change from white to black goes through other colours, some work has to be done in order to spell out how exactly the constitutive account is supposed to be applied. For the constitutive account suggests that there are properties which are the result of the composition of other properties in different amounts. But how is a composition of properties supposed to work? There seem to be two options. One could take this at face value and claim that properties as such can be combined with each other in varying quantities. Or one could take Aristotle's account as a simplified way to say that the stuff out of which the subjects of those properties are made can be mixed in different amounts; one can speak of composition of properties only derivatively and, to a certain extent, improperly. The first option is unpromising, among other reasons because Aristotle himself rejects the idea that properties can mix or be composed in their own right (*GC* I.10, 327b10–22; cf. I.2, p. 84). But if it is only the material objects to which qualities belong that can be mixed and composed with each other, then some work has to be done in order to spell out in what sense the composition of contrary differences is the basic ontological fact accounting for the coming about of ranges of qualities. For if one says that yellow is a certain ratio of white and black, what gets quantified in the ratio is not white and black in their own right, but the material components that are, respectively, white and black, and which, once mixed, produce a yellow object. For a detailed account of how this might work in the case of colour see Kalderon 2015, Ch. 6. Note that, if one reads I.7 with the correct account of composition in mind, one may come up with a fairly coherent view about how ranges of perceptible qualities of material objects are ultimately determined by the mixture of the four elements in that the elements are characterized by basic contrary features (along the lines of *GC* II.2 and *DS*; cf. Introduction, pp. xxxiv–xxxv, xl–xli).

These considerations show that, if I.7 provides a useful tool for the analysis of the ontology of qualities, it can only do so in conjunction with Aristotle's theory of composition. According to such a theory, it is only the material subjects of qualities that can be mixed and quantified strictly speaking. But it is difficult to tell whether I.7 is supposed to be read with such a theory in view. Perhaps Aristotle's insistence on the dynamic account of intermediates, with its embedded reference to a substratum of qualities, serves the purpose of drawing the attention to the more complex picture which is necessary in order to make sense of the composition of properties. I.7, however, mainly emphasizes the formal side in the constitutions of intermediate qualities: these qualities are always qualities of certain material objects, but they come to be in that the material components of those material objects have certain more basic qualitative features.

1057b29–32: The passage states the conclusions of the argument. Aristotle seems to draw a picture of the structure of genera and species such that (for each genus) there is a pair of primary contrary differences which determines intermediate differences (if any), contrary species, and intermediate species (if any).

I.7 as such does not provide evidence to tell whether the point is that, at each step in the division of a genus into its species, there is a pair of prior contrary differences, or whether a grander plan is alluded to in which some basic pair of contraries determines the whole structure of being (or, at least, of relatively large parts of it) into genera and species. Depending on the stand we take on this issue, we can take *panta* ('all things') at b31 and *prōtōn* ('primary' or 'first') at b32 as more or less metaphysically loaded. If we go for the more metaphysically loaded interpretation, then Aristotle is alluding to some pair of primary contraries which would be principles of all things that are (for the philosophical background of this idea see Introduction, section II.2). If we go for the more deflationary interpretation, then Aristotle would be saying that, for each division of a genus into contrary and intermediate species, the contrary differences affecting the genus are what determines intermediate differences, contrary and intermediate species with respect to that particular division.

The clause at b29–30 is very difficult. Perhaps it picks up option (d) at 1057b4, and is meant to emphasize that, in the case of contrary differences, there is no prior genus and there are no prior contraries dividing a genus out of which contrary differences themselves are made. In particular it is difficult to understand what 'of the same kind' (*homogenē*) means in this context.

The adjective *homogenes* does not necessarily mean 'belonging to one and the same genus' in the technical sense (which, as it appears, would not be appropriate to contrary differences) but, more generally, 'of the same kind or general character' (LSJ *s.v.*: Cf. *GA* I.1, 715a23; *Cat.* 6, 5b18–29: 'a mountain can be said to be small, and a millet can be said to be big, in virtue of the fact that the one is bigger than things of the same kind, and the other is smaller than things of the same kind'). For some discussion of the homogeneity of contraries see Introduction, section II.1.

1057b32–34: The closing lines sum up the three results of the chapter in the order in which they have been argued for (i.e. (4), (5), and (3)). The logical dependence of (3) on (4) and (5) is not emphasized, although the order of the list seems to allude to it.

There are some general problems concerning the argumentative strategy and the results of the chapter. As for the argumentative strategy, it is not clear in what sense (3) can be argued for on the basis of (4) and (5). Is Aristotle suggesting that (3) is a necessary condition for (4) and (5)? In other words, does I.7 work backwards in arguing that (3) should be regarded as the (only?) way to explain why (4) and (5) are the case? If so, the underlying train of thought of the chapter would be: we have reasons to say that, if x is an intermediate between C1 and C2, x is in the same genus as C1 and C2 and C1 and C2 are contraries. This must be due to the way in which the intermediates are ontologically constituted—and (3) spells out one basic ontological fact about the intermediates.

However, Aristotle does not prove (3) for all intermediates. In the course of the chapter, Aristotle considers two cases of ontological constitution: the constitution of intermediate differences out of contrary differences and the constitution of species out of genus and differences. I.7 does not establish that all intermediates are out of the contraries of the same kind (species out of species and differences out of differences). Rather, it shows that those intermediates which are in the same genus as species are not constituted out of the contraries that are in the same genus, i.e. contrary species, whereas the intermediates which are not in the genus but are linked to the genus by differentiating it are out of the corresponding contraries.

Accordingly, one might try to find a reading of (3) compatible with the differences between intermediate species and intermediate differences. One way to do this would be by taking (3) as a claim primarily about differences (possibly in analogy with properties assumed by changing subjects) and only derivatively about species (possibly in analogy with subjects determined by certain contrary properties). (3) would be true of intermediate species by being true of their differences. If so, the reference to the genus in (4) should be taken rather loosely, not in the sense that intermediates are species of one and the same genus but in the sense that they are the same kind of property as the opposites between which they are—either by being the same kind of thing (e.g. colours) or by being formally comparable features of the same kind of things (e.g. of colours or of the genus colour).

CHAPTER 8

I.8 spells out what it is for something to be other in species (*heteron tōi eidei*) than something else. In doing this, I.8 attempts an account of the ontological interaction of genus and differences in the constitution of species and of the role of contrariety in the division of the genus (for some introductory notes about the conceptual framework of genera, species, and differences, see introduction to I.7, pp. 170–7).

Some of the difficulties in I.8 may be at least partly concealed by the translation, but they should be taken into account in approaching the text and the commentary. Two problems in particular, while clearly emerging in connection with specific textual points, bear more general relevance to our overall understanding of the chapter. First, I translate *tōi eidei* systematically as 'in species'. 'Species' is the standard translation of *eidos* in contexts where the articulation through genera and differences is at stake. But *eidos* can also be translated as 'form'. 'Form', in its turn, and depending on the context, can indicate a rather general qualitative characteristic, a more or less observable feature of things (cf., for instance, *Met.* Δ.6, 1016a17–24), or can be used in a more philosophically loaded way. In particular, *eidos* is usually translated as 'form' when it occurs in opposition to *hulē*, 'matter' (this is relevant, for instance, at 1058a21–28). There are advantages in translating *eidos* consistently throughout the chapter, but I shall note in the commentary instances in which the connection with 'form' may be significant.

Secondly, and connected with the way in which we understand *eidos*, there is an issue as to the range of things Aristotle has in mind as things that can be said to be other in *eidos*. 'Other in species', as its opposite 'same in species', usually ranges over individuals: this horse and this man are other in species; Socrates and Plato are the same in species (see, p. 203). However, pretty much everything Aristotle says in I.8 seems to apply to species as well as to individuals and it is not that obvious that he would not be willing to apply the predicate 'other in *eidos*' to species as well, at least in this context. If this is correct, however, it would be better not to translate *eidos* with 'species', as long as saying that two species are other in species than each other may sound as a category mistake. But, e.g., it does not seem wrong to say that species are different 'in form': it is precisely in virtue of the differences and of the contraries which enter the determination of the form corresponding to each species that species differ from each other (see, by way of contrast, I.9 on the contraries which determine a difference in individual matter only and, therefore, fail to yield a division of a genus into species). In fact, explaining how it is that species differ 'in *eidos*' from each other looks like a more basic task than explaining what it is for things to be other in species: for the property of being other in species applies to things in virtue of the way in which their species are determined by some genus and specific differences. Perhaps the more basic explanation is what we find in I.8. Note that the question whether I.8 is primarily about particulars or about universals (species) cannot be answered on the basis of linguistic formulation. See notes on pp. 202–8 for further details on this point.

Aristotle seems to treat the locutions 'other in species' and 'different in species' as equivalent, although he may regard 'different in species' as more technical than 'other in species', given his account of the distinction between difference and otherness in I.3, 1054b23–27.

1057b35–36: The very first claim of the chapter reads (with the addition of indices):

(o) What is other in species is something$_1$ other than something$_2$.

What corresponds to 'something$_1$' in the Greek text is the indefinite pronoun *ti*, which, in this context, can be taken in two ways. (i) We can take *ti* as an accusative of respect. This would yield a different translation: 'What is other in species is other than something with respect to something'. This translation would be perfectly plausible and we could paraphrase it as: 'If we say of x that it is other in species, then x is other in species than something y (=something$_2$) with respect to something z (=something$_1$)'. This reading can be supported by the use of the accusative of respect at 1058a12. (ii) Alternatively, we can take *ti* as part of the predicate saying what the subject (i.e. 'what is other in species') is. This is the way in which I take it, in analogy with the constructions at 1057b36 and at 1058a4. At 1057b36 I take the predicate *zōion heteron tōi eidei* ('animal other in species') to be obtained from the preceding line by substituting *ti* with *zōion* ('animal'); in this case, *ti* cannot be taken as an accusative of respect. (I do not think that the addition of *tōi eidei*, 'in species', here makes any difference, since at b35 *ti heteron* ('something other') can be taken as an elliptic expression for *ti heteron tōi eidei* ('something other in species') which can be easily supplied on the basis of the very beginning of the sentence.) Similarly, at 1058a4 *touto to koinon heteron... tōi eidei* ('this common thing, other in species [. . .]') displays the same construction. On this reading, we could paraphrase the first sentence of the chapter as: 'What is other in species is a different kind of something than something else'. 'Something$_1$' in (o) would have the function of a placeholder (in the paraphrase, 'a different kind of *something*') for the name of the relevant genus. For instance, if a horse is other in species, it is one other animal than (i.e. a different kind of animal than), say, a man.

It is important to stress that (ii) immediately introduces the idea that, if x is other in species than y, there is something z which both x and y are, and that x and y are z's of different kinds. This common thing z would be what 'this' (*touto*) at b35 refers to by picking up the first 'something' (*ti*) in the translation ('something$_1$' in (o)). Option (i) may, but need not, be taken in this sense. The respect in which x is other in species than y need not be something that x and y have in common. If x differs from y

with respect to z, z may pick out something that x and y have in
common (x and y differ with respect to the way in which they are z),
but it may also pick out that by which they differ (x and y differ
with respect to their species). We saw in I.3, 1054b25–31, that
Aristotle does not fully resolve the ambiguity between the aspect
in which x is different from y (and y is different from x), which can
either be the species or the genus, and what x and y have in
common. The same ambiguity affects (i). Note, in any case, that
the respect in which x and y are different from each other in I.3 is
expressed with the dative and not with the accusative. As we will
see, in the rest of the chapter Aristotle does not focus on the
respect in which x is other than y (i.e. in species), but, rather, on
what x, being other in species than y, has in common with y.

The claim that:

(1) 'this must belong to both of them'

is illustrated by the immediately following example. In particular,
the text suggests that the following two claims are two ways to
express the same thing:

(1a) A belongs (*huparchei*) to both x and y.

(1b) x is A and y is A.

(1a) and (1b) are two ways Aristotle uses to express predication.
They are not always interchangeable, as emphasized in *Top.* II.1,
109a10–26, where Aristotle comments on the fact that if the
predicate expresses an incidental feature of the subject, it is not
always possible to move from (1a) to (1b). For instance, we can
say that colour belongs to Socrates, but we cannot say that
Socrates is colour. In the case of the genus, however, it is always
possible to move from (1a) to (1b) and vice versa.

Aristotle's reliance on this feature of the predication of the
genus points to the specific way in which the genus is common
to things that are other in species: the genus is not simply a
common incidental feature of both of them, but it is (part of)
what each of them is.

1057b37–1058a6: The conclusion at 1057b37 ('therefore', *ara*),
that things that are other in species are in the same genus, is
supported by what precedes in conjunction with the account of

the genus at 1057b37–1058a2. This account can be analysed into three components. If x is other in species than y, then the genus of x and y is **(2)** the one and the same thing that both x and y are said to be, **(3)** which has a difference not incidentally, **(4)** be it as matter or in another way. (2) links to (1a) and (1b). In particular (1a) and (1b) are regarded as equivalent to 'x and y are said to be one and the same thing, e.g. animal'. I shall leave aside claim (4) for now (see notes on 1058a21–28) and focus on (3). (2) and, most of all, (3) are spelled out at 1058a2–6, as 'for' (*gar* at a2) points out. It is not only the case that the genus must belong to both items which are other in species, but the genus must belong to each of them in a different form. In this context one of the difficulties mentioned at the beginning of the notes to I.8 becomes apparent. For that the genus belongs to both items which are other in *eidos* and belongs to each of them in a different way is true independently of whether we take the two items at issue to be species or to be individuals that fall under different species. Any interpretative choice on this point is underdetermined by textual evidence.

Starting with 1058a2–6, we can see in what way the text is ambiguous in the following way. Greek lacks indeterminate articles. This is a syntactical feature of the language, which is not a problem in itself. The problem arises when Greek sentences presenting predicates without articles ('animal of this sort', 'horse', 'human being') are translated into English, which, unlike Greek, cannot avoid the use of indeterminate articles in sentences such as the one in question. Accordingly, we have: 'So they will be in their own right the one *an* animal of this sort, the other *an* animal of this other sort—for example, the one will be *a* horse, the other will be *a* human being'. The translation with the articles strongly suggests that the objects we are talking about (the objects that differ in species and have the same genus) are individuals: this human being is other in species than this horse; Socrates is other in species than Bucephalus. The problem is that the Greek sentence may, but need not, be about individuals. In fact, it could be about the species of the genus—and the species of horses is *not a* horse. (Note that this is the case independently of the precise way in which we think of a species: we can think of it as a universal property shared by all horses or as the collection of all horses, but neither of these is a horse or an animal.) If Aristotle is talking about species, a translation without the indeterminate articles would be better, provided that the general terms 'animal', 'horse', and 'human being' are understood as names of genus and species respectively: 'So they will be in their own right the one animal of this sort, the other animal of this other sort—for example, the one will be horse, the other will be human being'.

Not only does the text leave room for both options, but independent evidence can be gathered in support of both. In support of the individuals-reading, one could say that the opposite predicate of 'other (or different) in species', namely 'the same in species', is usually applied to individuals and not to species as such: Socrates and Callias are the same in species. In support of this view see, for instance, *Top.* I.7, 103a10–13: '<The same> in *eidos* (*eidei*) are those things that, being many, do not differ with respect to the *eidos* (*pleiō onta adiaphora kata to eidos esti*), just as a man <is the same in *eidos*> as a man and a horse as a horse; for such things are said to be the same *tōi eidei* which are under the same *eidos*' (cf. *Met.* Z.8, 1034a5–8). Starting from this account of sameness in species, one may wonder whether analogous considerations apply to the case of otherness or difference in species (on this point see also notes on 1058a17–21). For this account seems to imply that 'the same in *eidos*' can only be predicated of a plurality of things, and these can only be a plurality of individuals belonging to the species. If 'the same in *eidos*' and 'other in *eidos*' range over the same objects, then it looks like these objects must be individuals.

This argument may look strong, but there is enough textual evidence to disarm the basic assumptions on which it is built. First of all, the plurality of subjects which can be said to be the same in *eidos* does not seem to be such a strong requirement as *Top.* I.7 may suggest. In *Met.* Δ.6, 1016b31–36 Aristotle claims that also what is one in number (the single individual) can be said to be one in *eidos*. If one takes 'one in *eidos*' as equivalent to 'the same in *eidos*' (which seems plausible), this seems to drop the requirement of plurality for predicating sameness in *eidos*. In addition, if sameness in *eidos* amounts to having the same definition (cf. *Met.* Δ.6, 1016b33; see also notes on I.1, 1052a29–b1), certainly a species is the same in *eidos* as itself. Furthermore, since I.7 Aristotle has been mainly concerned with the mutual relations between genus, differences, and species. It is, of course, possible that I.8 picks up a different aspect and turns to the way in which the ontology of genus, differences, and species applies to individuals (cf. I.9), but it is also possible that I.8 carries on the discussion of genera, species, and contrariety which was the main topic in the previous chapter.

These considerations should induce us to at least take into account the possibility that *eidos* here does not simply indicate the species, but also the formal qualitative features fixing the identity of one species and distinguishing one species from another species in the same genus. Consider the two sentences:

(i) (The species) horse and (the species) human being are different in species (*eidos*).

(ii) (The species) horse and (the species) human being are different in form (*eidos*).

Even if one may feel inclined to regard (i) as possibly ill-formed on the basis of some category mistake, (ii) should give us a moment's pause. Certainly (ii) is not straightforwardly ill-formed (on this point see also notes on 1058a21–28).

Furthermore, in *Met.* Δ.10, 1018a38–b8 Aristotle provides a fairly liberal list of things which can be said to be other in species: '(a) Those things are said to be other in species which, being of the same genus (*tautou genous onta*), are not under each other, and (b) those which, being in the same genus (*en tōi autōi genei onta*), have a difference, and (c) those which have a contrariety in their substance; and (d) the contraries are other in species than each other—either all or those which are said to be contraries primarily—and (e) those things in the last species of the genus (*en tōi teleutaiōi tou genous eidei*) <are other in species> whose accounts are other (e.g. man and horse are atomic things in the genus (*tōi genei*) and their accounts are other), and (f) those things which, being in the same substance (*en tēi autēi ousiai onta*), have a difference. The same in species are things which are said in the opposite ways to these.' Of these accounts, (a) seems to apply to species rather than to individuals since individuals belonging to the same species belong to the same genus and are not under each other (neither of them is the result of a subdivision of the other), but are not, by definition, other in species. (b), (c), (e), and (f) equally apply to different species of the same genus and to individuals falling under them. I take (e) to be about species which are on the last level of division of a genus and/or to the individuals falling under two such species. (f) is very difficult. I suggest that 'in the same substance' simply means 'in the same genus'; this reading can be supported with reference to some of Aristotle's views on the relation between genus and difference according to which the genus, rather than the differences, expresses what the things falling under it are (their essence or substance), whereas the difference rather adds a further qualitative feature (see introductory notes to I.7, pp. 174–5). Things 'in the same substance' could be individuals belonging to the same species and differing in other respects, too. In this case the relevant differences would be incidental properties of the individuals. This reading cannot be excluded, but it would require a rather unusual understanding of difference. As for (d), the contraries which 'are said to be contraries primarily' are presumably general properties (see Introduction, pp. xxxi–xxxv; I.4, pp. 128–9; see I.7, pp. 191–2 about whether differences or species of a genus have a stronger claim to being primary contraries). This seems to confirm the general impression that Aristotle does not distinguish sharply between the application of the predicates 'other in *eidos*' and 'the same in *eidos*' to universals and their application to individuals.

In light of these considerations, it may not be particularly surprising that I.8 does not draw any sharp distinction as to the kinds of object over which 'other in species' ranges (cf. notes to 1058a17–21). Keeping this point in mind, we can now try to make sense of the three aspects mentioned in the account of the genus at 1058a37–b2.

I shall start with (2). If x is other in species than y, then the genus of both x and y is what both x and y are. This should be understood in conjunction with the complementary claim that the same genus is different for each of the species. The upshot of the latter claim seems to be that any animal is an animal by being a specific kind of animal. Human beings are animals by being human beings, horses are animals by being horses and the way in which humans are animals is different from the way in which horses are animals. Nonetheless, the differentiation of the genus into its species does not imply that the genus is an ambiguous predicate. In particular, Aristotle thinks that, if S_1 and S_2 are different species of a genus G, both the name and the (same) account of G will be predicated of S_1 and S_2. For instance, let us assume that the account of the genus animal is 'living being endowed with sense perception'. Both the name 'animal' and the account will be predicated of all the species of the genus. Both human beings and horses are living beings endowed with sense perception. In this sense the genus is a univocal predicate. This general property can only be grasped by making abstraction of the more specific features that any animal has, and it is not possible for any animal to have this property without having it in a more specific form.

We can now turn to (3), i.e. the claim that the genus has a difference 'not incidentally'. The claims at a5–6 are about what falls under the genus G and the property of being a G of such and such a kind. This further property belongs to each G 'in its own right'. For example, if x is an animal, x is an animal of such and such a kind not incidentally. In the phrase 'animal of such and such a kind', 'animal' indicates the genus, whereas 'of such and such a kind' is a generic way to indicate the relevant specific difference. On the distinction between differences that belong to a genus in its own right and differences that belong to the genus incidentally, see notes to I.9. Note that in these lines Aristotle speaks of the difference as a contrariety, whereas in I.7 he speaks of contrary differences (in the plural). I take it that when he uses the plural he refers distributively to the two or more properties (the specific differences) which attach to the genus, whereas when he uses the singular he refers collectively to the set of specific differences which determine one division of the genus (cf. notes on I.7, pp. 174–5). For instance, rational and irrational are differences of the genus animal; the opposition rational–irrational is a difference of the genus animal.

Aristotle seems to believe that if human being is biped animal in its own right and horse is quadruped animal in its own right, then the two differences biped and quadruped (or the difference given by the set of biped and quadruped) belong to the genus animal in its own right. In fact, at 1058a5–6 he seems to resort to claims about the species such as (iii) and (iv) below as providing support for a claim such as (3a) (a particular instance of (3)) about the genus:

(iii)   Human being is biped animal in its own right.

(iv)   Horse is quadruped animal in its own right.

(3a) Animal has the difference {biped, quadruped} not incidentally.

Since the conjunction of (iii) and (iv) (henceforth: (iii) & (iv)) spells out the content of (2), we can investigate the relation between (iii) & (iv) and (3a) in order to spell out the relation between (2) and (3). One could take (3a) as a necessary condition for (iii) & (iv). If so, then (iii) & (iv) is not equivalent to (3a). Alternatively, we could take (3a) as both necessary and sufficient for (iii) & (iv). If so, one might wonder whether (iii) & (iv) is simply an alternative way (possibly: an easier way) to express (3a), or whether Aristotle takes (iii) & (iv) on the one hand and (3a) on the other hand as expressing different facts, one of which is more basic than the other. This difficulty and a series of closely related issues will be better explored in I.9 and further details can be found in the notes to that chapter. One point is worth anticipating here, though. Let us consider the following pair of claims:

(v)   the species is the result of the composition of genus and differences;

(vi) genus and differences are the result of the analysis of the species.

Of course, the nature of both composition and analysis should be specified, and, of course, one could take (v) and (vi) as equivalent. But (v) and (vi) could be taken to express opposite claims, i.e. that the genus and differences are basic, or that the species is. These claims could be understood as ontological or epistemic. If we take them both as ontological claims, they are incompatible. They would not necessarily be incompatible if one took both as epistemic or if one took one of them as ontological and the other as epistemic. Taking them both as epistemic claims, one could resort to Aristotle's distinction between what is better known to us and what is better known by nature and in its own right (e.g. *Phys.* I.1, 184a16–23) and apply the distinction to dissolve the apparent incompatibility between (v) and (vi). One could argue that either (v) or (vi) must be understood in the sense that species (or genera and differences) are better known to us, whereas genera and differences (or species) are better known in themselves. Alternatively, one could take (vi) as an ontological claim and (v) as an epistemic claim, or vice versa. I shall return to these remarks in

I.9, where I will suggest that Aristotle's analysis there may mark a shift from a rather Platonic commitment to (v) as an ontological claim to (vi) as an ontological claim.

1058a6–8: Aristotle establishes, on the basis of 1057b37–1058a6 and 1058a7–8, that the difference of the genus is the 'otherness of the genus' he has been talking about so far. In particular, at 1058a7–8 Aristotle introduces a terminological point concerning what we should call 'the difference of the genus'. The difference of the genus is what makes the genus 'other', i.e. what differentiates the genus into things that are other in species. I take the point of the passage to be that it is in this sense that the difference of the genus is also said to be an 'otherness' of the genus. On Aristotle's use of technical terminology in these chapters see remarks on p. 171.

1058a8–16: In these lines Aristotle argues for the further claim that **(5)** 'this' difference, i.e. the difference of the genus, is contrariety. At 1058a8 the Greek for 'contrariety' is *enantiōsis*. In the course of the chapter Aristotle uses both *enantiōsis* (here and at 1058a16, 18, 19, 20, 26) and *enantiotēs* (1058a11, which I also translate as 'contrariety'). The two words seem to be used interchangeably (cf. also 1054b32), but see notes on 1055b14–15.

(5) is stated at the beginning of the passage (a8–9) and restated at the end of it (a16) in the form of a conclusion (a16: *ara*, 'therefore') following from the lines in between. The argument in support of this conclusion starts immediately (cf. *gar*, 'for', at a10) and I take it to include a9–13, while I take the parenthetical remark at a13–16 as the explanation of an additional point which is not crucial for the main argument.

Before looking at the argument in support of (5), note that (5) can be read in different ways, and namely either as an identity claim:

(5a) the differences of a genus are the same as contrarieties,

or as a predicative statement:

(5b) all differences of a genus are contrarieties.

(5b), unlike (5a), leaves open the possibility that there be contrarieties which are not differences of a genus (cf. I.7, p. 193).

At a9 Ross puts the remark 'and this is clear also from induction' into brackets. I take it that this move rests on the following reading: what Aristotle is saying is that we could show (5) by way of induction, i.e. by showing that the differences of any genus we consider are contraries, but this is not the argument that he is going to provide. 'For' (*gar*) at a11 would then refer back to the initial statement of (5). However, an alternative reading is possible. On the alternative reading, we could take the remark as part of a more complex argument that Aristotle provides in support of (5) and, in particular, we could take induction as what shows us that all genera are divided by the opposites (a9–10). In this case *gar* at a11 would refer back to the claim 'and this is clear also from induction' by spelling out what it is that induction makes clear, i.e. that all genera are divided by the opposites. The translation I provide follows this reading, without brackets.

We can now take a closer look at how the argument at a9–13 unfolds. The text is quite compressed and, as in the previous section, there is a series of clauses introduced by *gar* ('for') introducing different parts of the explanation in support of the main claim (5). I shall start with a list of claims in the order in which they appear in the text and then propose a reconstruction of the arguments supplying missing premises and implicit steps.

(5) The difference of the genus is contrariety.

For:

(6) All <genera> are divided by the opposites.

(7) Contraries are in the same genus.

For:

(8) Contrariety is complete difference.

(9) Difference in species is from something with respect to something.

(10) That with respect to which two things differ in species is the same and is the genus of both (e.g. horse and human being differ from each other with respect to the way in which each of them is animal).

I take (8)–(10) to explain (7), while (6) and (7), in conjunction with the account of the difference of the genus as otherness at a7–8, lead to (5). I shall deal with the main argument, whose conclusion is (5), first and then move on to the argument presented in (8)–(10) in support of (7).

As for (6), in the translation I supply the substantive 'genus' where the Greek simply has a neuter plural: I therefore translate 'for all <genera>' instead of the more literal 'for all things'. It seems that in any case some restriction must be introduced on the unqualified 'all things'. I propose to restrict the claim to those things which can be divided in the relevant sense, i.e. genera (note that *genos* in Greek is neuter too). If this is correct, (6) says that, for any genus G, if a pair of opposites applies to G in some way to be specified, then G is divided by them. In order to make full sense of this claim, one has to spell out the relevant way in which the opposites 'apply' to a genus and yield a division of the genus. This will be useful also to understand (7) and the claim that the opposites or the contraries can be *in* something—and, in particular, *in* a genus. I.9 will add substantive materials to the discussion of this issue.

As we have already seen in I.7, Aristotle suggests that the genus can be thought of as a substrate determined by the differences. I.7 may suggest an analogy between the genus, which can assume the various differences, and the substrate of change. This, in turn, may lead to an understanding of the relation between opposites and genus as analogous to the relation between opposite properties and their subject. However, if one tries to explore this suggestion, one pretty soon finds out that the analogy (*if* an analogy is there) cannot be pushed very far. For, unlike the substrate of change, the genus does not change from one difference to another, but is simultaneously determined by all of them. Furthermore, a substratum persists through change. Is there any sense in which the genus 'resists' its differentiation without being completely swallowed up by its differences? (See introduction to I.7, pp. 172–7, 189).

One could try to make sense of the relevant way in which the opposites apply to a genus (or are in it) and of the way in which they divide the genus in extensional terms. According to this view, the genus animal would simply be the set of individual animals. The opposites in question would be opposite properties ranging over the set of animals such that no animal can have both properties and each animal must have either of those properties. The opposite properties would then issue a partition of the set of animals into two subsets. Although this account has the advantage of being relatively clear, it has the disadvantage of implying that any pair of opposite properties ranging over the genus and complying with the criterion just given would count as a pair of specific differences. The problem with this perspective is that, as I.9 will make clear, Aristotle does not think that this is the case. It is certainly true that Aristotle takes extensional aspects of the relation between genus, differences, and species into account (see, e.g., *Top.* IV.2, 122b36–123a19; 6, 128a22–23), but a merely extensional approach does not exhaust Aristotle's views on the matter.

The difficulties we have just considered impact on the interpretation of (7). (7) is needed to draw the implicit intermediate conclusion that the genus is divided by the contraries. Aristotle has said before that the difference of the genus is 'the otherness which makes one and the same genus other' (1058a6–8). It seems reasonable to assume that 'making one and the same genus other' amounts to the same as 'dividing the genus'; and that 'contrariety' is the abstract noun which refers collectively to a pair of contraries. So, if the difference of the genus is what divides the genus, and contrariety is what divides the genus, we can say that the difference of the genus is contrariety, which was the conclusion we wanted to reach, i.e. (5).

Let us now try to see how (7) follows from (8)–(10). Let me anticipate that, while it is possible to reconstruct an argument from (8)–(10) to (7), the argument conveys an interpretation of (7) that is at odds with other Aristotelian tenets about the contraries. I shall start by formulating the argument.

(8) is the definition of contrariety provided in I.4: contrariety is complete difference. As we have seen in I.7, Aristotle considers the possibility of intermediate differences dividing the genus. Intermediate differences along with contrary differences yield all the species (respectively, intermediate and contrary species) of the genus. So, it is possible for something x to differ in species from something else y in various degrees, depending on how close the species of x and the species of y are in the spectrum of the species of a genus (let's assume, for the sake of the argument, that this picture makes sense). On the basis of these considerations and of (9) we can infer that:

> **(9*)** Complete difference in species is from something with respect to something.

Furthermore,

(10*)   The second 'something' in (9*) refers to the genus in both things that differ in species.

The rest of the argument can be spelled out in the following way:

(11)   If x is completely different in species from y, then there is something which both x and y are and this is the genus of both x and y. {from (9*) and (10*)}

(12)   Something is the genus of both x and y iff x and y are in the same genus. {by definition}

(13)   If x is completely different in species from y, then x and y are in the same genus. {from (11) and (12)}

(14)   If x and y are contraries, then x and y are in the same genus. {from (13), by definition of contrariety}

If (14) is what (7) really means, then (7) would commit Aristotle to the view that all contraries belong to the same genus. As I argue in the Introduction, section II.1 and as we have seen in I.7, there are some basic difficulties in understanding Aristotle's insistence on linking the contraries to one genus. If the link is understood in the sense that all contraries are species of a genus, this is incompatible with Aristotle's claims about the existence of contrary genera (if such claims have to be understood in the sense that there is no higher genus which is the genus of both contraries), and it is not obvious how contrary differences should be accounted for. Taken in isolation, (7) could also mean that contraries are the only kind of opposites which can be in the genus. If this is the appropriate interpretation of (7), however, a different reconstruction of the whole argument is called for since the claim that contraries are the only kind of opposites which can be in a genus does not seem to follow from (8)–(10).

The parenthesis at 1058a13–16 provides a fuller account of Aristotle's remark in I.3, 1054b35–1055a2. In I.3 Aristotle said that all contraries are different, i.e. other in some respect. There Aristotle commented that some are other in genus, whereas 'some are in the same series of predication, so that they are in the same genus, i.e. the same in genus'. Here in I.8 the description of contraries that are in the same series of predication is applied to contraries that differ in species and not in genus. In particular, a13–16 rely on the twofold characterization of contraries that differ in species as at the same time (15) having something in common (i.e. the genus) and (16) being completely different. On the one hand, (15) contraries that differ in species are in the same series of predication (i.e. they fall under a common genus); on the other hand, (16) being contrary, (16a) they differ in the highest degree and (16b) they do not come to be at the same time.

I take (16b) to mean that contraries do not come to be at the same time in the same subject in the same respect (cf. *Cat.* 6, 5b39–6a4; 11, 14a10–14). The only other way to understand this claim would be by taking it as an ontological claim about contrary species coming to be out of the genus and the differences. But in this case the passage would be in plain contrast with Aristotle's explicit remarks in *Cat.* 13, 14b33–15a4, where he says that things 'that are out of the same genus according to the same division are together (*hama*) by nature'.

1058a17–21: The account of what is it to be the same in species here may suggest that the chapter is about individuals; but see pp. 202–5.

A full account of what it is to be other in species is given. The construction with the substantival infinitive of the verb *einai* ('to be') and the dative of the thing whose being is at issue ('being for what is other in species') is one of Aristotle's usual constructions to indicate the essence of the object picked up by the expression in the dative. The use of this construction, however, need not imply that there is an essence corresponding to being other in species, given that being other in species is a cross-categorial feature (i.e. pairs of items in any category can be said to other in species). Aristotle's interest in providing a full-fledged account of otherness in species, i.e. an account that sums up the basic results of the philosophical investigation into this notion, may go back to the project of enquiry outlined in *Met.* B.1 and Γ.2 (see Introduction, pp. xii–xix), where Aristotle prompts the enquiry into what the one, the same, the other, the contrary, etc. are, and into what their attributes are. The structure of I.8 complies with the programmatic indications of B.1 and Γ.2. First, Aristotle reaches a fully articulated account of what it is to be other in species; secondly and on the basis of that account, he explains some of the features of things that are other in species such as the restrictions on the kinds of pairs of items that can be said to be other in species (1058a21–28).

With respect to what has already been said, i.e. that things that are other in species belong to the same genus and have/display contrariety, this final account adds the specification that **(17)** things that are other in species are 'indivisible' (*atoma*). In different contexts this expression is used by Aristotle to indicate the lowest species, which are not further divisible into lower species (e.g. *Met.* Z.8, 1034a8), or the particulars that are members of a lowest species (e.g. *Cat.* 2, 1b6–9).

In the parenthesis at a18–19 Aristotle makes the point that those things are the same in species which 'do not have a contrariety' and are indivisible. This characterization of things that are the same in species, while perhaps intuitive for items belonging to categories such as quality, is less clear with respect to other categories. For instance, Aristotle stresses that nothing is contrary to substances—and, a fortiori, no substance is contrary to any other substance (*Cat.* 5, 3b24–27). So, Socrates and Bucephalus, while being other in species, do not have or display any obvious contrariety. Similarly for one litre and one centimetre: they are quantities that differ in species, but it is not clear in what sense they may display a contrariety. And surely Aristotle does not want to say that Socrates and Bucephalus or this litre and this centimetre are the same in species. However, in I.9, 1058a35–36, winged and footed are introduced as contraries that divide the genus animal (which is a genus of substances) and in *Cat.* 8, 10b12–15 Aristotle makes room for the possibility that the winged thing and the footed thing be regarded as contrary (if winged and footed are contraries), even if in a derivative way. Furthermore, in his attempt to improve on the method of division for classificatory purposes, Aristotle will emphasize that each natural substance can be described by a cluster of properties of its parts. Even if the clusters as such are not contrary to each other, each of the properties (i.e. differences) constituting one cluster may be contrary to (or intermediate between contrary differences homogeneous with) a corresponding property in the other cluster. The picture of the dihairetic role of contrariety conveyed in I.7–9 might therefore be somewhat simplified without being fundamentally misleading.

1058a19–20 is meant to explain something of what precedes (cf. *gar*, 'for', at 19), but it is not completely clear what it is supposed to explain. One possibility is that it explains how contrariety comes about in atomic things, be they individuals or lowest species. If the atomic things Aristotle is talking about are individuals, a19–20 could voice the worry that it does not make sense to say of individuals that they are contrary as long as contrariety seems to be a relation of opposition between properties. The point would be that individuals can be said to belong to different species only in virtue of the way in which the species under which they fall are obtained through division. In particular, whether individuals are characterized by contrary features or appear to be contrary to each other is a derivative fact, depending on some features of the division through which the species under which they fall have been obtained. The point would be similar if the atomic things are the lowest species: lowest species can be said to have a contrariety as long as they are the result of a division through contrary differences (cf. I.7, pp. 190–2).

Alternatively, a19–20 could be taken as a comment (by Aristotle) on the claim that things that are other or the same in species are atomic. The point would then be that the use of 'other in species' or 'the same in species' should be restricted to things which cannot be further divided. All things at each stage of a dihairetic process are obtained by means of contrary differences from a common genus. But (and this would be Aristotle's point) we do not refer to any results of a division through contrary differences at any level in a dihairetic tree as other in species or the same in species. This description should only be applied to atomic subjects.

1058a21–28: Based on the characterization of being other in species achieved in the previous part of the chapter, Aristotle draws some consequences concerning the pairs of subjects that can be said to be other in species.

The final remarks add further material for the discussion of whether the chapter is mainly concerned with lowest species or with particulars. At 1058a22 the subject of the whole sentence is *outhen tōn hōs genous eidōn*, literally: 'none of the *eidē* as of a genus'. (*eidē* is the plural of *eidos*—on the translation of this as 'species' in this chapter see below and pp. 198–9). This expression (also occurring in I.7, 1057b7: *eidē hōs genous*) seems to push the interpretation of the chapter towards taking species as the proper subject of the properties at issue. However, sticking to rigid terminology could be misleading here. In order to appreciate the difficulties involved in the use of the Greek terminology I shall refer to the grammatical subject of the sentence as 'none of the *eidē-as-of-a-genus*', which is obviously non-transparent, but has the advantage of making the difficulties evident. For the same reason I shall leave *eidos* untranslated.

The first pair of items which cannot be said to be the same or other in *eidos* are **(a)** *eidē-as-of-a-genus* and **(b)** the so-called genus (1058a21–25). The second pair of items which cannot be said to be the same or other in *eidos* are **(c)** *eidē-as-of-a-genus* and **(d)** things which are not in the same genus (1058a25–28). The reasons why neither (a)–(b) nor (c)–(d) can be regarded as cases of sameness or otherness in *eidos* are different.

As for (a)–(b), Aristotle refers to the nature of the genus as the reason why a genus cannot be said to be the same in *eidos* as or other in *eidos* than any of its species (or any of the particulars belonging to its species). The reason is that the genus is regarded as the matter of what it is a genus of (cf. p. 210). Note that at 1058a1–2 Aristotle is more cautious about the relation between genus and matter (see (4) on p. 202).

The reason why the genus is assimilated to matter is that the relation between a genus and what it is a genus of is regarded as analogous to the relation between matter and what it is matter of. The very fact (on which see pp. 198–9) that *eidos* is used to indicate both what the genus is a genus of and what matter is matter of might provide a reason to come up with the analogy in the first place. The basic idea is that matter is shown by way of negation, i.e. by removing form(s) (*eidos/eidē*) from it (cf. *Met.* Z.3, 1029a10 ff.) and the genus is the matter of that whose genus it is, i.e. presumably, its *eidē* (cf. 1058a22). Note, however, that if this is the way in which the relation between genus as matter and its species is construed, then the passage may rest on a different reading of the relation between genus and species than other places, where the genus is regarded as analogous to matter in that the differences (rather than the species) are regarded as analogous to form (see e.g. Z.12 and H.6, pp. 176 and 189). If, on the other hand, we think of the species as forms that the genus takes on or 'as forms of the genus' (which is a possible translation for *hōs genous eidē*, cf. 1058a22), then species should be identified with differences (as in Z.12). Be this as it may, the argument leading to the conclusion that the genus cannot be other in *eidos* than any of its *eidē* presupposes that the genus as such, like matter as such, has no *eidos* and that, if x and y are the same in *eidos* or other in *eidos*, then each of x and y must have an *eidos*.

The remark at 1058a24–25 is meant as a disambiguation of the sense in which Aristotle is talking of the *genos* ('genus'). In *Met.* Δ.28 Aristotle distinguishes three main senses of *genos*. In one sense, *genos* is said with reference to 'the continuous generation of things that have the same *eidos*', e.g. the *genos* of humans is the human stock or the human kind. In the second sense, *genos* is said with reference to the first mover or the initiator (the first progenitor) of a race or clan or family. This is the sense in which the Heraclides are a *genos* (i.e. the *genos* whose progenitor was Heracles). The third sense is that in which 'plane is the *genos* of plane figures and solid is the *genos* of solid figures; for each of the figures is a plane of this kind or a solid of this kind. And this is the substrate (*to hupokeimenon*) of the differences (*tais diaphorais*). Furthermore, <*genos* is said> in the sense of the first constituent of accounts, which is said in the what it is; for this is the *genos* of which differences are said to be qualities (*poiotētes*).' The characterizations of *genos* in the quotation are gathered at 1024b8 under one single label: *genos* can be said *hōs hulē*, 'as matter'. I am not sure why the contrast between the *genos* as in 'the *genos* of the Heraclides' and the relevant sense of *genos* is drawn by saying that the latter is 'in nature'. Perhaps there is an implicit contrast here between *nomos* ('law', but also 'convention') and *phusis* ('nature'): while the membership in a clan is (or may be) a matter of social convention, the division of genera into species (at least as far as natural kinds are concerned) is not a matter of convention, but is based on the nature of things. Quarantotto (2005, p. 184) takes this to mean that the function of the genus in its species is the same as the function of matter in natural beings. One could perhaps say that being something that is determined by differences is a matter of nature in the sense that it depends on the kind of thing that the *genos* is. Alternatively, *genos* in the relevant sense is understood as 'in nature' in that the role of the genus as a sort of matter that can be further determined by differences is displayed in certain natural processes. For example, in cases where the offspring does not belong to the species of its parents (e.g. when a horse and an ass generate a mule) the closest common genus of the parents is what is displayed in what is generated (*Met.* Z.8, 1033b33–1034a2). Cf. *GA* II.8, IV.3.

As for (c)–(d), the reason why, if x and y belong to different genera, they cannot be said to be the same in *eidos* is obvious: if x and y belong to different genera, a fortiori they belong to different species (i.e. they do not belong to the same *eidos*). The reason why they cannot be said to be other in *eidos* is expressed in a very puzzling way. On the face of it, Aristotle's argument seems to be that, if x and y are other in *eidos*, **(18)** they differ in *eidos* and **(19)** the kind of difference by which they differ is contrariety. But **(20)** contrariety belongs only to things that are in the same genus. Therefore, **(21)** if x and y are in different genera, then contrariety cannot belong to them. Therefore, **(22)** things belonging to different genera cannot differ in *eidos*.

(22) is equivalent to saying that only things belonging to the same genus can be said to differ in *eidos* strictly speaking. However, there is a looser sense of otherness in species in which otherness in species is implied a fortiori by otherness in genus. For some discussion of the issues involved in (22) see notes to I.10. As for the reasons why (20) might be problematic see p. 212.

CHAPTER 9

In I.8 Aristotle has given an account of what it is for things to be other in species (1057b35). According to the summary at 1058 a17–19, things that are other in species are in the same genus, are characterized by a contrariety, and each of them is indivisible or atomic (*atomon*). Contrariety is the relation of opposition obtaining between the differences by which the genus is divided in its own right (see 1057b37–1058a16); conversely, the differences of the genus are contrarieties belonging to the genus non-incidentally.

I.9 is devoted to the analysis of some problematic cases of pairs of contraries which, despite apparently meeting the formal requirements for being specific differences, fail to yield a differentiation of the genus into species. From the point of view of the overall structure of the book, I.9 stands to I.8 in a similar relation as I.5 and I.6 stand to I.4: it deals with problematic cases with respect to the general account given in I.8.

I.9's structure is clear: the chapter opens with the introduction of two difficulties (1058a29–36); a solution is proposed in two steps (1058a36–b3) and a series of examples is analysed accordingly (1058b3–15). Finally, an objection to the proposed solution is raised and solved (1058b15–21) before a general conclusion wraps up the discussion of I8–9 (1058b21–25).

1058a29–36: The opening lines present the difficulties setting the agenda for the whole chapter. We can distinguish three formulations characterized by an increasing degree of generality: **(a)** Why is it not the case that woman and man differ in species? (a29–31); **(b)** Why is it not the case that the female animal and the male animal differ in species? (a31–34); **(c)** Why is it the case that some contrarieties yield a difference in species, whereas some others do not? (a34–36). Aristotle regards (a) and (b) as two ways to formulate the same problem, whereas (c) is regarded as 'almost the same' difficulty as the one raised in (a) and (b) (1058a34).

At 1058a30–34 Aristotle spells out two main features of the pair male/female: **(1)** they are contraries; **(2)** the distinction (or difference) between male and female belongs to animal 'in its own right' or 'in so far as it is animal'. Furthermore, we know from the previous chapters that **(3)** contraries differentiate the genus. The general truth in (3) is that the basic differences dividing any genus are contraries; this does not imply, though, that all contraries behave as specific differences even with respect to the genus over which they range. I.9 addresses precisely some such cases.

With respect to (1), male and female figure in the list of basic contraries Aristotle ascribes to the Pythagoreans in *Met.* A.5, 986a22 ff. This might shed some light on Aristotle's motivation for singling out this pair of contraries for the discussion of a more general problem (see also *Met.* A.6, 988a2–7, where Aristotle discusses the similarities obtaining between male and female on the one hand and form and matter on the other; more generally on male and female as principles of generation see *GA* I.2). However in I.9 Aristotle does not seem to be interested in explaining in what sense male and female can or cannot be regarded as principles; rather, he uses this pair of contraries as an example to illustrate a more general point about the relation between a genus and pairs of contraries which, while belonging to it in its own right, do not differentiate it into species.

(2) makes clear why the cases under consideration are problematic. On the face of it, the pair male/female complies with the formal requirements specified in I.8 for contrarieties that divide the genus: animals can be distinguished into male and female precisely insofar as they are animals—or, conversely, male and female are a contrariety that belongs to the genus animal non-incidentally.

The point of the difficulty can be best understood by way of contrast. There are other features dividing the domain of animals into subgroups, but such features belong to animals insofar as they are something else. For instance, animals can be divided according to their colour, but colours belong to animals insofar as animals are objects with a surface. Colours are properties of surfaces in their own right and they are properties of animals by being properties of the surfaces of animals (in the same way in which they are properties of any other object with a surface). While objects that are not animals have colours, only animals can be said to be male or female (let's assume for the sake of the argument that this is true). This lends credence to the idea that there is some specific tie between something's being an animal and its being male or female—pretty much in the same way in which there seems to be some specific link between something's being an animal and its being winged or footed. Why is it the case, then, that, while apparently sharing significant features with the contraries which do differentiate the genus into species, the pair male/female behaves like the pair pale/dark with respect to differentiation into species? (For the translation of colour words see comments on p. 83.) A similar problem is raised in Plat., *Pol.* 262b–264b, which touches upon the difficult issue of what parts of the genus can be said to be its species.

In formulating the difficulty in I.9 Aristotle relies on three different partitions of properties with respect to their relation to a certain genus: **(D1)** the distinction between specific differences (contrary properties which differentiate the genus into different species) and contrary properties which apparently meet the formal requirements for being specific differences but fail to differentiate the genus into species; **(D2)** the distinction between contrary properties belonging to the genus in its own right and contrary properties belonging to the genus incidentally; **(D3)** the distinction between pairs of contraries that differentiate the genus and pairs that do not. (D3) is more general than (D1) in that contrary properties which apparently meet the formal requirements for being specific differences but fail to differentiate the genus into species (e.g. male and female with respect to animal) are a subset of the contrary properties which do not differentiate the genus (e.g. pale/dark do not differentiate the genus animal and do not comply with the general formal requirements for differences). Furthermore, (D2) is different from (D3) in that there are some properties belonging to a genus in its own right (i.e. in some sense: not incidentally; see below) without differentiating it (e.g. again, male and female with respect to animal).

The second difficulty (question (c) on p. 219), which is 'almost the same' as the first one, is built on (D3). In the course of the chapter Aristotle will spell out (D1) and in this way he will also provide a general account of (D3), but he will not say much more about (D2) as such. Rather, (D2) and, more generally, the distinction between properties belonging to a subject in its own right and properties belonging to a subject incidentally is taken for granted throughout the chapter. It might therefore be useful to spell it out at the start.

The minimal requirement for properties belonging to a genus G in its own right, as opposed to properties belonging to it incidentally, is the following:

(i)   A property P belongs to G in its own right iff (i.a) for any x that is P, G is the genus of x and (i.b) G is the smallest genus of x for which condition (i.a) holds.

Conversely, clause (i.a) says that P does not belong to G in its own right if there is some x that is P and G is not the genus of x. Clause (i.b) is meant to restrict the attention to the smallest genus of x for which (i.a) holds. (i.b) is important insofar as non-incidental properties are co-extensive with their subject and it is therefore important that the subject is picked out in the appropriate way. For instance, all animals are substances; therefore, there is nothing which is male or female and which is not a substance. If (i.a) was the only requirement for being a non-incidental property, then male and female could be taken as non-incidental properties of substance. However, not all substances are male or female (e.g. the unmoved movers have no sexual determination) and this suggests that it is not insofar as something x is a substance that x is male or female. This in turn suggests that there might be some more specific features that substances must have in order to be male or female. This more specific feature is captured by a more specific genus which is the smallest genus for which (i.a) applies. This is the genus animal and this is the subject of male and female in its own right.

The account just given can be extended to pairs of contrary properties:

(ii)   The pair of contrary properties C_1–C_2 belongs to G in its own right iff (ii.a) for any x that is C_1 or C_2, G is the genus of x and (ii.b) G is the smallest genus of x for which condition (ii.a) holds.

For the sake of brevity, I shall refer to the contrary properties satisfying (ii) as per se contrary properties. This general account of per se contrary properties covers both per se contraries which do not differentiate the genus and per se contraries which do differentiate the genus. Contrary properties which do differentiate the genus answer to a stronger condition (for the sake of simplicity I ignore the possibility that C_1–C_2 have intermediates):

(iii) C_1–C_2 are contrary properties which differentiate the genus G iff for any x that is C_1 or C_2, G is the genus of x, and, for any x whose genus is G, x is essentially C_1 or C_2.

Note that (ii) is compatible with the possibility that some x is G without being C_1 or C_2—and, in particular, it is compatible with the possibility that there is some time at which some x is a G and is neither C_1 nor C_2. This possibility is not compatible with (iii). This will be important with reference to the remarks at 1058b21–25, where it is suggested that properties belonging to the genus in its own right (henceforth: per se properties of the genus) which are not specific differences of it need not belong to each individual falling under the genus for the individual's whole ontological career.

The threefold partition of contraries with respect to the genus (D_1)–(D_3) can be expressed in terms of some distinctions Aristotle provides in *APo* I.4, where he analyses the different uses of the expression *kath' hauto* ('in its own right' or 'per se'). Two of those uses are pertinent to the discussion in I.9: something x belongs per se_1 to y iff x appears in the definition of y (cf. *Met.* Δ.18, 1022a25–29); something x belongs per se_2 to y iff y appears in the definition of x (cf. *Met.* Δ.18, 1022a29–32).

Specific differences are those contrarieties which are per se_2 of the genus and per se_1 of the species. (D1) is the distinction between specific differences and contrary properties which are per se_2 of the genus without being per se_1 of the species. (D2) is the distinction between contrary properties that are per se_2 of the genus and those properties which are neither per se_1 nor per se_2 of the genus. (D3) is the distinction between specific differences and all other properties. Although the distinction between per se_1 and per se_2 is useful in drawing the boundaries between the three groups of properties considered in I.9, it does not tell us much about the ontological underpinning for (D1)–(D3) and, in particular, it does not tell much about why the two kinds of contraries distinguished in (D1) behave differently with respect to the genus. I.9 can be read as an attempt at filling in these gaps.

1058a36–b3: Aristotle advances a reply to the puzzles introduced in the first part of the chapter. The reply is divided into two parts. The first part (a36–37) introduces the idea that properties can be more or less 'proper' or 'related' (see below) to their subject; the second (a37–b2) spells out the degrees of 'relatedness' or 'kinship' of properties to their subjects by distinguishing between properties belonging in the form and properties of the compound of form and matter. Although the relation between the two parts of the explanation is not spelled out in this section of the chapter, at b21–24 it becomes clear that some properties are 'proper affections' of their subject only in virtue of its body and matter. This seems to imply that, of 'proper affections', some belong to their subject in virtue of its form or by constituting its form, whereas others belong to their subject in virtue of its matter. The idea of degrees of relatedness or kinship is not taken over in the conclusion of the chapter and it is difficult to tell whether Aristotle wants to keep it and spell it out in terms of form and compound, or whether he rather intends to replace it by introducing a more precise distinction.

At a36–37 the Greek adjective *oikeion*, which I have translated with 'proper', has the same root as *oikia*, 'house' (understood not only in the sense of the building, but also in the sense of the household—the properties and people belonging to or living in the house). Accordingly, the first meaning of the adjective is that of 'belonging to the house' and by extension it comes to indicate what belongs to one's property and what is proper to a thing. Following this train of thought, this reply introduces the idea that different properties can pertain to the same subject genus according to different degrees of relatedness or kinship. About male and female as *oikeia pathē* of the genus animal cf. *Met.* M.3, 1078a6–9 and a16.

The first part of the answer does not specify any ground for the distinction of degrees of relatedness. Such a ground is introduced in the second part of the answer and is based on the distinction between *logos* and matter: contrarieties in the *logos* make a difference in species, whereas contrarieties characterizing the compound of *logos* and matter do not. *Logos*, which I have translated as 'account', here, as often in Aristotle, indicates the formula expressing the essence or substance of something and, therefore, its form. Cf. 1058b22, where *ousia*, 'substance', is used instead.

This solution is more problematic than it might appear at first. For it is not completely clear whether Aristotle is introducing a distinction between *logos* and matter with respect to the genus (in the example: animal), to the species or to the individual falling under the genus. In either of the last two cases, how exactly is a fact about the species or the individuals supposed to explain something about the relation between the genus and its differences (i.e. the fact that some contrarieties differentiate it, whereas others do not)?

Possible answers to this question link to more general intuitions about the ontology of genera and species, with respect to which two radically different approaches can be adopted. One could adopt a top-down approach, assuming that more general items and their features have priority and explain the features of less general items. According to this view, we should start with an understanding of the relation between the genus and its differences in order to account for the features of species and individuals falling under the genus as deriving, at least in part, from the features of the genus and its differences. This would amount to saying that the fact that the species human being (as any other species falling under the genus animal) is not further differentiated into female and male human being has to be explained by resorting to the relation obtaining between the genus animal and the properties male and female. Following this line of thought, one should make sense of the idea that we can distinguish between form and matter of the genus or between genus understood as form and genus understood as a compound. Aristotle's claim would then be that only the properties modifying the form of the genus count as specific differences. Some support for the idea that one might be able to distinguish the form of the genus from the genus as a compound can be found in Aristotle's distinction, at least at the level of species, between the essence of the species (possibly: the kind of soul that is characteristic of the species) and the generalized notion of the compound (cf. *Met.* Z.11, 1036a5–10; 1036b21–32; H.3, 1043a34–b4, on which see pp. 226–7). One might wonder whether a similar distinction applies to the genus, although some imagination will be required in order to come up with an account of the generic form of the animal soul and the generalized notion of the compound of soul and body which would be the form of the genus taken together with its matter.

Alternatively, one could adopt a bottom-up approach and think that what we regard as features of the genus are the result of some process of generalization which we carry out on more specific items. The idea would be that the distinction between male and female animals is a distinction which can only be observed and explained by looking at what happens to the matter of the single individual animals (possibly in their process of generation: cf. 1058b21–25). The homogeneous distribution of these two contrary features over the domain of animals might suggest that, if we want to explain this feature of animals, we have to look at some factor that animals have in common rather than at features of the single species or individuals. In this way, we would end up with an explanation of this pair of contraries' belonging to animals with an adequate degree of generality. This approach can do without the assumption of some general items (the genus, its differences, and other properties) as prior and independent from the individuals falling under them. In I.9

Aristotle seems to make a choice in favour of the bottom-up approach. As in I.8, there is some ambiguity as to whether the starting point of the bottom-up approach is the level of the species or that of individuals. However, the development of the argument in I.9 strongly suggests that individuals rather than species are what is needed. If this is correct, the matter and form Aristotle is talking about turn out to be the matter and form of the individuals falling under the genus.

1058b3–15: Aristotle resorts to three examples to illustrate the distinction between differences in the compound of matter and form, which do not yield a difference in species, and differences in the formula, which yield a difference in species. The pale human being and the dark human being do not differ in species (b3–12); the brazen circle and the wooden circle do not differ in species (b12–13); the brazen triangle and the wooden circle differ in species not because of their matter, but because of the contrariety which is in their *logos* (b13–15).

The only example which Aristotle fully unpacks is the first one (b3–12). Paleness and darkness (or whiteness and blackness: for the translation of colour words see notes to I.2, p. 83) do not differentiate the human being into subspecies. We can distinguish two steps in the explanation of this case: first Aristotle introduces the notion of properties or contrarieties that belong to a certain subject understood as matter or compound (b3–10) and then he spells out how we come to ascribe properties to a subject when they are properties of its matter (b10–12).

When we say that the pale human being is different from the dark human being, 'human being' refers to the compound of form and matter, and not to the form alone. Being a human being is being an animal capable of performing certain functions, in particular, to exercise rationality. This characterization (or something along these lines) is the account which captures the form of human being. The colour of the skin does not make any difference as to whether something is a human being or not. Rather, being pale or dark is a feature distinguishing particular compounds of flesh and bones from each other.

The remark that in these cases the human being is understood as the matter (b5–6) may be meant to avoid a possible misunderstanding. In *Met.* H.3, 1043a29–b4 Aristotle says that sometimes the same noun (say 'human being') can be used to indicate the compound of matter and form (the human being in flesh and bones) or the form alone (the human soul). In the example at stake, when we tell the pale human being from the dark human being, what we tell apart is human beings in flesh and bones and not their forms (i.e. their souls). In other words: when we distinguish pale human beings and dark human beings, we cannot make sense of the distinction by taking 'human being' in the sense of 'human soul'. This would amount to a sort of category mistake (souls do not have colours). The only option left is that the distinction is a distinction concerning the compounds, i.e. human beings in flesh and bones. But this sort of differentiation, which does not apply to the form, does not yield any differentiation into species.

For the remark at b5, 'even if one assigned one name <to each of them>', cf. *Met.* Z.4, 1029b27 on introducing one single name to indicate an incidental compound. I take the point to be that, even if we had a noun to indicate the dark human being and/or a noun to indicate the pale human being (as we have 'man' and 'woman' to indicate the male and the female human being respectively), each of those nouns would still indicate a compound of substance + incidental feature, which would not differ from the other in species, but only in some incidental respect. It is more difficult to figure out what is the point of the remark with respect to the unfolding of the argument. Perhaps the idea is that the existence of a noun for something (as in 'woman' and 'man') might suggest that there is one unified object, possibly a kind, that the noun picks out. But—Aristotle points out—it does not make any difference if there is one noun to designate a compound: one should look at the ontology of the object at issue.

I take b6–9 as introducing uncontroversial evidence in support (*gar*, 'for', at b6) of the claim that distinctions concerning the matter of individual compounds, such as differences in colour for human beings, do not correspond to specific differences. When we consider the distinction between single human beings in virtue of the fact that they have different pieces of matter, we do not describe the distinction by saying that human beings are different in species from each other. Rather, the compounds (of matter and form) are different from each other, while two human beings are not different in species. When we give an account of what it is to be a human being for each of them, we come up with the same formula and not with two formulas differing from each other in that one contains a predicate which is contrary to a corresponding predicate in the other (for accounts displaying a contrariety cf. notes to I.8, p. 214). Schematically, Aristotle's point is the following: suppose that F is the formula of a kind K. Suppose also that two contrary properties, C_1 and C_2, range over Ks. Let's call FC_1 and FC_2 the accounts of Ks that are C_1 and of Ks that are C_2 respectively. If, for any values of C_1 and C_2, it is not the case that FC_1 and FC_2 are formulas of appropriately unified kinds, then K is atomic and indivisible—its formula does not split up into formulas involving contrary properties (cf. I.8, 1058 a17–18).

I take *touto*, 'this', at b9 to refer back to what 'is not other in species, because there is no contrariety in the formula'. Here Aristotle seems to make a point about objects (two human beings of different colour are not other in species) based on a feature of their account ('because there is no contrariety in the formula'). This may seem to convey the wrong relations of priority, if we take the point about the definition to ground the point about the defined objects. This can be avoided in two ways. One could take the 'formula' to indicate the form or the essence of the defined things (rather than the definition as a linguistic formula); or one could take the reference to formulas as spelling out why it is appropriate to say that the objects at issue are other in species without implying that facts about their definition are more basic than facts about their ontology. However, it is not unusual for Aristotle to introduce claims about the objects of definition starting from claims about their definition: see notes on I.1, pp. 40–2.

At b8 *sunholon*, 'compound', is Aristotle's technical term to indicate the compound of form and matter.

I take it that the point of the following section (b10–12) is to explain how it is possible that properties belonging to individuals in virtue of their matter come to be ascribed to general terms (such as 'human being' or 'animal') under which individuals fall. As noted above (see notes to I.8, pp. 202–3), Greek does not have indeterminate articles. A singular general noun can be used to signify individuals (a human being or an animal) or universals (the species human being or the genus animal). Similar considerations apply to general nouns preceded by the determinate article. Usually, a predicative sentence with a singular general subject (such as 'the human being' or 'the animal') is regarded as true if the predicate can be universally predicated of the individuals falling under the subject. For instance, '(the) human being is animal' is usually understood as equivalent to a universal affirmative sentence 'all human beings are animal'. I take it that Aristotle's point in this chapter is to show that, in some cases, the conditions of truth of statements about genera and species are given by the conditions of truth of corresponding statements about individuals. In particular, Aristotle's analysis shows that, once we have reached the level of the 'last indivisible thing', i.e. of the indivisible species which is not further differentiated by some contrariety, all distinctions below that level have to be accounted for primarily in terms of the ontology of the individuals belonging to the species. It is only in a derivative way that we can ascribe to a subject picked out by the name of the corresponding genus the properties that can strictly speaking only belong to individuals falling under the genus.

Aristotle's account of how accidents can be ascribed to universal subjects and of how incidental compounds can be said to be is helpful to make sense of Aristotle's account of the distinction between per se properties of a genus that are not its specific differences and per se properties of a genus that are also its specific differences. Let's take a closer look at the example of Callias. Callias is a compound of form (his soul) and matter (his flesh and bones). Callias is pale on account of his matter, i.e. by having a body which is delimited by surfaces which are receptive of colour. Callias is also a human being. The basic subject to which the property of being pale belongs is Callias, i.e. an individual substance falling under the species human being. The universal human being is not the kind of object which can be coloured. Nonetheless, we can say that (the) human being is pale or dark because there are individual human beings, like Callias, who happen to have those properties. It is only in a derivative way and because of the two more basic facts, that Callias is pale and that Callias is a human being, that we can say that (the) human being is pale incidentally or, as Aristotle puts it, that 'the pale human being is'. The pale human being is an incidental being and is one only incidentally (cf. *Met.* Δ.7, 1017a8–25; Δ.6, 1015b28–34; Δ.9, 1017b27–1018a4).

I take the point of 'the pale human being is because Callias is pale—therefore the human being is pale incidentally' to be the following: the compound of an accident (such as pale) and a species (such as human being) can be said to be because there is an individual substance, Callias, which is a human being, and which is pale incidentally. An entity such as the pale human being is and is something one if and only if the property of being pale belongs to some particular human being. If this is not the case, there is nothing linking paleness to the general subject picked out by 'human being': what it is for something to be pale has nothing to do with what it is for something to be a human being (cf. *Met.* Z.12, 1037b14–18). The same analysis applies to the pale animal.

On the basis of this account we can now analyse the cases of the female animal (where female is a per se property, but not a difference, of the genus animal) and of the biped animal (where biped is a specific difference of the genus animal). Unlike the case of merely incidental compounds, the subject (animal) to which the properties of being female and of being biped are ascribed belongs in the definition of both properties (i.e. both in the definition of female and in the definition of biped). This is what makes them both per se properties of the genus animal. Nonetheless, the basic ontological facts accounting for the claims that the animal is per se female (or that the female animal is) are facts concerning some particular animals: Rigel is female and Rigel, being a horse, is an animal. By way of contrast, in the case of specific differences, the basic ontological facts accounting for the truth of claims such as 'the animal is biped' or 'the biped animal is' can remain at a higher level of generality: all human beings are biped and all human beings are animals.

Note that, despite differences, all these predications are derivative. We have seen what this means in the case of incidental predicates and of per se properties which do not differentiate the genus. Partially similar considerations apply to the case of specific differences: specific differences cannot be predicated of the genus without qualification. For example, biped cannot be predicated of animal if the claim 'animal is biped' is understood as equivalent to a universal sentence: for it is not true that all animals are biped. Rather, each difference is predicated of (some of) the objects of which the genus is predicated ('biped' is predicated of some of the objects of which 'animal' is predicated).

Ross reads b10–12 differently and takes it as an elliptical formulation for 'the pale man, then, is also definition + matter, for it is the individual Callias that is pale' (Ross 1924, II p. 304). Ross does not expand on this proposal, but it seems to me that, if taken in this way, the point of the passage would be rather different. The point would be that, when we talk of the pale man, we have to talk about a compound, because it is only the compound that can be pale. This is certainly part of what Aristotle wants to say here, but on this reading the passage would not take us much farther in explaining how we can talk of pale man in the first place, given that the universal man is not the kind of thing that can be pale. Nor would this reconstruction provide any explanation of why man is pale incidentally. For these reasons, I think my interpretation is preferable. On my interpretation the passage tells us something on how we come to ascribe properties such as male and female to the genus animal and it helps us to unpack the difference between properties which are specific differences of the genus and properties which are not.

Still, the passage does not lead us very far in distinguishing between incidental properties *tout court* and per se properties which do not differentiate the genus. The basic idea is that, if we have a subject x whose species is S and whose genus is G, if x has a certain property P, we can say that S (or G) is P. For example, if we consider Callias, who is a man, if Callias is pale, we can also say that (the) pale human being is or that (the) pale animal is. What we have to focus on now is the ontology of x. In particular, we want to check whether x is P on account of its form or on account of its matter. Callias, who is a human being, is male; Helena, who is a human being, is female. But Callias and Helena are, respectively, male and female on account of their matter (depending on the different degree of heat their seeds received in their mother's womb—see p. 236). Accordingly, (the) human being can be said to be male or female because each individual human being happens to be male or female. Furthermore, since being male or being female is a property belonging to individual human beings in virtue of their matter, the pair of contrary properties male/female does not differentiate human being into two subspecies.

Given that Callias and Helena are also animals (animal is their genus), we could also say that the animal is male or female by following the same reasoning. But what is the difference between pale/dark and male/female with respect to the species human being and to the genus animal? In order to make room for the distinction we have to take a further step and see how male/female and pale/dark behave with respect to the domain of human beings and of animals. At first glance and if we consider the domain of human beings (a species of the genus animal), no crucial difference seems to emerge: each human being is either male or female and each human being has skin of some colour; human beings are not the only beings to be male or female nor are they the only ones to have a colour (this table and this chair have a colour too). So, with respect to the species human being it might look like both sexual determination and colour are incidental.

If we look at the domain of the genus, though, we can see some differences: there are no things that are not animals and are male or female, but there are things that are not animals and have colours. If animals only present a differentiation into male and female, there must be something about animals explaining this connection between a pair of contrary properties and their subject genus. The idea would be that, even if male and female are not specific differences of the genus animal because they belong to animals in virtue of their matter, there must be something at the level of generality of the genus animal which accounts for the fact that only animals are male or female. This consideration may induce us to revise the hypothesis that there is no difference in the relation that sexual differentiation and colours bear to the species human being.

The problem with this procedure is that it ends up removing any ground for the distinction between per se and incidental properties of individual objects: we could move up to an appropriate level of generality and find a genus of the species human being, e.g. material object, which would then be co-extensive with the property of being coloured and, following the same reasoning as before, we would end up with the result that there is a genus of the human being of which being coloured is a per se property. In other words, there is a general difficulty in drawing a neat partition between per se and incidental properties of an object.

There is a further difficulty concerning the distinction between properties which differentiate the genus and properties which do not differentiate the genus in terms of form and matter. The difficulty can be seen by looking at the examples Aristotle uses to illustrate the distinction: some concern living beings, some others concern geometrical objects. While it is clear that the particular matter in which the triangle and the circle are instantiated, be it bronze or wood, is not part of the definition of triangle and circle, the case of geometrical figures might well be rather different from the case of natural beings which are always made of the same kind of matter, which enables them to perform their vital functions in the way that is characteristic of their species (cf. Z.10, 1035b14–27; Z.11, 1036b22–32). Furthermore, the differentiation of animal species is at least in part based on corporeal features, such as being footed or being winged, which certainly belong to animals also, if not exclusively, in virtue of the fact that they have a body. For some discussion of the complex problems involved in the distinction of essential, necessary and incidental features in natural beings, in connection with I.9, see Balme 1987b; Quarantotto 2005.

1058b15–21: Before concluding the chapter, Aristotle raises a doubt about the proposed solution. Is it really the case that matter does not count at all in differentiating things into species or is there a sense in which it does? What is interesting here is the kind of example Aristotle resorts to in order to illustrate the problem: if we consider two individuals belonging to different natural species (b16–17)—say: Vegliantino, a horse, and Orlando, a man—what we look at are things whose matter is clearly different, not only in the sense that Vegliantino's body and Orlando's body are two distinct chunks of matter, occupying different places, but also in the sense that their bodies have different material features (differences in composition, weight, etc.). Is it really the case that, in giving an account of what makes of Vegliantino a horse and of Orlando a human being, i.e. in the account of what makes them belong to different species, the features of their body and matter do not count?

The clause at b17–18, 'in truth their accounts are with matter', is ambiguous for some of the reasons we have already considered. The claim could be taken in either of two ways: **(i)** the individual form which is present in each individual is with matter, in the sense that, in the individual, it cannot be separated from matter;

(ii) the general form which is expressed in the definition of the species is with matter (i.e. includes reference to matter or to material features). The emphasis on individuals in the examples pushes towards (i), but (ii) cannot be excluded and carries interesting philosophical implications. On reading (i), the individual form of this horse and the individual form of this man are in the particular matter which constitutes this horse and the particular matter which constitutes this man respectively. On reading (ii), the form of the species of horse and the form of the species of human being are with matter, i.e. their form includes material features. Reference to the matter which is characteristic of the species (henceforth: specific matter) is not the same as reference to the concrete chunks of matter which compose the individuals. The latter certainly cannot be referred to or exhibited in a general account of what something is, but nothing prevents specific matter, i.e. the kind of matter in which the form of the species must be in order for the members of the species to perform the functions and the activities determined by their form, from being part of the essence of species.

Aristotle's reply (b18–21) insists on the point already made in the first part of the chapter, but the example introduces a new way to look at the distinction. The example is the following: if we take a dark horse and a pale human being, difference in colour does not contribute anything to their belonging to different species since they would belong to different species even if they were both pale. The reply suggests the following generalization: contrary properties P_1 and P_2 characterizing two subjects S_1 and S_2 that are different in species do not contribute to the differentiation of the species of S_1 and S_2 as long as S_1 and S_2 would still differ in species if they were both characterized by P_1 or both by P_2. The generalization is useful as long as it emphasizes the intuition that none of the properties that S_1 and S_2 can possibly share can be responsible for their difference in species. This is, in a way, trivial, but it raises the issues whether all properties that things have in virtue of their matter are of this sort. This need not be the case, but the choice of the example in the reply suggests an analogy between the relations obtaining between matter and form on the one hand, and incidental features and substance on the other hand, in that Aristotle seems to suggest that all properties that subjects have in virtue of having a body behave as the property of being pale with respect to being a horse or a man.

Saying that the properties belonging to individuals in virtue of the particular chunk of matter which is their body are incidental properties of the individuals is not incompatible with the idea that those properties range over the genus of the individuals they characterize and are therefore to be regarded as per se properties of the genus. Being male or being female belongs to each individual animal depending on the particular features of the process its matter went through in the period of its gestation. Still, male and female are properties belonging to animals only and, in this sense, they are per se properties of the genus animal. Furthermore, the view that properties due to individual matter are all incidental does not exclude that there be some properties belonging to individual members of a species in virtue of their specific matter and these properties (unlike those due to individual matter) may well be part of what defines the species. For instance, all birds are biped and have wings, but not all of them are male or red. Sexual determination, colour, precise size, etc. are features determined only for each single individual of the species in virtue of its matter. Being winged or being biped are properties of the body belonging to all members of the species and can therefore belong in a general account of the features of the species. This view is compatible with (ii).

If, on the other hand, one takes the analysis of the example to be about material properties in general, then the point would be that all material properties without restriction (be they due to individual or specific matter) resemble incidental properties in some relevant sense. The relevant sense is that, like incidental properties, they are not the kind of properties which determine a difference in species. This does not exclude that some material properties be necessary for the members of the species in order to perform the functions and carry out the activities characteristic of their species. But these material properties would then turn out to be necessary properties of their subjects (e.g. having fins for fishes or feet for humans), in contrast with material properties which do not affect the basic capacity of individuals to engage in their specific functions and activities (being more or less fat, having eyes and hair of a determinate colour, etc.). Neither class of properties, though, would belong to the set of specific differences.

If this is what Aristotle has in mind, then in I.9 he endorses the view that no material property can be part of the essence of a species and this would lead to the rejection of option (ii).

1058b21–25: The conclusion of the discussion is divided into two parts corresponding to the two parts of the solution to the difficulties at 1058a36–b3. Male and female are proper affections of the animal, but they are such by being in the body and matter of individual animals. That the argument refers to the matter of the single animal can be gathered by the reference to the way in which the matter is affected in the process of generation of the animal which determines the sex of the outcome. Aristotle hints briefly at his doctrine that one and the same seed (provided by the father and bearing the formal determination of the new individual), depending on the thermic state of the mother (providing the matter of the new individual) turns into a male rather than a female individual. In this sense whether an individual animal is male or female is not determined by its form, but by some incidental conditions of its matter. For the claim that the same seed becomes male or female, depending on how it is affected see *GA* I.18, 723a33–34; for a full discussion of sexual differentiation see *GA* IV.3 and V.1 with Kosman 2010.

The final lines at b24–25 close the discussion of I.8 and I.9. About the relation between the end of I.9 and the beginning of I.10 see pp. 237 and 242.

One can give two rather different readings of the overall strategy of I.9. On one reading, the chapter prescribes a general method to establish whether a given property belongs to one or the other of the classes of properties distinguished in (D1)–(D3) (see pp. 220–1). On the second reading, the goal of the chapter is that of describing the difference between three classes of properties which are assumed as different (incidental properties, per se properties which are not differences, specific differences). If the intent of the chapter is prescriptive, i.e. if the chapter is meant to tell how properties should be sorted into the three classes and, possibly, which properties should be taken as specific differences, Aristotle faces a problem: for the distinction is based on the distinction between matter and form and it looks like we should already know what the properties belonging to the form of the species are in order to sort out specific differences from other properties ranging over the genus. This procedure is circular. On the other hand, if the intent of the chapter is that of describing some intuitions about some (at the time) current distinctions between properties which do figure as specific differences and properties which do not, then the chapter is stressing that the line is drawn along the boundary between individuals and specific determinations. Since what differentiates an individual from the others is its particular matter, none of the properties belonging to the individual in virtue of its particular matter works as a specific difference. According to this reading, the distinctions into species, genera, and differences are a given and what has to be explained is why certain properties, which seem to range over the genus in the same way in which specific differences do, are not regarded as specific differences. I take it that the descriptive reading makes better sense of the chapter as a whole and of the difficulties raised at the beginning. On the idea that Aristotle is raising some difficulties and spelling out the ontological under-pinning of a conceptual framework already in use see introductory notes to I.7, p. 171.

CHAPTER 10

After the discussion of otherness in species in I.8–9, I.10 explores the relation of opposition obtaining between perishable and imperishable. This relation turns out to be a relation of otherness in genus. The beginning of the chapter ('Since contraries are other in species') provides an apparently clear thematic link to the end of I.9, but it remains to be seen whether the discussion in I.10 is genuinely resting on the results of the former chapters for the reasons that will become apparent in the course of the commentary.

1058b26–29: Leaving the parenthesis aside, the most natural reading of the opening lines is the following: **(1)** since the contraries are other in species and **(2)** the perishable and the imperishable are contraries, **(3)** it is necessary that the perishable and the imperishable be other in genus. This looks like an argument with two premises and one conclusion, but the shift from being other in species in (1) to being other in genus in (3) is puzzling and different interpreters have come to grips with it by following different strategies.

There are two main overarching issues. First, does Aristotle intend to provide a deductive argument in support of (3)? If so, are (1) and (2) necessary and sufficient to establish (3) or are we supposed to supply further premises, possibly from the rest of the chapter? Secondly, there is an issue as to the overall interpretation of I.10 and the relation between the bulk of the chapter and 1059a10–14, where Aristotle criticizes Platonic Forms based on what has been previously established. Is the whole of I.10 supposed to be read as an attack on Forms? Or is the argument in I.10 meant to be a general one, with a coda about Platonic Forms? The two issues of the argumentative structure of (1)–(3) and of I.10's general goal are intertwined: for if one takes the whole chapter as an attack on Platonic Forms, one might wonder whether this has any consequence as to the reconstruction of the initial argument. In particular, the anti-Platonic reading of the chapter may suggest a preferred interpretation of (1)–(3) in that the argument would be about (perishable) sensible particulars and (imperishable) Forms rather than about perishable and imperishable things in general.

Before getting to the possibility of a preferred interpretation for (1)–(3), there are some issues about the logical structure of 1058b26–29. The most natural reading of the section is that it presents a deductive argument. However, most interpreters have gone beyond this and assumed that the argument is meant to be a syllogism in Aristotle's technical sense—but, unfortunately, fails to be one. A syllogism in the technical sense is a deductive argument with two premises and one conclusion such that both premises and the conclusion are in standard predicative form (a predicate is ascribed to a subject); the subject and the predicate of the conclusion appear each (either as the subject or as the predicate) in one of the premises; the further term which appears (either as the subject or as the predicate) in the premises is in common between the two premises. The common term (the middle term) ties the subject and the predicate of the conclusion in that either it appears as the predicate of the one and the subject for the other, or as the predicate of both, or as the subject of both in the two premises.

Given this account of what a syllogism is, it is clear that what we read at 1058b26–29 is not a syllogism, even if it was originally meant to be one (which we have no way to establish). For the argument simply does not comply with the formal requirements for being a syllogism: the predicate of the conclusion ('other in genus') does not appear in either of the premises. Most interpreters, instead of dropping the assumption that we have to do with a syllogism, have tried to explain away the obvious difficulties by following different strategies. One strategy is that of textual emendation: one could try to emend 1058b28 by replacing *genei* ('in genus') in (3) with *eidei* ('in species') (Bonitz 1849, p. 449). This solution, apart from clashing with the apparently unanimous manuscript tradition, does not take into account the fact that at 1059a10 Aristotle establishes his conclusion and formulates it, as in (3), in terms of *genei* (and not of *eidei*). Alternatively one could think of emending *eidei* at b26 in order to have *genei* both in (1) and (3) (Aubenque 1997, p. 315). This solution, too, is not supported by the manuscripts and has the additional problem that, unlike (1), the emended claim 'since the contraries are other in genus' has not been prepared by anything Aristotle has said so far nor is it generally true (as to whether (1) as it stands is generally true, see below).

A different strategy consists in claiming that *eidos* and *genos* are not being used in their technical sense and are, therefore, interchangeable (Ross 1924, II p. 305; Jaeger 1957, apparatus *ad* 1058bb28; Elders 1961, p. 187; and Schmitz 1985, pp. 540–1; on the technical and non–technical use of these terms, see introductory notes to I.7, p. 171). However, at 1059a10–14 the two expressions are used in their technical sense, and the advocates of this strategy are aware of this. Their way out consists in taking 1059a10–14 as a later addition. This kind of hypothesis can be hardly established or rejected with certainty, but should be a last resort. Note that, since I.7–9 are quite technical, the hypothesis of the later addition of 1059a10–14 implies two stages of revision of the text: the last lines of I.10 would be a later addition to the rest of the chapter, but I.10 as a whole (with or without the later addition) would be an extrinsic addition to the rest of Iota—or, at least, to the immediately preceding chapters. Furthermore, it is not obvious that *eidos* at 1058b31 is not used in a technical sense, given that the argument at 1058b29–35 deals with cases similar to those considered in I.9. Even if *eidos* and *genos* are used in a technical way, however, one should further establish whether they are used according to the absolute or the relative distinction (cf. p. 172). In I.8, 1058a25–26 things that belong to different genera (and therefore are other in genus) cannot be said to be other in species. This suggests that the absolute distinction is in play. Is the absolute distinction what is at issue in I.10? In the course of the commentary I shall suggest that one could drop the absolute distinction between being other in species and being other in genus in order to reconstruct (1)–(3) as a relatively plausible argument without dropping a technical distinction between species and genus.

Along textual emendation and resort to non-technical vocabulary, a third strategy consists in taking the refutation of the Platonic claim that perishable particulars and the corresponding imperishable Form are the same in *eidos* as the goal of the chapter, and in explaining the initial formulation of (1) as 'betraying' Aristotle's chief interest in the chapter (Centrone 2002; Fronterotta 2005). The idea would be that in the course of the argument Aristotle would switch to the strongest claim that he can establish, i.e. (3), which, a fortiori, will allow him to refute the Platonic claim. This strategy differs from the first one in that it does not plead textual corruption as the reason for the unsatisfactory formulation of the argument, but provides a sort of psychological explanation for it. On this reading, 1059a10–14, where Aristotle formulates his argument against Forms, provides the key to reading the opening lines and I.10 as a whole. The psychological explanation can hardly be confirmed or rejected on the basis of undisputable evidence, but if there are alternative ways to make sense of the argumentative structure of the chapter without resorting to the psychology of the author, I think those should be preferred. And there seem to be alternative ways.

The first three strategies have one feature in common: they assume that 1058b26–29 is meant to be a syllogism. They accordingly try to explain why it does not look like one. However, one could try to make sense of the text by dropping the assumption that the opening lines were meant to be a syllogism. This can be done in more or less radical ways.

The most radical option consists in dropping the assumption that the text at 1058b26–29 is a deductive argument altogether.

This option has been endorsed, in different ways, by Andrenacci and Palpacelli (2003), and by Quarantotto (2004). Andrenacci and Palpacelli (2003) follow Centrone (2002) in their general interpretation of I.10, but take the opening words of I.10 as a brief summary of the results achieved in I.8–9. On this reading, *epeidē de* introducing (1) should be taken in the temporal sense, which would refer back to the results summed up in I.9, 1058b25. Furthermore, (2) should not be taken as coordinate with (1), but as introducing a new syntactically independent period. This would yield the translation: 'After having said that the contraries are different in species; however, perishable and imperishable are contraries [. . .], it is necessary that perishable and imperishable be other in genus'. This proposal eliminates the problem of the logical structure of the opening lines by eliminating its syntactical unity. Fragmentary or anacoluthic sections are certainly not completely unusual in Aristotle, but the results of this approach are clearly suboptimal.

Quarantotto (2004, pp. 43–9) follows a different and more interesting route. She takes *epeidē* at the very beginning of the chapter as introducing a concessive clause: 'Although the contraries are other in species [. . .]' (cf. Centrone 2005, p. 35). Quarantotto refers to texts where *epei* is apparently used with a concessive value (*HA* V.6, 541a32; VII.11, 587b31; *GA* II.5, 741a16; III.6, 756b26; III.7, 757a35; see also notes on I.1, 1053a32 for another case where one is tempted to take *epei* as concessive), but there might be independent reasons for resisting the causal reading of *epeidē*. Quarantotto argues that the causal reading implies that **(a)** there is at least some sense in which perishable and imperishable are different in species and that **(b)** difference in species can ground the claim that perishable and imperishable are different in genus. She claims that neither (a) nor (b) is the case, so the causal reading should be dismissed (Quarantotto 2004, p. 48).

However, (a) and (b) cannot be the case only if being different in species is taken as incompatible with being different in genus; but it need not be incompatible. Quarantotto relies on I.8, where it is true that difference in species requires sameness in genus, but it is not obvious that this has to be the case in general. In fact, in *Met.* Δ.6, 1017a1 we read that if x and y are one in *eidos*, then x and y are one in *genos*; but this implies (even if Aristotle does not state this explicitly), that if it is not the case and x and y are one in

241

genus, then it is not the case that x and y are the same in *eidos*. In the latter case, it does not seem to be false that x and y are other in species. Of course, otherness in species in this sense should be taken in the relatively loose sense which does not imply sameness in genus. This immediately raises the question of the relation between I.10 and the discussion in I.8–9. We saw above (p. 236) that the last lines of I.9 wrap up the discussion in I.8–9. This leaves an open question as to whether the conceptual framework and the vocabulary employed in I.8–9 and I.10 are used consistently throughout the three chapters. I shall return to (b) in the course of the commentary (see p. 243 ff.).

Given the advantages and the disadvantages of the radical options, one could question the traditional assumption that the beginning of I.10 is supposed to present a syllogism in a less radical way. One could take the beginning of the chapter as a (sketchy) deductive argument, without assuming that it has to be a syllogism. I shall explore the possibility of taking (1)–(3) as the synthetic version of a deductive argument in which the conclusion that the perishable and the imperishable are other in genus rests on the claims that contraries are other in species and that the perishable and the imperishable are contraries. Although the reading I propose is certainly not problem-free, it has the advantage of showing where the problems are if we take (1)–(3) to present (the sketch of) a deductive argument in the first place.

I assume that (3) states exactly what Aristotle wants to show (as at 1059a10 and a14). The parenthesis at b27–28 provides support for the claim that perishable and imperishable are contraries by emphasizing that the determinate incapacity (the incapacity to perish) which is imperishability is the privation (i.e. presumably, not simply the contradictory negation) of its opposite. One might wonder why imperishability is the privation and not the contradictory of perishability. Ross (1924, II pp. 304–5) suggests that imperishability is not a feature of everything that does not perish, but a feature of things that might conceivably perish (cf. 1055b8). I am not sure what the restriction to things that might conceivably perish amounts to. One reason why perishable and imperishable are opposed as possession and privation rather than as contradictories is that they range over things that are (as opposed to perishable and not perishable: cf. I.3, 1054b18–22). Given that in any pair of contraries one opposite is the complete privation of the other, this analysis of imperishability supports claim (2). According to Elders (1961, pp. 188–9) b27–28 should be deleted since he takes privation to be always the privation of a good property, but the privation of perishability is hardly the privation of something good. Although it is true that in some contexts privation retains a negative connotation (see pp. 99 and 119), we have already seen that at other places in Iota the notions traditionally taken as the opposites of privations turn out to be privation (I.3, 1054a26–29, about the one as indivisible; I.5, 1056a17–18, about the equal as privative negation of the great and the small). I take it that b27–28 are exactly where they are supposed to be.

In order to reconstruct the argument leading to (3), it is important to specify what sort of items the argument is about. Different kinds of objects can be said to be contraries (see Introduction, pp. xxv–xxvi; I.4, pp. 124, 128–9; see also introductory notes on I.1, pp. 21–2, about the use of the neuter adjective with the determinate article) and 'the perishable' and 'the imperishable' can, in principle, indicate different kinds of object: the perishable and the imperishable could be properties (imperishability—perishability), instances of properties (this instance of imperishability—this instance of perishability), or the particular subjects that receive those properties (the imperishable thing—the perishable thing). The way in which the argument is built and the formulation at 1058b30–31 (*hotioun aphtharton kai phtharton hetera einai tōi eidei*, 'that anything which is imperishable and anything which is perishable be other in species') strongly suggest that 'other in species' is used as a predicate of the particular things that are imperishable and perishable respectively. Accordingly, I take the general thesis of the chapter as well as the first part of the chapter down to 1058b35 to be about contrary things and not about contrary properties as such (however, at 1058b36–59a4, the perishable and the imperishable indicate the properties belonging to their subjects; this oscillation is made clear by the context). More precisely, perishable and imperishable objects are not simply perishable or imperishable, but are objects of a determinate kind. We know from I.9 that (1) is not generally true with respect to things of a determinate kind: male and female, pale and dark do not determine a difference in species in the genus animal. For while it is true that this particular instance of pale qua pale is different in species from this particular instance of dark qua dark (they are two colours differing in species), it is not true that this pale man is different in species from this dark man. What is generally true is that, if a and b differ in species, then a and b fall under species determined by contrary specific differences, while it is not necessarily the case that, if a and b instantiate contrary properties, they also differ in species. 1058b29–35 will then raise the question whether it is possible that the imperishable thing and the perishable thing, while being instantiations of contrary properties, do not differ in species (let alone in genus).

As for the intended generality of the argument, one might wonder whether the argument need be construed with any specific kind of imperishable or perishable objects in view. For instance, one might think that the argument must be understood with reference to the opposition between (imperishable) celestial bodies and (perishable) sublunary substances (Elders 1961, pp. 185–7) or with reference to the opposition between (imperishable) Platonic Forms and (perishable) particulars (Centrone 2002; Fronterotta 2005). I shall return to these options in the course of the commentary, but I aim at providing a reconstruction of the argument according to which the argument is completely general.

1058b29–35: This section unpacks a possible worry about the claim that any perishable thing differs in species from any imperishable thing. Note that the worry is formulated as an objection not so much to the generality of (1), but to the idea that the perishable thing and the imperishable thing may not differ in species. Aristotle's response to this will be to show that the difference between a perishable and an imperishable thing is never an incidental one, but is always based on their essence.

At 1058b29–30 we find what reads like a back-reference: 'Now, then, we have spoken with reference to universal names as such'. It is hard to tell whether this is a reference to the introduction of the problem in the previous lines, to I.9 or to a previous discussion which is now lost. 'Universal' is used in a rather technical sense in the parenthesis at b32–35, where Aristotle distinguishes between the attribution of contrary predicates to universal subjects and to particular subjects. If we keep the parenthesis as is printed in modern editions, the very fact that both cases are used to illustrate the point about 'universal names as such' makes it difficult to take 'universal names' outside the parenthesis in the same technical sense as within the parenthesis. Following this line of thought 'with reference to universal names as such' could perhaps be taken in the sense of 'speaking in general'. It seems, however, unlikely that this is the sense of 'with reference to universal names'. Alternatively, we could take the two occurrences of 'universal' inside and outside the parenthesis in the same technical sense and regard the reference to the case of individuals as an addition in support of the general point (which is in any case already made clear by looking at universals) that one and the same subject can receive contrary predicates. If so, then perhaps the parenthesis could be eliminated.

Aristotle considers two kinds of relation between a subject and a pair of contrary properties. In both cases it makes sense to say that the subject can receive the contrary properties without going through a differentiation into species. The first case is that of a universal subject, e.g. human being. As we have seen in I.9 (pp. 229–31), there is a derivative sense in which we can ascribe the properties of individuals falling under a certain universal species or genus to the species or genus itself (or, more precisely, to a general subject picked out by the species-term or by the genus-term). If different individuals falling under the universal have different contrary properties, each of the two contrary properties can be derivatively ascribed to the universal subject. Such pairs of properties do not determine the specific identity of the individuals and can be incidentally predicated of the universal term indicating the species of those individuals. For instance, there are individual human beings who are pale, there are individual human beings who are dark, and these two states of affairs can hold at the same time. In this sense, we can say that (the) human being is pale and dark at the same time. But we can also consider the case of contrary incidental features affecting the same individual over time. In this case, the contraries are not attributed to the same individual subject at the same time, but we can say that the same individual is pale and dark (i.e. tanned), at different times. The capacity to receive contrary properties at different times while remaining one and the same individual is a characteristic feature of individual substances (*Cat.* 5, 4a10–b19).

Both examples make it clear that Aristotle is thinking of pairs of contrary properties in their interaction with a subject *of a certain kind*. There are contraries which do not affect the kind of thing their subject is. The issue is whether perishable and imperishable are the sort of contraries that affect the kind of thing their subject is. For one could think that perishable and imperishable, like pale and dark, can be ascribed to a universal subject without yielding a differentiation into species and/or to a particular subject at different times or in different respects without modifying the kind of thing it is.

Although the issue whether perishable and imperishable are the sort of contraries that affect the essence of their subject is a general one, Aristotle's motivation for tackling the issue might derive from reflection on some particular cases. For instance, the view that perishable and imperishable can be ascribed to a universal without a corresponding differentiation in species can be found in the allegedly Platonic claim that the perishable particulars which participate in a Form and the corresponding eternal Form have the same *eidos* (they share the same definition: cf. 1059a10–14; cf. *Met.* B.2, 997b7–12). As for the idea that the same individual might change from being perishable to being imperishable, in *LBV* 3 Aristotle addresses the question whether any change of place can affect things' perishability by making them imperishable. The issue is tackled in connection with the general problem of how the surroundings can affect the length of things' life. In particular, the example of fire is considered. For Aristotle each of the sublunary elements (earth, water, air, and fire) naturally occupies a certain region of the universe, and the four regions are concentric spheres about the centre of the universe (from the centre to the extremity of the sublunary world: earth, water, air, fire). Each of the elements is essentially characterized by a pair of two properties belonging to two basic pairs of contraries: hot/cold, wet/dry. Earth is cold and dry, water is cold and wet, air is hot and wet, fire is hot and dry. Elements are the cause of corruption of each other in virtue of the mutual disruption of the contraries in some substrate. One of the ideas in play here is that what is hot will not survive long in a cold environment (and similarly for the other contraries). The question Aristotle asks is then the following: once fire has reached its region, where no wetness or coldness can be found, will fire become imperishable, given that in that region there will not be anything able to make it perish? Aristotle's answer is quite complex, but the gist of it seems to be that this is not the case: if fire is perishable, it will eventually perish by changing into another element. Aristotle's views on why this is so are complex and have to do with the view that the matter of perishable things has the potentiality to be and not to be and things cannot retain such a potentiality forever without actualizing it (on this point see 1058b36–1059a10). Favourable surroundings can affect the length of the ontological career of things, but they cannot modify the intrinsic nature of perishable things. Furthermore, in *Met.* B.4, 1000a11–14, Aristotle mentions the inadequacy of traditional mythological accounts according to which immortality (i.e. imperishability) is caused by the assumption of a certain kind of food (nectar and ambrosia). Although the case of the gods' losing their immortality if deprived of nectar and ambrosia is clearly fictional, Aristotle stresses that an account of what determines mortality and immortality must be given.

1058b36–1059a10:   This section shows why perishable and imperishable are not the kind of contraries which are irrelevant to the differentiation into species. Aristotle starts by distinguishing between contraries that can belong to some of their subjects incidentally and contraries that cannot belong to any of their subjects incidentally only (58b36–59a1). He then shows that the property of being perishable can only be a necessary property of perishable things and that it must have something to do with the essence of the things to which it belongs (59a1–7). The same argument is extended to the imperishable (59a7–8); finally (59a9–10) the conclusion is reached that perishable and imperishable are different in genus.

The first distinction we encounter is that between contraries which can belong incidentally to some of their subjects and contraries which cannot belong incidentally to any of their subjects. The properties of being perishable and imperishable fall into the second group. In spelling out this distinction Aristotle shows that the intuition behind the doubts raised in the former section, that perishable and imperishable might belong to the first group, is wrong.

Before taking a closer look at the development of the argument, some preliminary distinctions may be useful to disentangle the problems raised by the argument. There are different non-equivalent accounts of what it is for something to belong incidentally to a subject. On one account, a property is an incidental property (*sumbebēkos*) of a subject if it belongs to it neither necessarily nor for the most part (*Met.* Δ.30, 1025a4–30). This kind of properties are properties that the subject can lose or acquire while remaining the individual it is. On this account, x belongs incidentally to y (or: x is an accident of y) if y can lose x without ceasing to be (alternatively: x can belong or not belong to y) (cf. *Top.* I.5, 102b6–9). In a different sense, x belongs incidentally to y if it does not belong per se to y in either of the two senses of per se, i.e. x belongs incidentally to y if x does not figure in the definition of y and y does not figure in the definition of x (see I.9, p. 223). According to the third account, x belongs incidentally to y if x is not part of the essence of y; in this case, one might want to distinguish per se accidents of a subject (necessary but not essential features which can be scientifically accounted for) from merely incidental features (accidents *tout court*), for which there is no explanation (*Met.* Δ.30, 1025a30–34). In the course of the argument Aristotle seems to move from the claim that being perishable/imperishable are necessary properties to the claim that they are the substance or in the substance of their subjects. This suggests that the distinction between essential and necessary properties is not at work in I.10.

Properties of a certain subject can turn out to be incidental according to one account and not according to another. For instance, whiteness belongs to snow incidentally in the second sense, but not in the first (such properties are sometimes referred to as inseparable accidents). Being female or male belongs incidentally to animals according to the third account, but not according to the second. We will have to sort out in what sense perishable and imperishable are never incidental to their subjects.

Furthermore, the same general features can belong to different subjects in different ways. For instance, being hot belongs essentially to fire, but belongs only incidentally to stones or to Socrates. Being odd is a necessary feature of number five, but is an incidental feature of the group of people in this room. Being pale is an incidental feature of Socrates, but being pale is essential to the instance of paleness which incidentally inheres in Socrates. Aristotle intends to argue that being perishable and being imperishable do not belong in different ways to different subjects. In particular, it is not the case that they belong incidentally to some of their subjects and non-incidentally to other subjects. Rather, they do not belong incidentally to any of their subjects.

Doubts about the claim that it is necessary that the perishable and the imperishable are other in genus were raised on the basis of two grounds. First, there are pairs of contraries which, while ranging over a certain unified domain, do not differentiate it into species. Second, there are pairs of contraries which can belong at different times to the same individual (which, remaining the same individual, remains, a fortiori, an individual of the same kind). The same pair of contraries (pale and dark) was used to illustrate both cases and there is a link between the two: the properties according to which the individuals of a species can change cannot be properties that define the species to which those individuals belong.

At a1–6 we find an argument meant to show that nothing is perishable incidentally. Aristotle adds without further comments that a similar argument would apply to the imperishable at 1059a7–8. The argument is the following: (4) nothing is perishable incidentally, because (5) it is possible for an incidental feature to fail to belong to its subject, and (6) being perishable is a property which belongs to its subjects by necessity. For (7) if it were possible for the property of being perishable to fail to belong to its subject, one and the same thing would turn out to be perishable and imperishable.

The whole argument rests on (7) and on the assumption that, if a property belongs to its subject by necessity, it cannot be an incidental feature of it (see the first account of incidental properties, p. 248). The argument raises a few crucial problems. In the first place, Aristotle does not explain why the consequence that one and the same thing turns out to be perishable and imperishable in (7) is unacceptable. Furthermore, the argument alluded to in (7) (see below) focuses on individual subjects in that it is supposed to show that it is not possible for one and the same individual to change with respect to its perishability (or imperishability). The argument does not show that it is not possible for individuals of the same species to differ by being the one perishable and the other imperishable. However, Aristotle seems to rely on this argument to argue that being perishable and being imperishable are properties 'in the substance' of their subjects. Although the interpretation of this claim raises some issues on its own, the claim suggests that being perishable and being imperishable have something to do with the kind of thing that their subjects are (see pp. 252–3). But it is not immediately clear that the argument about individuals justifies Aristotle's further move to the claim that perishable and imperishable are in the substance of their subjects.

In (7) Aristotle alludes to an argument supposed to establish that it is not possible for one and the same thing to change from being perishable to being imperishable and vice versa. Although the argument is not spelled out in I.10, Aristotle can avail himself of at least two arguments to establish the desired conclusion. The first argument can be reconstructed on the basis of *DC* I.11–12, the second one can be construed by working on iterated modalities. As for the first argument, Aristotle seems to entertain the view that, if x has the potentiality not to be, x cannot retain that potentiality forever without ever actually ceasing to be; otherwise said, any potentiality not to be is actualized given an infinite time (*DC* I.12, 281a28–b25; 283a24–28; there are some issues with the generalization of this view to all potentialities, but I take it that all Aristotle needs is the claim about the specific potentiality not to be which is perishability). In *DC* I.11, 280b20–281a1 Aristotle distinguishes different ways in which things are said to be perishable or imperishable, but only one way (i.e. the way in which things are properly said to be perishable or imperishable: cf. *DC* I.11, 280b32–33; 281a3–4; I.12, 282a27–30) is relevant to I.10. Things can be said to be perishable (*phtharton*) if they are at some time and are such as to be able not to be at some later time. Correspondingly, things can be said to be imperishable (*aphtharton*) if they are and are not such as to be able to perish, i.e. if they are such that it is not the case that they are at some time and have the potentiality not to be. Simplifying, if perishability can be regarded as the potentiality not to be at some point in the future and if such a potentiality is actualized in an infinite time, if x is perishable, there will be a time when x has perished. It is not possible that x is perishable and just stays perishable forever, without ever being actually perished. For, if x were perishable for an infinite time, x would be now and it would never be true in the future that x is not. But this formulation, i.e. x is now and it will never be true in the future that x is not, is a sufficient condition of x's being imperishable. So, if x were forever perishable, x would be at the same time actually perishable and actually imperishable; since being imperishable is the opposite of being perishable, this would amount to saying that x is and is not perishable, which is a contradiction.

In *Met.* I.10 Aristotle does not directly deny the claim that something perishable can exist forever without ever perishing. Rather, he addresses and refutes the claim that something can change from being perishable into being imperishable. However, an argument similar to the one sketched above can be easily supplied. If x is perishable at time t1, there will be a time tn, posterior to t1, after which it will be true to say that x is not. But if x changes from being perishable to being imperishable there will not be any tn after which it will be true to say that x is not. An argument in support of the claim that it is not possible for something perishable to turn into something imperishable could then run like this: if 'This human being is imperishable' is false now, then 'This human being is perishable' is true now. 'This human being is perishable' means that this human being has the potentiality not to be, and such a potentiality will be actualized at some point in the future. But this is incompatible with the truth of 'This human being is imperishable' at any point in the future.

A different argument could be supplied based on iterated modalities (I owe this suggestion to Lindsay Judson). The idea would be that if something cannot perish, it cannot become perishable—for if it did, then it would have been perishable all along. Similarly, if something is the kind of thing that can perish, it is hard to see how it could remain the same kind of thing and turn into something which could not perish. Aristotle would, I think, endorse this argument, especially given that he claims that perishability and imperishability are grounded in things' natures. However, I do not think that he could avail himself of this argument at this stage without begging the question, if what he is looking for is an argument in support of the claim that being perishable and being imperishable are properties grounded in things' essence (for more comments see pp. 252–3 about the 'physical' and the 'logical' approach).

We have seen above (p. 245) that there are two kinds of subject with respect to which one can test whether a pair of contrary properties affects the kind of thing the subject is: universals and particulars. Contraries that do affect the kind of thing their subject is cannot belong at different times to the same individual subject and yield a differentiation into species in their universal subject. From the beginning of the chapter it is not clear whether Aristotle takes these two accounts of contraries modifying the essence of their subject as equivalent. In general, they are not equivalent: for while a property determining the species to which an individual belongs is also a property with respect to which the individual cannot change over time, it is not necessarily the case that a property with respect to which an individual cannot change over time is also a property which determines the essence of its species. However, if the argument for (7) and the argument resting on (7) are meant to provide support for the further claim that being perishable and being imperishable belong in the essence of their subjects, Aristotle should regard the two accounts as equivalent. For the argument he gives is about the application of the properties of being perishable/imperishable to single individuals: not much is said about the possibility that two different individuals of the same kind (e.g. two human beings) be the one perishable and the other imperishable. It would still be true that neither of them changes with respect to its being perishable or imperishable, but from this one could not infer anything about human beings in general and their nature and essence.

Why is it not possible that some human beings are perishable whereas some others are imperishable then? Aristotle could make this point by referring to his understanding of what it is to be a human being, which is being a rational animal with a body of such and such a sort, and by explaining how the presence of a body of such and such a sort affects material beings' perishability. Since such an account must apply to all human beings, either they will all be perishable or they will all be imperishable. Aristotle considers this approach and labels it 'physical' in *DC* I.12, 283b17–22 (cf. *LBV* 3). Such an approach is contrasted with a 'logical' approach which, in *DC* I.11–12, is displayed by the first argument given above in support of (7). I.10's stance on the 'physical' approach is left unclear. It is likely that the bridge between the impossibility of change from perishable to imperishable (and vice versa) in an individual and the differentiation in genus of perishable and imperishable is built on the idea that otherness in genus has something to do with an ontological gap which cannot be bridged by any process of change and with some basic differentiation in the 'matter' of things (see below; cf. I.3, 1054b28–30; I.4, 1055a6–7; Δ.28, 1024b9–16). However, even if we grant that being perishable and being imperishable are necessary properties of species, it still does not follow that being perishable must be the substance or 'in the substance' of all things that are perishable, as Aristotle infers at 1059a6–7. Perhaps the alternative 'the substance or in the substance' introduces a note of caution: even if being perishable is not the essence or part of the essence of something, it is a (necessary) property grounded in the essence of things.

1059a9–10 states the general conclusion of the argument (ara, 'therefore'). I have suggested the possibility that what Aristotle means is not necessarily that being perishable and imperishable belong to the essence of their subjects, but, more generally, that they are properties grounded in the essence of their subjects. Even if this were the case, one might wonder how Aristotle reaches the conclusion that perishable and imperishable differ in genus. The argument of the former section emphasizes that being perishable and being imperishable are never incidental properties of their subjects and concludes that they are at least grounded in their subjects' essence. An implicit premise could be added that things that can be said to be perishable or imperishable (i.e. all things) belong to different species (note that Aristotle shows interest in the idea that not only substances, but also non-substantial beings go out of being: *Phys.* V.4, 228a6–19; *LBV* 1, 465a19–26). Furthermore, being perishable and imperishable in their primary or proper sense are said non-equivocally of all things of which they are said (i.e. being perishable is the same property for all things that are perishable, and the same holds for being imperishable). If this is true, then there are two contrary properties, being perishable and being imperishable, which are said of things that differ in species in a non-equivocal way and which are grounded in the essence of all of them. This situation makes room for the idea that the grounds of perishability and imperishability respectively are determined at a level of higher generality than that of the species, i.e. at the level of the basic partition between perishable things and imperishable things.

At a9–10 it is not clear whether the 'primary thing' on account of which perishable things are perishable and imperishable things are imperishable has to be matter or, more generally, whatever the basic ontological factors are which are responsible for the distinction. If the point is that there is a basic distinction in matter as the factor determining perishability or imperishability, then the passage is about a distinction between kinds of matter (cf. *Met.* Θ.8, 1050b20–28; Λ.2, 1069b24–26). If so, then the distinction is about perishable and imperishable material objects (presumably: perishable sublunary substances and imperishable celestial substances; for this interpretation see Elders 1961, pp. 85–187 and 201–9). However, the point of the argument could be more general: perishable and imperishable things belong to two primitively distinct domains of being, which cannot be bridged by change and do not have any substratum or matter or genus in common. Note that this argument, together with the (controversial) claim in I.2, 1053b22–24 (see notes *ad loc.*) that substance is not a genus, provides the main evidence on the basis of which Berti 1975 argues against the univocity of substance and the unification under one genus of the three kinds of substance (*Met.* Λ.1, 1069a30–33 and Λ.6, 1071b3–4: eternal, sensible and imperishable, sensible and perishable).

1059a10–14: Aristotle turns the result of the chapter into a point of criticism against Platonic Forms. Forms, according to their supporters, are imperishable beings; sensible particulars participating in Forms are perishable. At the same time, Forms and particulars participating in them are not homonymous, i.e. the definition of the Form is supposed to apply to all particulars participating in it (the definition of what it is to be beautiful applies to both the Form of the Beautiful and the beautiful particulars—or this, at least, is part of what Aristotle takes as distinctive of the theory of Forms). Things sharing the same definition are one in species. But this is not possible, if perishable and imperishable items belong to different genera.

The thesis that perishable and imperishable are two primitively distinct genera or domains of reality is a distinctively Platonic thesis in *Tim.* 27d5–28a4 (cf. *Leg.* X 894a) and is an underlying assumption in *Phaed.* 78b–84b. Furthermore, the two fundamental claims that Forms and particulars share the same account and that Forms are imperishable, while particulars are perishable, can be led back to what Aristotle takes to be the two basic motives leading Plato to the introduction of Forms with their peculiar features (*Met.* A.6, 987a32 ff.; M.4, 1078b12 ff.; M.9, 1086a24 ff.; for a more detailed account of the interplay between these two lines of thought, see Castelli 2013). One the one hand, Aristotle says, Plato followed Socrates in feeling the need for objects of definition and knowledge, in opposition to sensible particulars which, following Heraclitus and Cratylus, he regarded as being in flux. On the other hand, Plato felt the need to introduce imperishable causes of perishable beings. Aristotle follows both Socrates and Plato in acknowledging the need for objects of definition and scientific knowledge and for imperishable causes of perishable beings. However Aristotle thinks that Socrates's and Plato's needs can only be met by two different kinds of objects: universals and separate imperishable substances respectively. Plato's mistake, according to Aristotle, is that of introducing the same entities, i.e. Forms, as a response to both theoretical needs. In this way, Plato ends up with only one candidate (Forms) with both functions of universals and separate imperishable substances. In this way Plato's universals turn out to be separate substances and imperishable substances turn out to be nothing more than eternal duplicates of sensible particulars. For Aristotle universals, while being what can be defined in particulars, are not separate; and imperishable substances, while being separate, do not share their definitions with perishable beings. In I.10 Aristotle spells out one of the problems involved in the introduction of the hybrid entities Aristotle takes Forms to be. And, in doing this, he sets a basic requirement for any theory making room for both perishable and imperishable beings.

NOTES ON THE TEXT

The translation is based on the Greek text edited by Ross 1924. The data of a new collation of all the manuscripts regarded as independent by Harlfinger 1979 have been made available to me by Oliver Primavesi in the form of a complete apparatus. A new critical edition of Iota is not yet available. I signal here the places where I depart from Ross's text in addition to a few other places where interesting textual issues emerge, where textual issues impact on the translation and/or the general meaning. As a matter of fact, all places where I depart from Ross turn out to be places at which I accord preference to the α-text (whereas Ross tends to accord preference to the β-text). A full analysis of the *stemma codicum* and of the textual history of the *Metaphysics* together with an assessment of the relations between the α-text and the β-text can be found in Primavesi 2012. Sigla are used as in Harlfinger 1979.

I.1, 1052a18 reading πρώτων with the manuscripts (and Ross), but see notes on 1052a15–19, pp. 25–6.

I.1, 1052a29 ᾖ (in οὕτως ἓν ᾖ συνεχὲς ἢ ὅλον) is a conjecture by Christ; β simply has η (which is of course compatible with ᾖ), whereas the α-text reads ἓν συνεχὲς ἢ ὅλον. Jaeger 1957 suggests in the apparatus *ad loc.* that ᾖ συνεχὲς ἢ ὅλον could be a gloss.

I.1, 1052b7 reading τῇ δυνάμει with Ross, who follows α; δυνάμει in β seems *facilior*. See notes on pp. 45–6.

I.1, 1052b17–18 reading ἀχωρίστῳ ἢ τόπῳ ἢ εἴδει ἢ διανοίᾳ ἢ καὶ τῷ ὅλῳ καὶ διωρισμένῳ, μάλιστα δὲ τῷ μέτρον εἶναι πρῶτον instead of ἰδίᾳ χωριστῷ ἢ τόπῳ ἢ εἴδει ἢ διανοίᾳ, ἢ καὶ τὸ ὅλῳ καὶ ἀδιαιρέτῳ, μάλιστα δὲ τὸ μέτρῳ εἶναι πρώτῳ.

These lines and the textual problems they present are by far the most complex and rich of consequences in the whole book. I refer to the commentary for a full discussion of the philosophical implications of the different versions of the text.

At **b17**, ἰδίᾳ χωριστῷ is the β-text; ἀχωρίστῳ is the α-text (cf. *Met.* Δ.6, 1016b2; see the commentary, p. 47, for the use of the language of inseparability to indicate indivisibility). A third reading is well attested: ἀδιαχωρίστῳ in δ. The only other occurrence of the word in Aristotle according to the TLG is in *EE* 1219b34, where it indicates the inseparability of the concave and the convex in what is curved. At b17 ἀδιαχωρίστῳ in δ looks like an attempt at correcting ἰδίᾳ χωριστῷ in light of ἀχωρίστῳ. However, according to Harlfinger's stemma, the earliest contaminations between α and β would be later than δ. One

257

could perhaps suppose that both variants were present in α. The presence of ἀδιαχωρίστῳ in δ does in any case call out for an explanation.

At **b17–18**, τῷ ὅλῳ καὶ διωρισμένῳ instead of τὸ ὅλῳ καὶ ἀδιαιρέτῳ: all manuscripts read τῷ, while τὸ is a conjecture by Bonitz. Bonitz's intentions are clear: he takes τὸ ὅλῳ καὶ ἀδιαιρέτῳ in the sense of τὸ ὅλῳ καὶ ἀδιαιρέτῳ <εἶναι> and as a further way to spell out what it is to be one at b16: 'being one is being indivisible [...] and being a whole and indivisible'. But the construction τῷ + dat. + <εἶναι> does not seem impossible here since the phrase τὸ + dat. + εἶναι can be inflected. What we obtain is not an identity statement anymore, but a further respect in which what is one and indivisible is inseparable, i.e. with respect to the essence of a whole.

As for διωρισμένῳ instead of ἀδιαιρέτῳ, from the stemmatic point of view the two readings have the same value. However, διωρισμένῳ seems preferable from the point of view of the meaning (what is distinctive of wholes is that they are something with a determinate form) and in order to avoid repetition (cf. b16).

At **b18**, τῷ μέτρον εἶναι πρῶτον instead of τὸ μέτρῳ εἶναι πρώτῳ: all manuscripts read μέτρον εἶναι πρῶτον and it would be good to preserve this if possible. With τό this makes no sense, whereas with τῷ we would have an infinitive introduced by an instrumental dative. τό is well attested in that it is in β and in E, but in E it is inserted as a correction on τῷ. τῷ is further preserved by J and, more generally, by the manuscripts depending from γ. See the commentary pp. 48–9 for the interpretation of the two texts.

I.1, 1052b23 reading ᾧ πρώτῳ γιγνώσκεται with α instead of ᾧ πρώτῳ ποσὰ γιγνώσκεται; the general meaning of the sentence is not affected since ποσόν or ποσά must be understood.

I.1, 1053a23 reading ἐθέλει with the manuscripts instead of θετέον. θετέον is a conjecture by Forster accepted by Ross. The manuscripts preserve two readings: ἐθέλει is the α-text, whereas Aᵇ has θέλει. I follow Jaeger 1957, who prints ἐθέλει and refers to Bonitz, *Index*, 216b6 (*s. v.* ἐθέλειν), which registers a use of *verba volendi* in the sense of πέφυκεν.

I.1, 1053a35 I read ἡμῶν with α (followed by Ross). β and δ, however, have ἡμῖν, which would yield the translation: '[...] that the cubit-rule applies to us for so much'.

I.1, 1053b4–5 reading ἀφορίζουσι (dat. masc. plur. pres. part.) with α and M, instead of ἀφορίζοντι (dat. masc. sing.). No difference in meaning.

I.2, 1053b14 Christ secludes πῶς, coordinate with the interrogative at b11 ('[...] how we ought to think of it [...] and how it should be spoken of more intelligibly [...]'). The seclusion makes sense in that b14 ff. seem to further specify the view of the philosophers of nature introduced at b13 rather than introduce a further issue.

I.2, 1053b33 τίνων: Christ and Jaeger opt for the indefinite τινῶν. This does not seem necessary, but cf. 1054a7.

I.2, 1054a8 reading αὐτοῦ as in α instead of αὐτό. The translation of Ross's text would be: 'and yet this very thing is not substance'.

I.3, 1054a24 Bonitz follows A^b and reads οὔτε ('neither') instead of τουτῶν ('of these'), which is the α-text (followed by Ross). Probably the reason for Bonitz's choice is that he takes Aristotle to be giving the following argument: the oppositions are of four kinds; divisible and indivisible are neither opposed as possession and privation nor as contradictories nor as relatives; therefore, divisible and indivisible are opposed as contraries. Apart from the fact that, as Bonitz acknowledges, this reading would require the additional displacement of the following lines excluding the opposition of divisible and indivisible as contradictories and as relatives, Bonitz himself recognizes that the reading τουτῶν can be kept if we consider I.4, 1055b14–16, where Aristotle states that contrariety is an opposition of possession and complete privation.

I.3, 1054a33–34 reading κατ᾽ ἀριθμὸν ὃ λέγομεν with α instead of κατ᾽ ἀριθμὸν λέγομεν; see commentary pp. 111–13.

I.3, 1054b2 reading καὶ ἰσογώνια with Ross, but see notes p. 106 for the implication of the α-text καὶ τὰ ἰσογώνια.

I.3, 1054b12–13 reading ἢ χρυσῷ πῦρ with α. Ross's conjecture ἢ λευκόν instead of ἢ χρυσῷ, (followed by the β-text: χρυσὸς δὲ πυρί) as well as Jaeger's insertion <ἢ λευκόν> (followed by the α-text) do not seem necessary.

I.3, 1054b34 Ross's text διαφέροντα φαίνεται καὶ ταῦτα makes good sense and I keep it. However, α has διαφέροντά τε and E and δ have καὶ ταῦτά, which, put together, would give διαφέροντά τε φαίνεται καὶ ταῦτά.

In Ross's text, the closing lines of I.3 are about the contraries to which πάντα (...) καὶ ταῦτα ('all these too', i.e. 'all the contraries too') refer. In the alternative text Aristotle would return to the characterization of what is different after a brief remark about contrariety. From the point of view of the sense, the first reading seems preferable not only because it provides a smoother transition to I.4, but also (and mainly) because so far Aristotle has not said that in all cases of difference the different items are, in some sense, the same. Rather, in the immediately following lines he distinguishes the two cases of items that are different in genus and of items that are in the same genus; only the latter are, in some sense, the same. See commentary p. 118.

I.4, 1055b18 reading θατέρου (α-text) instead of θάτερον.

I.4, 1055b25 ἔτι: Bonitz corrects in ὅτι. See pp. 133–4 for discussion.

I.5, 1055b32 reading τὸ γάρ (α-text) instead of εἰ γὰρ τό.

I.5, 1056a13 reading μεταξύ with α; μεταξὺ οὐδεμία is Ross's text; the β-text is οὐδεμία μεταξύ.

I.6, 1056b22 reading μέτρον, καὶ τὸ μετρητόν with the manuscripts instead of μέτρον [καὶ τὸ μετρητόν].

I.6, 1056b30 ἔδει δ' εἰπεῖν ἀντὶ τοῦ καὶ μικρότητι is omitted in the venerable Y (Parisinus Suppl. gr. 687).

I.6, 1056b32–33 reading τοῖς πολλοῖς with α and Y instead of καὶ τὰ πολλὰ τὰ ἐν ἀριθμοῖς as in A^b and M, followed by Ross and Jaeger. The text in A^b spells out the sense in which τοῖς πολλοῖς must be understood. Note that if one keeps τοῖς πολλοῖς the two pairs of terms figuring in the comparison display the same construction ('the one is opposed to the many as measure to measurable', where both 'to the many' and 'to measurable' are in the dative case).

I.6, 1056b34 ὅσα μὴ καθ' αὐτὰ τῶν πρός τι is only in the α-text. For an account of the significance of portions of text which are only in α see Primavesi 2012, pp. 439–56.

I.6, 1057a3 I follow Ross and read οἷον γένος; the α-text is οἷον ὡς γένος, which may be redundant in that οἷον already suggests that plurality is, in some sense, a sort of genus of number.

I.7, 1057a23 I follow Ross and read τῷ ὀλιγίστῳ (see pp. 182–3 about why I think this is preferable from the point of view of the meaning); the α-text is τῷ ὀλιγίστῳ λόγῳ. λόγῳ could be an α-supplement of Pythagorean origin, analogous to those discussed in Primavesi 2012, pp. 447–9.

I.7, 1057b6 reading ποιήσασαι with the manuscripts instead of ποιήσουσαι. No difference in meaning.

GLOSSARY

ENGLISH–GREEK

account	λόγος	*logos*
accurate	ἀκριβής	*akribēs*
to add	προστιθέναι	*prostithenai*
to add in predication	προσκατηγορεῖσθαι	*proskatēgoreisthai*
affection	πάθος	*pathos*
articulate sound	φθόγγος	*phthongos*
atomic	ἄτομος	*atomos*
bad	κακός	*kakos*
beginning	ἀρχή	*archē*
being	ὄν	*on*
black	μέλας	*melas*
blackness	μελανία	*melania*
bond	δεσμός	*desmos*
	σύνδεσμος	*sundesmos*
capacity	δύναμις	*dunamis*
category	κατηγορία	*katēgoria*
cause	αἴτιον	*aition*
to change	μεταβάλλειν	*metaballein*
change	μεταβολή	*metabolē*
colour	χρῶμα	*chrōma*
column	συστοιχία	*sustoichia*
(process of) coming to be	γένεσις	*genesis*
common	κοινός	*koinos*
complete	τελεῖος	*teleios*
composite	συγκείμενος	*sunkeimenos*
	σύνθετος	*sunthetos*
to be composed	συγκεῖσθαι	*sunkeisthai*
compound	σύνολος	*sunholos*
constituent	ἐνυπάρχος	*enhuparchos*
contact	ἁφή	*haphē*
continuous	συνεχής	*sunechēs*
contracting	συγκριτικός	*sunkritikos*
contradiction	ἀντίφασις	*antiphasis*
contrariety	ἐναντιότης	*enantiotēs*
	ἐναντίωσις	*enantiōsis*
contrary	ἐναντίος	*entantios*

cubit-rule	πῆχυς	*pēchus*
dark	μέλας	*melas*
darkness	μελανία	*melania*
to define	ἀφορίζειν	*aphorizein*
definition	ὅρος	*horos*
	ὁρισμός	*horismos*
depth	βάθος	*bathos*
diagonal	διάμετρος	*diametros*
to differ	διαφέρειν	*diapherein*
difference, differentia	διαφορά	*diaphora*
different	διάφορος	*diaphoros*
discourse	λόγος	*logos*
dissimilar	ἀνόμοιος	*anhomoios*
dissimilarity	ἀνομοιότης	*anhomoiotēs*
distance, interval	διάστημα	*diastēma*
to divide	διαιρεῖν	*dihairein*
divisible	διαιρετός	*dihairetos*
downwards inclination	ῥοπή	*rhopē*
element	στοιχεῖον	*stoicheion*
end	τέλος	*telos*
equal	ἴσος	*isos*
equality	ἰσότης	*isotēs*
even	ἄρτιος	*artios*
exceeded	ὑπερεχόμενος	*huperechomenos*
exceeding	ὑπερέχων	*huperechōn*
excess	ὑπεροχή	*huperochē*
extreme	ἔσχατος	*eschatos*
fast	ταχύς	*tachus*
female	θέλυς	*thelus*
few	ὀλίγος	*oligos*
figure	σχῆμα	*schēma*
to follow	ἀκολουθεῖν	*akolouthein*
	παρακολουθεῖν	*parakolouthein*
force	βία	*bia*
form	εἶδος	*eidos*
genus	γένος	*genos*
glue	κόλλη	*kollē*
good	ἀγαθός	*agathos*
great	μέγαλος	*megalos*
	μέγας	*megas*
greater	μείζων	*meizōn*
to imitate	μιμεῖσθαι	*mimeisthai*
imperishable	ἄφθαρτος	*aphthartos*

in its own right	καθ᾽ αὑτό	kath' hauto
in the strictest sense	κυριώτατα	kuriōtata
incapacity	ἀδυναμία	adunamia
incidental (feature)	συμβεβηκός	sumbebēkos
incidentally	κατὰ συμβεβηκός	kata sumbebēkos
incomparable	ἀσύμβλητος	asumblētos
incomposite	ἀσύνθετος	asunthetos
indivisible	ἀδιαιρετός	adiairetos
induction	ἐπαγωγή	epagōgē
inequality	ἀνισότης	anisotēs
inseparable	ἀχώριστος	achōristos
intermediate	μεταξύ	metaxu
it itself	αὐτό	auto
kind	γένος	genos
of the same kind	ὁμογενής	homogenēs
belonging to the same kind	συγγενής	sungenēs
knowledge	ἐπιστήμη	epistēmē
that can be known	γνωστός	gnōstos
last	ἔσχατος	eschatos
to lead back	ἀνάγεσθαι	anagesthai
length	μῆκος	mēkos
less	ἐλάττων	elattōn
	ἥττων	hēttōn
light (adj.)	κοῦφος	kouphos
line	γραμμή	grammē
liquid	ὑγρός	hugros
long	μακρός	makros
magnitude	μέγεθος	megethos
male	ἄρρην	arrēn
many	πολλά	polla
matter	ὕλη	hulē
measurable	μετρητός	metrētos
measure	μέτρον	metron
to measure	μετρεῖν	metrein
measured	μεμετρημένος	memetrēmenos
more	μᾶλλον	mallon
motion	κίνησις	kinēsis
circular motion	κυκλοφορία	kuklophoria
local motion	φορά	phora
much	πολύ	polu
multiple	πολλαπλάσιος	pollaplasios
nail	γόμφος	gomphos
name	ὄνομα	onoma

263

nature	φύσις	*phusis*
by nature	φύσει	*phusei*
negation	ἀπόφασις	*apophasis*
joint negation	συναπόφασις	*sunapophasis*
number	ἀριθμός	*arithmos*
odd	περιττός	*perittos*
one	εἷς / μία / ἕν	*heis / mia / hen*
opposites	ἀντικείμενα	*antikeimena*
to be opposed	ἀντικεῖσθαι	*antikeisthai*
opposition	ἀντίθεσις	*antithesis*
in opposition	ἀντικειμένως	*antikeimenōs*
other	ἄλλος	*allos*
	ἕτερος	*heteros*
otherness	ἑτερότης	*heterotēs*
pale	λευκός	*leukos*
paleness	λευκότης	*leukotēs*
particular	καθ' ἕκαστον	*kath' hekaston*
perception	αἴσθησις	*aisthēsis*
perishable	φθαρτός	*phthartos*
piercing	διακριτικός	*diakritikos*
place	τόπος	*topos*
plurality	πλῆθος	*plēthos*
possession	ἕξις	*hexis*
power	δύναμις	*dunamis*
precise	ἀκριβής	*akribēs*
predication	κατηγορία	*katēgoria*
to be predicated	κατηγορεῖσθαι	*katēgoreisthai*
something predicated	κατηγόρημα	*katēgorēma*
primary, first	πρῶτος	*prōtos*
prior	πρότερος	*proteros*
principle	ἀρχή	*archē*
privation	στέρησις	*sterēsis*
proper	οἰκεῖος	*oikeios*
(of some) quality	ποιός	*poios*
(of some) quantity	ποσός	*posos*
ratio	λόγος	*logos*
receptive	δεκτικός	*dektikos*
to reduce	ἀνάγεσθαι	*anagesthai*
reduction	ἀναγωγή	*anagōgē*
relative	πρός τι	*pros ti*
(the) same	τὸ αὐτό	*to auto*
semitone	διέσις	*diesis*
separate	χωριστός	*chōristos*

264

shape	μορφή	morphē
short	βραχύς	brachus
side	πλευρά	pleura
to signify	σημαίνειν	sēmainein
similar	ὁμοῖος	homoios
similarity	ὁμοιότης	homoiotēs
simple	ἁπλοῦς	haplous
slow	βραδύς	bradus
small	μικρός	mikros
smaller	ἐλάττων	elattōn
solid	ξηρός	xēros
species	εἶδος	eidos
speed	τάχος	tachos
stade	στάδιον	stadion
subject	ὑποκείμενος	hupokeimenos
substance	οὐσία	ousia
substrate	ὑποκείμενος	hupokeimenos
to subtract	ἀφαιρεῖν	aphairein
talent	τάλαντος	talantos
thought	διάνοια	dianoia
	νόησις	noēsis
time	χρόνος	chronos
tune	μέλος	melos
to underlie	ὑποκεῖσθαι	hupokeisthai
undifferentiated	ἀδιάφορος	adiaphoros
unequal	ἄνισος	anisos
uniform	ὁμαλός	homalos
unit	μονάς	monas
unity	ἑνότης	henotēs
universal	καθόλου	katholou
unjoinable	ἀσύμβλητος	asumblētos
vocal element	στοιχεῖον	stoicheion
vocal sound	φωνή	phōnē
way	τρόπος	tropos
weight	βάρος	baros
white	λευκός	leukos
whiteness	λευκότης	leukotēs
whole	ὅλος	holos
width	πλάτος	platos
without qualification	ἁπλῶς	haplōs
woman	γυνή	gunē

265

GREEK–ENGLISH

ἀγαθός	agathos	good
ἀδιαιρετός	adiairetos	indivisible
ἀδιάφορος	adiaphoros	undifferentiated
ἀδυναμία	adunamia	incapacity
αἴσθησις	aisthēsis	perception
αἴτιον	aition	cause
ἀκολουθεῖν	akolouthein	to follow; to correspond
ἀκριβής	akribēs	precise, accurate
ἄλλος	allos	other
ἀνάγεσθαι	anagesthai	to reduce, to lead back
ἀνήρ	anēr	man
ἄνθρωπος	anthrōpos	human being
ἄνισος	anisos	unequal
ἀνισότης	anisotēs	inequality
ἀνόμοιος	anhomoios	dissimilar
ἀνομοιότης	anhomoiotēs	dissimilarity
ἀντίθεσις	antithesis	opposition
ἀντικείμενα	antikeimena	opposites
ἀντικειμένως	antikeimenōs	in opposition
ἀντικεῖσθαι	antikeisthai	to be opposed
ἀντίφασις	antiphasis	contradiction
ἁπλοῦς	haplous	simple
ἁπλῶς	haplōs	without qualification
ἀπόφασις	apophasis	negation
ἀρετή	aretē	virtue
ἀριθμός	arithmos	number
ἄρρην	arrēn	male
ἄρτιος	artios	even
ἀρχή	archē	principle; beginning
ἀσύμβλητος	asumblētos	unjoinable; incomparable
ἀσύνθετος	asunthetos	incomposite
ἄτομος	atomos	atomic
ἀφαιρεῖν	aphairein	to subtract
ἀφή	haphē	contact
ἄφθαρτος	aphthartos	imperishable
ἀφορίζειν	aphorizein	to define
ἀχώριστος	achōristos	inseparable
βάθος	bathos	depth
βάρος	baros	weight

βία	bia	force
βραδύς	bradus	slow
βραχύς	brachus	short
γένεσις	genesis	process of coming to be
γένος	genos	genus
γνωστός	gnōstos	that can be known
γόμφος	gomphos	nail
γραμμή	grammē	line
γυνή	gunē	woman
δεκτικός	dektikos	receptive
δεσμός	desmos	bond
διαιρεῖν	dihairein	to divide
διαιρετός	dihairetos	divisible
διακριτικός	diakritikos	piercing
διάμετρος	diametros	diagonal
διάνοια	dianoia	thought
διάστημα	diastēma	distance; interval
διαφέρειν	diapherein	to differ
διαφορά	diaphora	difference; differentia
διάφορος	diaphoros	different
διέσις	diesis	semitone
δύναμις	dunamis	power; capacity
εἶδος	eidos	form; species
εἷς μία ἕν	heis / mia / hen	one
ἐλάττων	elattōn	smaller; less
ἐναντίος	entantios	contrary
ἐναντιότης	enantiotēs	contrariety
ἐναντίωσις	enantiōsis	contrariety
ἑνότης	henotēs	unity
ἐνυπάρχος	enhuparchos	constituent
ἕξις	hexis	possession
ἐπαγωγή	epagōgē	induction
ἐπιστήμη	epistēmē	knowledge
ἔσχατος	eschatos	extreme; last
ἕτερος	heteros	other
ἑτερότης	heterotēs	otherness
ἧττων	hēttōn	less
θέλυς	thelus	female
ἴσος	isos	equal
ἰσότης	isotēs	equality
καθ' αὑτό	kath' hauto	in its own right
καθ' ἕκαστον	kath' hekaston	particular
καθόλου	katholou	universal

κακός	*kakos*	bad
κατὰ συμβεβηκός	*kata sumbebēkos*	incidentally
κατηγορεῖσθαι	*katēgoreisthai*	to be predicated
κατηγόρημα	*katēgorēma*	something predicated
κατηγορία	*katēgoria*	category; predication
κίνησις	*kinēsis*	motion
κοινός	*koinos*	common
κόλλη	*kollē*	glue
κοῦφος	*kouphos*	light
κυκλοφορία	*kuklophoria*	circular motion
κυριώτατα	*kuriōtata*	in the strictest sense
λευκός	*leukos*	pale; white
λευκότης	*leukotēs*	paleness; whiteness
λόγος	*logos*	account; ratio; discourse
μακρός	*makros*	long
μᾶλλον	*mallon*	more
μέγαλος	*megalos*	great
μέγας	*megas*	great
μέγεθος	*megethos*	magnitude
μείζων	*meizōn*	greater
μελανία	*melania*	darkness; blackness
μέλας	*melas*	dark; black
μέλος	*melos*	tune
μεμετρημένος	*memetrēmenos*	measured
μεταβάλλειν	*metaballein*	to change
μεταβολή	*metabolē*	change
μεταξύ	*metaxu*	intermediate; between
μετρεῖν	*metrein*	to measure
μετρητός	*metrētos*	measurable
μέτρον	*metron*	measure
μῆκος	*mēkos*	length
μικρός	*mikros*	small
μιμεῖσθαι	*mimeisthai*	to imitate
μονάς	*monas*	unit
μορφή	*morphē*	shape
νόησις	*noēsis*	thought
ξηρός	*xēros*	solid
οἰκεῖος	*oikeios*	proper
ὀλίγος	*oligos*	few
ὅλος	*holos*	whole
ὁμαλός	*homalos*	uniform
ὁμογενής	*homogenēs*	of the same kind
ὁμοῖος	*homoios*	similar

ὁμοιότης	*homoiotēs*	similarity
ὄν	*on*	being
ὄνομα	*onoma*	name
ὅρος	*horos*	definition
οὐσία	*ousia*	substance
πάθος	*pathos*	affection
παρακολουθεῖν	*parakolouthein*	to follow
περιττός	*perittos*	odd; extraordinary
πῆχυς	*pēchus*	cubit-rule
πλάτος	*platos*	width
πλευρά	*pleura*	side
πλῆθος	*plēthos*	plurality
ποδιαῖος	*podiaios*	a foot long
ποιός	*poios*	of some quality
πολλαπλάσιος	*pollaplasios*	multiple
πολλά	*polla*	many
πολύ	*polu*	much
ποσός	*posos*	of some quantity
πρός τι	*pros ti*	relative
προσκατηγορεῖσθαι	*proskatēgoreisthai*	to add in predication
προστιθέναι	*prostithenai*	to add
πρότερος	*proteros*	prior
πρῶτος	*prōtos*	primary; first
ῥοπή	*rhopē*	downwards inclination
σημαίνειν	*sēmainein*	to signify
στάδιον	*stadion*	stade
στέρησις	*sterēsis*	privation
στοιχεῖον	*stoicheion*	element; vocal element
συγγενής	*sungenēs*	belonging to the same kind
συγκείμενος	*sunkeimenos*	composite
συγκεῖσθαι	*sunkeisthai*	to be composed
συγκριτικός	*sunkritikos*	contracting
συμβεβηκός	*sumbebēkos*	incidental
συναπόφασις	*sunapophasis*	joint negation
σύνδεσμος	*sundesmos*	bond
συνεχής	*sunechēs*	continuous
σύνθετος	*sunthetos*	composite
σύνολος	*sunholos*	compound
συστοιχία	*sustoichia*	column
σχῆμα	*schēma*	figure
τάλαντον	*talanton*	talent
τάχος	*tachos*	speed
ταχύς	*tachus*	fast

τὸ αὐτό	to auto	the same
τελεῖος	teleios	complete
τέλος	telos	end
τόπος	topos	place
τρόπος	tropos	way
ὑγρός	hugros	liquid
ὕλη	hulē	matter
ὑπερεχόμενος	huperechomenos	exceeded
ὑπερέχων	huperechōn	exceeding
ὑπεροχή	huperochē	excess
ὑποκείμενος	hupokeimenos	object; subject
ὑποκεῖσθαι	hupokeisthai	to underlie
φθαρτός	phthartos	perishable
φθόγγος	phthongos	articulate sound
φορά	phora	local motion
φύσις	phusis	nature
φύσει	phusei	by nature
φωνή	phōnē	vocal sound
χρόνος	chronos	time
χρῶμα	chrōma	colour
χωριστός	chōristos	separate

SELECT BIBLIOGRAPHY

ACKRILL, J.L. (1963), *Aristotle. Categories and De Interpretatione*, Oxford: Clarendon Press.

AERTSEN, J.A. (2012), *Medieval Philosophy as Transcendental Thought*, Leiden: Brill.

ALLAN, D.J. (1936), *Aristotle. De Coelo*, OCT, Oxford: Clarendon Press.

ANDRENACCI, E. AND PALPACELLI, L. (2003), 'Una possibile soluzione del rebus di *Metafisica*, I 10, 1058b26–29', Rivista di Filosofia Neo-Scolastica 95 (3/4), pp. 615–25.

ANNAS, J. (1975), 'On the "Intermediates"', Archiv für Geschichte der Philosophie 57 (2), pp. 146–66.

ANNAS, J. (1976), *Aristotle's Metaphysics: Books M and N*, Oxford: Clarendon Press.

ANTON, J.P. (1957), *Aristotle's Theory of Contrariety*, London: Routledge & Kegan Paul.

AUBENQUE, P. (1979), (ed.), *Études sur la Métaphysique d'Aristote*, Actes du VIe Symposium Aristotelicum, Paris: Vrin.

AUBENQUE, P. (1997, 3rd edn), *Le problème de l'être chez Aristote* (1962, 1st edn), Paris: Presses universitaires de France.

BALME, D.M. (1962), 'ΓΕΝΟΣ and ΕΙΔΟΣ in Aristotle's Biology', Classical Quarterly, New Series 12, pp. 81–98.

BALME, D.M. (1987a), 'Aristotle's Use of Division and Differentiae', in GOTTHELF–LENNOX (1987), pp. 69–89.

BALME, D.M. (1987b), 'Aristotle's Biology Was Not Essentialist', in GOTTHELF–LENNOX (1987), pp. 291–312.

BALME, D.M. (1991), *Aristotle. History of Animals VII–X* (prepared for publication by A. Gotthelf), Aristotle XI, Loeb, Cambridge, Mass.: Harvard University Press.

BARKER, A. (1989), *Greek Musical Writings, Vol. 2: Harmonic and Acoustic Theory*, Cambridge: Cambridge University Press.

BARKER, A. (2004), 'Theophrastus and Aristoxenus: Confusions in Musical Metaphysics', Bulletin of the Institute of Classical Studies 47, pp. 101–17.

BARKER, A. (2007), *The Science of Harmonics in Classical Greece*, Cambridge: Cambridge University Press.

BARNES, J. (1984), (ed.), *Complete Works of Aristotle. The Revised Oxford Translation*, 2 vols, Princeton: Princeton University Press.

BARNES, K.T. (1977), 'Aristotle on Identity and its Problems', Phronesis 22, pp. 48–62.

BÄRTHLEIN, K. (1972), *Die Traszendentalienlehre der alten Ontologie, I: Die Traszendentalienlehre im Corpus Aristotelicum*, Berlin/New York: de Gruyter.

BEERE, J. (2009), *Doing and Being. An Interpretation of Aristotle's* Metaphysics *Theta*, Oxford/New York: Oxford University Press.

BELL, I. (2000), 'Are Being and Unity Substances of Things: On the Eleventh Aporia of Metaphysics B', Southern Journal of Philosophy 38, pp. 1–17.

BERTI, E. (1973), 'La "riduzione dei contrari" in Aristotele', *Zetesis, Bijdragen E. de Strijcker*, Antwerpen-Utrecht: De nederlandsche Boekhandel, pp. 122–46.

BERTI, E. (1975), 'Logical and Ontological Priority among the Genera of Substance in Aristotle', in MANSFELD–DE RIJK (1975), pp. 55–69.

BERTI, E. (1978), 'The Intellection of 'Indivisibles' According to Aristotle, *De Anima* III 6', in LLOYD–OWEN (1978), pp. 141–63.

BERTI, E. (1979), 'Le problème de la substantialité de l'être et de l'un dans la *Métaphysique* d'Aristote', in AUBENQUE (1979), pp. 181–208.

BERTI, E. (1990), 'L'uno ed i molti nella Metafisica di Aristotele', in V. Melchiorre (a c. di), *L'uno e i molti*, Milano: Vita e Pensiero 1990, pp. 155–80.

BERTI, E. (2003), 'L'essere e l'uno in *Metaph*. B 998b17–28', in V. Celluprica, *Il libro Beta della Metafisica di Aristotele*, Napoli: Bibliopolis 2003, pp. 103–25.

BERTI, E. (2005), 'Aristotele, Metaphysica Iota 1–2: univocità o polivocità dell'uno', in CENTRONE (2005), pp. 65–74.

BERTI, E. (2009), 'Aporiai 6-7', in CRUBELLIER–LAKS (2009), pp. 105–33.

BETEGH, G. (2012), 'The Next Principle. (*Metaphysics* A 3–4, 984b8–985b2)', in STEEL (2012), pp. 105–40.

BODÉÜS, R. (2002), (ed.), *Aristote. Catégories*, Paris: Les Belles Lettres.

BODÉÜS, R. and STEVENS, A. (2014), (trans.) *Aristote:* Métaphysique, *Livre Delta,* Paris: Vrin.

BOGEN, J. (1991), 'Aristotle's Contraries', Topoi 10, pp. 53–66.

BOGEN, J. (1992), 'Change and Contrariety in Aristotle', Phronesis 37, pp. 1–21.

BOLTON, R. (1976), 'Essentialism and Semantic Theory in Aristotle: *Post. An. II 7–10*', Philosophical Review 85, pp. 515–44.

BONITZ, H. (1848), *Aristotelis Metaphysica recognovit et enarravit H.B.*, vol. I, Bonn: Ad Marcus.

BONITZ, H. (1849), *Commentarius in Aristotelis Metaphysicam*, Bonn: Ad Marcus (repr. Hildesheim: Olms Verlag 1992).

BONITZ, H. (1870), *Index Aristotelicus*, Berlin: Reimer.

BOTTANI, A., CARRARA, M., AND GIARRETTA, P. (2002), (eds), *Individuals Essense and Identity*, Leiden/New York: Brill.

BOWMAN, A.A. (1916), 'Aristotle, Metaphysics X (I) 6, 1056b27–32', The Classical Review 30, pp. 42–4.

BRANDIS, Ch. A (1834), *Ueber die aristotelische Metaphysik*, Abhandlungen der Preussischen Akademie der Wissenschaften zu Berlin, pp. 63–87.

BRENTANO, M. (1948), *Die Bedeutungen des "Hen" als Grundbegriff der aristotelischen Metaphysik*, Freiburg (unpublished dissertation).

BRETON, S. (1981), 'De l' "élément neutre" en philosophie', Revue des Sciences philosophiques et théologiques 61, pp. 593–607.

BROWN, L. (1986), 'Being in the *Sophist*: A Syntactical Enquiry', Oxford Studies in Ancient Philosophy 4, pp. 49–70.

BROWN, L. (1994), 'The Verb "to Be" in Greek Philosophy: Some Remarks', in S. Everson (ed.), *Language. Companions to Ancient Thought* 3, Cambridge: Cambridge University Press, pp. 212–36.

BRUNS, I. (1892), (ed.), *Alexandri Aphrodisiensis praeter commentaria scripta minora. Quaestiones, De fato, De mixtione*, Supplementum Aristotelicum vol. II, Berlin: Reimer.

BRUNSCHWIG, J. (2007), *Aristote. Topiques*, Tome II, Paris: Les Belles Lettres.

BRUNSCHWIG, J. (2009), *Aristote. Topiques*, Tome I, Paris: Les Belles Lettres.

BURNYEAT, M. (2001), *A Map of Metaphysics* Zeta, Pittsburgh: Mathesis Publications.

BYWATER, I. (1911), *Aristotelis De Arte Poetica*, OCT, Oxford: Clarendon Press.

BYWATER, I. (1920), *Aristotelis Ethica Nicomachea*, OCT, Oxford: Clarendon Press.

CASTELLI, L.M. (2005), 'Metaphysica Iota 6: alcuni aspetti dell'opposizione uno/molti', in CENTRONE (2005), pp. 139–56.

CASTELLI, L.M. (2008), '*to hen legetai pollachōs*. Questioni aristoteliche sui significati dell'uno', Antiquorum Philosophia 2, pp. 307–33.

CASTELLI, L.M. (2010), *Problems and Paradigms of Unity. Aristotle's Accounts of the One*, Sankt Augustin: Academia Verlag.

CASTELLI, L.M. (2011), 'Greek, Arab, and Latin Commentators on Per Se Accidents of Being qua Being and the Place of Aristotle, Metaphysics, Book Iota', Documenti e studi sulla tradizione filosofica medievale 22, pp. 153–208.

CASTELLI, L.M. (2013), 'Universals, Particulars and Aristotle's Criticism of Plato's Forms', in G. Galluzzo and R. Chiaradonna (eds), *Universals in Ancient Philosophy*, Pisa: Edizioni della Scuola Normale, pp. 139–84.

CASTELLI, L.M. (forthcoming), '*Physics* I.3', in QUARANTOTTO (forthcoming).

CATTANEI, E. (1996), *Enti matematici e metafisica. Platone, l'Accademia antica e Aristotele a confronto*, Milano: Vita e Pensiero.

CATTANEI, E. (2005), 'Quale matematica per Iota? L'antitesi dell'uguale al grande e al piccolo e il possibile retroterra matematico di Iota 5', in CENTRONE (2005), pp. 117–38.

CAVINI, W. (2009), 'Aporia 11', in CRUBELLIER–LAKS (2009), pp. 175–88.

CENTRONE, B. (2002), 'La critica aristotelica alla dottrina delle Idee. L'argomento di *Metafisica* I 10, 1058b26–1059a14', in M. Migliori (a c. di), *Gigantomachia. Convergenze e divergenze tra Platone e Aristotele*, Brescia: Morcelliana 2002, pp. 191–203.

CENTRONE, B. (2005), (ed.), *Il Libro Iota (X) della Metafisica di Aristotele*, International Aristotle Studies 6, Sankt Augustin: Academia Verlag.

CHARLES, D. (2000), *Aristotle on Meaning and Essence*, Oxford: Clarendon Press.

CHARLTON, W. (1970), *Aristotle's* Physics *Books I and II*, Oxford: Clarendon Press.

CHIARADONNA, R. (2005), 'I contrari e i termini intermedi: Metaphysica Iota 7', in CENTRONE (2005), pp. 157–70.

CLARKE, T. (forthcoming), '*Physics* I.2', in QUARANTOTTO (forthcoming).

CLEARY, J. (1985), 'On the Terminology of 'Abstraction' in Aristotle', Phronesis 30, pp. 13–45.

CLEARY, J. (1995), *Aristotle and Mathematics. Aporetic Method in Cosmology and Metaphysics*, Leiden: Brill.

COHEN, S.M. (2008), 'Aristotle's Ontology: Kooky Objects Revisited', Metaphilosophy 39, pp. 3–19.

COHEN, S.M. (2013), 'Incidental Beings in Aristotle's Ontology', in G. Anagnostopoulos–F.D. Miller Jr (eds), *Reason and Analysis in Ancient Greek Philosophy: Essays in Honor of David Keyt*, Dordrecht: Springer 2013, pp. 231–42.

COULOUBARITSIS, L. (1983), 'L'être et l'un chez Aristote', Revue de Philosophie Ancienne 1, pp. 49–88, 143–95.

COULOUBARITSIS, L. (1990), 'La métaphysique s'identifie-t-elle à l'ontologie?', in R. BRAGUE–J.-F. COURTINE (ed.), *Herméneutique et ontologie*, Paris: Presses Universitaires France 1990, pp. 295–322.

COULOUBARITSIS, L. (1992), 'Le statut de l'Un dans la «Métaphysique»', Revue philosophique de Louvain 88, pp. 497–522.

CRAGER, A. (in progress), 'Three Ones in Aristotle's *Metaphysics*'.

CRIVELLI, P. (2002), 'Sameness in Aristotle's Topics', in BOTTANI–CARRARA–GIARRETTA (2002), pp. 239–46.

CRUBELLIER, M. AND LAKS, A. (2009), (eds), *Aristotle's Metaphysics Beta. Symposium Aristotelicum*, Oxford: Oxford University Press.

DE HAAS, F.A.J. (2009), 'Aporiai 3-5' in CRUBELLIER–LAKS (2009), pp. 73–104.

DEMOS, R. (1946), 'Types of Unity According to Plato and Aristotle', Philosophical and Phenomenological Research 6, pp. 534–46.

DEMOSS, D. AND DEVEREUX, D. (1988), 'Essence, Existence, and Nominal Definition in Aristotle's *Posterior Analytics* II 8–10', Phronesis 33, 133–54.

DESLAURIERS, M. (1990), 'Plato and Aristotle on Division and Definition', Ancient Philosophy 10, pp. 203–19.

DI GIOVANNI, M. AND PRIMAVESI, O. (2016), 'Who Wrote Alexander's Commentary on *Metaphysics* Λ? New Light on the Syro-Arabic Tradition', in HORN (2016), pp. 11–66.

EINARSON, E. (1936), 'On Certain Mathematical Terms in Aristotle's Logic', The America Journal of Philology 57, pp. 33–54 and 151–72.

ELDERS, L. (1961), *Aristotle's Theory of the One. A Commentary on Book X of the Metaphysics*, Assen: Van Gorcum.

FAIT, P. (2005), 'L'identico, l'uguale e il simile nella filosofia prima: una lettura di Iota 3', in CENTRONE (2005), pp. 76–95.

FALCON, A. (1996), 'Aristotle's Rules of Division in the 'Topics': The Relationship between Genus and Differentia in a Division', Ancient Philosophy 16, pp. 377–87.

FOWLER, D. (1987), *The Mathematics of Plato's Academy*, Oxford: Oxford University Press.

FORSTER, E.S. (1961), *Movement of Animals. Progression of Animals*, 3rd edn. Aristotle XII, Loeb, Cambridge, Mass.: Harvard University Press.

FREGE, G. (1884), *Die Grundlagen der Arithmetik*, Breslau: Verlag W. Koebner.

FRONTEROTTA, F. (2005), 'Corruttibile e incorruttibile. L'argomento di Metaphysica Iota 10 nella critica di Aristotele alla teoria platonica delle idee', in CENTRONE (2005) pp. 187–203.

FURTH, M. (1985), *Aristotle. Metaphysics Books VII–X* translated by M.F., Indianapolis: Hackett.

GALLAGHER, R.L. (2014), '*Anthiphasis* as Homonym in Aristotle', History and Philosophy of Logic 35, pp. 317–31.

GALLUZZO, G. AND MARIANI, M. (2006), *Aristotle's Metaphysics Book Z. The Contemporary Debate*, Pisa: Edizioni della Scuola Normale.

GILL, M.L. (2010), 'Unity of Definition in *Met*. H 6 and Z 12', in LENNOX–BOLTON (2010), pp. 97–121.

GLOY, K. (1985), 'Aristoteles' Theorie des Einen auf der Basis des Buches I der Metaphysik', in GLOY–RUDOLPH (1985), pp. 73–101.

GLOY, K. AND RUDOLPH, E. (1985), (Hrsg.), *Einheit als Grundfrage der Philosophie*, Darmstadt: Wissenschaftliche Buchgesellschaft.

GOHLKE, P. (1954), *Die Entstehung der aristotelischen Prinzipienlehre*, Tübingen: Mohr Siebeck.

GOTTHELF, A. AND LENNOX, J. (1987), (eds), *Philosophical Issues in Aristotle's Biology*, Cambridge: Cambridge University Press.

GRAESER, A. (1987), (ed.), *Matemathics and Metaphysics in Aristotle*, Symposium Aristotelicum, Bern: P. Haupt.

GRANGER, H. (1984), 'Aristotle on Genus and Differentia', Journal of the History of Philosophy 22, pp. 1–23.

GUARIGLIA, O. (1978), *Quellenkritische und logische Untersuchungen zur Gegensatzlehre des Aristoteles*, Hildesheim: Georg Olms.

HALPER, E. (1984), '*Metaphysics* Z 12 and H 6: The Unity of Form and Composite', Ancient Philosophy 4, pp. 146–59.

HALPER, E. (1985), 'Aristotle on the Convertibility of One and Being', The New Scholasticism 59, pp. 213–27.

HALPER, E. (2005), *One and Many in Aristotle's Metaphysics. The Central Books*, Las Vegas: Parmenides Publishing (1st edn: Ohio State University Press, 1989).

HALPER, E. (2007), 'Aristotle's Paradigmatism: *Metaphysics* I and the Difference It Makes', Proceedings of the Boston Area Colloquium 22, pp. 69–103.

HALPER, E. (2009), *One and Many in Aristotle's Metaphysics Alpha-Delta*, Las Vegas: Parmenides Publishing.

HARLFINGER, D. (1979), 'Zur Überlieferungsgeschichte der Metaphysik', in AUBENQUE (1979), pp. 7–33.

HARTE, V. (1996), 'Aristotle, *Met.* H 6: A Dialectic with Platonism', Phronesis 41, pp. 276–304.

HAYDUCK, M. (1891), *Alexandri Aphrodisiensis in Aristotelis Metaphysicam Commentaria*, CAG I, Berlin: Reimer.

HERTLING, G. (1864), *De Aristotelis notione unis*, Berlin: Schade.

HORN, C. (2016), (ed.), *Aristotle's Metaphysics* Lambda. *New Essays*, Boston, Berlin: de Gruyter.

ISNARDI-PARENTE, M. (2012), *Senocrate e Ermodoro. Testimonianze e frammenti, edizione traduzione e frammenti*—edizione rivista e aggiornata a cura di T. Dorandi, Pisa: Edizioni della Scuola Normale.

JAEGER, W. (1912), *Studien zur Entstehungsgeschichte der Metaphysik des Aristoteles*, Berlin: Weidmann.

JAEGER, W. (1923), *Aristoteles. Grundlegung einer Geschichte seiner Entwicklung*, Berlin: Weidmann.

JAEGER, W. (1957), (ed.), *Aristotelis Metaphysica*, OCT, Oxford: Clarendon Press.

JEANNOT, Th.M. (1986), 'Plato and Aristotle on Being and Unity', New Scholasticism 80, pp. 404–26.

JUDSON, L. (forthcoming), '*Phys.* I 5', in QUARANTOTTO (forthcoming).

JUDSON, L. (in progress), 'First Philosophy'.

KAHN, Ch.H. (2003), *The Verb 'Be' in Ancient Greek*, Indianapolis: Hackett (originally published: *The Verb 'Be' and its Synonyms*, vol. 6, Dordrecht/Boston: D. Reidel 1973. With a new introduction).

KALDERON, M.E. (2015), *Form without Matter: Empedocles and Aristotle on Color Perception*, Oxford: Oxford University Press.

KEELING, E. (2012), 'Unity in Aristotle's *Metaphysics* H 6', Apeiron 45, pp. 238–61.

KIRWAN, Ch. (1993), *Aristotle. Metaphysics: Books Gamma, Delta, and Epsilon*, 2nd edn. Oxford: Clarendon Press.

KOSLICKI, K. (2006), 'Aristotle's Mereology and the Status of Form', Journal of Philosophy 103, pp. 715–36.

KOSLICKI, K. (2008), *The Structure of Objects*, Oxford: Oxford University Press.

KOSMAN, A. (2010), 'Male and Female in Aristotle's *Generation of Animals*', in LENNOX–BOLTON (2010), pp. 147–67.

KRÄMER, H.J. (1968), 'Grundbegriffe akademischer Dialektik in den biologischen Schriften von Aristoteles und Theophrast', Rheinisches Museum 112, pp. 293–333.

KRÄMER, H.J. (1973), 'Aristoteles und die akademische Eidoslehre. Zur Geschichte des Universalienproblems in Platonismus', Archiv für Geschichte der Philosophie 55, pp. 118–90.

KÜHNER, R. (1890), *Ausführliche Grammatik der griechischen Sprache. Erster Teil: Elementar- und Formenlehre.* (1890 3rd edn), 2 vols, Hannover: Hahnsche Buchhandlung.

LEE, H.D. (1952), *Aristotle. Meteorologica*, Aristotle VII, Loeb, Cambridge, Mass.: Harvard University Press.

LENNOX, J. (1980), 'Aristotle on Genera, Species, and The More and The Less', Journal of the History of Biology 13, pp. 321–46 (repr. in LENNOX (2001a), pp. 160–81).

LENNOX, J. (2001a), *Aristotle's Philosophy of Biology*, Cambridge: Cambridge University Press.

LENNOX, J. (2001b), *Aristotle: On the Parts of Animals I–IV*, Oxford: Clarendon Press.

LENNOX, J.G. AND BOLTON, R. (2010), (eds), *Being, Nature, and Life in Aristotle: Essays in Honor of A. Gotthelf*, Cambridge: Cambridge University Press.

LEWIS, F. (1982), 'Incidental Sameness in Aristotle', Philosophical Studies 42, pp. 1–36.

LLOYD, G.E.R. AND BURNYEAT, M., ET AL., *Notes on Book Iota of Aristotle's Metaphysics* (minutes of the London Group Seminar meetings 1982–4, unpublished).

LLOYD, G.E.R. AND OWEN, G.E.L. (1978), (eds), *Aristotle on Mind and the Senses. Proceeding of the Seventh Symposium Aristotelicum*, Cambridge: Cambridge University Press.

LOUIS, P. (1961), *Aristote. De la génération des animaux*, Paris: Les Belles Lettres.

LOUIS, P. (1982), *Aristote. Météorologiques*, Paris: Les Belles Lettres.

LOUIS, P. (2002–3), *Aristote. Problèmes*, 3 vols, Paris: Les Belles Lettres.

LOUX, M.J. (1973), 'Aristotle on the Transcendentals', Phronesis 18, pp. 225–39.

LOWE, M.F. (1977), 'Aristotle on Being and the One', Archiv für Geschichte der Philosophie 59, pp. 44–55.

MADIGAN, A. (2007), 'Commentary on Halper', Proceedings of the Boston Area Colloquium 22, pp. 104–8.

MAKIN, S. (1988), 'Aristotle on Unity and Being', Proceedings of the Cambridge Philological Society, New Series 34, pp. 77–103.

MANSFELD, J. AND DE RIJK, L.M. (1975), (eds) *Kephalaion. Studies in Greek Philosophy and its Continuation Offered to C.J. de Vogel*, Philosophical Texts and Studies 23, Assen: Van Gorcum.

MARIANI, M. (2000), 'Numerical Identity and Accidental Predication in Aristotle', Topoi 19, pp. 99–110.

MARIANI, M. (2005), 'Identità e indiscernibili in Aristotele', in CENTRONE (2005), pp. 97–116.

MATHIESEN, Th.J. (1985), 'Rhythm and Meter in Ancient Greek Music', Music Theory Spectrum 7, pp. 159–80.

MATTHEWS, G.B. (1982), 'Incidental Unities', in M. Schofield and M. Craven Nussbaum (eds.), *Language and Logos: Studies in Ancient Greek Philosophy*, Cambridge: Cambridge University Press, pp. 223–40.

MEIXNER, U. (1992), 'On Negative and Disjunctive Properties', in K. Mulligan (ed.), *Language, Truth and Ontology*, Dordrecht: Kluver 1992, pp. 28–36.

MENDELL, H. (2004), 'Aristotle and Mathematics', Stanford Encyclopedia of Philosophy (http://plato.stanford.edu/entries/aristotle-mathematics/).

MENN, S. (1995), 'Metaphysics, Dialectic, and the *Categories*', Revue de Métaphysique et de Morale 100 (3), pp. 311–37.

MENN, S. (2011), 'Fârâbî in the Reception of Avicenna's Metaphysics: Averroes against Avicenna on Being and Unity', in D. Hasse and A. Bertolacci (eds), *The Arabic, Hebrew and Latin Reception of Avicenna's Metaphysics*, Berlin/Boston: de Gruyter, pp. 51–96.

MENN, S. (in progress), *The Aim and the Argument of Aristotle's Metaphysics*, available at http://www.philosophie.hu-berlin.de/de/lehrbereiche/antike/mitarbeiter/menn/ig1neu.pdf (last access: August 2016).

MIGNUCCI, M. (2002), 'On the Notion of Identity in Aristotle', in BOTTANI–CARRARA GIARRETTA (2002), pp. 217–38.

MILLER, F.D. (1973), 'Did Aristotle Have the Concept of Identity?', Philosophical Review 82, pp. 483–90.

MINIO-PALUELLO, L. (1963), *Aristotle. Categoriae et Liber de Interpretatione*, OCT, Oxford: Clarendon Press.

MORISON, B. (2002), *On Location. Aristotle's Concept of Place*, Oxford: Oxford University Press.

MORRISON, D. (1992), 'The Taxonomical Interpretation of Aristotle's Categories: A Criticism', in A. Preus and J.P. Anton, *Essays in Ancient Philosophy V. Aristotle's Ontology*, Albany: State University of New York Press, pp. 19–46.

MORRISON, D. (1993a), 'The Place of Unity in Aristotle's Metaphysical Project', Proceedings of the Boston Area Colloquium in Ancient Philosophy 9, pp. 131–56.

MORRISON, D. (1993b), 'Le statut catégoriel des différences dans l'*organon*', Revue philosophique 2, pp. 147–78.

MÜLLER, I. (1991), 'peri tōn mathēmatōn', Apeiron 24 (4), 1–251.

PAKALUK, M. (1993), 'Commentary on Morrison', Proceedings of the Boston Area Colloquium in Ancient Philosophy 9, pp. 157–65.

PECK, A.L. (1961), *Aristotle. Parts of Animals*, 3rd edn. Aristotle XII, Loeb, Cambridge, Mass.: Harvard University Press.

PECK, A.L. (1965), *Aristotle. History of Animals I–III*, Aristotle IX, Loeb, Cambridge, Mass.: Harvard University Press.

PECK, A.L. (1970), *Aristotle. History of Animals IV–VI*, Aristotle X, Loeb, Cambridge, Mass.: Harvard University Press.

PELLEGRIN, P. (1982), *La Classification des animaux chez Aristote: Statut de la Biologie et unité de l'aristotélisme*, Paris: Les Belles Lettres.

PELLEGRIN, P. (1986), *Arisototle's Classification of Animals. Biology and the Conceptual Unity of the Aristotelian Corpus*, Berkeley/Los Angeles/London: University of California Press (translation of Pellegrin (1982) by A. Preus).

PELLEGRIN, P. (1987), 'Logical Difference and Biological Difference: the Unity of Aristotle's Thought', in GOTTHELF–LENNOX (1987), pp. 313–38.

PELLEGRIN, P. (1991), '*Le Sophiste* ou de la division. Aristote-Platon-Aristote', in P. Aubenque and M. Narcy (eds), *Études sur le Sophiste de Platon*, Paris 1991, pp. 389–416.

PELLETIER, Y. (1991), 'Sameness and Referential Opacity in Aristotle', Nous 13, pp. 283–311.

PERAMATZIS, M. (2011), *Priority in Aristotle's Metaphysics*, Oxford: Oxford University Press.

PFEIFFER, C. (forthcoming), *Aristotle's Theory of Body*, Oxford: Oxford University Press.

PINES, S. (1961), 'A New Fragment of Xenocrates and its Implications', Transactions of the American Philological Association 51, pp. 3–34.

PRIMAVESI, O. (2012), 'Aristotle, Metaphysics A: A New Critical Edition with Introduction', in STEEL (2012), pp. 387–464.

QUARANTOTTO, D. (2004), 'Dalla diversità per specie alle condizioni di possibilità dell'essenza. Aristotele, *Metaphysica* I 8, 9, 10', Methexis 17, pp. 25–53.

QUARANTOTTO, D. (2005), 'Metaphysica Iota 8–9: le cose diverse per specie e lo status dei principi', in CENTRONE (2005), pp. 171–86.

QUARANTOTTO, D. (forthcoming), (ed.), *Aristotle. Physics I*, Cambridge: Cambridge University Press.

RASHED, M. (2005), *Aristote. De la génération et la corruption*, Paris: Les Belles Lettres.

REALE, G. (1965), *Il concetto di filosofia prima e l'unità della Metafisica di Aristotele*, Vita e Pensiero.

REALE, G. (1994), 'Struttura paradigmatica e dimensione epocale della metafisica di Aristotele: "henologia" e "ontologia" a confronto', in A. Bausola and G. Reale (a c. di), *Aristotele. Perché la metafisica*, Milano: Vita e Pensiero 1994, pp. 37–57.

ROBERTS, W.R. (1910), *Dionysius of Halicarnassus: On Literary Composition*, London: MacMillan & Co.

ROSS, D.W. (1924), *Aristotle's Metaphysics*, 2 vols, Oxford: Oxford University Press.

ROSS, D.W. (1936), *Aristotle. Physics*, Oxford: Oxford University Press.

ROSS, D.W. (1949), *Aristotle's Prior and Posterior Analytics*, Oxford: Oxford University Press.

ROSS, D.W. (1955), *Aristotle. Parva Naturalia*, Oxford: Oxford University Press.

ROSS, D.W. (1958), *Aristotle's Topics*, OCT, Oxford: Clarendon Press.

ROSS, D.W. (1959), *Aristotelis Ars Rhetorica*, OCT, Oxford: Clarendon Press.

ROSS, D.W. (1961), *Aristotle. De Anima*, Oxford: Oxford University Press.

ROSSITTO, C. (2000), 'Problemi di dialettica nell'Accademia antica: il *peri antikeimenōn* di Aristotele', in C. Rossitto, *Studi sulla dialettica in Aristotele*, Napoli: Bibliopolis 2000, pp. 287–324.

RUNGGALDIER, E. (1989), 'Einheit und Identität als formale Begriffe in der Metaphysik des Aristoteles', Theologie und Philosophie 64, pp. 557–66.

SATTLER, B.M. (2017), 'Aristotle's Measurement Dilemma', Oxford Studies in Ancient Philosophy 52, pp. 257–302.

SCALTSAS, Th., CHARLES, D., AND GILL, M.L. (1994), *Unity, Identity, and Explanation in Aristotle's Metaphysics,* Oxford: Clarendon Press.

SCHMITZ, H. (1985), *Die Ideenlehre des Aristoteles*, Bd. I: *Aristoteles, Teil II: Ontologie, Noologie, Theologie*, Bonn: Bouvier Verlag.

SCHWEGLER, A. (1847–8), *Die Metaphysik des Aristoteles*, Tübingen: Fues (repr. Frankfurt am Main 1960).

SHIELDS, Ch. (1999), *Order in Multiplicity. Homonymy in the Philosophy of Aristotle*, Oxford/New York: Oxford University Press.

SORABJI, R. (1972), 'Aristotle, Mathematics, and Colour', The Classical Quarterly 22, pp. 293–308.

SORABJI, R. (1976), 'Aristotle on the Instant of Change', Proceedings of the Aristotelian Society. Suppl. vol. 50, pp. 69–89.

STEEL, C. (2012), (ed.), *Symposium Aristotelicum. Aristotle's Metaphysics Alpha*, Oxford, New York: Oxford University Press.

STOKES, M.C. (1971), *One and Many in Presocratic Philosophy*, Cambridge, Mass.: Harvard University Press.

TRENDELENBURG, U. (1828), 'Das *to heni einai, to agathoi einai* etc. und das *to ti ēn einai* bei Aristoteles', Rheinisches Museum 2, pp. 457–83.

VAN OPHUIJSEN, J.M (1987), *Hephaestion on Metre*, Leiden/New York: Brill.

WALZER, R.R. AND MINGAY, J.M. (1991), *Aristotelis Ethica Eudemia*, OCT, Oxford: Clarendon Press.

WEIN, S. (1983), 'Are Being and Unity the Genera of All Things? A Note on *Met*. 998b21–26', The Modern Schoolman 61, pp. 49–52.

WHITE, N.P. (1971), 'Aristotle on Sameness and Oneness', The Philosophical Review 80, pp. 177–97.

INDEX LOCORUM

GENERAL INDEX